NICHO

ORDNANC

GUIDE TO THE

WATERWAYS

2: CENTRAL

Series editor: David Perrott

Nicholson

An Imprint of Bartholomew
A Division of HarperCollins*Publishers*

Also available in this series:

Nicholson/Ordnance Survey Guide to the Waterways 1. South
Nicholson/Ordnance Survey Guide to the Waterways 3. North
Nicholson/Ordnance Survey Guide to the River Thames
Nicholson/Ordnance Survey Guide to the Broads & Fens
Nicholson/Ordnance Survey Inland Waterways Map of Great Britain

The indication of a towpath in this book does not necessarily imply a public right of way. If you are in any doubt, check before you proceed with the latest published Ordnance Survey Map.
Pathfinder Series (2½ in to 1 mile scale or 1:25 000). These OS walker and rambler maps show the countryside in great detail, including rights of way in England and Wales.
Landranger Series (1¼ in to 1 mile scale or 1:50000). This OS series covers the country in 204 sheets and is ideal for detailed exploring by car or on foot.

First published in 1983 by
Nicholson
77–85 Fulham Palace Road
Hammersmith, London W6 8JB
and
Ordnance Survey,
Romsey Road, Maybush,
Southampton SO9 4DH

5th edition 1991
Reprinted 1992

Nicholson
An Imprint of Bartholomew
A Division of HarperCollins*Publishers*

The series editor gratefully acknowledges the help given by British Waterways and their staff. Thanks is also due to CAMRA representatives and branch members for their help in recommending real ale pubs.

Research: Jane Bruton, Ray Butler

Cover photograph: Derek Pratt

Typeset by Rowland Phototypesetting Limited, Bury St Edmunds, Suffolk
Printed in Great Britain by HarperCollinsManufacturing Glasgow

Ordnance Survey ISBN 03190 0251 9
Nicholson ISBN 07028 1260 9

84/5/512

INTRODUCTION

The canals and navigable rivers of Britain were built as a system of new trade routes at a time when roads were virtually non-existent. After their boom period in the late 18th and early 19th centuries, they gradually declined in the face of fierce competition from the new railway companies, and large-scale commercial carrying ended by the time of the Second World War, when many of the routes had slipped into decay and ruin. It is true that in a few areas goods continue to be carried profitably to this day, but for the majority of canals it was the new traffic of pleasure boats that provided the impetus for rescue and restoration.

The founding of the Inland Waterways Association by L.T.C. Rolt and Robert Aickman in 1946 brought together enthusiasts from all over the country who were to campaign to save and restore these 2000 miles of navigable waterways that are so much a part of our history. There is something for everyone in the canals: engineering feats like aqueducts, tunnels and flights of locks (which at the time of their construction amazed a world that had seen nothing like it since Roman days); the brightly decorated narrowboats which used to throng the waterways; the wealth of birds, animals and plants on canal banks; the mellow, unpretentious architecture of canalside buildings like pubs, stables, lock cottages and warehouses; and the sheer beauty and quiet isolation that is a feature of so many canals.

This edition contains full information and large scale maps covering the entire Birmingham Canal Navigations, the most exciting concentration of canals on the national network. Why not plan a trip to include the rural delights of the Wyrley & Essington, the industrial archaeology of the Dudley and the Walsall, the superb Farmer's Bridge Locks and the grand Netherton Tunnel. There are plenty of good safe moorings and friendly Black Country pubs.

So use this book to discover the waterways for yourself; it is one of five volumes covering the South, Centre and North of England and Wales; the Rivers Thames and Wey; and the Norfolk Broads, Ouse, Nene and Middle Level Navigations. There is also a full colour Nicholson/Ordnance Survey *Inland Waterways Map*, to help you plan your route.

CONTENTS

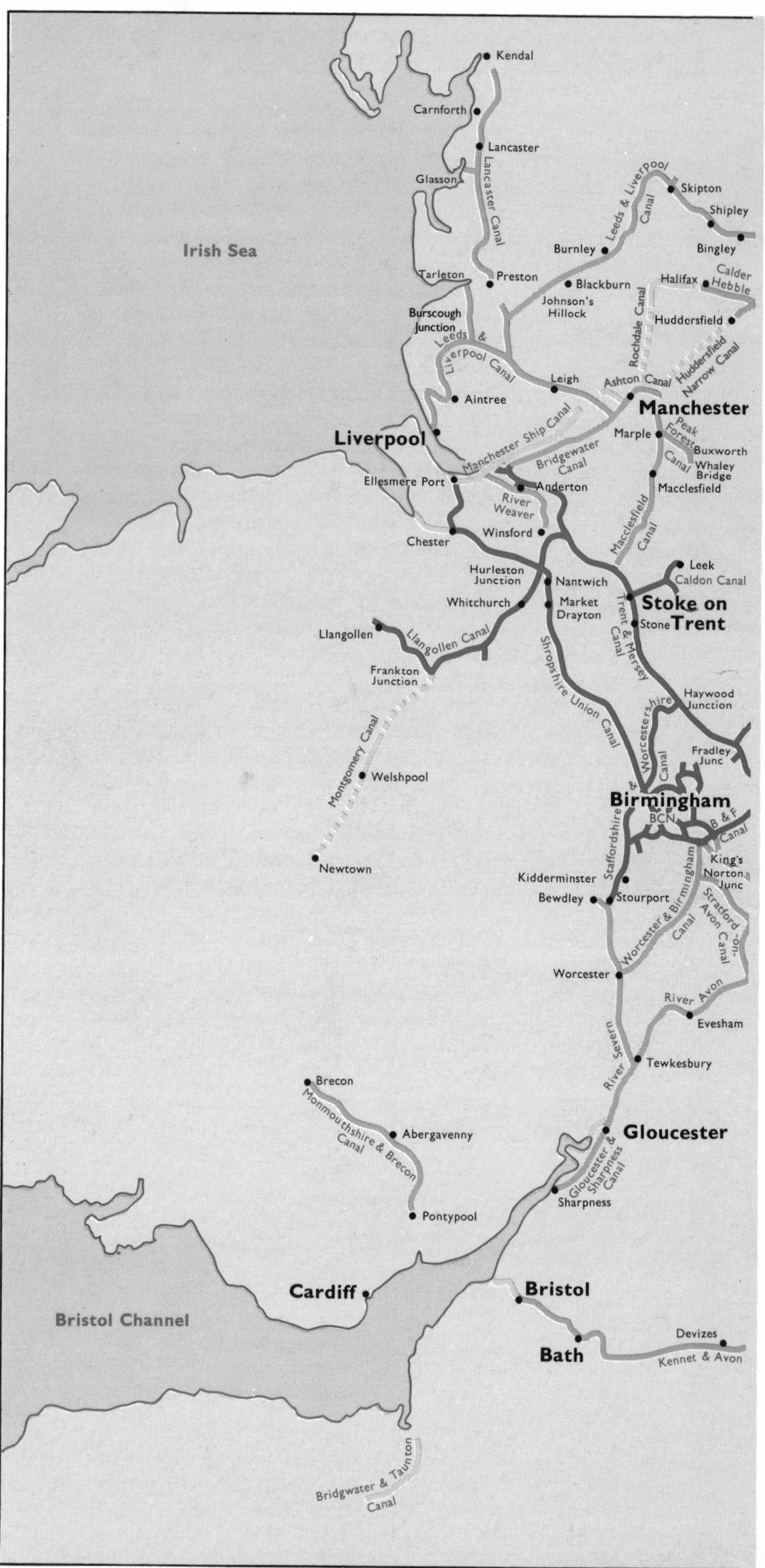

Kendal
Carnforth
Lancaster
Glasson
Lancaster Canal
Irish Sea
Skipton
Leeds & Liverpool Canal
Shipley
Bingley
Burnley
Tarleton
Preston
Blackburn
Halifax
Calder Hebble
Johnson's Hillock
Burscough Junction
Rochdale Canal
Huddersfield
Leeds & Liverpool Canal
Huddersfield Narrow Canal
Leigh
Ashton Canal
Aintree
Manchester
Liverpool
Manchester Ship Canal
Marple
Peak Forest Canal
Buxworth
Bridgewater Canal
Whaley Bridge
Ellesmere Port
Anderton
Macclesfield
River Weaver
Winsford
Chester
Macclesfield Canal
Leek
Hurleston Junction
Nantwich
Caldon Canal
Whitchurch
Market Drayton
Stoke on Trent
Stone
Llangollen
Llangollen Canal
Trent & Mersey Canal
Frankton Junction
Shropshire Union Canal
Haywood Junction
Staffordshire & Worcestershire Canal
Fradley Junc
Montgomery Canal
Welshpool
Birmingham
BCN
B & F Canal
Newtown
King's Norton Junc
Kidderminster
Bewdley
Stourport
Worcester & Birmingham Canal
Stratford-on-Avon Canal
Worcester
River Avon
Evesham
River Severn
Tewkesbury
Brecon
Abergavenny
Gloucester
Monmouthshire & Brecon Canal
Gloucester & Sharpness Canal
Sharpness
Pontypool
Cardiff
Bristol
Bristol Channel
Devizes
Bath
Kennet & Avon
Bridgwater & Taunton Canal

Waterways Map showing Nicholson Guide Areas
Waterways covered in this guide
Waterways covered in other guides in the series
Other Waterways
Waterways unnavigable at present time
North Sea
Ripon
Ripon Canal
York
River Ouse
Leeds
Aire & Calder Navigation
Selby Canal
Selby
Pocklington Canal
Market Weighton Canal
River Hull
Hull
Castleford
Wakefield
Goole
Keadby
River Ancholme
Stainforth
Sheffield & South Yorkshire Navigation
Doncaster
River Trent
River Idle
West Stockwith
Rotherham
Gainsborough
Sheffield
Worksop
Chesterfield Canal
Torksey
Fossdyke & Witham Navigations
Lincoln
Newark
Erewash Canal
Gunthorpe
Boston
Nottingham
Trent & Mersey Canal
Burton upon Trent
Grand Union Canal
River Soar
Loughborough
Kings Lynn
Wisbech
Tamworth
Coventry Canal
Ashby Canal
Leicester
Peterborough
River Nene
Foxton
Market Harborough
Marston Junction
Rugby
Oxford Canal
Grand Union Canal Leicester Section
Welford
Bedford Rivers
Coventry
Kingswood Junc
Crick
River Great Ouse
Norton Junction
Napton Junction
Braunston Turn
Gayton Junction
Northampton
River Cam
Cambridge
Stratford-upon-Avon
Stoke Bruerne
Cosgrove
Banbury
Leighton Buzzard
Bishops Stortford
Thrupp
Aylesbury
Marsworth
Hertford
River Stort
Berkhamstead
Oxford
Watford
Lee Navigation
LONDON
River Thames
Slough
Reading
Hungerford
Crofton
Canal
Newbury
Aldershot
Basingstoke Canal
River Wey
Guildford
River Medway
Chatham
Maidstone

HOW TO USE THIS GUIDE

The maps are drawn at a scale of 2 inches to 1 mile. Adjacent to each map section is a description of the countryside and places of interest together with a commentary on the course of the canal or river. Details of the boatyards and pubs marked are also given, adjacent to each map, and are arranged in order from the top of the page to the bottom.

Symbols and abbreviations used in the text:

Ⓑ	Boatyard or boatyard services
R	Refuse disposal
S	Sewage or 'Elsan' disposal
W	Water
P	Petrol
D	Diesel
E	Electric boat recharging
☕	Public house
✕	Restaurant
!	Licensed to sell alcohol
L	Open for lunch
D	Open for dinner
EC	Early closing
MD	Market day
BW	British Waterways
IWA	Inland Waterways Association
NT	National Trust

Symbols used on maps:

Ⓑ	Boatyard or boatyard services
☕	Public house
R	Refuse disposal
S	Sewage or 'Elsan' disposal point
W	Water point

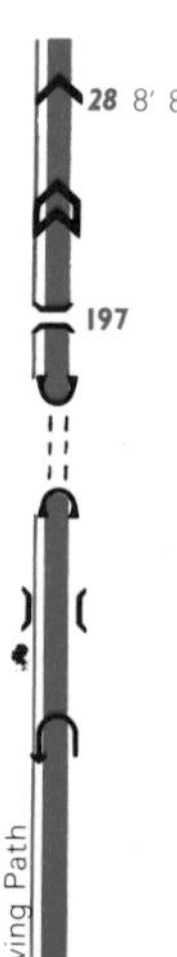

Locks, with number and 'rise'. The symbol points uphill.

Staircase locks.

Bridge and its number. Many are named.

Tunnel – often described in the text.

Aqueduct – often described in the text.

Winding hole – turning point for boats longer than the ordinary width of the canal (it's pronounced as in the wind that blows). Canal junctions are also good places to 'wind'.

Weir.

Scale and north point
The strip maps are drawn at 2 inches to 1 mile. North is indicated on each map.

Navigational notes
These appear where necessary to point out potential hazards, navigational limits or other vital information.

Boatyards
Services listed are those usually available; do not, however, expect a hire base to stop what they are doing on fleet 'turn around' day (usually Saturday) to help you – *they will be extremely busy*. Any other day you are sure to be made to feel welcome. Remember also that moorings get filled very quickly, so do not assume that there will be space for your boat. Always ask.

A feature of these guides is the 'milestone' which appears on every map thus:

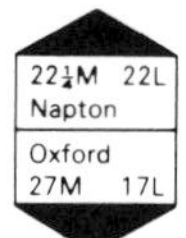

This performs many useful functions. It reminds you of your direction of travel – in this example **up** the page is towards Napton, **down** the page is towards Oxford; it denotes distances and indicates the number of locks between the milestone and strategic points (usually junctions) along the waterway – in this example, Napton is 22¼ miles (M) with 22 locks (L) from the 'milestone', and Oxford is 27 miles and 17 locks from the milestone. By deducting the miles and locks on one milestone from those on the next, distances from page to page can be accurately estimated. Using the 'lock-miles' system (see **Planning a cruise**, page 165) the time your journey will take can be calculated, and with a little experience based on your speed of travel and lock operation, your own time formula can be arrived at.

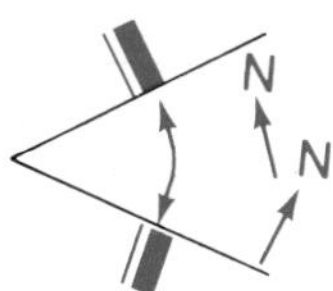

Where this device occurs on a map it simply means that the actual route of the waterway would not fit neatly onto the page, so the cartographer has 'bent' the map, using two north points. The navigator on the water, or the walker on the bank, will notice nothing amiss. Distances in this book should be measured along the thick blue line only, not including these gaps.

LOCKS AND THEIR USE

The different locks and their attendant machinery are a source of endless fascination for all waterway users. Understanding why they are there and the principle upon which they work will help you in their use.

A lock is a device for transporting craft from a higher water level to a lower level, or vice versa, for example when a canal crosses a range of hills. It consists of a box with gates at each end, and a separate means of letting water in at the top (higher level) and out at the bottom (lower level). This is controlled by paddles. These paddles may simply open and shut holes in the gates (gate paddles), or they may open and shut underground culverts (ground paddles). A windlass (carried on the boat) is used to wind the paddles open and shut. Whilst locks differ in detail, the following instructions will apply in the case of the vast majority of *narrow* canal locks. Some extra points regarding wide locks are covered later.

A typical narrow lock

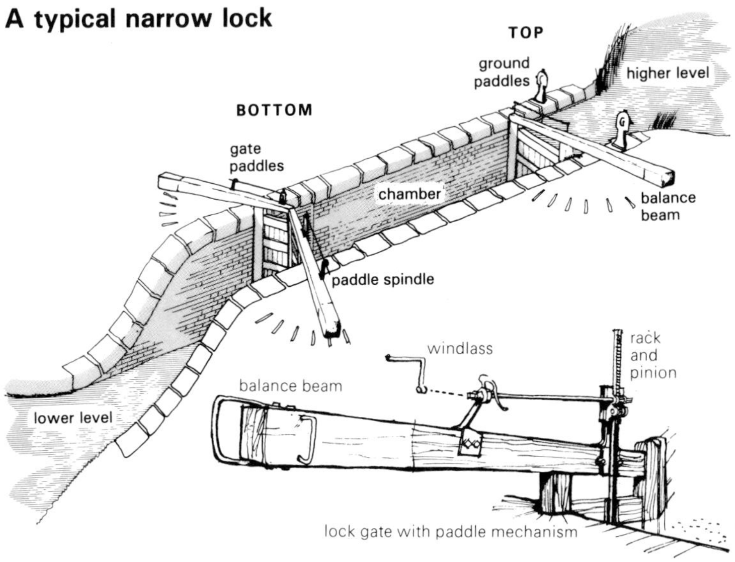

How to go through a lock

PRELIMINARIES

Stop the boat well outside the lock and secure it. If members of your crew can get off the boat before the lock (at the narrow point under a bridge for example) and run ahead to prepare the lock, this will save time.

GOING UP IN A LOCK (LOCKING UP)

Lock empty – ie water at lower level

Open bottom gate(s)
Drive boat in
Close bottom gate(s)
Check bottom paddles closed
Keep boat near to the bottom of lock
Open top paddles to fill lock
Open top gate(s) when lock is full
Drive boat out
Close top gate(s)
Close top paddles

Lock full – ie water at higher level

Check top gate(s) and paddles closed
Open bottom paddles to drain lock
Open bottom gate(s)
Drive boat in
Close bottom gate(s) and paddles
Keep boat near to the bottom of lock
Open top paddles to fill lock
Open top gate(s) when lock is full
Drive boat out
Close top gate(s)
Close top paddles

GOING DOWN IN A LOCK (LOCKING DOWN)

Lock full – ie water at higher level

Open top gate(s)
Drive boat in
Close top gate(s)
Check top paddles closed
Keep boat near to the bottom of the lock
Open bottom paddles to empty lock
Open bottom gate(s)
Drive boat out
Close bottom gates and paddles

Lock empty – ie water at lower level

Check bottom gate(s) and paddles closed
Open top paddles to fill lock
Open gate(s)
Drive boat in
Close top gate(s) and paddles
Keep boat near to the bottom of the lock
Open bottom paddles to empty lock
Open bottom gate(s)
Drive boat out
Close bottom gate(s) and paddles

If you have to drain or fill a lock in order to enter it, make sure there is no boat approaching that could usefully use the lock before you. Always try to conserve water, which is being continually passed down the canal from its summit and thus requires constant replenishment at a higher level.

SOME GENERAL DO'S AND DON'TS AT LOCKS

Do not leave your windlass slotted onto the paddle spindle – if something slips it could be thrown off and cause injury.

Always leave all gates and paddles closed when you leave, but look out for notices which may give other instructions for the proper operation of a particular lock.

Always wind the paddles down – letting them drop is bad practice, and causes damage.

Beware of protrusions in the side walls of the lock chamber that may damage the boat, and don't use fenders in narrow locks – they may jam.

When opening and closing lock gates, keep to the landward side of the balance beam.

Don't rush around at locks, especially in wet weather, when the sides are slippery. Never jump across partly opened gates.

Always make the safety of the crew and boat your prime concern and remember that if things do start to go wrong, you can stop everything by closing the paddles.

There is no reason why your children, wearing buoyancy aids and properly supervised, should not help at locks – it is all part of the fun, after all – but impress upon them the potential dangers, and establish some commonsense rules. You have no authority over other people's children, and their participation should be discouraged. Great difficulties could ensue should they be injured in any way.

Beware of fierce top gate paddles, especially in wide locks.

Don't leave your windlass behind; hundreds are lost this way each year.

WIDE LOCKS

Taking a narrowboat (7ft beam) through a wide lock (14ft) can present special difficulties, especially when locking up. If all the top paddles were to be opened fully at the same time, the boat would be buffeted considerably. The diagram below illustrates one method of ensuring a smooth passage. The stern line held ashore will provide added security.

Locking up in a wide lock

(a suggested technique)

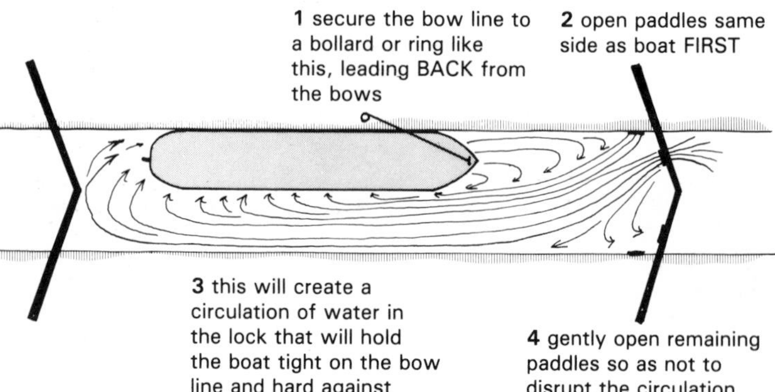

1 secure the bow line to a bollard or ring like this, leading BACK from the bows
2 open paddles same side as boat FIRST
3 this will create a circulation of water in the lock that will hold the boat tight on the bow line and hard against the side of the lock
4 gently open remaining paddles so as not to disrupt the circulation already established

STAIRCASE LOCKS

Where the top gates of one lock are the bottom gates of the next. Usually there is a board nearby giving operating instructions – read it carefully and make sure you understand it before you start. And remember: in a narrow staircase you can't pass a boat coming the other way.

GENERAL CRUISING INFORMATION

All the waterways covered in this book are controlled by British Waterways. All craft using BW canals must be licensed and those using BW rivers must be registered. Charges are based on the length of the boat and a canal craft licence covers all the navigable waterways under BW's control. Permits for permanent mooring on the canals are also issued by BW. Apply in each case to the British Waterways Offices listed on page 173 or to:

Customer Services,
British Waterways,
Greycaine Road,
Watford,
WD2 4JR
(0923 226422).

Getting afloat

There is no better way of discovering the joys of canals than by getting afloat. The best thing is to hire a boat for a week or a fortnight from one of the boatyards on the canals (each boatyard has an entry in the text, and most of them offer craft for hire; brochures may be easily obtained from such boatyards). Or, go on one of the many trip boats for a couple of hours, or longer.

General cruising

Most canals are saucer-shaped in section and so are deepest in the middle. Very few have more than 3–4ft of water and many have much less. Try to keep to the middle of the channel except on bends, where the deepest water is on the *outside* of the bend. When you meet another boat, the rule is to keep to the right, slow down, and aim to miss the approaching boat by a couple of yards: do not steer right over to the bank or you will most likely run aground. The deeper the draught of the boat, the more important it is to keep in the middle of the deep water, and so this must be considered when passing other boats. If you meet a loaded working boat, keep right out of the way. Working boats should always be given precedence, for their time is money. If you meet a boat being towed from the bank, pass it on the outside rather than intercept the towing line. When overtaking, keep the other boat on your starboard, or right, side.

Speed

There is a general speed limit of 4mph on most British Waterways canals. This is not just an arbitrary limit: there is no need to go any faster, and in many cases it is impossible to cruise even at this speed. Canals were not built for motor boats, and so the banks are easily damaged by excessive wash and turbulence. Erosion of the banks makes the canal more shallow, which in turn makes running aground a more frequent occurrence. So keep to the limits and try not to aggravate the situation. It is easy to see when a boat is creating excessive turbulence by looking at the wash – if it is 'breaking' or causing large waves, you are going too fast and should slow down.

Slow down also when passing moored craft, engineering works and anglers.

Slow down when there is a lot of floating rubbish on the water: old planks and plastic bags may mean underwater obstacles that can damage a boat or its propeller if hit hard. Try to drift over obvious obstructions in neutral.

Slow down when approaching blind corners, narrow bridges and junctions.

Running aground

The effective end of commercial traffic on the narrow canals has resulted in canals being shallower than ever. Running aground is not uncommon, but is rarely serious, as the canal bed is usually soft. If you run aground, try first of all to pull the boat off by gently reversing the engine. If this fails, use the pole as a lever against the bank or some solid object, in combination with a tow rope being pulled from the bank. Do not keep revving the engine in reverse if it is obviously having no effect. Another way is to get your crew to rock the boat from side to side while using the pole or mooring lines. If all else fails, lighten your load; make all the crew leave the boat except the helmsman, and then it will often float off quite easily.

Remember that if you run aground once, it is likely to happen again as it indicates a particularly shallow stretch – or that you are out of the channel. If you are continually bumping the bottom in a shallow stretch, it may be that you are going too fast, causing the boat to 'dig in' at the back. Going less fast may make things more comfortable.

In a town it is not uncommon to run aground on sunken rubbish; this is most likely to occur near bridges and housing estates. Use the same methods, but be very careful as these hard objects can easily damage your boat or propeller.

Remember that winding holes are often silted up – do not go further in than you have to.

Mooring

All boats carry metal stakes and a mallet. These are used for mooring when there are no rings or bollards in sight, which is usually the case. Generally speaking you may moor anywhere to

BW property but there are certain basic rules. Avoid mooring anywhere that could cause an obstruction to other boats; do not moor on a bend, in a winding hole or a narrow stretch, do not moor abreast boats already moored. Never moor in a lock, and do not be tempted to tie up in a tunnel or under a bridge if it is raining. Pick a stretch where there is a reasonable depth of water at the bank, otherwise the boat may bump and scrape the canal bed – an unpleasant sensation if you are trying to sleep. For reasons of peace and quiet and privacy it is best to moor away from main roads and railway lines.

Never stretch your mooring lines across the towpath; you may trip someone up and face a claim for damages.

There is no need to show a riding light at night, except on major rivers and busy commercial canals.

Beware of mooring at unrecognised sites in cities – you may attract the unwelcome attention of vandals.

So long as you are sensible and keep to the rules, mooring can be a pleasant gesture of individuality.

Knots

A simple and easy way of securing a rope to a bollard or mooring stake is to use a couple of round turns and a half hitch or two made with a loop and pulled tight. This can be released quickly by pulling the loose end, which will have been left tidily coiled.

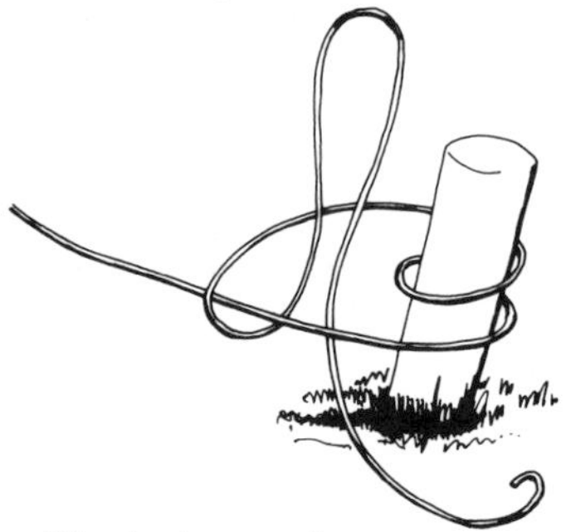

When leaving a mooring, coil all the ropes up again. They will then be out of the way, but ready if needed in a hurry. Many a sailor has fallen overboard after tripping on an uncoiled rope.

Fixed bridges

At most bridges the canal becomes very narrow, a means of saving building costs developed by the engineers. As a result, careful navigation is called for if you are to avoid hitting either the bridge sides with the hull, or the arch with the cabin top. As when entering a lock, the best way to tackle 'bridgeholes' is to slow down well in advance and aim to go straight through, keeping a steady course. Adjustments should be kept to a minimum for it is easy to start the boat zig-zagging, which will inevitably end in a collision. One technique is to gauge the width of the approaching bridgehole relative to the width of the boat, and then watch one side only, aiming to miss that side by a small margin – say 6in; the smaller you can make the margin, the less chance you have of hitting the other side of the bridge. If you do hit the bridge sides when going slowly it is not likely to do much damage; it will merely strengthen your resolve to do better next time.

Moveable bridges

Swing and lift bridges are an attractive feature of some canals and cannot be ignored as they often rest only 2 or 3ft above the water. They are moved by being swivelled horizontally, or raised vertically. Operation is usually manual, although some have gearing to ease the movement. There are one or two mechanised versions; these have clear instructions at control points. Before operating any bridge make sure that approaching road traffic is aware of your intention to open the bridge. Use protective barriers if there are any and remember to close the bridge again after you.

Some *lift bridges are very unstable*, and could close while your boat is passing underneath, with disastrous consequences. For this reason it is prudent to have your strongest (or heaviest) crew member hold it open until the boat is clear. Many swing bridges are very heavy to operate, and require two strong people to move them. Keep your crew off the sides of the boat when you are negotiating narrow bridges – they could easily be knocked off, and seriously injured.

Tunnels

Many people consider a canal incomplete without one or two tunnels, and certainly they are an exciting feature of any trip. Nearly all are easy to navigate, although there are a few basic rules:

Make sure your boat has a good headlight in working order and *always* use it.

If it is a narrow tunnel (ie 7ft) make sure there is no boat coming the other way *before* you enter. Craft of 7ft beam can pass in some wide tunnels – slow right down when you meet to lessen the almost inevitable bump.

In most tunnels the roof drips constantly, especially under ventilation shafts. Put on a raincoat and some form of hat before going in.

A notice on the tunnel portal will give its length, in yards, and will say whether unpowered craft are permitted to use it.

Where there are restrictions on time of entry, and one-way systems, these must be adhered to. To meet head on half way through a long narrow tunnel would create great difficulties.

Care of the engine

Canal boats are generally powered by either diesel, petrol or two-stroke engines. If you have a hire craft, the boatyard will give you instructions for your daily maintenance, which will no doubt include some or all of the following:

Every day before starting off, you should:

Check the oil level in the engine.
Check the fuel level in the tank.

If your engine is water-cooled, check that the filter near the intake is clean and weed free. Otherwise the engine will over-heat, which could cause serious damage.

Check the level of distilled water in the battery, and ensure that it is charging correctly.

Lubricate any parts of the engine, gearbox or steering that need daily attention.

Check that the propeller is free of weeds, wire, plastic bags and any other rubbish. The propeller and the water filter should be checked whenever there is any suspicion of obstruction or overheating – which may mean several times a day.

Pump the bilges every day.

If there is a stern gland greaser, screw it down a turn at the end of each day's cruising.

When navigating in shallow water, keep in mind the exposed position of the propeller. If you hit any underwater obstruction put the engine into neutral immediately. When running over any large floating object put the engine into neutral and wait for the object to appear astern before re-engaging the drive.

Fuel

Petrol engines and petrol/oil outboards are catered for by some boatyards and all road-side fuel stations. Running out is inconvenient; remember you may have to walk several miles carrying a heavy can.

Diesel-powered craft, and narrowboats in particular, can usually cruise for over two weeks before needing to be refilled. Those using diesel-powered hire craft rarely need to be concerned about fuel. Those with their own boats, however, should bear in mind that boatyards are few and far between on some parts of the network, and should a diesel-powered boat run out of fuel, the system will need to be bled before the engine can run again. Most boatyards sell marine diesel (indicated D in the text), which is cheaper than the road fuel.

Electrically powered boats

These are becoming increasingly popular on the inland waterways, in view of their quietness and lack of environmental pollution. Indicated E under the **BOATYARD** heading are those establishments known to offer recharging facilities – polite enquiry by electric boat users will certainly reveal more. If you are lucky enough to be using this form of power, please note the following.

All boats using this information are assumed to have a battery charger on board and 50 metres of cable fitted with standard 13 amp terminals.

It is essential for the safety of the boater, the owner of the supply and the general public that a proper residual current circuit breaker (RCD) be carried by the boat and fitted between the boat's cable and the supply unless the supply is already so protected. The RCD must be tested for correct operation before battery charging starts.

Water

Fresh water taps occur irregularly along the canals, usually at boatyards, BW depots, or by lock cottages. These are marked on the maps in the guide. Ensure that there is a long water hose on the boat (BW taps have a ½-inch slip-on hose connection). Fill up every day.

Lavatories

Some canal boats are fitted with chemical lavatories which have to be emptied from time to time. Never empty them over the side or tip them into the bushes. Use the sewage disposal points marked on the map S, for which you will need a BW key, or at boatyards. Many boats now have pump-out toilets, which must be emptied with a special machine – usually at boatyards and indicated in the text. This symbol at the canalside indicates just such a 'pump-out station' (although not all boatyards with the facility display it). Expect to have to pay.

Some BW depots and boatyards have lavatories for the use of boat crews; again, you may need your BW key.

Litter

Some canals are in a poor state today because they have long been misused as unofficial dumps for rubbish, especially in towns. Out of sight is only out of mind until some object is tangled round your propeller. So keep all rubbish until you can dispose of it at a refuse disposal point, indicated R on the map, or at a boatyard equipped to deal with it.

By-laws

Although no-one needs a 'driving licence' to navigate a boat, boat users should remember that they have certain responsibilities to others on the waterways and should abide by the Waterways Code (available from BW offices). Prospective navigators are advised to obtain a copy of the by-laws relevant to the waterways on which they are to travel.

Stoppages

Although BW and other navigation authorities plan their maintenance for the winter months, it often becomes necessary to carry out repairs during the cruising season. Many of the structures on the canal system are beginning to show their age (especially the tunnels) and repairs are a lengthy and costly affair, sometimes resulting in stoppages lasting many years. A long dry spell can lower water levels and restrict lock operation, and of course a canal embankment can breach at any time.

To avoid disappointment it is wise to check that your planned route is clear before you set off, and that there are no time restrictions on locks that may upset your schedule. Those using hire craft may be able to get this information from their boatyard, although some are surprisingly lax. It is best to check for yourself by ringing the BW Area Offices (listed on page 173) or the relevant navigation authority. News of any last minute stoppages is available on 'Canalphone', as a recorded message. Ring 071-723 8486 for the North and Midlands, or 071-723 8487 for the South and Midlands. Check before you go.

ASHBY

Maximum dimensions

Length: 72′
Beam: 7′
Headroom: 6′ 6″

Manager:

(0203) 392250

Mileage

MARSTON JUNCTION (Coventry Canal) to
Burton Hastings: 3
Hinckley Wharf: 6
Stoke Golding Wharf: 8¾
Dadlington: 10
Shenton Aqueduct: 13
Market Bosworth Wharf: 15
Congerstone: 17¼
Shackerstone: 18¼
Snarestone Tunnel: 21
CANAL TERMINUS: 21¾

No locks

Looking at this canal on a map it appears to be very much out on a limb. In fact the Ashby Canal – often referred to as the Ashby de la Zouch Canal – was originally intended to be a through route from the River Trent at Burton to the Coventry Canal near Bedworth, but this plan was repeatedly shelved. In 1792 however an Ashby Canal Company was formed and a Bill promoted, mostly by the owners of Leicestershire limeworks and the new coalfields near Ashby de la Zouch, who decided that an outlet southwards was required from their various works. The problem that soon arose was that while the proposed canal could be built level for 30 miles from the junction with the Coventry Canal at Marston Jabbett, near Bedworth, to Moira, the section north of Moira would require expensive and complicated works including locks, reservoirs, pumping engines and possibly a tunnel. Part of this cost was in fact avoided by building an extensive system of tramroads to and around the various coalmines and limeworks. However, while the canal was still being built (by a succession of engineers – Jessop, Outram, Whitworth senior and junior, and Thomas Newbold), the new coalmines near Ashby Woulds were found to be less productive than had been hoped. This, combined with the fact that the canal was never extended north to the Trent, was instrumental in preventing the Ashby Canal from making a profit for 20 years. However a new coal mine sunk at Moira in 1804 (two years after the completion of the canal) eventually produced coal of such excellent quality that it became widely demanded in London and southern England. The canal flourished at last.

In 1845 the Midland Railway bought up the Ashby Canal – with the approval of all concerned except the Coventry and Oxford Canal companies, who stood to lose a lot in tolls if the coal traffic from Moira switched to rail carriage. These two companies managed to hamstring the Midland Railway so effectively over its management of the canal that instead of switching to carriage by rail, the coal traffic from Moira continued along the canal at a substantial level right through to the turn of the century. It is therefore hard to see what real benefit the railway company gained from buying the canal.

Subsidence from the coal mines near Measham has caused great damage in this century to the canal that served them. This subsidence has brought about the abandonment of over 9 miles of the canal, so that the canal now terminates just north of Snarestone, outside the coalfield. There is no regular trade left on the canal, the last load of coal being carried to Croxley (Herts) from Gopsall Wharf in 1970.

Bosworth Wharf on the lock-free Ashby Canal. *Derek Pratt.*

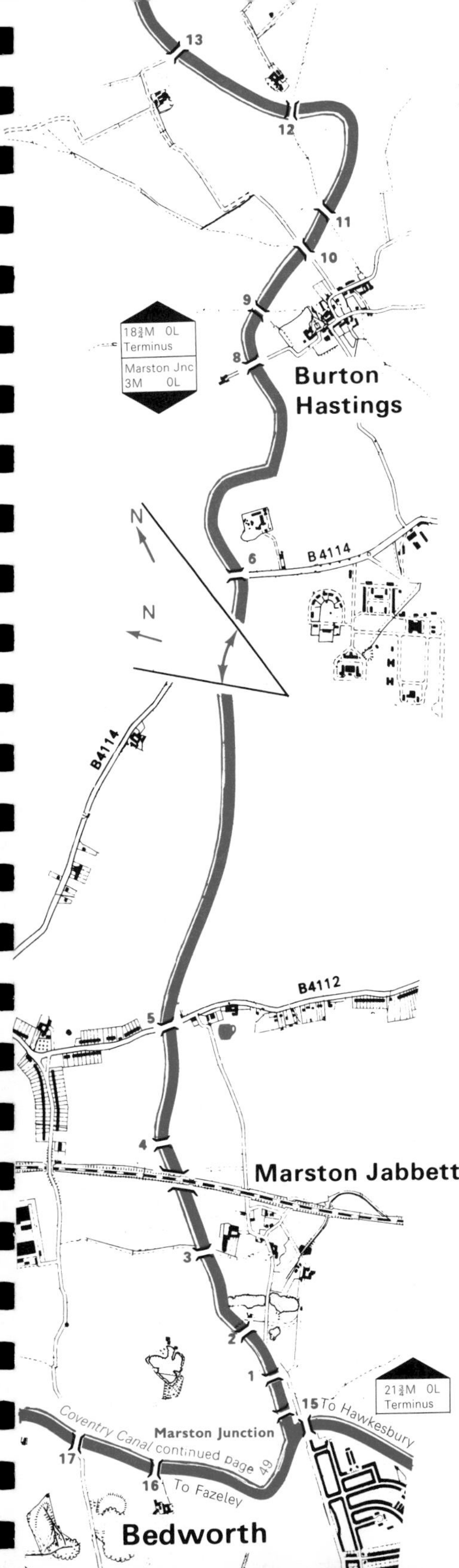

Burton Hastings

At Marston Junction the Ashby Canal branches east off the Coventry. Free guides to the canal are kept in a box at the junction (BW key required). As soon as it leaves Marston, the canal changes completely and dramatically. The industry and housing estates that had accompanied the Coventry Canal through the Nuneaton–Bedworth conurbation suddenly vanish to be replaced by green fields, farms and trees. In this way the character of the Ashby Canal is established at once: also the first of the typical stone-arched bridges occurs which, together with the shallow and clear water, suggests a rurality far from the industrial Midlands. Only the power lines that criss-cross this stretch are a memory of the other world to the west. A long wooded cutting leads the canal towards Burton Hastings, a typical farming village. Then the canal turns north, setting a course for Hinckley passing, to the east of bridge 13, Stretton Baskerville, a 'lost' village. In many places along the canal the towpath disappears, making walking very difficult. The B4114 and the B4112 cross the canal.

Burton Hastings
Warwicks. PO, tel. Quiet village set on a hill in open farmland. The pretty, well-placed church has a decorated font of 1300.

PUBS

Corner House Hotel Bulkington Lane, Marston Jabbett. Very large friendly pub with a public bar and a vast wood-panelled lounge. Marstons real ale, good bar meals, garden with unusual pets.

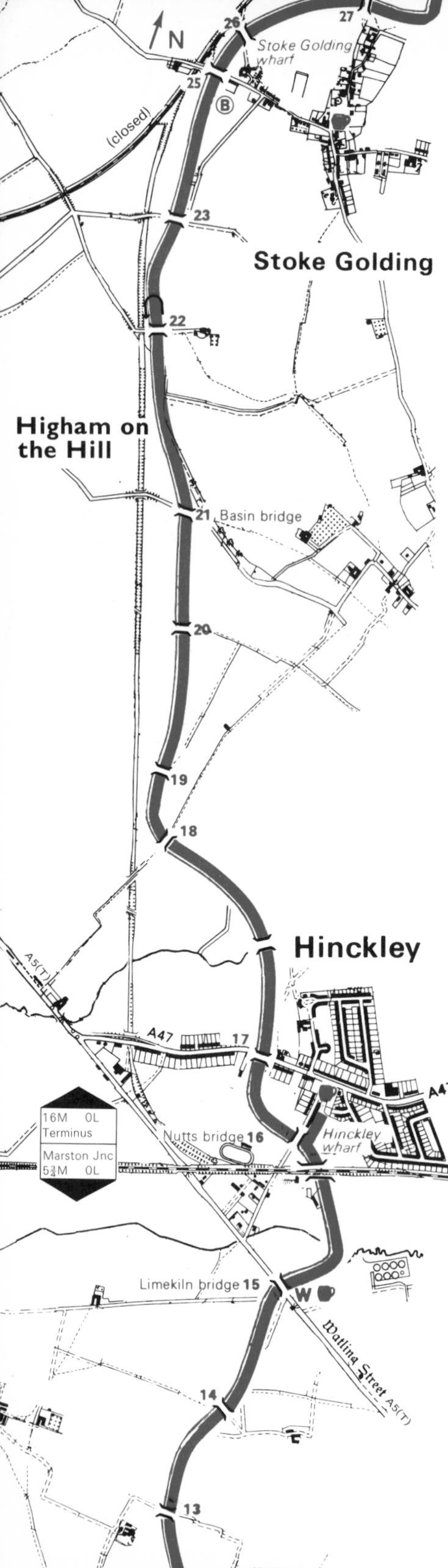

Hinckley

Keeping west of Hinckley, the canal continues through the fine rolling farmland that typifies the Ashby Canal; a short arm runs east to the town wharf. The canal then runs fairly straight to Stoke Golding where there is one of the finest churches in Leicestershire. There are no locks, but the typical Ashby accommodation bridges occur regularly. Throughout its length the Ashby Canal is remote and rural, a haven from the industry that surrounds it, and an ironic contrast to its *raison d'être*, the Ashby coalfields. The A5 (Watling Street) and the A47 cross near Hinckley. There is no navigation on the Hinckley Wharf Arm, which is used as a boat club mooring. The towpath is non-existent between bridges 17 and 18.

Stoke Golding
Leics. EC Wed. PO, tel, stores, garage. The church is very beautiful, full of original 13th and 14thC work. It is large, on a hill, and the spire dominates the landscape. The carving of the windows and the column capitals is especially fine. Crown Hill, near the wharf, marks the place where Henry Tudor was crowned king after the battle of Bosworth Field in 1485. There are good moorings between bridges 27 and 28.

Higham on the Hill
Leics. PO, tel, stores. 1 mile west of bridges 21 and 23. Quiet village on a hill overlooking the canal. To the west is the huge proving ground used by the Motor Industry Research Association for testing new vehicles. The end of the banking can be seen from the canal.

Hinckley
Leics. EC Thur. MD Mon. PO, tel, stores, garage, station, cinema. A hosiery manufacturing town that can boast of having installed the first stocking machine in Leicestershire, in 1640. There are few buildings of interest, and only the mound of the castle remains. A row of timber-framed thatched cottages survives in Bond Street, a memento of a pre-industrial era.

BOATYARDS

Ⓑ **Ashby Narrowboat Company** The Canal Wharf, Stoke Golding, Nuneaton. (0455 212671). [R][S][W][D] Pump-out, narrowboat hire, gas, day hire craft, overnight mooring, long-term mooring, winter storage, slipway, chandlery, books and maps, boat building, boat sales, engine repairs, toilets, gifts. *Closed Sun.*

PUBS

- **George & Dragon** Stoke Golding. Food.
- **White Swan** Stoke Golding. Food.
- **Wharf Inn** Hinckley. Marstons real ale, food. Snacks, garden. Good general store and butcher's shop nearby.
- **Lime Kilns Inn** Watling Street, Hinckley. Canalside. Marstons real ale in an unself-consciously preserved pub, with a tap room and a large basic public bar; traditional pub games and lively conversation are the entertainment. Food, moorings for patrons, garden. [W]
- **Three Horse Shoes** Stoke Golding. Food. Children welcome.

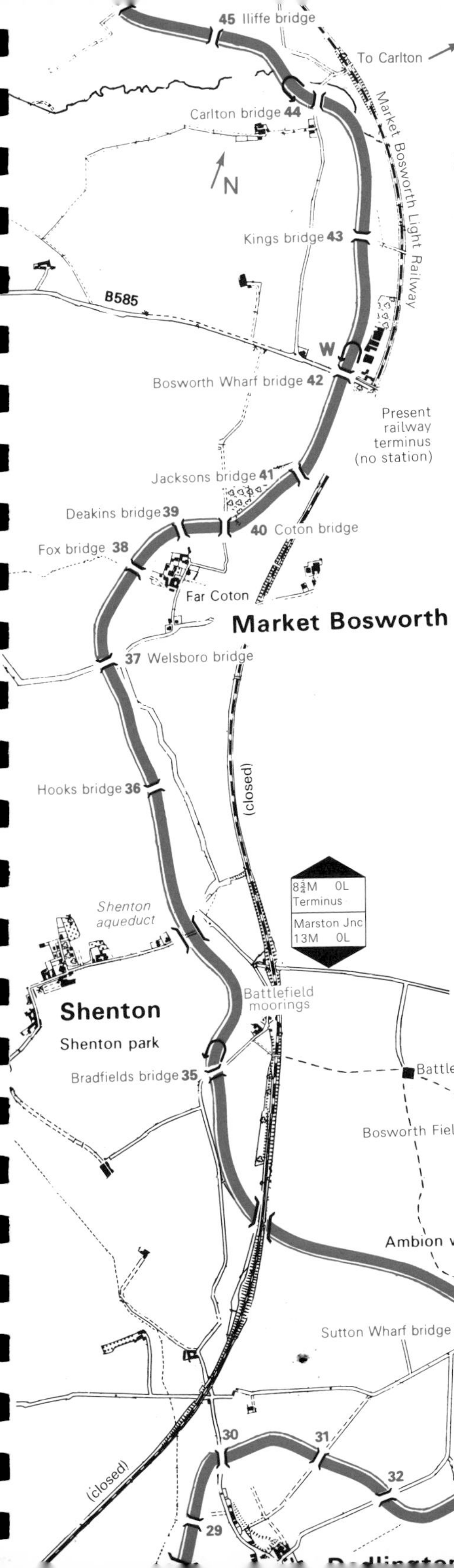

Market Bosworth

After Stoke Golding the contours cause the canal to meander, passing Dadlington and Shenton, where there are good moorings for the Battlefield Centre. After Shenton it resumes a general north west course. Shenton Park is passed on an embankment, and then an aqueduct carries the canal over the road to Shenton village. It then continues through light woods towards Congerstone, Market Bosworth and Carlton being set away to the east. All the Ashby characteristics are present: no locks and a quiet, remote and wholly rural environment.

Market Bosworth
Leics. EC Wed. MD Wed. PO, tel, stores, garage, wine bar. 1 mile east of its wharf. Small market town remaining much as it was in the 18thC. The size and style of the church reflect the one-time importance of the town. The Hall was extensively altered in the late 19thC. There are several good pubs.

Shenton
Leics. PO box, tel, stores. Well-preserved estate village clustered around the Hall, a house of 1629 much rebuilt in the 19thC. The Victorian church has a good 17thC monument. The predominance of farming in this area is shown by the large amount of home produce offered for sale in the village.

Battle of Bosworth Field 22 August 1485
Ambion Hill, Sutton Cheyney. The battlefield where Richard III, last of the Plantagenets, was killed by Henry Tudor who thus became Henry VII. An excellent ¾ mile walk from Shenton Embankment across rolling countryside to the Battlefield Centre, housed in a splendid group of red-brick farm buildings. Trails lead through Ambion Wood and plaques along the way explain the battle. *Open afternoons Mar–Oct.* Café, toilets, picnic area, souvenirs. Admission charge.

Dadlington
Leics. PO box, tel. Village built around a green with much new development. The church dates from the 13thC.

BOAT TRIPS

Bosworth Field Boat Trips From bridge 34, ¾ hour trips by Battle of Bosworth site *on Sun afternoons*. Ring (0455) 847667 for details. Also private charter.

PUBS

- **Gate** Carlton. Food.
- **Dog & Hedgehog** Dadlington. Food.
- **Hercules Inn** Sutton Cheyney. Food.

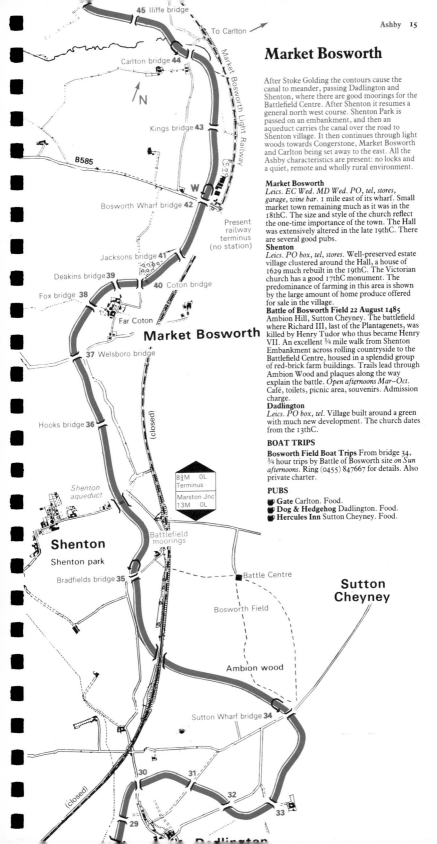

45 Iliffe bridge
To Carlton
Market Bosworth Light Railway
Carlton bridge 44
N
Kings bridge 43
B585
W
Bosworth Wharf bridge 42
Present railway terminus (no station)
Jacksons bridge 41
Deakins bridge 39
40 Coton bridge
Fox bridge 38
Far Coton
Market Bosworth
37 Welsboro bridge
Hooks bridge 36
(closed)
$8\frac{3}{4}$M 0L Terminus
Marston Jnc 13M 0L
Shenton aqueduct
Shenton
Shenton park
Battlefield moorings
Bradfields bridge 35
Battle Centre
Sutton Cheyney
Bosworth Field
Ambion wood
Sutton Wharf bridge 34
30
31
32
33
29
(closed)

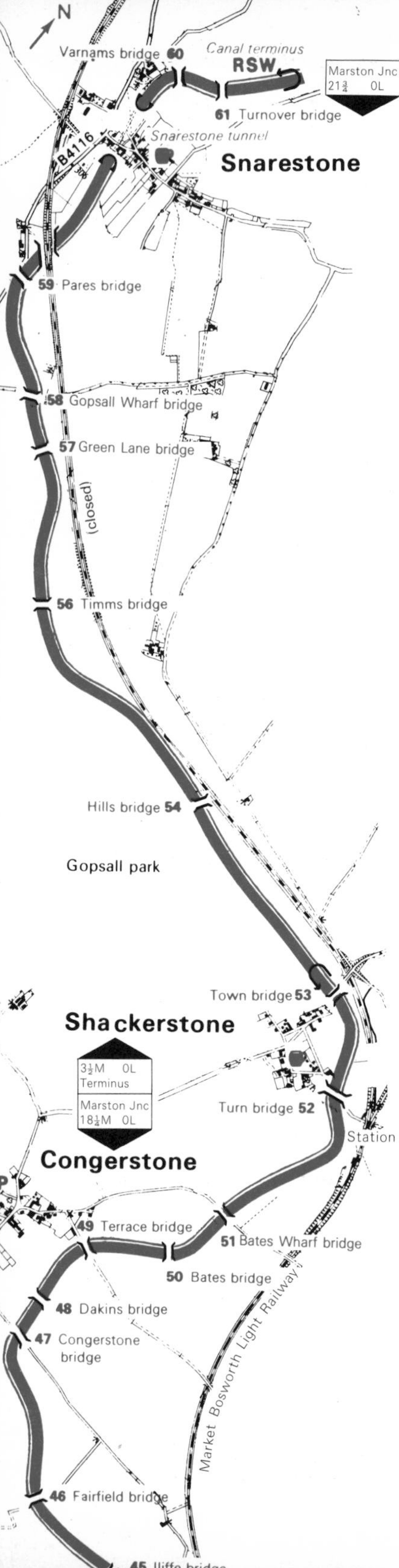

Snarestone

Continuing north west, the canal passes Congerstone and Shackerstone, crossing the River Sence. After Gopsall Park the hills become more prominent, although the quality of the landscape does not change. Snarestone sits on a ridge at right-angles to the canal, which passes beneath the village through the tunnel, the only one on the canal. After the tunnel there are two more stone arched bridges, and then the present terminus is reached. There is a winding hole, sanitary station and picnic area. The canal once continued for another 9 miles to Moira, passing through Measham on the way; constant trouble from subsidence made it impossible to retain this last section. The same subsidence may account for the rather poor state of the towpath in places. The present terminus means that the Ashby Canal is idyllic and rural throughout its length. There is no hint of the coal mines and heavy industry that prompted its creation.

Snarestone
Leics. PO, tel, stores, garage. An 18thC farming village built over the top of the canal, which passes underneath through the crooked tunnel (250yds). The Victorian Gothic waterworks, ½ mile north, mark the end of the canal.
Shackerstone
Leics. PO, tel, stores. Undeveloped and unchanged, Shackerstone is a farming village that reflects the pre-industrial feeling of the whole of the Ashby Canal. West of the village the canal flanks Gopsall Park; the house where Handel is reputed to have composed the 'Messiah' was pulled down in 1951, and the park has since lost its original dignity and quality.
Market Bosworth Light Railway Although the railway line that follows the Ashby Canal is now closed, the former Shackerstone Junction station (near canal bridge 82) has come to life again as a small railway museum and a depot for preserved steam locomotives which run trips on *Sun afternoons and B. Hols Easter to Oct.* Café.
Congerstone
Leics. PO, tel, stores, garage. Scattered village of small interest. 1 mile west of the village is a gibbet put up in 1800 to hang a local murderer.

PUBS

Globe Inn Snarestone. Food.
Rising Sun Shackerstone. Food, garden.
Horse & Jockey Congerstone. Food. Day tickets for fishing.

BIRMINGHAM CANAL NAVIGATIONS (BCN)

Maximum dimensions

Length: 71′ 6″
Beam: 7′
Headroom: 6′ 6″

Manager:

021-456 2723

Mileages

Birmingham Canal new main line
BIRMINGHAM Gas Street to
SMETHWICK JUNCTION (old main line): 2⅞
BROMFORD JUNCTION: 4⅞
PUDDING GREEN JUNCTION (Wednesbury Old Canal): 5⅝
TIPTON FACTORY JUNCTION (old main line): 8¾
DEEPFIELDS JUNCTION (Wednesbury Oak loop): 10
Bradley Workshops: 2¼
HORSELEY FIELDS JUNCTION (Wyrley & Essington Canal): 13
Wolverhampton Top Lock: 13½
ALDERSLEY JUNCTION (Staffordshire & Worcestershire Canal): 15⅛

Locks: 24 (3 up, 21 down)

Birmingham Canal old main line
SMETHWICK JUNCTION to
SPON LANE JUNCTION: 1½
OLDBURY JUNCTION (Titford Canal): 2½
BRADESHALL JUNCTION (Gower Branch): 3½
Aqueduct over Netherton Tunnel Branch: 4⅜
TIPTON JUNCTION (Dudley Canal): 5½
FACTORY JUNCTION (new main line): 6

Locks: 3

Dudley No. 1 Canal
TIPTON JUNCTION to
Dudley Tunnel (north end): ⅜
PARK HEAD JUNCTION: 2⅜
Delph Bottom Lock (Stourbridge Canal): 4½

Locks: 12

Dudley No. 2 Canal
PARK HEAD JUNCTION to
WINDMILL END JUNCTION: 2⅝
HAWNE BASIN: 5½

No locks

Netherton Tunnel Branch
WINDMILL END JUNCTION to
DUDLEY PORT JUNCTION: 2⅞

No locks

Wednesbury Old Canal
PUDDING GREEN JUNCTION to
RYDER'S GREEN JUNCTION: ⅝

No locks

Walsall Canal
RYDER'S GREEN JUNCTION to
Ryder's Green Bottom Lock: ¼
TAME VALLEY JUNCTION: 1⅜
WALSALL JUNCTION: 6⅞

Locks: 8

Walsall Branch Canal
WALSALL JUNCTION to
BIRCHILLS JUNCTION (Wyrley & Essington Canal): ⅞

Locks: 8

Wyrley & Essington Canal
HORSELEY FIELDS JUNCTION to
SNEYD JUNCTION: 6¼
BIRCHILLS JUNCTION (Walsall Branch Canal): 8
PELSALL JUNCTION (Cannock Extension): 12⅞
Norton Canes Docks: 1½
CATSHILL JUNCTION: 15⅜
OGLEY JUNCTION (Anglesey Branch): 16⅜
Anglesey Basin and Chasewater: 1½

No locks

Daw End Branch
CATSHILL JUNCTION to
LONGWOOD JUNCTION (Rushall Top Lock): 5¼

No locks

Rushall Canal
LONGWOOD JUNCTION to
RUSHALL JUNCTION: 2¾

Locks: 9

Tame Valley Canal
TAME VALLEY JUNCTION to
RUSHALL JUNCTION: 3½
Perry Barr Top Lock: 5½
SALFORD JUNCTION: 8½

Locks: 13

BIRMINGHAM CANAL NAVIGATIONS

The Birmingham Canal Company was authorised in 1768 to build a canal from Aldersley on the Staffordshire & Worcestershire Canal to Birmingham. With James Brindley as engineer the work proceeded quickly. The first section, from Birmingham to the Wednesbury collieries, was opened in November 1769, and the whole 22½-mile route was completed in 1772. It was a winding, contour canal, with 12 locks taking it over Smethwick, and another 20 (later 21) taking it down through Wolverhampton to Aldersley Junction. As the route of the canal was through an area of mineral wealth and developing industry, its success was immediate. Pressure of traffic caused the summit level at Smethwick to be lowered in the 1790s (thus cutting out six locks – three on either side of the summit), and during the same period branches began to reach out towards Walsall via the Ryder's Green Locks, and towards Fazeley. Out of this very profitable and ambitious first main line there grew the Birmingham Canal Navigations, more commonly abbreviated to BCN. After a long dispute about the building of the canal from Birmingham to Fazeley, the Birmingham Company bought up the embryonic Birmingham & Fazeley Canal Company; in 1794 the cumbersome title created by this merger, 'The Birmingham and Birmingham & Fazeley Canal Company', was changed to the simpler BCN. The battle for the right to build the Fazeley line was long and hard, and was fought with considerable intrigue and bitterness, a pattern of behaviour that tended to surround all the activities of the Birmingham Company. Being first in the field, it generally behaved in a high-handed manner, holding the whip hand over rivals when extensions and developments were proposed. Generally it exacted high compensatory tolls, and exercised strict controls over water rights – habits that pleased the shareholders but infuriated competitors.

The BCN network that exists today developed from three rival companies each seeking to capture traffic from the others. This intense competition resulted in a very intricate network, which was thus able to cater for all the material and distribution needs of the developing industries in the area. The web of lines forming the BCN became the veins of the Black Country, carrying the life blood of its commerce and wealth.

Apart from the Birmingham Company, there were two other companies instrumental in the creation of the BCN network. Over the other side of the Rowley Hills, the Dudley and Stourbridge Companies had set up a rival route to the Staffs & Worcs, to the annoyance of the Birmingham Company. Thomas Dadford, who had worked with Brindley earlier, was appointed engineer, and in three years (1776–79) it was completed as planned to a point just below the present Blower's Green Lock. Immediately there were plans to extend it underground to link with Lord Ward's private canal, and with the Birmingham at Tipton. After several setbacks this extension was completed between 1785 and 1792, including the long Dudley Tunnel. Then once again the directness of the Dudley Company prompted it to undertake a further extension to link with the recently authorised Worcester & Birmingham Canal at Selly Oak, a means of avoiding the severe compensation tolls exacted by the Birmingham Company for the junction at Tipton. This new line, 11 miles long, was opened in 1798. It included two tunnels, that at Lappal being the fifth longest in Britain. Cut through rock strata with great difficulty, this tunnel suffered continuously from subsidence and roof falls, and had to undergo frequent closure for repairs. The financial strain of this last extension nearly crippled the Dudley Company, and it only just managed to survive until 1846, when it was absorbed by the BCN. Lappal Tunnel was finally closed in 1917.

Up in the north, the Wyrley & Essington Company joined the fray, completing a line from Wolverhampton to Wyrley in 1795 under the direction of William Pitt. This company also grew quickly, extending initially to Brownhills, and then to join the Coventry Canal at Huddlesford via the Ogley flight of 30 locks. Several branches were added to serve the rich coalfields around Cannock and Brownhills, which were destined to serve the BCN and West Midlands well when the Black Country pits began to decline. Indeed the meandering line of the Wyrley & Essington saw some of the last commercial traffic on the whole BCN network. The Birmingham Company had spread northwards to Walsall, but because of ill-feeling and rivalry, the logical link with the Wyrley & Essington line was not made until 1840, when the Walsall Branch Canal was built.

Traffic continued to increase, and with it the wealth of the BCN. The pressures of trade made the main line at Smethwick very congested, and brought grave problems of water supply. Steam pumping engines were installed in several places to recirculate the water, and the company appointed Thomas Telford to shorten Brindley's old main line. Between 1825 and 1838 he engineered a new main line between Deepfields and Birmingham, using massive cuttings and embankments to maintain a continuous level. These improvements not only increased the amount of available waterway (the old line remaining in use), but also shortened the route from Birmingham to Wolverhampton by 7 miles.

Serious congestion had also arisen at Farmer's Bridge Locks, which could not keep up with the traffic although they operated 24 hours a day and seven days a week. Land was not available for a duplicate flight in the immediate area, and so an earlier plan to build a canal following the valley of the River Tame was revived. However, it was not until railway control and amalgamation with the Wyrley & Essington came in 1840 that the necessary impetus was found to promote the Tame Valley Canal, and the whole series of extensions and improvements to the network that accompanied it. These developments led to the building of a relief for the narrow Dudley Tunnel: the Netherton Tunnel, cut on a parallel course, included a towpath on each side and gas lighting throughout. The last addition to the network was the Cannock Extension Canal to Hednesford Basin, with its link to the Staffs & Worcs Canal via Churchbridge Locks.

Railway control of the BCN meant an expansion of the use of the system, and a large number of interchange basins were built to promote outside trade by means of rail traffic. This was of course quite contrary to the usual effect of railway competition upon canals. Trade continued to grow in relation to industrial development, and by the end of the 19thC it was topping 8½ million tons per annum. A large proportion of this trade was local, being dependent upon the needs and output of Black Country industry. After the turn of the century this reliance on local trade started the gradual decline of the system as deposits of raw materials became exhausted. Factories bought from further afield, and developed along the railways and roads away from the canals. Yet as late as 1950 there was over a million tons of trade, and the system continued in operation until the end of the coal trade in 1967 (although there was some further traffic for the Birmingham Salvage Department), a pattern quite different from canals as a whole. Nowadays there is no significant commercial traffic – a dramatic contrast to the roaring traffic on the new Birmingham motorways.

As trade declined, so parts of the system fell out of use and were abandoned. In its heyday in 1865, the BCN comprised over 160 miles of canal. Today just over 100 miles remain. However, all the surviving canals of the BCN are of great interest; excellent for leisure cruising, they represent a most vivid example of living history and will reward exploration – one of the most important monuments to the Industrial Revolution.

Much has been done in recent years in landscaping waste land (as at the south end of Dudley Tunnel), dredging old basins (such as at the top of the Wolverhampton '21'), and restoring disused buildings (such as the Pump House at Smethwick). The Birmingham Inner City Partnership (British Waterways; Birmingham City Council; Department of the Environment; West Midlands County Council) is implementing a programme of improvements, having recognised the unique recreational potential of the canal system and its value as an area of retreat for the harassed city dweller and as a new area of exploration for the canal traveller.

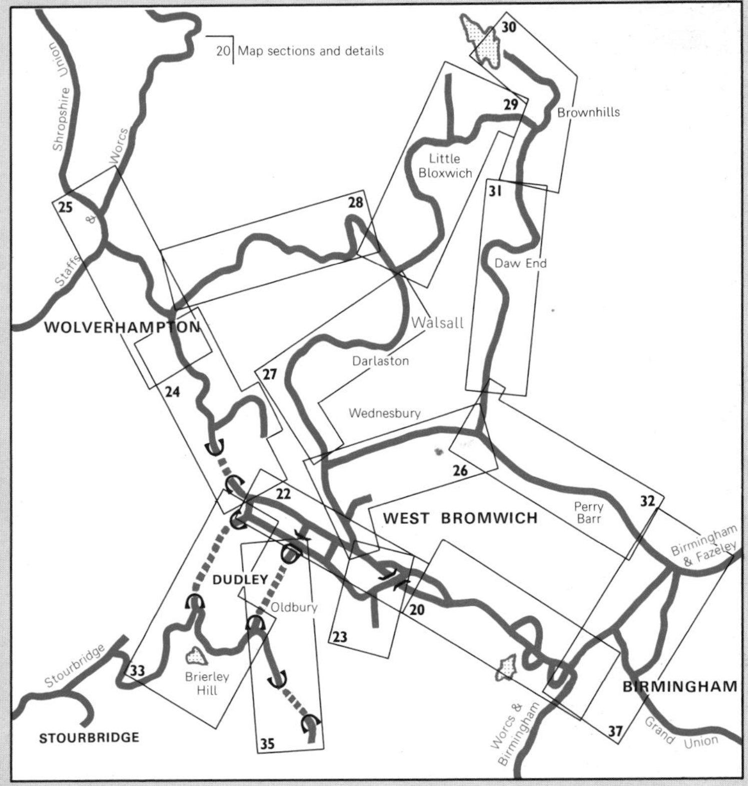

Smethwick

The Worcester & Birmingham Canal terminates in Gas Street Basin, at the famous Worcester Bar. The main line of the Birmingham Canal Navigations (BCN) leaves the basin, passing immediately under Broad Street Bridge, which has been extended so many times that it is now virtually a tunnel; the towpath continues beside the canal. North of Broad Street is Farmer's Bridge Junction, a canal crossroads where the Old Turn Island was rebuilt in 1985 in a new position. Here the Birmingham & Fazeley Canal swings away to the east, passing immediately Cambrian Wharf and the Longboat pub, and then starting the descent through 13 very tidy locks to Aston Junction (see page 37). The main line turns west at Farmer's Bridge, while the short Oozells Street loop goes to the south, quickly disappearing behind old warehouses. This loop, which now houses a hire fleet base and moorings, and the others further along, are surviving parts of Brindley's original contour canal, now known as the Birmingham Canal Old Main Line, which pursued a rather meandering course. The delays caused by this prompted the Birmingham Canal Company to commission Telford to build a straighter line, the Birmingham Canal New Main Line. This was constructed between 1823 and 1838, and when completed reduced Brindley's old 22½-mile canal to 15 miles. The Oozells Street loop reappears from the south, and then, after two bridges, the Icknield Port loop leaves to the south. This loop acts as a feeder from Rotton Park reservoir; adjoining it are the BW maintenance yard and area offices. Originally built to supply water to the BCN in the 1830s, the reservoir is now used for water sports and recreation as well. The loop rejoins after ¼ mile at another canal crossroads – the Winson Green or Soho loop, which leaves the main line opposite the Icknield Port loop. This last loop is the longest of the three, running in a gentle arc for over a mile before rejoining the main line again. It is also the only loop to have a towpath throughout its length. At its eastern end are Hockley Basins, formerly railway-owned but now a recreational area for the young people of Birmingham. There are house boats, a community hall, dry docks with an interesting guillotine gate and workshops. At the point where the loop rejoins, there is an island in the middle of the canal, the site of one of the many toll offices that existed throughout the system. The main line continues towards Smethwick, being crossed by the railway which accompanies the canal all the way to Wolverhampton, and then a gentle curve leads to Smethwick Junction. Here there is a choice of routes; Brindley's old main line swings to the right, while Telford's new main line continues straight ahead – the old line is the more interesting of the two. The two routes run side by side, but the old line climbs to a higher level via the three Smethwick Locks. Here there were two flights of locks side by side, the extra flight built by Smeaton to overcome the traffic hold-up. Brindley's original flight is now built over although traces remain. Beyond the junction, Telford's new line enters a steep-sided cutting. This 40ft-deep cutting enabled Telford to avoid the changes in level of the old line, and thus speed the flow of traffic. The two routes continue their parallel courses, the one overlooking the other, until the lower line passes under the Telford Aqueduct. This elegant single span cast-iron structure carries the Engine Branch, a short feeder canal that leaves the old line, crosses the new line, and then turns back to the south for a short distance. This arm is named after the first Boulton & Watt steam pumping engine to be bought by the Birmingham Canal Company. This continued to feed the old summit level for 120 years. It was then moved to Ocker Hill for preservation and demonstrations, until the 1950s, when it was finally retired. (It is now in the Birmingham Museum of Science & Industry.) The sides of the cutting are richly covered with wild flowers and blackberry bushes, and the seclusion of the whole area has turned it into an unofficial nature reserve. The old pumping station at Brasshouse Lane is being restored after years of disuse as part of the new Galton Valley Canal Park development. A Tangyes Engine is being installed to replace the original. The New Main Line continues through natural wilderness to Galton Tunnel. Telford's Galton Bridge crosses the cutting in one magnificent 150ft cast-iron span. This bridge is preserved as an ancient monument.

BOATYARDS

Ⓑ **Brummagem Boats** Sherborne Street Wharf, on the Oozell's Street Loop. (021-455 6163/0691). R S W D Pump-out, gas, narrowboat hire, day hire boats, overnight mooring, wet dock, winter storage, chandlery, books and maps, souvenirs, boat building, boat sales, toilets. 50-seat executive charter boat.
BW Icknield Port Yard (021-454 2240).

BOAT TRIPS

Brummagem Boats have two trip boats with buffet and bar, for 48 persons. Ring 021-445 6163/0691.

PUBS AND RESTAURANTS

Old Navigation Smethwick Bottom Lock.
Smiths Arms Asylum Bridge. Useful food shop and PO next door. Note the gents urinal built into the bridge here.
Moilliet Arms Cranford Street, Smethwick. Courage real ale in a renovated pub. *Lunchtime* food.
Bellefield Winson Street, Winson Green. Davenports real ale. The cosy lounge and snug has a fine ceiling. Food, including samosas.
Unspoilt by Progress Five Ways Shopping Centre, south of Farmer's Bridge. Modern Banks' real ale pub. Food.
Crown Broad Street, south of Farmer's Bridge. Spacious well appointed pub dispensing M & B real ale and *lunchtime* food.
Prince of Wales Cambridge Street, north of Gas Street Basin. Comfortable classic pub saved from demolition. Ansells and Tetley's real ale, snacks.
Shakespear Summer Row, north of Gas Street Basin. M & B and Bass real ale in a good basic pub. Snacks.
Plaka New Street, east of Farmer's Bridge. (021-643 6601). Lively Greek taverna. *L & D, closed Sun.*
Hawkins King Edward's Buildings, 205–219 Corporation Street, east of Farmer's Bridge Locks. (021-236 2001). Imaginative light meals in an atmospheric wine bar decorated with the screen from a now demolished church. *L & D, closed Sun.*
Chun Ying 16–18 Wrottesley Street, east of Gas Street Basin. (021-622 5669). Classic Cantonese food in a cavernous restaurant. *L & D.*
Long Boat Cambrian Wharf. Canalside at Farmer's Bridge top lock. Large modern pub with a crane on the terrace and good moorings. Ansells real ale, food usually available.
James Brindley Attractive pub at Gas Street Basin. Seafood *lunchtime and early evening.*

Industrial sunset at Smethwick, Birmingham Canal. *Derek Pratt.*

Dudley

The old and the new Birmingham canal lines continue their parallel course, and soon the pleasant semi-rural isolation of the cutting ends, to be replaced by a complex meeting of three types of transport system. The M5 motorway swings in from the east, carried high above the canal on slender concrete pillars; the railway stays close beside Telford's new line; and the canals enter a series of junctions that seem to anticipate modern motorway practice. The new line leaves the cutting, and continues in a straight line through industrial surroundings. It passes under Stewart Aqueduct, and then reaches Bromford Junction. Here a canal 'sliproad' links the old and the new lines via the three Spon Lane Locks, joining the new at an angle from the east. Note the unusual 'split' bridge at Spon Lane top lock, which was rebuilt in 1986. The old line swings south west following the 473ft contour parallel to the M5, crossing the new line on Stewart Aqueduct. Thus canal crosses canal on a flyover. Spon Lane Locks, the linking 'sliproad', survive unchanged from Brindley's day, and are among the oldest in the country. The old and the new lines now follow

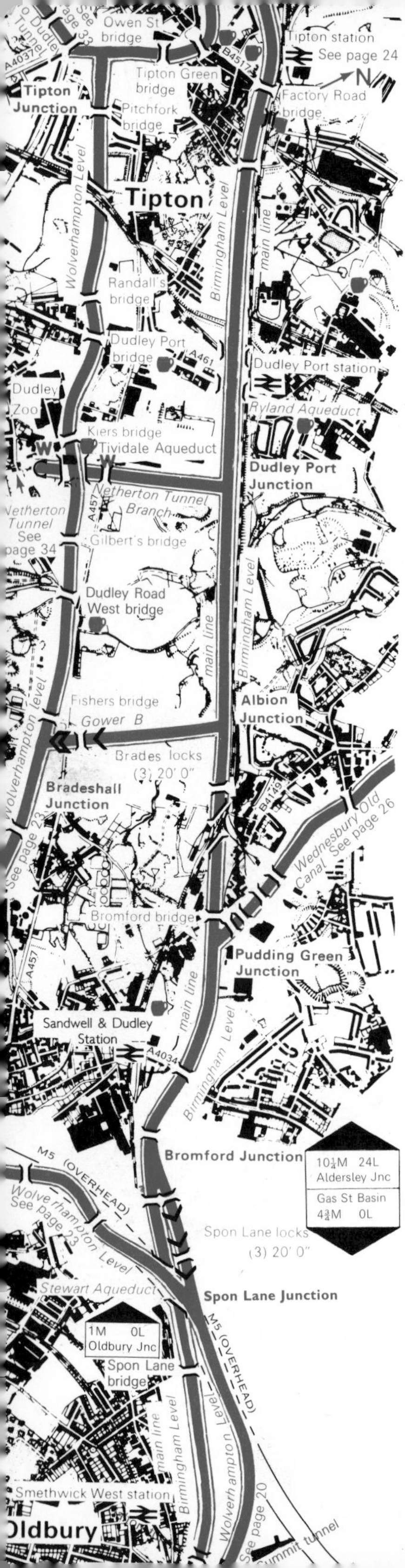

Dudley

separate courses. The old line continues below the motorway to Oldbury Locks Junction. Here the short Titford Canal (see page 23) climbs away to the south via the six Oldbury Locks; this canal serves as a feeder from Titford Pools to Rotton Park reservoir. After the junction the old line swings round to the north west, and continues on a parallel course to the new line once again passing Les Allens boatbuilding yard. At Bradeshall Junction the Gower Branch links the two lines, descending to the lower level of the new line through three locks, two of which are a staircase, unique on the BCN. At Tividale the old line crosses the Netherton Tunnel Branch on an aqueduct, another canal flyover, and then continues to Tipton Junction. To the south west is the branch leading to the Black Country Museum and the Dudley Tunnel (see page 33), reopened in 1973 after joint restoration by volunteers, BWB and Dudley Corporation. This branch connects with the Dudley Canal, the Stourbridge Canal, and thus with the Staffs & Worcs, but is not, at present, a through route – Netherton Tunnel must be used. The old line turns north at the junction, turning towards the new line which it rejoins at Factory Junction. After Bromford the new line continues its straight course towards Wolverhampton. At Pudding Green Junction the main line goes straight on; the Wednesbury Old Canal forks right to join the Walsall Canal, which in turn joins the Tame Valley Canal at Tame Valley Junction (page 26). Beyond Pudding Green the railway crosses to the north bank, staying beside the canal. At Albion Junction the Gower Branch turns south to join the old line at Bradeshall. At Dudley Port Junction the Netherton Tunnel Branch joins the main line, having passed under the old line at Tividale. The tunnel mouth can be seen from the junction. The Netherton Tunnel Branch goes through the tunnel to Windmill End Junction; from here boats can either turn south down the old Dudley Canal to Hawne Basin, or west towards the Stourbridge Canal, and thus to the Staffs & Worcs (see page 122). North of Dudley Port the new line crosses a main road on the Ryland Aqueduct; this structure was completely rebuilt in 1968, because the narrowness of the old aqueduct was hindering a road rebuilding scheme. Continuing its elevated course the new line reaches Tipton, where there are attractive landscaped moorings with shops close by, and a small basin still in use for boat repairs. Tipton station is right by the canal, and it is possible to walk from platform to towpath. Leaving the station, Factory Bottom Lock comes into view, the first of three which carry the new main line up to join the old Wolverhampton level.

PUBS

Noah's Ark Wood Street, Tipton. Access from Wood Street Footbridge near bottom of Factory Locks. Modernised and extended local decorated with old canal photographs. Hansons real ale.

Fountain Owen Street, Tipton (corner of Factory Road). Canalside pub which was once the headquarters of William Perry, a prizefighter known as the 'Tipton Slasher'. Originally a canal boatman, he became champion in 1850 and held the title for seven years. The building has now been renovated in the old Black Country style. Open fires, *lunchtime* meals and Holts real ale. Moor by Coronation Gardens on the other side of Owen Street Bridge.

Old Court House Lower Church Lane. North east of Dudley Port Station. There are usually eight different real ales available in this friendly one-roomed pub.

Dudley Port Inn 200yds east of Dudley Port Bridge. Refurbished two-room pub offering Holts real ale and local food.

Horseley Tavern 150yds east of Ryland Aqueduct. Traditional unspoilt local offering Hansons real ale. Games room.

Boat Inn Near Dudley Road West Bridge. The plush lounge of this large modern pub has a canal theme. Banks' real ale.

Railway Inn Next to Sandwell and Dudley Station. M & B real ale in an old local.

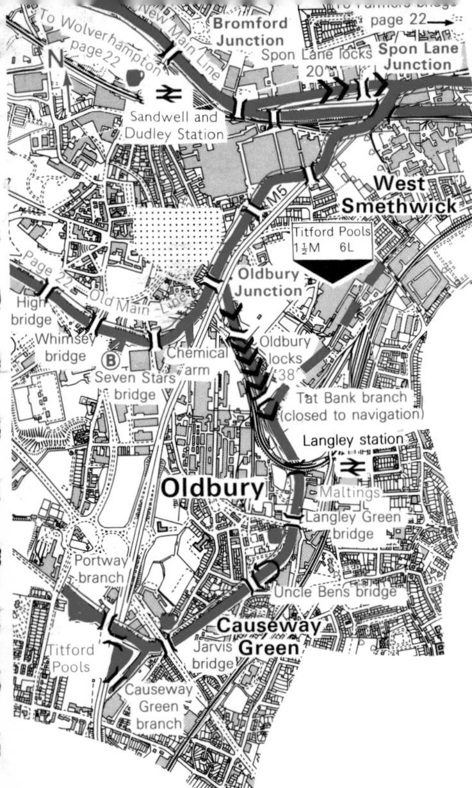

The Titford Canal

Built in 1837 as part of the original Birmingham Canal scheme, acting as a feeder to Spon Lane, the Titford Canal served Causeway Green. This must have been a very busy canal in its heyday, with many branches, wharves and tramways connecting it to the surrounding mines and engineering works. Today it survives in shortened form and has the distinction of being the highest navigable part of the BCN, with a summit level above Oldbury Locks of 511ft. The locks are sometimes referred to as 'The Crow' – a branch which left the canal above the third lock served the alkali and phosphorous works of a local industrialist and benefactor 'Jim Crow'. The last surviving recirculatory pumping station can be seen by the top lock. The canal now terminates at the wide expanse of water of Titford Pools, scene of IWA Rallies in 1978 and 1982. It is well worth making the short diversion off the main line (see navigational note), and walkers will find the towpath in good condition and access easy.

Navigational note
Since this is the highest level on the BCN, it is advisable to ring the BW Canal Manager (021-456 2723) to check that there is adequate water before you make your trip.

The Titford Canal leaves the Old Main Line at Oldbury Junction, under the M5 Motorway. What is now a sterile place was once the base of Thomas Claytons of Oldbury, one of the last carriers to operate on the BCN, finally ending operations in 1966. Their boats carried mainly liquid cargoes of crude tar and gas water to the Springfield Tar Distillery, whose wharf can be seen to the left below the first lock. There is an attractive lock cottage, and the locks themselves are handsome, with wooden balance beams and traditional paddle gear. Locks 2 to 5 are enclosed by large side ponds. Above the third lock the sealed off entrance to the Jim Crow Arm can be seen on the towpath side. By the top lock stands a pumping station, which is still in use although electric pumps have replaced the old beam engine. The Tat Bank Branch was one of the last narrow canals to be built, and now serves as a feeder from Rotton Park reservoir. The canal now becomes typically urban, with houses on the towpath side faced by industrial buildings on the other. Notable amongst these are Langley Maltings, which date from the 1890s. These imposing buildings were once known as Showells Maltings, but are now owned and used by the Wolverhampton and Dudley Breweries, makers of Banks' fine ales. Beyond the next bridge are the old buildings of Langley Forge, where castings are still produced. A 1½ ton steam drop hammer, installed in 1900, is still in use here. After passing through Jarvis Bridge the canal splits into the old Causeway Green and Portway Branches, connecting with Titford Pools. The M5 motorway passes high above, on stilts.

PUBS

Railway Inn Next to Sandwell and Dudley Station. M & B real ale in an old local.
Holt Brewery Inn Canalside at Langley Green Bridge. A local pub tastefully refurbished in old fashioned Black Country style, with a cast iron range in the parlour and snob screens between the bars. A glass panel in the rear passageway offers a view of the brewery. Real ale and *lunchtime* food.
New Navigation Jarvis Bridge. Ansells real ale and *lunchtime* snacks in a canalside hostelry. Tudor-style frontage.

Bilston

The new line climbs the three Factory Locks, flanked by the old boatmen's mission and weigh-house, now industrial premises, and then immediately reaches Factory Junction, where the old line comes in from the south. The long parallel course of the two canals is over. At Coseley there is a short tunnel, another sign of Telford's new route, for the old canal used to wind round Coseley Hill. The tunnel is of wide bore, with a towpath on each side; the style is the same as the much longer Netherton Tunnel, opened in 1858, and indeed Coseley was cut to the same specification, as a trial run. There are good moorings here, at Coseley Stop. Beyond the tunnel, the canal continues straight to Deepfields Junction. Here the old canal swings away to the east on the Wednesbury Oak Loop (see below). The junction now has a pleasant garden, with small trees and seats. To the north the main line continues its wandering course towards Horseley Fields Junction, its twisting and turning revealing that Brindley's original line was not altered by Telford north of Deepfields.

The Wednesbury Oak Loop
This was the original course of the Old Main Line which followed the contour route around Coseley Hill, and was bypassed in 1837 with the building of Coseley Tunnel. Leaving the main line at Deepfields Junction, the canal passes through an area of flattened coal mines, either landscaped or in the process of reclamation, with wide views to south and north. Factories then line most of the south bank, at one point extending over the canal to enclose it on both sides. Beyond Pothouse Bridge land which once reverberated to the sound of iron making is now a grassy field, accompanying the waterway on its last ¼ mile to the terminus at BW Bradley

Workshops. It is to this maintenance yard, where lock gates and boats are made and repaired, that the remaining section of the Loop owes its survival. There is now little trace of the length which once connected to the Walsall and Tame Valley Canals via the Bradley Locks Branch. The pumping station next to the BW Workshops draws water from an old colliery when extra is needed on the main line – the orange colour of the water hereabouts is caused by natural iron oxide.

PUBS

Boat Inn Canalside at Highfields Road Bridge on the Wednesbury Oak Loop. Hansons real ale in a basic local.
New Inn Ward Street. Walk west from the Coseley Stop moorings and cross the main A4123 road. Holdens real ale and food.
Painter's Arms Avenue Road. Walk north from the Coseley Stop moorings. Holdens real ale, which is brewed close-by in Dudley.
Old Bush By Factory Junction. Large pre-war pub offering Banks' real ale.

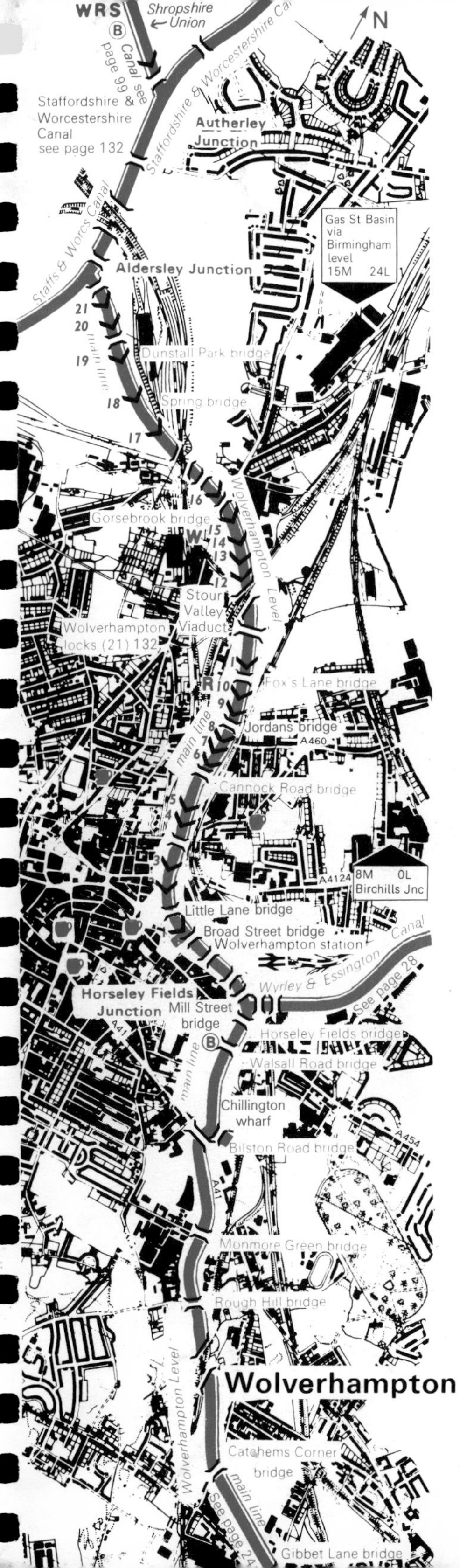

Wolverhampton

The canal continues its winding course through the heart of industrial Wolverhampton. Factories surround the canal, shutting it off from the rest of the town, but access is not difficult. Just north of Bilston Road Bridge there is a railway-canal interchange basin (Chillington Wharf), still intact, the sidings running beside the covered wharf. It is a reminder of the busy traffic that once filled the BCN. At Horseley Fields Junction, set in the middle of Wolverhampton, the main line goes straight on. To the east, the Wyrley & Essington Canal starts its meandering contour course towards Brownhills (see page 30). Soon after the junction the canal reaches the top lock of the Wolverhampton flight with its attendant BCN cottage, moored narrowboats and good moorings, now extending towards the junction by Broad Street Bridge where the canal was diverted in the early 1970s to accommodate road improvements. The original Broad Street Bridge now stands in the Black Country Museum. From here 21 locks carry the canal down to join the Staffordshire & Worcestershire Canal at Aldersley Junction. Half the locks are flanked by industry, and railways criss-cross over and around the canal, but gradually this background yields until the last three locks are virtually rural. Lock 20 was added in 1784 because the original bottom lock was excessively deep – note the single bottom gate. Access is possible at several places in the flight, but the most convenient services are near the Cannock Road Bridge and the Stafford Road (Gorsebrook) Bridge. Beyond the bottom lock there is a welcome old-fashioned brick arched bridge, and then the Birmingham Canal main line ends at Aldersley Junction, inconspicuous when approached from the Staffs & Worcs. (For the Staffordshire & Worcestershire Canal, see page 133.)

BOATYARDS

Ⓑ **Water Travel** Autherley Junction, Oxley Moor Road, Wolverhampton. (0902) 782371. R S W D E Pump-out, gas, narrowboat hire, overnight mooring, long-term mooring, winter storage, slipway, groceries, chandlery, books and maps, boat building, boat sales, engine repairs, toilets, telephone, licensed club house.

PUBS

Freemason's Arms Water Street, near the Springfield Brewery. M & B Springfield real ale in a friendly bar. Snacks.

Feathers Molineux Street, by the football ground. Banks' real ale local. Snacks.

Posada Lichfield Street. Renovated pub serving Holts real ale and meals.

Sir Tatton Sykes Lichfield Street. Large 'Toby Pantry' pub. M & B Springfield real ale, meals.

Wheatsheaf Market Street. Town centre pub offering Banks' real ale and snacks.

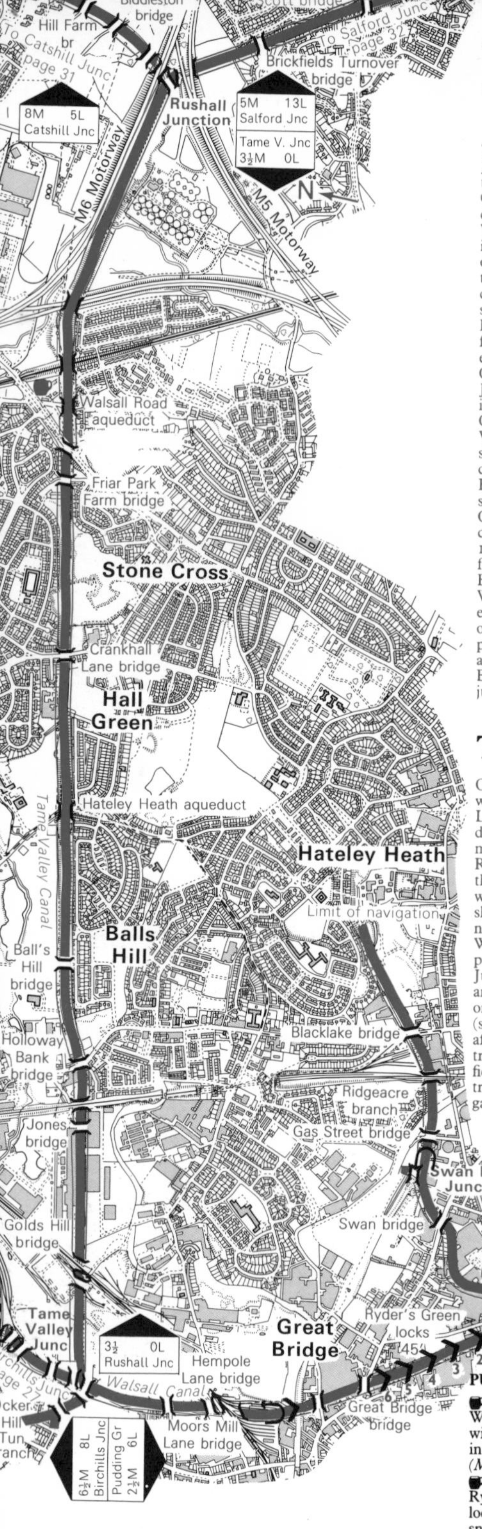

Walsall Canal

The Walsall Canal runs from Ryder's Green Junction to Birchills Junction, connecting with the Tame Valley and Wyrley & Essington Canals. Its construction to Walsall was completed in 1799, with the link with the Wyrley & Essington being made via eight locks in 1841. The Wednesbury Old Canal was opened prior to this, in 1769, and still provides the vital link with the Walsall Canal. These two canals are still heavily industrialised, and as such they give a good impression of what the BCN was like in its heyday. However, access for towpath walkers is not always as easy as elsewhere on the BCN. The Wednesbury Old Canal leaves the main line at Pudding Green Junction under a flurry of bridges and hemmed in by factories. Immediately after Ryder's Green Junction eight locks descend to Tame Valley Junction. Those making the passage should note the unusual guillotine gate which closes off the old basin in the Nelson Iron Foundry, between locks 4 and 5. Access to shops is easily made by walking west from Great Bridge Bridge. Hempole Lane Bridge is dated in Roman numerals – MDCCCXXV – 1825, and just beyond here time should be found for a look at the Ocker Hill Tunnel Branch, which once fed water to the Wednesbury Oak Loop via six pumping engines, a tunnel and shafts. It is now a little oasis, alongside a beautifully manicured cricket pitch with pavilion and gardens, and ending at a coal wharf beyond the bridge.
Black-and-white cast iron bridges mark the junction with the Tame Valley Canal.

Tame Valley Canal

Opened in 1844 to overcome the long delays which were occurring at Farmer's Bridge Locks, the canal is typified by its direct course, deep cuttings and high embankments. The 3½ mile section between Tame Valley Junction and Rushall Junction has the distinction of being the dreariest on the whole BCN. For those who would choose to stop along here, there are shops south of Hateley Heath Aqueduct and north of Crankhall Lane Bridge, and the pub at Walsall Road Aqueduct is an excellent place to prepare for the awesome approach to Rushall Junction, where motorways appear on all sides, and the sweet smells of a sewage farm spur you on. The Rushall Canal branches off to the north (see page 32) while the Tame Valley Canal, after passing under the motorway, undergoes a transformation little short of miraculous. Small fields with grazing horses replace the roads, trees line the towpath and colourful suburban gardens appear in the distance.

PUBS

New Navigation Navigation Lane, below Walsall Road Aqueduct. Friendly locals' pub with a comfortable modern wood and tile interior. M & B real ale, *lunchtime* food (*Mon–Fri*) and garden.

George Phoenix Street, north east of Ryder's Green Junction. Homely two-roomed local serving Hansons real ale and *lunchtime* snacks.

Fox & Goose Belper Bridge, Wednesbury Old Canal. Locals' pub serving Ansells real ale and snacks. There is a sweet shop opposite.

Eight Locks Hadley Bridge, Wednesbury Old Canal. A handsome pub with fine etched glass windows. *Lunchtime* food. Garden.

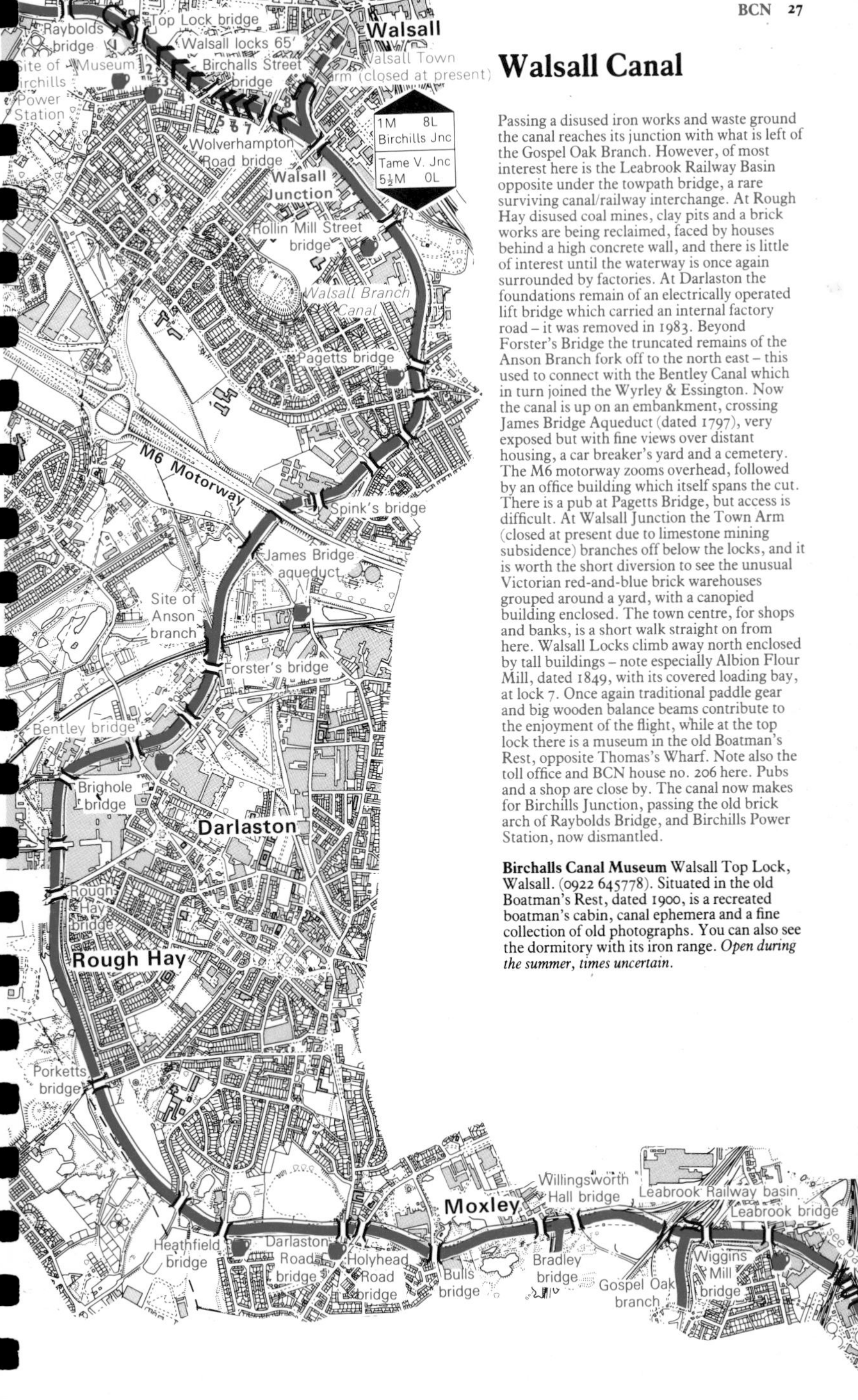

Walsall Canal

Passing a disused iron works and waste ground the canal reaches its junction with what is left of the Gospel Oak Branch. However, of most interest here is the Leabrook Railway Basin opposite under the towpath bridge, a rare surviving canal/railway interchange. At Rough Hay disused coal mines, clay pits and a brick works are being reclaimed, faced by houses behind a high concrete wall, and there is little of interest until the waterway is once again surrounded by factories. At Darlaston the foundations remain of an electrically operated lift bridge which carried an internal factory road – it was removed in 1983. Beyond Forster's Bridge the truncated remains of the Anson Branch fork off to the north east – this used to connect with the Bentley Canal which in turn joined the Wyrley & Essington. Now the canal is up on an embankment, crossing James Bridge Aqueduct (dated 1797), very exposed but with fine views over distant housing, a car breaker's yard and a cemetery. The M6 motorway zooms overhead, followed by an office building which itself spans the cut. There is a pub at Pagetts Bridge, but access is difficult. At Walsall Junction the Town Arm (closed at present due to limestone mining subsidence) branches off below the locks, and it is worth the short diversion to see the unusual Victorian red-and-blue brick warehouses grouped around a yard, with a canopied building enclosed. The town centre, for shops and banks, is a short walk straight on from here. Walsall Locks climb away north enclosed by tall buildings – note especially Albion Flour Mill, dated 1849, with its covered loading bay, at lock 7. Once again traditional paddle gear and big wooden balance beams contribute to the enjoyment of the flight, while at the top lock there is a museum in the old Boatman's Rest, opposite Thomas's Wharf. Note also the toll office and BCN house no. 206 here. Pubs and a shop are close by. The canal now makes for Birchills Junction, passing the old brick arch of Raybolds Bridge, and Birchills Power Station, now dismantled.

Birchalls Canal Museum Walsall Top Lock, Walsall. (0922 645778). Situated in the old Boatman's Rest, dated 1900, is a recreated boatman's cabin, canal ephemera and a fine collection of old photographs. You can also see the dormitory with its iron range. *Open during the summer, times uncertain.*

PUBS

New Navigation At Top Lock Bridge. M & B Springfield real ale in a convenient canalside pub. Snacks.

Rose & Crown Hotel 100yds west of Top Lock Bridge. An imposing traditional pub serving M & B Springfield real ale.

Forge Hammer West of Rolling Mill Street Bridge. M & B Springfield real ale, snacks.

Railway Tavern (The Hole) Cemetery Road, south of James Bridge Aqueduct. Fine pub with an open fire serving Bass and M & B real ale. Garden. *Opens 12.00.*

Boat Bentley Bridge. Welcoming local with a large, robust public bar and comfortable lounge with bench seats, iron tables and an open fire. Banks' real ale, very good and inexpensive bar meals. Garden, games room.

Royal George Heathfield Bridge. Large estate pub serving Banks' real ale.

Swan Near Darlaston Road Bridge. Enterprising M & B real ale pub. Shops nearby.

Bush Leabrook Bridge. Main road pub surrounded by factories.

Wyrley & Essington Canal

Opened throughout in 1797, the canal connected the Birmingham Canal with the Birmingham & Fazeley, running in a meandering contour line from Horseley Fields Junction to Huddlesford on the Coventry Canal, via Lichfield. Its construction was prompted by the coal trade, and there were several branches to serve the various coalfields. However, trade did not really develop until the Cannock fields were exploited in the 19thC. Its most important branch was the Daw End, running southwards from Catshill Junction, for this was later linked with the Tame Valley Canal via Rushall. In 1954 the main line between Ogley Junction and Huddlesford was abandoned, and much of this has now vanished. Leaving the main line at Horseley Fields Junction (see page 25) the Wyrley & Essington soon establishes its lazy roundabout course to Sneyd Junction, flanked by houses and factories but with enough pleasant breaks of grass and trees to maintain interest. At Wednesfield Junction, beyond a red brick turnover bridge, the remains of the Bentley Canal can be seen. This connected with the Walsall Canal but was abandoned in 1961. Church Bridge is overlooked by the red brick tower of St Thomas Church, and this is a very good place to gain access to all shops, banks and a very good pub. A little teashop here is *open Mon–Sat 9.15–16.30 (closed Wed)*. Gradually the buildings thin out – school playing fields provide open vistas and canalside gardens begin to acknowledge the presence of the water. There is a children's playpark by Perry Hall Bridge. Between this and the next bridge, on the towpath side, can be seen a cobbled overflow weir with no walkway over – presumably an interesting crossing after heavy rainfall. At Lane Head a triangular green is enclosed by terraced cottages on two sides, and grazed by donkeys. There are pubs and shops here. Reclaimed colliery land follows, landscaped with newly planted trees and scattered lakes and ponds. The M6 motorway accompanies the canal for a short way but is thankfully soon left well behind as Edwards Bridge, with its large gypsy encampment, is approached. At Sneyd Junction the main line turns sharp right under the bridge. Ahead, beyond the derelict lock, the old Wyrley Branch once linked with coal workings and the Essington Branch, at 533ft above sea level the highest point reached on the BCN. It was never successfully operated due to water supply problems. Beyond the attractive single storey BW buildings and wharf crane the canal makes a not very interesting journey to Birchills Junction (see page 29).

BOATYARDS

BW Sneyd Yard (0922 476851). R S W

PUBS

United Kingdom North of Lane Head Bridge. Banks' real ale, snacks.

Bridge South of Lane Head Bridge. Banks' and Hansons real ale, snacks.

Boat Wednesfield, canalside at Church Bridge. Terraced pub with a very fine sign.

Pyle Cock Rookery Street, Wednesfield. Round the corner from Church Bridge. Unspoilt traditional pub with fine etched glass windows serving handpumped Banks' real ale. Children's room, garden.

Bulls Head Wolverhampton Road, Heath Town. Plain main road pub. Not a good mooring.

Jolly Collier Old Heath Road, Heath Town. Hot meals, snacks, live music at *weekends*.

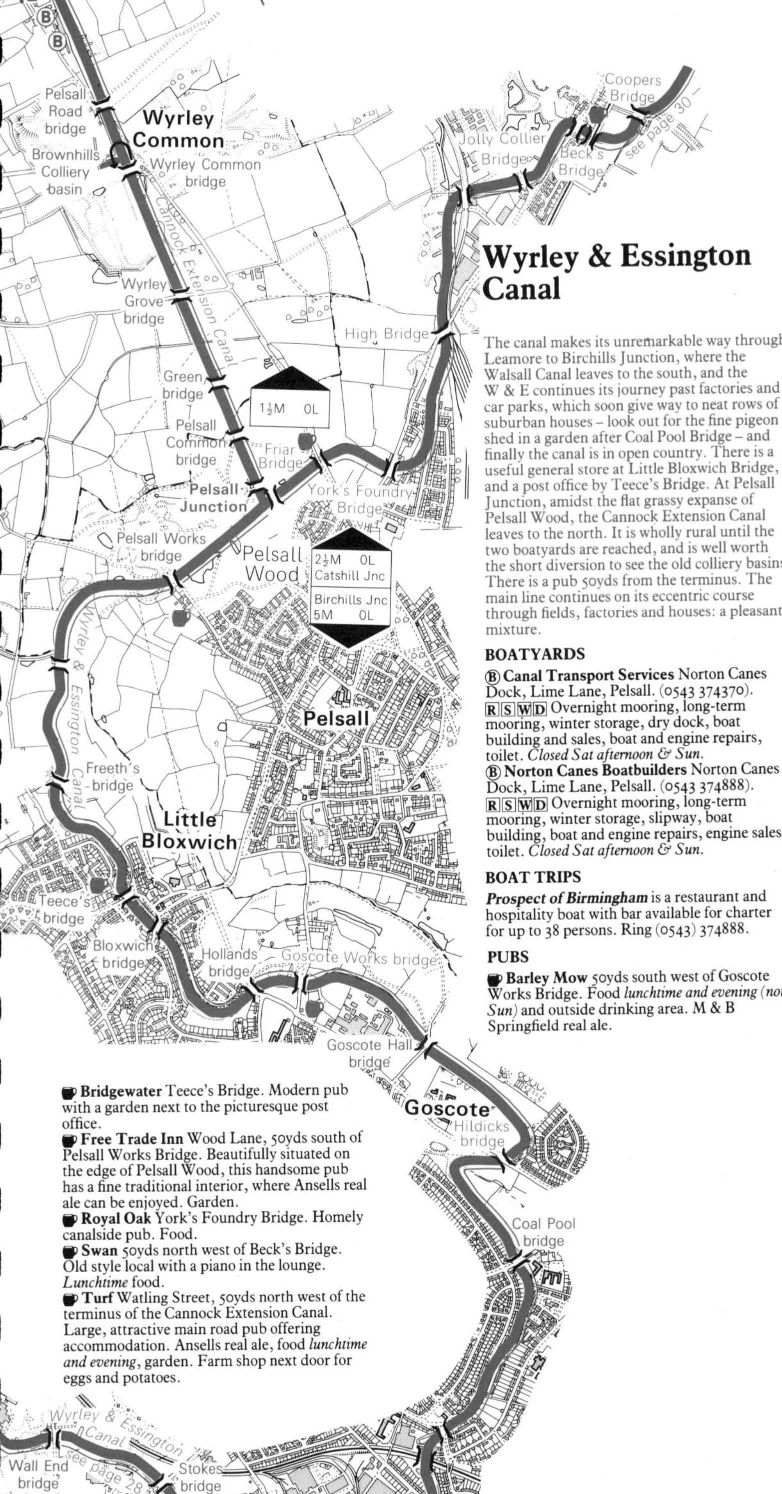

Wyrley & Essington Canal

The canal makes its unremarkable way through Leamore to Birchills Junction, where the Walsall Canal leaves to the south, and the W & E continues its journey past factories and car parks, which soon give way to neat rows of suburban houses – look out for the fine pigeon shed in a garden after Coal Pool Bridge – and finally the canal is in open country. There is a useful general store at Little Bloxwich Bridge, and a post office by Teece's Bridge. At Pelsall Junction, amidst the flat grassy expanse of Pelsall Wood, the Cannock Extension Canal leaves to the north. It is wholly rural until the two boatyards are reached, and is well worth the short diversion to see the old colliery basins. There is a pub 50yds from the terminus. The main line continues on its eccentric course through fields, factories and houses: a pleasant mixture.

BOATYARDS

Ⓑ **Canal Transport Services** Norton Canes Dock, Lime Lane, Pelsall. (0543 374370). R S WD Overnight mooring, long-term mooring, winter storage, dry dock, boat building and sales, boat and engine repairs, toilet. *Closed Sat afternoon & Sun.*

Ⓑ **Norton Canes Boatbuilders** Norton Canes Dock, Lime Lane, Pelsall. (0543 374888). R S WD Overnight mooring, long-term mooring, winter storage, slipway, boat building, boat and engine repairs, engine sales, toilet. *Closed Sat afternoon & Sun.*

BOAT TRIPS

Prospect of Birmingham is a restaurant and hospitality boat with bar available for charter for up to 38 persons. Ring (0543) 374888.

PUBS

Barley Mow 50yds south west of Goscote Works Bridge. Food *lunchtime and evening (not Sun)* and outside drinking area. M & B Springfield real ale.

Bridgewater Teece's Bridge. Modern pub with a garden next to the picturesque post office.

Free Trade Inn Wood Lane, 50yds south of Pelsall Works Bridge. Beautifully situated on the edge of Pelsall Wood, this handsome pub has a fine traditional interior, where Ansells real ale can be enjoyed. Garden.

Royal Oak York's Foundry Bridge. Homely canalside pub. Food.

Swan 50yds north west of Beck's Bridge. Old style local with a piano in the lounge. *Lunchtime* food.

Turf Watling Street, 50yds north west of the terminus of the Cannock Extension Canal. Large, attractive main road pub offering accommodation. Ansells real ale, food *lunchtime and evening*, garden. Farm shop next door for eggs and potatoes.

Anglesey Branch Daw End Branch Wyrley & Essington Canal

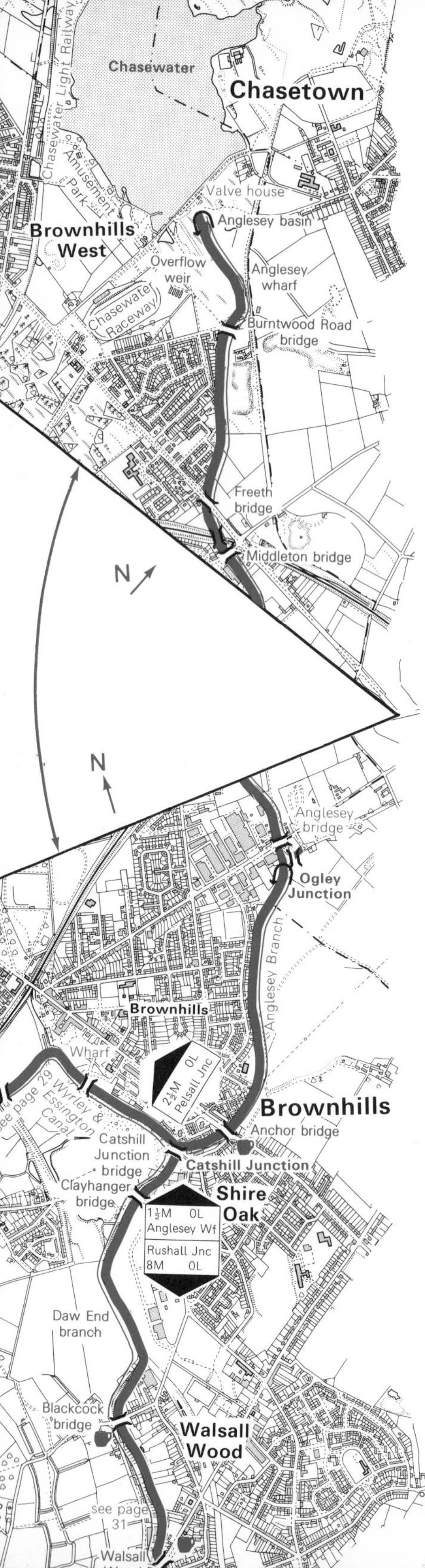

The wharf at Brownhills is now a tidy public area, with a large supermarket, market place and shops within easy reach. The Daw End Branch begins south of Catshill Junction – it was built in 1803 to carry lime from the workings around Daw End and Hay Head – and although built originally as a contour canal, mining and subsidence have frequently left it in a very high, exposed position. This is immediately apparent when approaching Walsall Wood Bridge, a good stop for shops and a post office. The Anglesey Branch last carried coal from the Cannock Mines in 1967, so those who make this worthwhile diversion may be surprised to find that the route is extremely rural, with open country to the north. An elegant grey cast-iron bridge spans Ogley Junction, where the main line of the W & E once descended through locks to join the Coventry Canal at Huddlesford Junction; the route, abandoned in 1954, is still traceable through much private land. What was once just a feeder from Chasewater now passes through sandy heathland to terminate at Anglesey Basin, a wide expanse where there are the remains of loading chutes and the ground is black with coal dust. Note the fine overflow weir, and the octagonal valve house high up on the dam. The Chasewater Amusement Park and Nature Reserve is only a short walk from here.

Chasewater Amusement Park Recreation Officer: (0922) 650000. The amusements include swings, climbing frames, children's boats, putting green, crazy golf. Rich bird life and nature trails. Steam railway operates *Sun & B. Hols in summer*. Watersports for clubs only on the reservoir. *Open daily*. No admission charge, but you must pay for rides, etc.

PUBS

Black Cock Blackcock Bridge, Walsall Wood. Banks' real ale and snacks in a modern local.

Anchor Canalside at Anchor Bridge. Small traditional Banks' real ale local with an open fire. Snacks, garden.

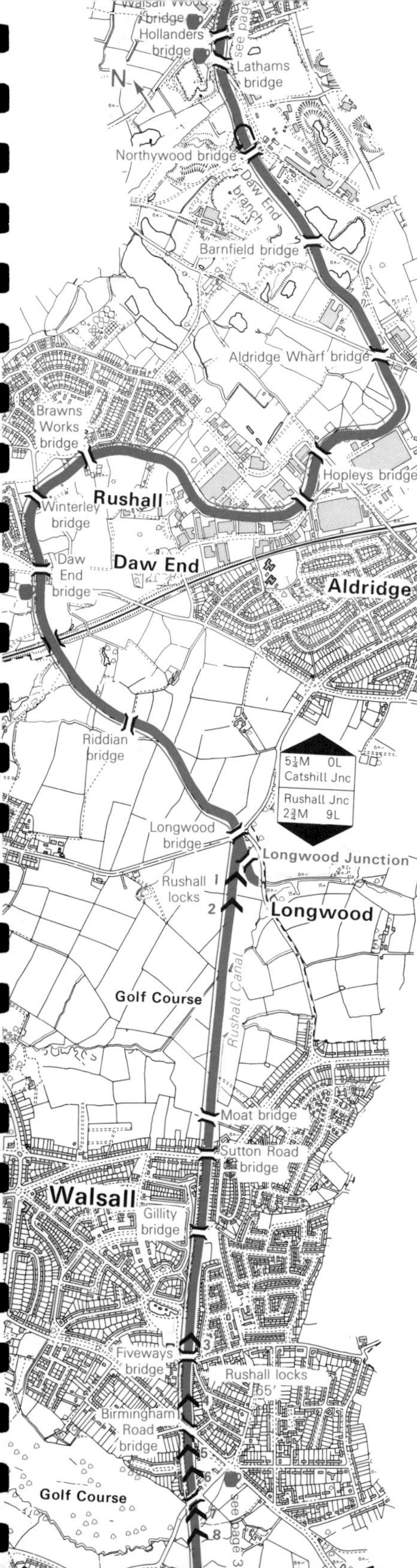

Daw End Branch Rushall Canal

Continuing south, the Daw End Branch of the Wyrley & Essington now finds itself high up on an embankment with very deep clay pits either side, some now partially flooded and landscaped, some still being worked. These dramatic surroundings give way to factories and sports grounds, which in turn are followed by a beautifully rural area which is to last until Walsall's smarter suburbs are reached. There is a remarkable stone cottage and red-brick arch bridge at Brawn's Works, and these red-brick arches reappear regularly, enhancing the canal's remote quality. At Longwood Junction the main line of the Daw End Branch used to continue to Hay Head – this is now abandoned and forms part of a nature reserve. Longwood Boat Club have their moorings at the junction, and their club house is in an old canal building next to BCN house 93 at the top lock. With pretty gardens, the whole is a very charming canal scene. Leaving Longwood the character of the route changes to that of a straight modern canal, revealing that the traveller is now on the Rushall Canal; this was built in 1847 to connect the Daw End Branch with the Tame Valley Canal in order to capture the coal trade from Cannock Mines. After the top two locks the canal passes a golf course; beyond Sutton Road Bridge the banks are lined with canalside gardens, and the towpath is overhung with willow, flowering currant and berberis. There is a children's playpark at Gillity Bridge. Another golf course accompanies the route through the next flurry of locks on this long, drawn-out flight, and still the surroundings are wholly amenable. This is truly a superb length of urban canal, which would stand comparison with any other in the country.

PUBS

Horse & Jockey Walsall Road, west of Hollander's Bridge or Walsall Wood Bridge. Straightforward Banks' real ale pub with a pool room. Hotel and restaurant opposite.

Manor Arms Park Road, Daw End Bridge. A welcoming canalside pub dating from the 18thC but first licensed in 1895. Unspoilt, its low beamed ceilings and open fires make for a warm and homely atmosphere. Bass and M & B real ale, excellent food *lunchtime and evening*, and canalside garden.

Bell North east of Bell Bridge. Attractive main road pub with a large garden. Food *lunchtime (Mon–Fri)* and snacks.

Tame Valley Canal

Leaving Rushall Junction, the Tame Valley Canal undergoes a startling transformation – the motorways disappear to leave the canal in its own secluded world – tree lined and with small fields either side. Colourful suburban gardens are glimpsed here and there before the waterway enters a steep wooded cutting crossed by the high modern Scott Bridge, and the more agreeable Chimney Bridge, a footbridge supported on substantial brick pillars. Emerging from the cutting, the traveller then finds himself on a high embankment, with wide views all around: two aqueducts are crossed. By the second, Piercy, there are shops and an off-licence. Again the canal enters a deep cutting, this time through sandstone some 200 million years old. After passing the handsome brick arch of Freeth Bridge, Perry Barr Top Lock is reached, set between a very fine red-brick BCN house (no 86), old stables and the Gauging Weir House. The lock flight is very spread out, and passes through an area of private back gardens, public open space and sports fields. Little industry intrudes, although the M6 motorway crosses twice. There are petrol stations by College Road Bridge and a telephone kiosk and post box by Brookvale Road Bridge, where factories and other industrial premises close in. The last two locks (shown on page 37) are both accompanied by BCN houses, the last being semi-detached and numbered 77 and 78. Their little gardens seem incongruous amidst such overpowering industry. The Tame Valley Canal joins the Birmingham & Fazeley and Birmingham & Warwick Junction Canals under Gravelly Hill motorway interchange, where cast iron towpath bridges are dwarfed by flyovers, and the air is full of dust and noise. A unique experience.

Dudley No I and No 2 Canals

The Dudley No I Canal was completed in 1792, its history and development being intimately connected with that of the Stourbridge Canal, which it joins at the bottom of Delph Locks. This flight, now designated a conservation area, is notable for its high waterfall overflows, which are very dramatic after a prolonged spell of wet weather. Known as the Nine Locks, seven of the original flight were rebuilt as six on the present line in 1858. Some remains of the old locks can still be seen to the east. Old stables by lock 3 have been converted into a museum and interpretive centre. Leaving the locks, the canal winds its way through the site of Round Oak Steelworks, which ceased production in 1983 after almost two centuries of steelmaking. However, other industries survive, and the canal is flanked by light industrial units, timberyards and the occasional surviving red brick warehouse. Immediately after Woodside Bridge a cast iron bridge marked 'Horseley Co, Tipton 1858' carries the towpath over what was, until subsidence caused its closure in 1909, the old Two Lock Line – a short cut which avoided the longer route via Park Head Junction. Now the canal passes along a side cut embankment with good views towards Netherton Hill as it approaches Blowers Green Lock, the deepest on the BCN, built to replace two earlier locks which suffered from subsidence. Note the disused pumphouse here.

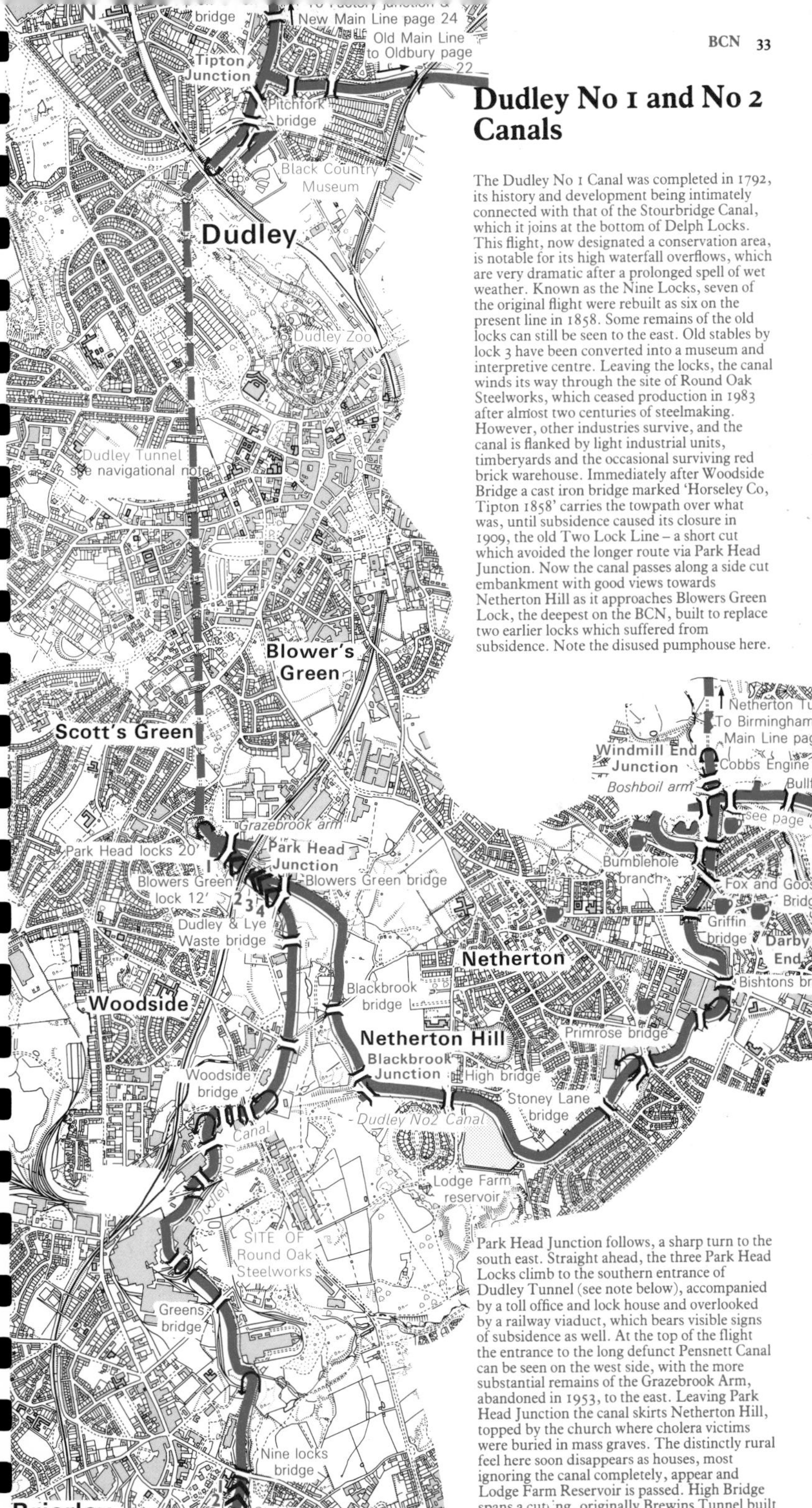

Park Head Junction follows, a sharp turn to the south east. Straight ahead, the three Park Head Locks climb to the southern entrance of Dudley Tunnel (see note below), accompanied by a toll office and lock house and overlooked by a railway viaduct, which bears visible signs of subsidence as well. At the top of the flight the entrance to the long defunct Pensnett Canal can be seen on the west side, with the more substantial remains of the Grazebrook Arm, abandoned in 1953, to the east. Leaving Park Head Junction the canal skirts Netherton Hill, topped by the church where cholera victims were buried in mass graves. The distinctly rural feel here soon disappears as houses, most ignoring the canal completely, appear and Lodge Farm Reservoir is passed. High Bridge spans a cutting, originally Brewins Tunnel built in 1838 but opened out only 20 years later. A large ship's anchor stands on the wharf by Primrose Bridge, recalling the times when Netherton was a centre for the manufacture of chains and anchors. This site was a testing house. Opposite, on the towpath side, fine wooden warehouses can be seen standing by an enclosed basin. A tall warehouse and covered loading bay overlooks Griffin Bridge, which is then followed by the Bumblehole Branch, a lovely urban environment of canalside gardens and old and new houses looking out over landscaped workings. The arm, which was the main line of the canal prior to the building of Netherton Tunnel, terminates in a 'Y' overhung with willows and served by an old-style pub. Cobbs Engine House and elegant black-and-white cast-iron bridge create great visual excitement in the midst of a reclaimed area of old workings, now rich in bird and insect life. Straight ahead is the grand entrance to Netherton Tunnel and the link with the Birmingham Canal Main Line. To the right is the Dudley No 2 Canal, a dead-end, but one worthy of exploration. The towpath on both Dudley canals is excellent.

Navigational note
Dudley and Netherton Tunnels
Internal combustion engines must not be used in Dudley Tunnel. At present there is no through traffic at all. Netherton Tunnel is wide bore, with ventilation shafts and a towpath each side. This is the only route through to the Birmingham Canal Main Line.

Dudley Tunnel
Reopened in 1973 with the rebuilding of Park Head Locks, Dudley Tunnel is one of the wonders of the BCN. This narrow tunnel, 3154yds long, was opened in 1792, after the usual delays and problems, to connect with the Birmingham Canal at Tipton. Inside there is a vast network of natural caverns, basins and branches serving old quarries and mines. In all there are over 5000yds of underground waterway, some cut off and abandoned, others still accessible. Internal combustion engines must not be used in this tunnel.
Netherton Tunnel
Opened in 1858, Netherton was the last canal tunnel to be built in Britain. 3027yds long, it was built with a bore sufficient to allow a towpath on both sides, and when opened it was equipped with gas lighting, later converted to electricity. The Netherton Tunnel Branch joins the Birmingham main line at Dudley Port. The tunnel was built to relieve congestion in the Dudley Tunnel, and runs on a parallel course.
Black Country Museum Tipton Road, Dudley. (021-557 9643). An open air museum of original buildings re-erected on the site. Workers' homes, shops, the Bottle & Glass pub (where you can buy a pint) and tram rides. There is a restored colliery, a replica Newcomen engine, and a chain-makers' workshop. Down by the canal there are limekilns, a boat dock, and trips into Dudley Tunnel. *Open 10.00–17.00 (reduced in winter) except Xmas*. Admission charge. Moorings by arrangement – telephone in advance.
Dudley Zoo (0384) 252401. Collections of animals, small children's fairground and chairlift. *Open daily except Xmas*. Admission charge.

BOAT TRIPS

Dudley Canal Trust (Trips) Unit 44, High Street, Tipton. (021-520 5321). Exciting trips from the Black Country Museum in an electrically powered narrowboat. The climax is the 'Singing Cavern', a large mine, reached through a new tunnel constructed in 1989. Also private charter.

PUBS AND RESTAURANTS

Dry Dock Inn Windmill End, between the Bumblehole Branch and Boshboil Arm. Within sight of Cobb's Engine House and the west portal of Netherton Tunnel, this pub is a remarkable renovation. Ansells, Gibbs Mew, Ind Coope (Burton) and Bathams real ales are dispensed from a salvaged Runcorn six-plank hull set inside an imitation galleon. Extensive range of food, including Desperate Dan Cow Pies.
The Boat Inn St Peter's Road, Netherton. At the end of the Bumblehole Branch. Old style Hansons real ale pub with fine etched glass windows.
Red Lion Darby End, 100yds east of Griffin Bridge. Pleasant modern Hansons pub with a brown and cream interior. *Food lunchtime Mon–Fri.*
Rose & Crown Darby End, 100yds east of Griffin Bridge. Traditional Home Brewery pub now dispensing Ansells real ale.
White Swan 50yds north of Primrose Bridge. Banks' real ale and bar snacks in a factory workers' local.
Old Swan ½ mile north of Bishtons Bridge, but well worth the walk to enjoy Doris Pardoe's recipe own brew beer. Potbellied stove and weighing machine in the bar. Known as 'Ma Pardoe's'.
Vine (Bull & Bladder) Delph Road, 400yds east of the bottom lock. Bathams famous unspoilt Black Country brewery tap. Note the quotation from *The Two Gentlemen of Verona* on the façade. Real ale, seafood and snacks *lunchtime and evening*.
Nine Locks & Chainmaker Amblecote Road, Brierly Hill. *Guinness Book of Records* candidate as the most expensive pub sold. Greenall Whitley real ale, meals and snacks.
Bell Canalside at the bottom of Delph Locks. Fine renovated local serving Holts real ale and *lunchtime* snacks.

Windmill End Junction on the Dudley Canal. *David Perrott.*

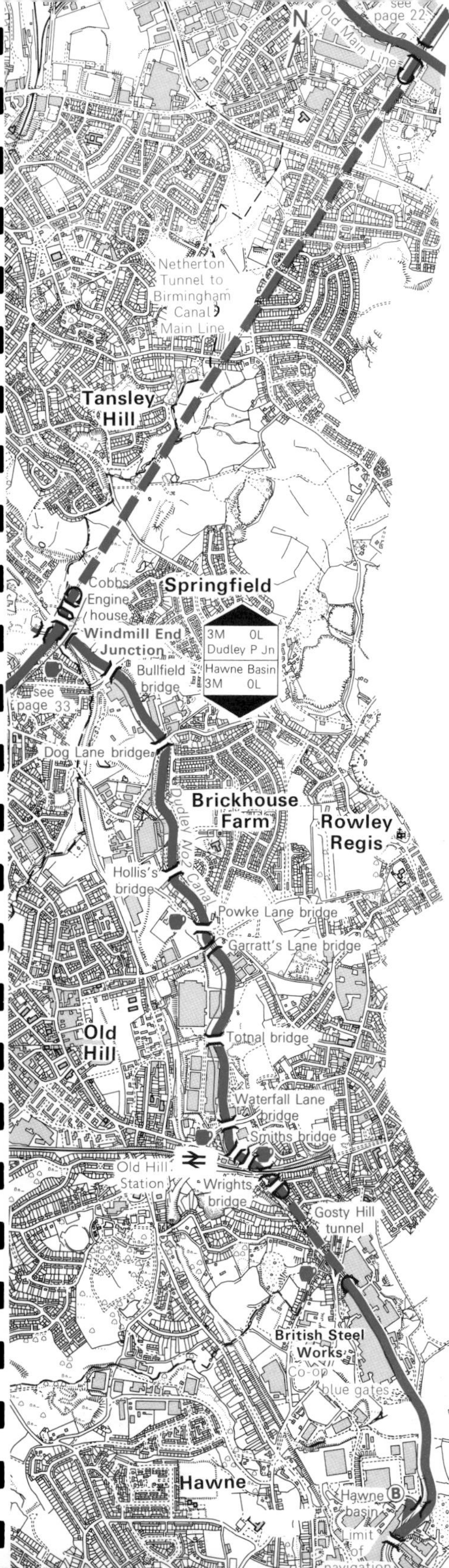

Dudley No 2 Canal

This route, now a dead-end, once continued in a wide loop to join the Worcester & Birmingham Canal via the notorious and claustrophobic Lappal Tunnel, which closed in 1917 due to subsidence. 3795yds long, this rocky tunnel was the longest in the BCN network and one of the narrowest in the country. The canal now terminates by Hawne Basin. Leaving Windmill End, there is a toll island and a disused colliery basin, one of many which once fed traffic onto the canal here, and soon the waterway is passing through houses, factories and playing fields interspersed with newly landscaped areas, the tidy legacy of these once thriving industrial areas. As this land matures, it will gradually assume a rural appearance. Beyond the quaint Totnal Bridge there is a small timberyard, followed by the remains of red-brick canalside buildings at Waterfall Lane where there is a good choice of pubs. At the entrance to the 577yd Gosty Hill Tunnel (no canoes) the 'lay-by' once used by the tunnel tug can be seen – regrettably the tughouse is now in ruins. Since there is no towpath through the tunnel, and the British Steel Works to the south is out of bounds, those walkers determined to make it to Hawne Basin will have to follow the long diversion indicated on the map. Look out for the tunnel ventilation shaft in the front garden of 171 Station Road. Those on the canal now pass through the steel works, under many factory bridges, and a trading estate to reach Hawne Basin, a canal/railway interchange until 1967 and now a friendly place full of moored narrowboats. It is safe to moor here, but a long walk along Hereward Rise to the shops and pubs.

BOATYARDS

Ⓑ **Coombeswood Canal Trust** Hawne Basin, Hereward Rise, Halesowen. (021-550 1355). R S WD Pump-out, gas, secure overnight mooring, secure long-term mooring, slipway (70ft trolley & track), boat building, inexpensive DIY facilities and advice, toilets, showers.

PUBS

Neptune Canalside at Powke Lane Bridge. Hansons real ale in a basic local.

Three Furnaces 100yds west of Waterfall Lane Bridge. A superb example of an unspoilt Black Country pub, with small rooms off a central passage. Hansons real ale.

Wharf (once the Sportsman & Railway) Station Road, Old Hill. At least four real ales are usually available in this renovated canalside pub. Food *lunchtime and evening*. Garden.

Boat Station Road, Old Hill. Close to the northern portal of Gosty Hill Tunnel. An old fashioned Black Country pub with a cosy bar and an open fire. Hansons real ale.

Anchor Coombe Road, above the south portal of Gosty Hill Tunnel. Traditional pub serving M & B Springfield real ale. Fish and chips opposite.

BIRMINGHAM & FAZELEY

Maximum dimensions

Length: 72′
Beam: 7′
Headroom: 7′ 6″

Mileage

FARMER'S BRIDGE JUNCTION (Birmingham Canal) to ASTON JUNCTION (Digbeth Branch): 1½
SALFORD JUNCTION (Tame Valley Canal): 3¼
Minworth Top Lock: 6¼
Curdworth Tunnel: 8½
Bodymoor Heath Bridge: 11½
FAZELEY JUNCTION (Coventry Canal): 15 miles
Hopwas: 17¾
Whittington Brook: 20½

Locks: 38

Digbeth Branch

ASTON JUNCTION (main line) to DIGBETH BASIN: 1 mile, 6 locks

Manager:

021-456 2723

The Birmingham & Fazeley has never been more than a useful junction canal. It was authorised in 1784, after a great deal of opposition from the well established Birmingham Canal Company (who very soon merged with it), as a link between Birmingham and the south east. Until then, London-bound goods from Birmingham had to go right round by the River Severn. Naturally the canal was useless until the Coventry Canal had at least reached Fazeley, but the new B & F company ensured – even before its enabling Act was passed – that the other canals important to its success were completed. Thus at Coleshill in 1782 the Oxford Canal Company agreed to finish its line to Oxford and the Thames; the Coventry Canal Company agreed to extend its line from Atherstone to Fazeley; the new B & F company agreed to build its proposed line and continue it along the defaulting Coventry route from Fazeley to Whittington Brook; and the Trent & Mersey Company pledged to finish the Coventry's line from Whittington Brook to Fradley Junction on the T & M.

This rare example of co-operation among canal companies paid off, when in 1790, the great joint programme was finished and traffic immediately began to flow along the system. The Birmingham & Fazeley employed John Smeaton to build their canal: he completed it in 1789. The flights of narrow locks at Farmer's Bridge and Aston became very congested, especially after the Warwick canals had joined up with the B & F at Digbeth; two new canals were built to bypass this permanent obstacle, one on each side. The Tame Valley Canal and the Birmingham & Warwick Junction Canal were opened in 1844, and traffic flowed more smoothly. After this the Birmingham & Fazeley Canal became more attractive to carriers and it continued to be an important link route – which it remains.

Birmingham

Turning north east off the main line of the Birmingham Canal, one arrives shortly at Cambridge Wharf – a canal basin with a modern canal pub and BW moorings. From this point the exciting Farmer's Bridge flight of 13 locks descends steeply into the heart of Birmingham. Many of the locks were built very close together and so the intervening pounds were expanded as much as possible in every direction. This results in one side of each lock becoming like a peninsula, flanked by water. Restoration work has made the passage through the locks a very attractive prospect and there is now a public viewing area at Newhall Bridge, by the Science Museum, an indication of how the forgotten world of the Birmingham canals is being opened up to the residents. After passing the base of Birmingham's Post Office Tower, the canal levels out as the locks come to an end. Moorings have been provided between the Farmer's Bridge and Aston flights. But soon comes Aston Junction, marked by the old iron turnover bridge, on which is cast 'Horseley Iron Works Staffordshire 1828'. To the north east is the main line of the Birmingham & Fazeley, falling through the 11 Aston locks to Salford Junction. The area of the junction by Ashted Top Lock has been landscaped and tidied up, another sign of the steady regeneration taking place on the Birmingham canals. The towpath is in excellent condition. Towards Salford Junction itself, the buildings become fewer and lower. Up above, motorways fill the sky.

PUBS

Long Boat Cambrian Wharf. Canalside near Farmer's Bridge top lock. Large modern pub, with a crane on the terrace and good moorings.

James Brindley Gas Street Basin. Attractive pub with seafood *lunchtime and early evening*.

Reservoir Cuckoo Bridge. Renovated pub serving M & B real ale and *lunchtime* food.

Swan & Mitre Lichfield Road, by Aston Station. Renovated in classic style. Ansells and Tetley's real ale.

Bartons Arms High Street, Aston. Well worth the ¾ mile walk west from the bottom of Aston Locks, to enjoy M & B real ale in a superb Edwardian pub which sparkles with stained glass and painted tiles. Cosy snugs, large saloons and snob screens. Excellent *lunchtime* food, including salads and seafood. Live music most *evenings*.

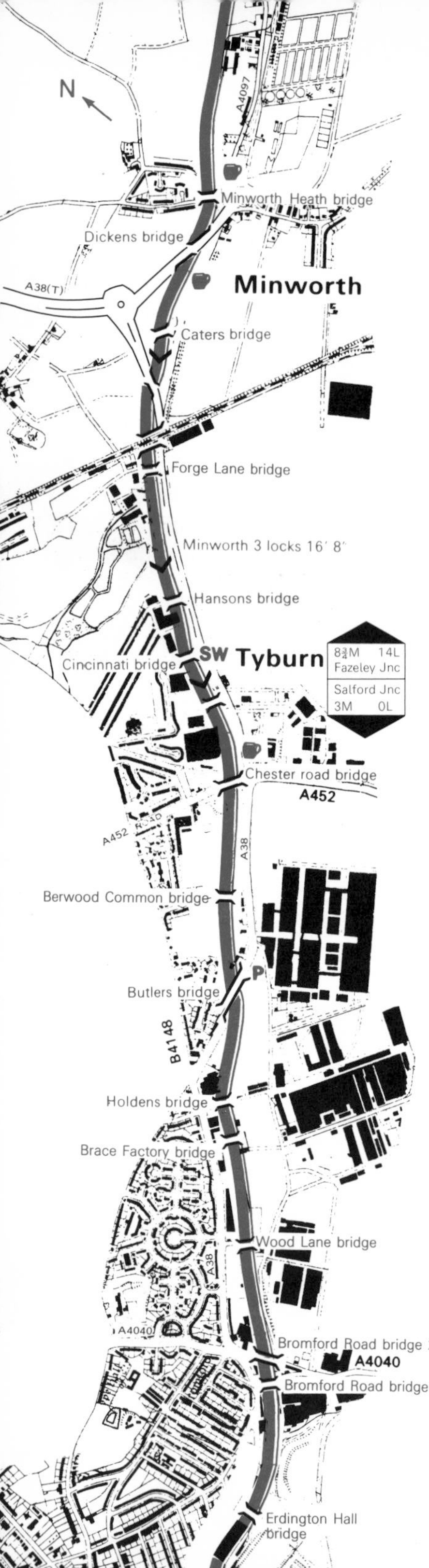

Tyburn

Leaving behind the motorway interchange at Salford Junction, the Birmingham & Fazeley Canal runs eastwards out of Birmingham. Power stations give way to industry, which in turn is slowly replaced by the spreading Birmingham suburbs. Named bridges are a feature of this stretch, a useful means of orientation, while at one point (near Erdington Hall Bridge) the canal is actually roofed over for 150yds by an enormous industrial building. As the canal progresses, the water becomes clearer. All facilities are readily available along the canal, although the factories limit the access; the bridge carrying the A452 across the canal at Tyburn is a convenient access point. Most of the factories ignore the canal, although the Cincinnati works are a laudable exception: landscaped lawns and gardens run down from the buildings to the water's edge. Minworth Locks start the descent.

PUBS

Hare & Hounds Minworth. Canalside, by Minworth Heath Bridge. Food.

Boat Minworth. Canalside, by Caters Bridge. Ansells real ale, snacks.

Tyburn House Chester Road Bridge (just above top lock). Canalside.

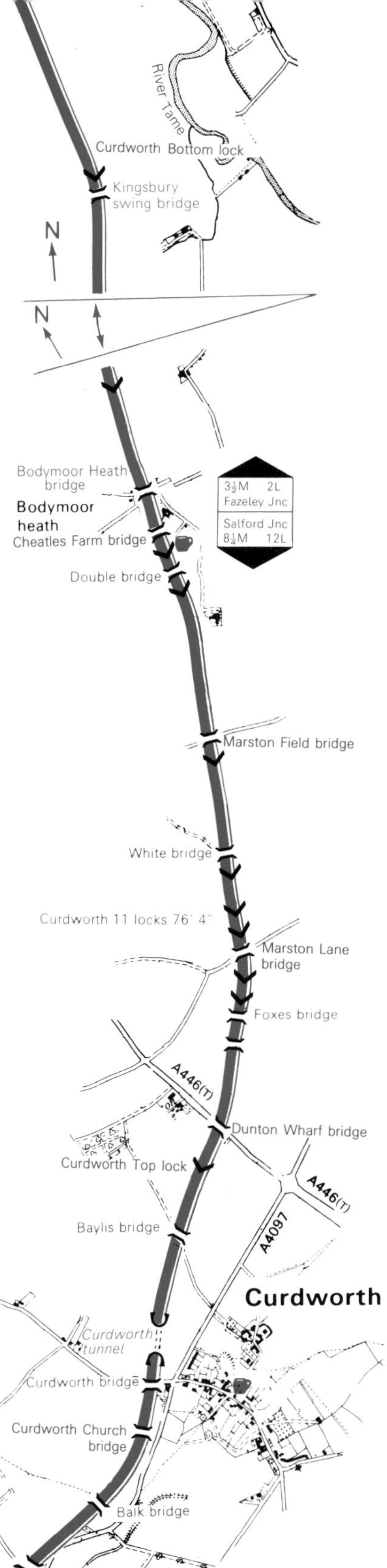

Curdworth

Continuing north east the canal leaves the industry that has followed it from Birmingham. A short cutting leads to Curdworth, whose church tower has been visible for some time. The cutting continues past the village, light woods screening it from view, and then the canal enters a short tunnel (57yds). The towing path passes through the tunnel, but it is very slippery. From now on until Fazeley the canal flows in complete isolation through the empty fields, only the 11 locks falling down to the junction breaking its journey. The lack of hedges is very noticeable, and partly explains the bleakness of this area; only the towing path hedge seems to have survived. As the canal swings to the north, hedges and trees reappear, and after Bodymoor Heath the trees line the canal on both sides for 2 miles. By the bottom lock there is a swing bridge, the first of two on this canal. The A4097 leaves the canal at Curdworth, where the A446 crosses.

Bodymoor Heath
Warwicks. PO, tel. A scattered village beyond which gravel pits, many flooded and overgrown, break up the fields. Yet amidst the dereliction are occasional 18thC buildings, surviving as a memory of the pre-industrial Midlands. The pub, the 'Dog & Doublet' is a fine example.

Curdworth
Warwicks. PO, tel, stores, garage. Set between two main roads in a predominantly industrial area. The squat church is partly Norman; note the finely carved font.

PUBS

Dog & Doublet Bodymoor Heath. Smart canalside pub serving M & B real ale, bar meals *lunchtime and evening* and restaurant meals *(L & D)*. Garden.

Beehive Curdworth. (0675 470223). Ansells real ale. Food.

White Horse Curdworth. M & B real ale. Food.

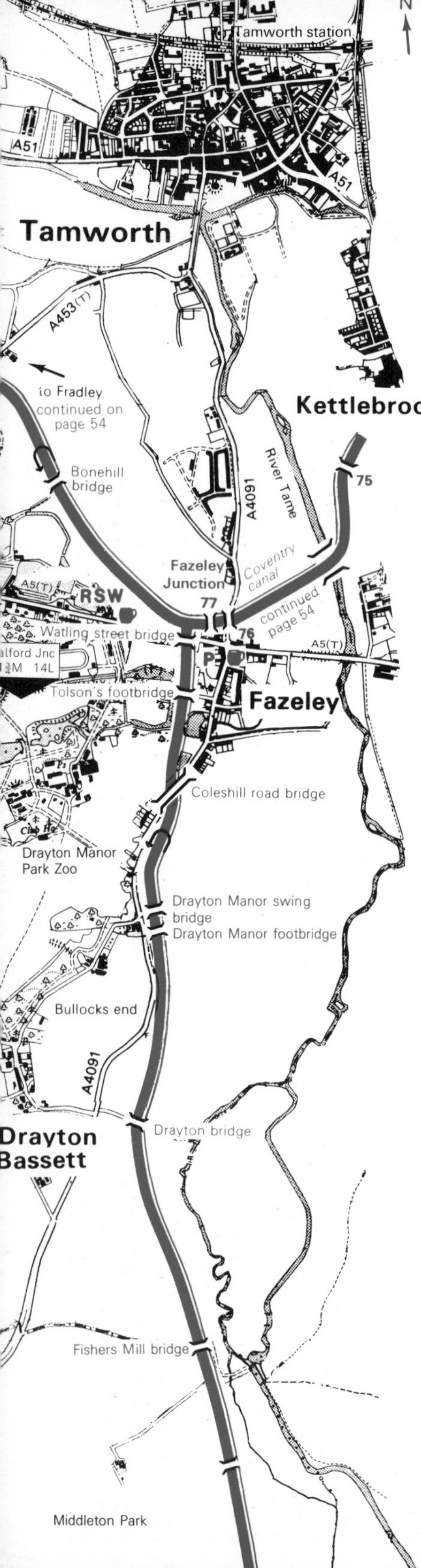

Fazeley

Continuing north, the canal runs through open farmland, flanked on both sides by oak trees, their roots projecting into the water. The isolation of the canal ends at Drayton Bassett where the A4091 swings in to run parallel to the canal as far as Fazeley. By Drayton Bassett is a curious footbridge, a marvellous folly, and immediately after it the second swing bridge. These features make the Birmingham & Fazeley Canal pleasantly eccentric, despite its unexciting course. The country gives way to the outskirts of Fazeley, which are quickly followed by the junction with the Coventry Canal. There are no locks. Fazeley is bisected by the A5 and A4091.

Fazeley
Staffs. EC Wed. PO, tel, stores, garage. Its importance as a road and canal junction determines the character of Fazeley; it is a small, industrial centre that has grown up around the communication network. From the canal the town appears more attractive than it really is. Useful as a supply centre, with a large number of garages and fish and chip shops.

Fazeley Junction
Staffs. The Birmingham & Fazeley Canal joins the Coventry which comes in from the east. Originally the Coventry was to continue westwards to meet the Trent & Mersey at Fradley; however the Coventry company ran out of money at Fazeley, and so the Birmingham & Fazeley continued on to Whittington. The Trent & Mersey company then built a linking arm from Fradley to Whittington, which was later bought by the Coventry company, thus becoming a detached section of their canal. The architecture of the buildings at the junction is in the best tradition of the canals and its recent restoration has made it a very pleasant place to moor.

Drayton Bassett
Staffs. EC Mon. PO, tel, stores, fish & chips. The village is set ½ mile to the west of the canal. The best feature is the charming and totally unexpected Gothic-style footbridge over the canal. Its twin battlemented towers would look quite commanding but for their ridiculously small size. This bridge is unique, and there seems to be no explanation for its eccentricity, thus greatly increasing its attraction.

Drayton Manor Park & Zoo Alongside the canal, off the A4091 at Drayton Manor Bridge. Formerly the house of Sir Robert Peel. 15 acres of wood and parkland with monkeys, birds, lions, pumas, llamas, sea lions and bears. Daily milking demonstration. *Open daily, Sun only in winter.*

BOATYARDS

BW Fazeley Wharf 200yds west of the junction. R S W

PUBS

Plough & Hare Watling Street, Fazeley. Food.

Three Tuns Fazeley. Manns real ale, bar food, garden. Overnight mooring for customers. W

CALDON

Maximum dimensions

Length: 72′
Beam: 7′
Headroom: 6′ 6″

Manager:

(0606) 40566

Mileage

ETRURIA TOP LOCK (Trent & Mersey Canal) to
Hanley: 2
Foxley: 4½
Stockton Brook Summit: 7
Hazelhurst Junction (Leek Branch): 9½
LEEK TERMINUS: 12¼
Cheddleton flint mills: 11½
FROGHALL TERMINUS: 17

Locks: 17

The Caldon Canal – or, more correctly, the Caldon Branch of the Trent & Mersey Canal – was designed as an outlet for the Caldon limestone quarries near Froghall on to the canal system. It was opened as a single branch to Froghall in 1779, tramways being constructed to bring the vast quantities of limestone down from Caldon Low quarries a couple of miles to the east. Froghall became a very busy terminus. 18 years later the Caldon's owners, the Trent & Mersey Canal Company, decided to build a secondary branch from the Caldon Canal to Leek, the main purpose of the extension being to use the line as a feeder from their new reservoir at Rudyard. The fact that the feeders from Rudyard had to enter the summit level of the canal, and the later advent of the railway, brought about significant changes in the layout of the canal between Endon and Hazelhurst, resulting in the exciting 'cross-over' junction that exists at Denford today.

In 1811 yet another branch was completed from Froghall down the Churnet Valley for 13 miles to Uttoxeter. This branch was shortlived, however. In 1845 a railway line was built, much of the track using the canal bed. One can still trace the remaining sections of the Uttoxeter branch near the railway.

The limestone from Froghall remained the chief commodity carried on the Caldon Canal for years. With its 17 locks and roundabout route the Caldon must have been an obvious target for railway competitors. However, the canal, with the rest of the Trent & Mersey, was owned by a railway company (the North Staffordshire Railway) from the 1840s onward, so presumably the NSR saw no point in competing against itself.

But at the beginning of the 20thC a new railway line was eventually opened and inevitably canal traffic slumped badly. After that time the canal gradually deteriorated until it became more or less unnavigable in the early 1960s.

The Caldon Canal Society led the struggle to reopen the canal; public interest grew and local authorities recognised the great recreational potential of this beautiful canal for the thousands of people living in the nearby Potteries. Much was achieved in the way of essential works by BWB and volunteer efforts and the canal was finally fully reopened to navigation in 1974, representing a splendid addition to the cruising network, and a much-needed 'linear park' for the Potteries.

Cheddleton Flint Mill. *David Perrott.*

Hanley

The Caldon Branch of the Trent & Mersey Canal leaves the main line at Etruria Top Lock, negotiating a series of amazing loops and turns that leave one wondering where the canal will go next. The first two locks up are 'staircase' locks – the only ones in north Staffordshire. All around, the little hills and valleys are crowded with terraced houses and factory chimneys. Planet Lock is soon reached; shops and pubs are close by. Now one passes through Hanley Park with its meticulously kept flower beds, lawns and bowling greens; east of the park, the canal twists round the built-up hillside that is topped by Hanley. As industrial stretches go, this is an interesting one, for several 'bottle' kilns still stand near the navigation, and the *Milton Maid*, *Queen*, or *Princess* may be moored along here. These narrowboats were specially built to carry pottery along the canal to Milton: the firm that operates them finds it substantially cheaper and safer than shifting the fragile goods by road. It is ironic to reflect that Josiah Wedgwood used precisely the same argument when supporting the proposed construction of the Trent & Mersey Canal over 200 years ago. Always give way to these craft. Ivy House lift bridge, once notoriously heavy to operate, has now been replaced by a new structure, operated by push buttons. You will need your BW key.

Hanley
Staffs. All services. Hanley is one of the six towns that were amalgamated in 1910 to form the present Stoke-on-Trent. It has been modernised and redeveloped as the shopping and business centre of the district. There is a rather unusual circular building housing Lewis's store, with a striking statue 'Fire' by David Wynne. Arnold Bennett was born here in 1867. Stoke City Museum and Art Gallery is in Bethesda Street, Hanley. (See page 155.)
Shirley's Bone Mill (0782 287577). By lock 39 on the Trent & Mersey. This Victorian potter's miller's works was built in 1857 and ground bone, flint and stone for the pottery industry until closure in 1972. It has now been restored as part of an industrial complex incorporating a blacksmith's shop with working steam-powered machinery. Originally the raw materials and ground products were transported by canal via the short arm, and present day canal travellers will find plenty of moorings available. A statue of James Brindley, the builder of the Trent & Mersey Canal, was erected at the junction of the Caldon Canal in 1989. *Open for guided tours Wed–Sun, closed Mon & Tue.* Free.

BOATYARDS

BW Etruria Yard at junction with Trent & Mersey Canal. (0782 215597). R S W Toilet.

PUBS

Duke of Wellington 227 Lichfield Street. Bass real ale in a comfortable lounge, where the organ is regularly played. Bar snacks.
Old Corner Cupboard 198 Caldon Road, opposite Hanley Park. Impressive collection of trophies in the public bar. Bass real ale, food *lunchtime*, snacks.
Norfolk 1–5 Norfolk Street, overlooking Planet Lock. Pub in a converted terrace. Marstons real ale, food *lunchtime and evening*. Mooring above and below the lock.
Duke of Bridgewater 1 Rectory Street, off Etruria Vale Road. Comfortable traditional local. Bass real ale, snacks.
Bird in Hand Etruria Vale Road. Close to the junction, this is a popular canal enthusiasts' pub. Ansells real ale, snacks, garden.

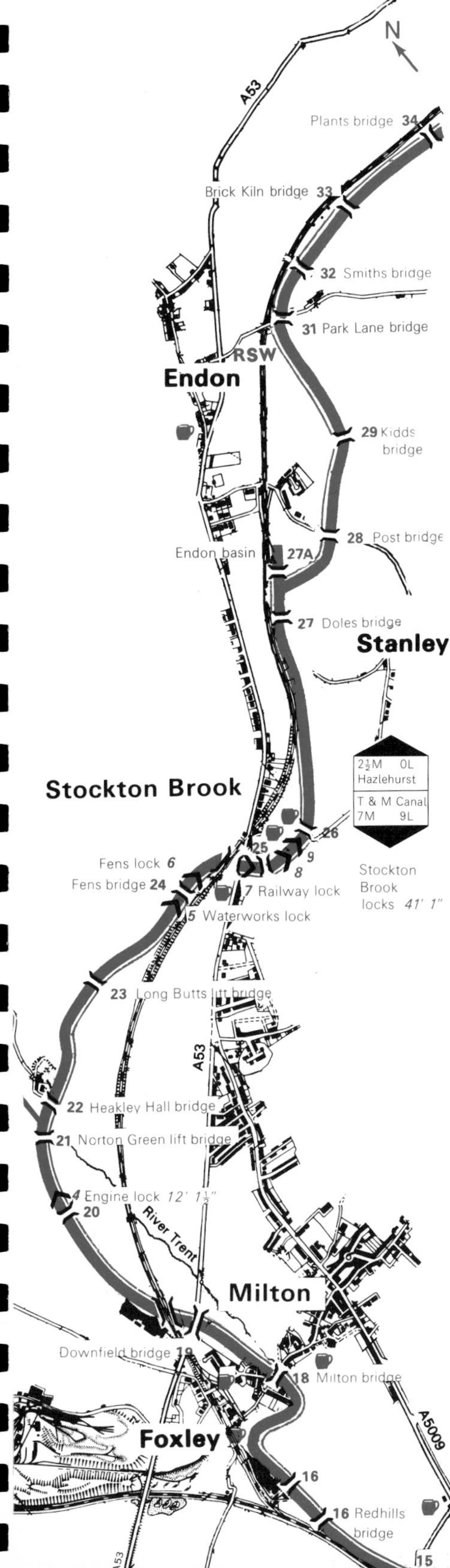

Stockton Brook

At Foxley the navigation turns sharp right: there is a pub on the corner, which is where the ½ mile-long Foxley Arm used to branch off: it is now filled in and difficult to trace. Engine Lock is not far off; it is so called because a huge beam engine used to be housed just up the hill, employed to pump water from mine workings. At the next pretty lift bridge the (unnavigable) feeder from Knypersley reservoir joins the canal. By now the countryside is thoroughly attractive, and the Potteries are safely distant. Five locks at Stockton Brook raise the canal up to the summit level 484ft above the sea. Soon the canal begins to hug once more the side of a hill.

Endon
Staffs. PO, tel, stores, garage, bank. The real village is up the hill just north of the main road and is attractive, especially during its traditional 'well-dressing' ceremony. Good views may be had from the Victorian church. Endon Basin (built in 1917, and once a canal/railway interchange basin) is the local wharf used as the Stoke-on-Trent Boat Club's base. Near the basin are the remains of a former light railway swing bridge over the canal, where it used to join the then busy main line.

Stanley
Staffs. PO, tel, stores. A stiff climb southwards from bridge 28 leads to a brown-stone hill village, still looking much as it did when farming predominated. There is, happily, little new development. There are fine views across the valley to Endon.

Stockton Brook
Staffs. PO, tel, stores. From the canal, a pleasant and useful place. The five locks have a charming position, with views back down the headwaters of the River Trent. There is a splendid Victorian waterworks at the bottom of the flight, and pubs and shops near the middle.

Knypersley reservoir
3½ miles north of Milton. This feeds water to the Trent & Mersey summit level via the Caldon Canal. The head of the River Trent is within its catchment area. Surrounded by woodland, the reservoir is a delightful setting for picnicking and rambling. The upper dam is covered with rhododendrons. Fishing rights are exercised by an angling club.

Milton
Staffs. PO, tel, stores, fish & chips. A little village on the side of a hill, forming an agreeable background to the canal.

PUBS

Black Horse Inn 381 Leek Road, Endon. Excellent local with a fine collection of toby jugs. Bass real ale, snacks.

Plough Leek Road, Endon. 18thC pub, now a Toby Inn with a smart lounge. Bass real ale, meals, snacks, garden.

Rose & Crown Stanley Road, Stanley. Friendly rural pub with an open fire, serving Ind Coope (Burton) and Tetley's real ale. Snacks, garden.

Travellers Rest Tompkin Road, Stanley. Comfortable 18thC cottage pub with an open fire and an enthusiastic landlord. A choice of Ansells, Ind Coope (Burton) and Tetley's real ale. *Lunchtime* food, snacks, garden.

Sportsman Stockton Brook, close to Railway Lock. A fine stone-built local serving Tetley's real ale and snacks. Garden.

Foaming Quart 5 Frobisher Street, Norton Green. Welcoming terrace local. Tetley's real ale, snacks and garden.

Holly Bush Stockton Brook. A spacious and smart pub with unusual etched windows. Bass real ale, bar food *lunchtime (not Sun)*, restaurant meals *Wed–Sun*. Bowling green, garden with playground, family room.

Miners Arms Milton. Terrace pub with a garden. Ind Coope (Burton) real ale.

Millrace Milton. Snacks. Surrounded by demolished buildings – luckily this handsome pub has survived. Shops nearby. Both the above by bridge 18.

Foxley Canalside at the junction with the former Foxley Arm. Food, children's room.

Leek Branch

At Hazelhurst the canal divides: the main line falls through three locks before turning east and south to join the River Churnet, while the Leek Branch bears right along the hillside, then crosses the main line on a large aqueduct. The railway and the Endon Brook are also traversed by aqueducts: thus the Leek Branch reaches the north side of the narrow valley. After this very interesting section, the canal clings to the hillside, flanked by beautiful, mature trees, as it follows the tortuous course of the River Churnet. The railway runs along the valley floor, but only the occasional goods train uses it. North of bridge 6 there is a tiny post office/store. There is a large 'lagoon' just before the 130yd Leek Tunnel. Beyond the tunnel, only a short stretch of canal remains, ending on a fine stone aqueduct over the River Churnet. The last ½ mile beyond the Churnet and straight along to Leek Basin has been filled in and covered with a new industrial estate. However, one can take a pleasant walk westwards by following the feeder that brings water down from Rudyard Lake into the navigation at its present terminus. An altogether delightful stretch of canal.

Leek
Staffs. EC Thur. MD Wed. All services. Essentially a textile town situated on the slope of a hill, and often referred to as the 'capital of the moors'. It was here that Thomas Parker, the first Earl of Macclesfield, was born in 1666, and his house can still be seen in the market place. James Brindley, the canal engineer, started in business as a millwright in Leek. The parish church of St Edward is 14thC, but was restored in 1856, and the chancel rebuilt in 1867.
Brindley Mill Macclesfield Road, Leek. (0538 384195). Turn right along the A53 from the canal feeder, follow signs to Macclesfield. The mill will be seen about 2 miles from the canal terminus, at the junction with the A523. A working corn mill equipped by James Brindley, the canal engineer, when he worked as a millwright in Leek. Milling display, Brindley's notebook and theodolite. *Open weekends and B. Hols, Easter–Oct, also Mon, Tue and Thur July & Aug. Afternoons only*. Modest charge.
Coombes Valley 3 miles south east of Leek. An attractive valley through which a trout stream runs. It is a reserve of the Royal Society for the Protection of Birds and it is possible to see kestrels, sparrowhawks, kingfishers, green and great spotted woodpeckers, dippers and redstarts. There are also a number of badger setts. *Open daily except Tue.* A nature trail has been laid out and guides may be obtained from the warden at Six Oaks Farm, Bradnop, near Leek, Staffs.
Rudyard Lake 3 miles north west of the canal terminus near Leek. A very long, thin reservoir in a pleasant wooded setting used for feeding water into the Trent & Mersey Canal summit level via the Caldon Canal. The Rudyard Hotel adjoins the reservoir headbank.

PUBS

Wheel Leek Road, Longsdon. Cosy pub with an open fire and decorated with much bric-a-brac. Ind Coope (Burton) real ale, *lunchtime* food and snacks. *Opens 12.00 and 19.00*. Grocery opposite.

New Inn Leek Road, Longsdon. Country local with an open fire, serving Marstons real ale and snacks.

Holly Bush Denford, near bridge 38. Small traditional 17thC canal pub with an open fire. Ind Coope (Burton) real ale, snacks and children's room. Mooring on the main (lower) line, although access from the Leek Branch is easy enough.

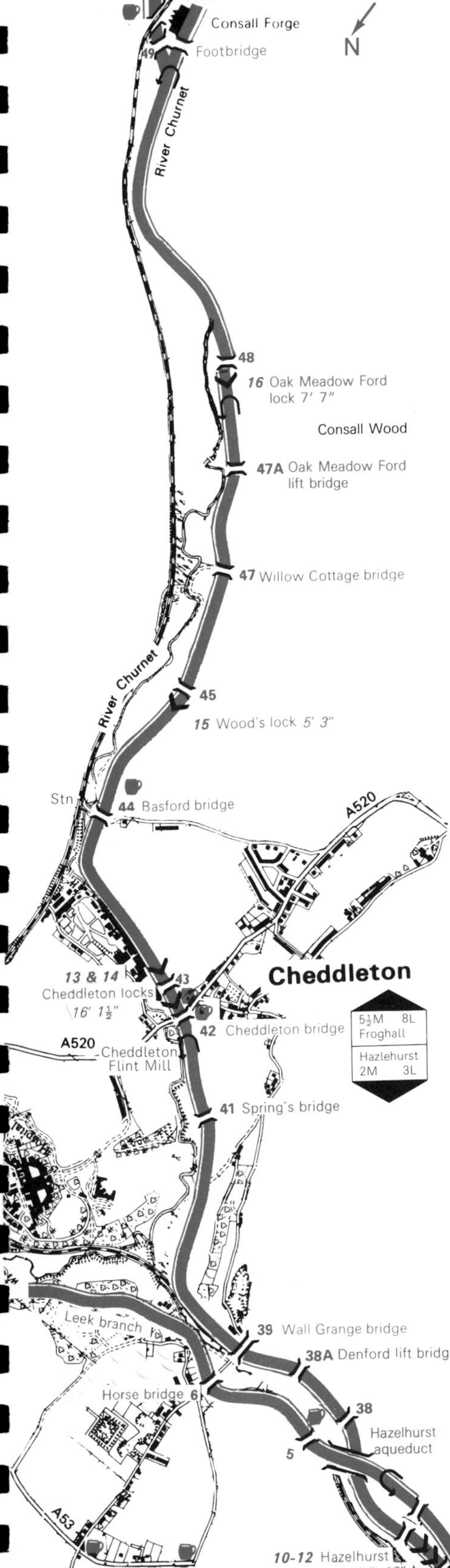

Cheddleton

Here the main line to Froghall drops down three attractive and isolated locks and passes under the Leek Branch, soon taking up a position at the foot of the hills. At the former canalside Wall Grange station, the railway veers off towards Leek: it is soon replaced by the River Churnet, and the two waterways flow side by side for the next 7 miles. This must be one of the most beautiful valleys in Staffordshire, and the canal makes its own special contribution to the scenery. At Oak Meadow Ford Lock the canal enters the River Churnet and the two waterways share the same course for 1 mile to Consall Forge. See Navigational note 2. For most of the way, the Churnet valley is enclosed by very steep and thickly wooded hills whose sides reach right down to the river and adjacent canal. It is a superlative landscape, almost untouched and unspoilt by man's incursions. Yet it has been busy in the past, when boats and trains laden with limestone from Caldon competed for trade. Now the canal carries only pleasurecraft and the railway a few trains a day, so there is little to break the peace of this splendidly secluded place.

Navigational note 1
If your boat does not fit the Froghall Tunnel profile displayed at Cheddleton, you will have to turn either at Consall Forge or just before the tunnel.

Navigational note 2
The canal and river share a common course between Oak Meadow Ford Lock and Consall Forge, and care should be exercised along here. If the river level is over 6in up on the gauge at Oak Meadow Ford Lock **do not enter this section.**

Cheddleton
Staffs. PO, tel, stores, garage, restaurant. A large main road rumbles through the village, but away from this are the two fine water mills hard by the canal as it enters the village. These flint-grinding mills were restored to their former glory and opened to the public in 1969: the big wooden water wheels now turn at the touch of a lever. (Ground flint has always been a vital raw material for the pottery industry.) The village proper is up the steep hill, grouped about the ancient stone church of St Edward the Confessor. Little of the original building remains but the 14thC work is worth examining.

Cheddleton Flint Mill Watch two waterwheels driving the flint grinding machinery in this charming and picturesque setting. A beautifully restored narrowboat is moored at the wharf. *Open weekend afternoons.*

North Staffordshire Railway Company Cheddleton Station. (0538 360522). Near bridge 44. Railway trips to Oakamoor, following the canal as far as Froghall, then alongside parts of the long abandoned Uttoxeter branch of the Caldon Canal. *Open summer Sun and Aug B. Hol.*

PUBS AND RESTAURANTS

Boat Canalside at bridge 44. Stone-built pub with long low-ceiling bar decorated with plates and handsome jugs. Marstons real ale, *lunchtime* food, garden. There is an old bridge across the River Churnet nearby.

Red Lion Near bridge 43, Cheddleton. Ansells and Ind Coope (Burton) real ale in a fine 18thC black and white pub with an open fire. *Lunchtime* food, snacks, garden.

Black Lion Cheddleton. Up the hill by the church. Traditional one-room local serving Marstons real ale and snacks.

Holly Bush Denford, near bridge 38. Small traditional 17thC canal pub with an open fire. Ind Coope (Burton) real ale, snacks and children's room. Mooring on the main (lower) line, although access from the Leek Branch is easy enough.

Flint Lock Canalside at Cheddleton Lock (0538 361032). *L & D, closed Mon.*

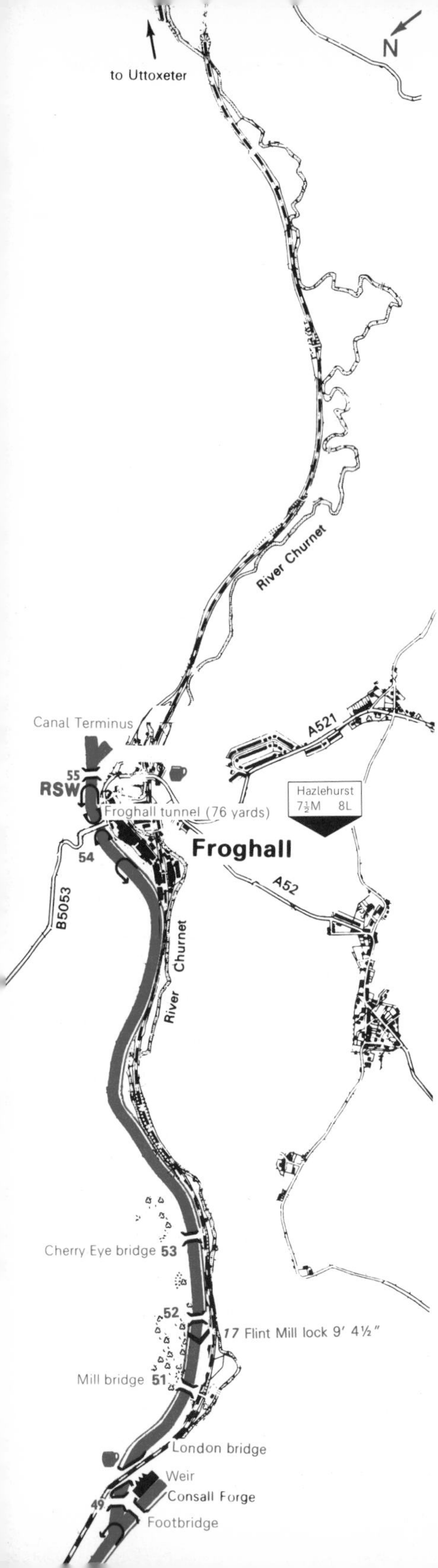

Froghall

This is another very beautiful and secluded length of canal. Passing along the wooded valley that contains the River Churnet, one arrives at Consall Forge. This, once bustling with various mineral works, is now a quiet backwater, ruffled occasionally by passing goods trains. In this unlikely situation the visitor will find a pub with no access by public road. The canal and the river split at Consall Forge, the canal proceeding along the north-east side of the steep valley to Flint Mill Lock and the adjacent flint mill. This is, in a way, another piece of living industrial archaeology, where Australian sand is ground to dust for use in glazing pottery. The machinery is still run entirely by water power: water from the canal drops 15ft to drive an underground turbine. The remains of the huge old waterwheel can still be seen. Beyond the mill, the navigation creeps along the side of a wooded hill as the valley floor drops away. Beyond here, one finds the large scale industrial works that dominate Froghall. There are moorings before the tunnel for those whose boat cannot pass through (your hire base will inform) and a winding hole. The terminus is just beyond the tunnel, where there is a full length winding hole, a fine small wharf house and stables.

Froghall
Staffs. PO, tel. Tucked away in the heart of unspoilt Staffordshire, Froghall has been an outpost of industry ever since the advent of the canal fostered the growth of the Caldon lime quarries a few miles east. The limestone was carted down the hills by a plate tramway, being transhipped into waiting canal boats at Froghall Basin. Much of the trade was later lost to the railways. Just west of the final bridge by the basin, one can still see the junction with the old canal arm to Uttoxeter: this locked down to the Churnet valley. The branch was closed in 1847 and the railway now occupies most of the canal's course, although much of the canal bed can still be traced. Froghall nowadays comprises almost entirely the factories and dwellings associated with Thomas Bolton's big copper works.

PUBS

Railway Hotel Bank View, Froghall. Recently altered pub offering Ansells, Ind Coope (Burton) and Tetley's real ale. *Lunchtime* food, snacks, garden.

Black Lion Consall Forge. A canalside pub of outstanding isolation in a beautiful setting. There is an open fire, and Marstons and Ruddles real ale to enjoy. *Lunchtime* food, snacks, garden. A popular place in summer.

COVENTRY

Maximum dimensions

Length: 72′
Beam: 7′
Headroom: 6′ 6″

Manager:

(0203) 392250

Mileage

COVENTRY BASIN to
HAWKESBURY JUNCTION (Oxford Canal): 5½
MARSTON JUNCTION (Ashby Canal): 8¼
Boot Wharf, Nuneaton: 10½
Hartshill: 14
Atherstone Top Lock: 16½
Polesworth: 21½
Alvecote Priory: 23¼
Glascote Bottom Lock: 25½
FAZELEY JUNCTION (Birmingham & Fazeley Canal): 27
Hopwas: 29¾
Whittington Brook: 32½
Huddlesford Junction: 34
FRADLEY JUNCTION (Trent & Mersey Canal): 38

Locks: 13

The Coventry Canal, whose enabling Act of Parliament was passed in 1768, was promoted with two main objectives: to connect the fast growing town of Coventry with the great new trade route called the Grand Trunk, now known as the Trent & Mersey Canal; and to provide Coventry with cheap coal from Bedworth coalfield 10 miles to the north.

The first, long-term objective was not achieved for some years until the company had overcome some financial difficulties, but – wisely – the stretch between Coventry and Bedworth was completed early on, so that the profitable carriage of local coal was quickly established along the canal, in 1769. It is interesting to note that several of the collieries in the Bedworth area had already used their own independent canal system for years: these were of course all connected to the main line of the new canal.

By the time the canal reached Atherstone in 1771, all the authorised capital had been spent and James Brindley, the original engineer of the canal, had been sacked. For these reasons – and because of an interminable wrangle with the Oxford Canal Company whose scheme to link Coventry with southern England had followed hard upon the original Coventry scheme – the Coventry Canal did not reach Fazeley (nearly 12 miles short of its intended terminus at Fradley) until 1790.

By this time, the Birmingham & Fazeley Canal had been built and was extending along the Coventry Canal's original proposed line to Whittington Brook, whence the Grand Trunk Canal Company carried it north to Fradley, thus completing the line. (The Coventry company later bought this section back, which explains the fact that there is now a detached portion of the Coventry Canal from Whittington Brook to Fradley Junction.)

In 1790 also, the Oxford Canal was completed through to Oxford and thus to London by the Thames. The profits of the Coventry Canal rose quickly, and rose even higher when the Grand Junction Canal was completed in 1799, shortening the route to London by 60 miles. Other adjoining canals contributed to the Coventry's prosperity: the Ashby, the Wyrley & Essington and the Trent & Mersey Canals. The extension of the Grand Junction via Warwick to Birmingham naturally dismayed the Coventry, but the numerous locks – and high tolls on the stretch of the Oxford Canal between Braunston and Napton Junctions – ensured that a lot of traffic to and from Birmingham still used the slightly longer route via the Coventry and Birmingham & Fazeley Canals, especially after the Oxford Canal was shortened by 14 miles between Braunston and Longford.

One could attribute the continuous financial success of the Coventry Canal first to its being part of so many long distance routes and secondly to the continued prosperity of the coal mines along its route. It was certainly one of the most persistently profitable canals ever built in Britain, paying a dividend up to 1947.

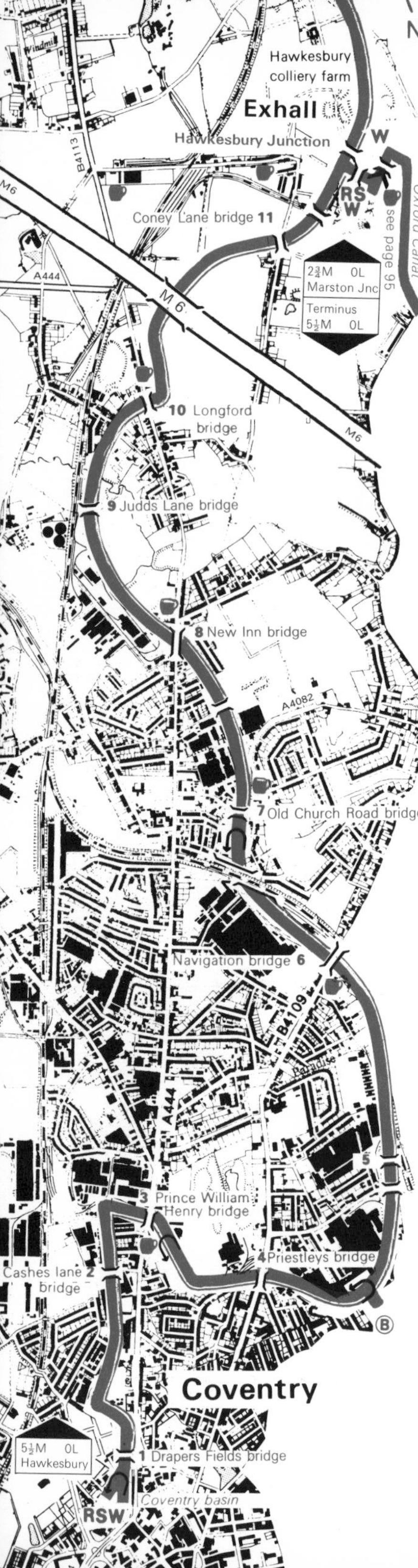

Coventry

The Coventry Canal begins at a large basin near the town centre. It is an interesting situation on the side of a hill: overlooked by tall new buildings and attractive old wooden canal warehouses; now restored as an arts, crafts and boat building centre and incorporating a canal museum. The old toll house is now a shop and information centre. Leaving the basin, the canal winds through industrial areas almost to Hawkesbury. The navigation is often narrow, and mostly flanked by buildings. Observant travellers will notice the course of another canal alongside the Coventry Canal between Longford Bridge and Hawkesbury Junction. This used to be the Oxford Canal running right beside the Coventry before actually joining it at Longford. In 1836 this was replaced by the present junction at Hawkesbury.

Hawkesbury Junction
Hawkesbury Junction is also known as Sutton Stop, after the name of the first lock keeper. It was always a busy canal centre, and remains so today, with plenty of narrowboats permanently moored at the junction. There are other things to see here: a canal pub, a stop lock and disused pumping house. The latter used to pump water up into the canal from a well. Its engine was installed in 1821, having been previously employed for nearly 100 years at Griff Colliery (a few miles up the canal towards Nuneaton). This Newcomen-type atmospheric steam engine, called 'Lady Godiva', is now in Dartmouth Museum. It ceased work in 1913. Supplies and calor gas are available every day from The Chandlery, 16 Sutton Stop.

Longford Bridge
West Midlands. PO, tel, stores, off-licence, chandlery.

Coventry
West Midlands. EC Thur. MD Wed/Fri/Sat. PO, tel, stores, garage, station, cinema, theatre. The town was largely destroyed during the Second World War and consequently today is a modern and well-planned city.

Herbert Art Gallery & Museum Jordan Well. Collections of local art including natural history, archaeology, industry. Frequent loan exhibitions. Collection of Sutherland sketches for the Coventry Cathedral tapestry. *Open Mon to Sat and Sun afternoons.*

Coventry Cathedral Designed by Sir Basil Spence and completed in 1962. The modern stained-glass windows all reflect their light towards the altar, behind which is a tapestry by Graham Sutherland. The font, a boulder from a hillside near Bethlehem, stands in front of the Baptistry window by John Piper.

Cathedral Church of St Michael Only the ruins of the old Cathedral destroyed by the Luftwaffe in 1940 still remain.

St John's Church Built in the 14thC and used as a prison when the Scots were defeated by Oliver Cromwell. From the incident comes the phrase 'sent to Coventry'.

BOATYARDS

Ⓑ **Club Line Cruisers** Swan Lane Wharf, Coventry. (0203 258864). R S WD Pump-out, gas, narrowboat hire, overnight mooring, long-term mooring, slipway, groceries, chandlery, books and maps, boat building, boat sales, engine sales and repairs, toilets.

PUBS

Black Horse Longford Road, Exhall. Single-bar pub with a garden, serving M & B and Bass real ale. Snacks.

Boat Black Horse Road, Exhall. Heritage Inn with unspoilt rooms and a cosy lounge. Ansells, Ind Coope (Burton) and Tetley's real ale, and *lunchtime* meals. Children allowed into the snug.

Greyhound Hawkesbury Junction. An interesting canalside pub offering Bass real ale and snacks. Outside drinking area, and groceries next door.

Engine by bridge 12.

Fiesta Canalside at bridge 8.

Royal Hotel near bridge 7.

Navigation Canalside, at bridge 6.

Prince William Henry by bridge 3.

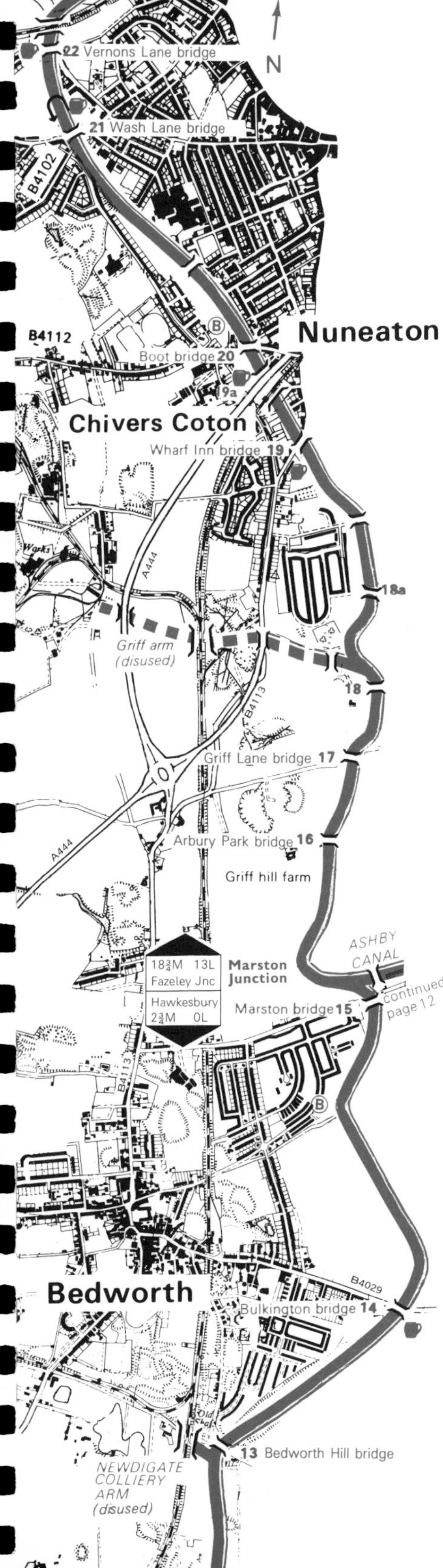

Nuneaton

Leaving Hawkesbury Junction, the canal runs through an open industrial wasteland, the only focal point being Hawkesbury Colliery Farm – a strange-looking survivor in this kind of landscape. The canal passes Bedworth via a long cutting: the town seems to be composed entirely of vast housing estates, but it is convenient as a supply centre. At Marston Junction the Ashby Canal branches to the east – a free guide to the canal is available from the dispenser (BW key required). The Coventry Canal continues north towards Nuneaton, passing a disused colliery arm to the west. There is a short stretch of open fields followed immediately by the suburbs of Nuneaton. There are good moorings and easy access to the town by Boot Bridge (20). The canal runs round the town and so its route is marked by a succession of housing estates and allotments.

Nuneaton
Warwicks. EC Thur. MD Sat. PO, tel, stores, garage, station, cinema. A rather typical Midlands town with much industrial development. On the derelict Griff colliery canal arm are the hollows said to be the origin of the Red Deeps of the *Mill on the Floss* by George Eliot, who was born here in 1819. *By bridge 21 there are stores, fish and chips and Chinese take-away.*
Nuneaton Museum & Art Gallery Riversley Park. Archaeological specimens of Nuneaton from prehistoric to medieval times, and also items from the local earthenware industry. Geological and mining relics, ethnography from Africa, Asia, America and Oceania. Paintings, prints and water colours. Personalia collection of the novelist George Eliot. *Open Mon–Fri afternoons, all day weekends.*
Arbury Hall 2 miles south west of canal off B4102. Originally an Elizabethan house, gothicised by Sir Roger Newdigate in 1750–1800 under the direction of Sanderson Miller, Henry Keene and Couchman of Warwick. Fine pictures, furniture, and china and glass. The Hall is in a beautiful park setting. *Open from Easter Sun–Oct on Sun, B. Hol Mon & Tue following B. Hol.*
Chivers Coton
Warwicks. Suburb of Nuneaton. Its church dates from 1946 and was designed by H. N. Jepson and built by German prisoners of war.
Bedworth
Warwicks. EC Wed. MD Tue/Fri/Sat. The most impressive parts of this mining town are its church by Bodley and Garner, 1888–90, and the almshouses built in 1840. Good shops.

BOATYARDS

Ⓑ **Gilbert Bros.** Charity Dock, Furnace Road, Bedworth. (0203 313122). S D Overnight mooring, long-term mooring, winter storage, crane, dry dock, boat building, boat sales, engine sales and repairs, toilets.
Ⓑ **Warwickshire Narrowboats** by Boot Bridge, Nuneaton. (0203 327107). R S W D Pump-out, gas, narrowboat hire, groceries, chandlery, books and maps, boat building, boat sales, engine repairs and sales, toilets.

PUBS

Board Inn Near bridge 22. Basic bar and small cosy lounge, where M & B real ale can be enjoyed. Snacks.
Cock & Bear By bridge 21. Large pub serving M & B real ale and snacks.
Boot Boot Wharf, Nuneaton. M & B real ale in a pub with a large bar and quiet lounge. The enclosed garden has swings for the children. *Lunchtime* meals.
Wharf Inn Canalside at bridge 19. M & B real ale, garden, snacks.
Fleur de Lys Two minutes' walk down the hill from bridge 19. There is a large bar and pleasant lounge where M & B real ale may be enjoyed. Meals *lunchtime and evening.*
Navigation Inn Bulkington Road, Bedworth. (0203 311990). Canalside at bridge 14. Large pub with a comfortable lounge, a restaurant, children's room and garden. Manns, Ushers and Wilson's real ale. Meals *lunchtime and evening*, booking advisable. Overnight moorings.

Coventry Canal at Hartshill. *Derek Pratt.*

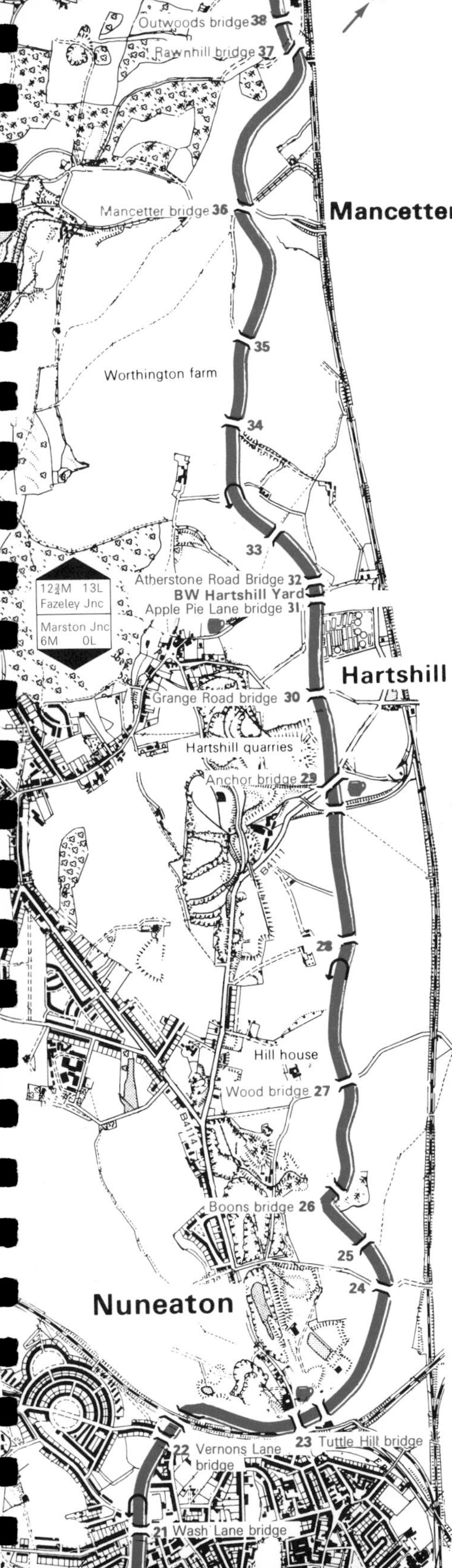

Hartshill

Continuing north west out of Nuneaton, the canal winds along the side of a hill into a landscape which is curiously exciting. Quarries and spoil heaps, now landscaped in part, are broken up by unexpected stretches of open countryside with fine views away to the north across the Anker valley. The earth has given the water a distinct rust colour. The canal passes below Hartshill; the attractive buildings in the BW yard are crowned by a splendid clock tower. The canal continues towards Mancetter leaving the quarry belt and moves temporarily into open rolling country backed by thick woods to the west. A railway follows the canal to the east, and the A4131 crosses at Hartshill.

Mancetter
Warwicks. PO, tel, stores, garage. ½ mile east of bridge 36. The church dates from the 13thC, but its best feature is the large collection of 18thC slate tombstones displaying all the elegance of Georgian incised lettering. There are some almshouses of 1728 in the churchyard, and across the road another row with pretty Victorian Gothic details. The manor, south of the church, is rather over restored.

Hartshill
Warwicks. PO, tel, stores, garage. A Nuneaton suburb and as such is hardly of interest. The canal passes through man-made surroundings now landscaped and reclaimed. It is hard to imagine that there was once a castle at Hartshill.

BOATYARDS

BW Hartshill Yard Clock Hill, Hartshill. (0203 392250). WD emergency only *in normal working hours.*

PUBS

Stag & Pheasant A short walk up the lane behind Hartshill BW Yard. Village green pub dispensing Flowers and Castle Eden real ale. Meals (*not Sun*) and children's room.

Anchor Hartshill. By bridge 29. Canalside pub with large garden and children's room. Ansells and Everards real ale, along with regular guest beers. Food.

Crazy Horse Nuneaton, near bridge 23. (0203 386690). Canalside pub with a large bar, pool room, restaurant and garden.

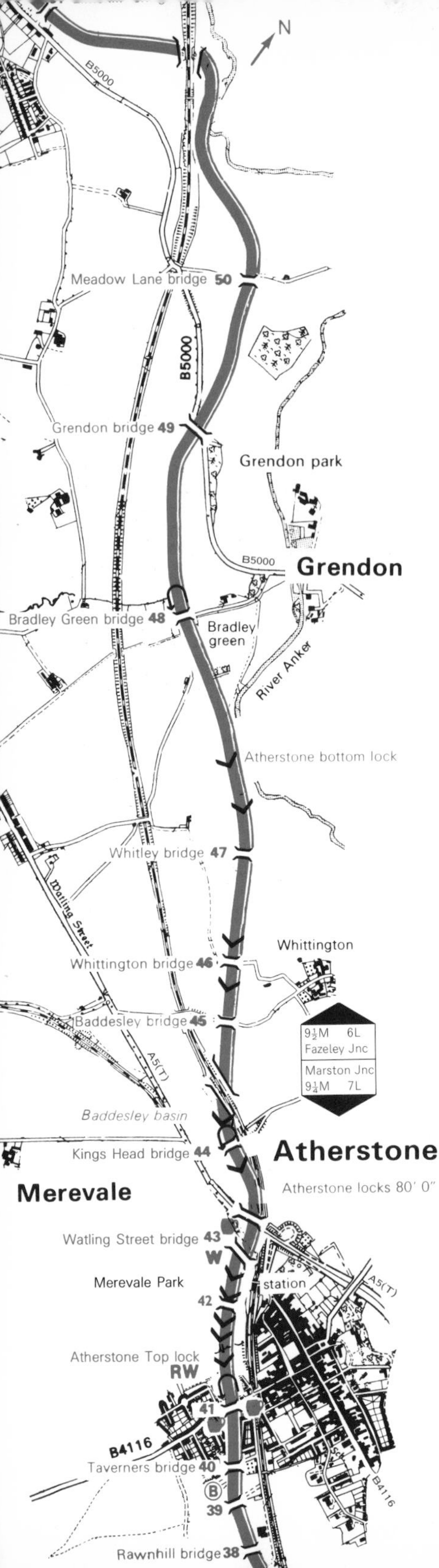

Atherstone

Continuing north west, the canal skirts to the south of Atherstone and begins to descend the locks. Wooded hills to the west reveal Merevale Hall overlooking a remote rural landscape. The 11 narrow locks empty at a remarkable speed, due to their outsize paddles. The flight is extremely attractive and varied, falling through housing, allotments and open countryside. The small basin at the top has been lovingly restored and is cared for by the lock keeper. When Rothens boat and butty (Buckden and Dipper) are moored there the scene is charming and complete. It is a pity that all except one of the side ponds on the flight are now sealed off. At the bottom, the River Anker converges with the canal from the east. A farm by bridge 48 is useful for supplies. Arable land accompanies the canal, lined with oak-trees as it passes Grendon. Only the skyline to the west reveals the industrial belt that is approaching. At this distance the skyline looks romantic, an 18thC vision of industry. As the canal turns towards Polesworth, it passes the remains of an iron swing bridge, a curiosity on this canal. The railway accompanies the canal, crossing from west to east after Grendon. The A5 runs through Atherstone and the B5000 crosses at Grendon.

Grendon
Warwicks. ½ mile north east of bridge 48. Grendon is just a small church set in very beautiful parkland. The woods and rolling fields are a last refuge before the industrial landscape that precedes Tamworth.

Atherstone
Warwicks. EC Thur. MD Tue, Fri. PO, tel, stores, garage, station, cinema. A pleasant town, with a strong 18thC feeling, especially in the open market place in front of the church, a large early Victorian building. There are interesting houses from the 16thC. On Shrove Tuesday medieval football is played in the town to commemorate the game originally played in Warwickshire and Leicestershire in the 12thC. Hundreds of people take part and there are no obvious rules or boundaries to the area of play. Shop windows are boarded up and all traffic is stopped in the town. The game is started by a famous sporting personality who throws the ball out of the window of the 'Three Tuns' pub.

Merevale A large battlemented house set among trees; high to the west is Merevale Hall, an early 19thC mock Tudor mansion. To the west are the remains of the 12thC abbey and the very pretty 13thC church which contains fine stained glass, monuments and brasses.

BOATYARDS

Ⓑ **Valley Cruises** Atherstone. (0827 712602). WD Pump-out, gas, narrowboat hire, overnight mooring, books and maps, boat building, boat sales, engine repairs, toilets, gifts.

PUBS

Red Lion Long Street, Atherstone. Bass real ale, snacks.

Kings Head Atherstone. By A5 bridge. Canalside. Davenports real ale, food.

Westwood House Atherstone. North of bridge 41. M & B real ale. Garden.

Maid of the Mill Atherstone. South of bridge 41. Friendly plain and homely pub with large games and children's room, and a cheerful public bar. The 'mill' is a felt hat factory next door. Davenports real ale and garden. Coleshill Road Stores opposite is useful for supplies.

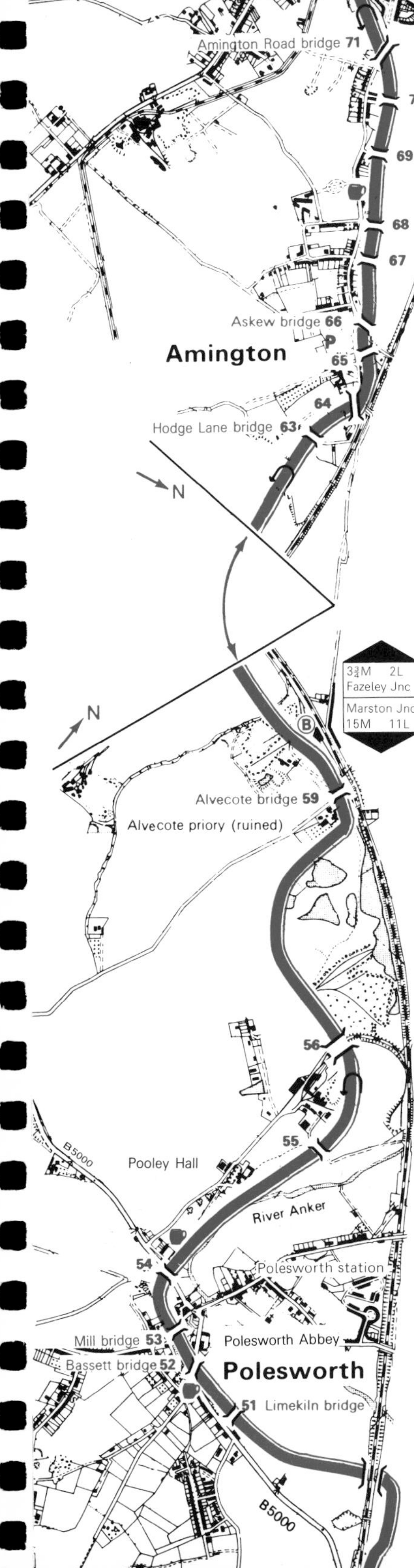

Polesworth

Now the canal runs along the side of a hill overlooking the Anker valley. Turning south of Polesworth it passes Pooley Hall, and an area of reclaimed spoil heaps, now a pleasant area of scrubland, with a golf course. Cows graze near Pooley Hall, and wildlife is filling the vacuum left by industry. Subsidence has affected the towpath which becomes difficult to follow at times. This landscape continues past Alvecote where the tree-surrounded ruins of the priory provide a sudden glimpse of history; and then at Amington it gives way to the suburbs of Tamworth. Throughout this stretch the views are striking across the valley to the hills beyond. The railway follows the canal; the B5000 crosses at Polesworth.

Amington
Staffs. PO, tel, stores, garage. A residential suburb of Tamworth notable for the church built by Street in 1864 which has a Burne-Jones stained glass window. To the south of bridges 68 and 69 is the Canal Craft Shop, where you can have 'Buckby' canalware painted to order.
Alvecote
Warwicks. PO, tel, stores. A mining village surrounded by the landscaped remains of industrialisation. The church has a weatherboarded bellcote and surviving Norman work inside.
Polesworth
Warwicks. EC Wed. PO, tel, stores, garage, fish & chips, station. The splendid gatehouse and the clerestory are all that remain of the 10thC abbey; most of the fragments are incorporated in the church. ½ mile to the north Pooley Hall, a Tudor brick mansion of 1509, overhangs the canal which is cut into the side of the hill.

BOATYARDS

Ⓑ **Narrowcraft** The Boatyard, Robey's Lane, Alvecote. (0827 898585). S W D Pump-out, gas, overnight mooring, long-term mooring, winter storage, books and maps, boat building, boat sales, toilets, showers. This base is situated in a converted colliery basin.

PUBS

Gate Inn Amington. Canalside. Marstons real ale, large garden, snacks. PO box, tel.
Royal Oak Polesworth. Food.
Bulls Head Tamworth Road, Polesworth. M & B and Bass real ale.

Tamworth

The canal runs through suburban housing, turning in a wide sweep south west past Tamworth towards Fazeley Junction. Houses and factories flank the canal as it passes Kettlebrook Wharf, and then it moves briefly into more open country, crossing the River Tame on an impressive aqueduct. At Fazeley Junction the Coventry meets the Birmingham & Fazeley Canal which then continues north west towards Fradley or south to Birmingham. Then follow lightly wooded open fields towards Hopwas Hill. The two Glascote Locks are the only ones on this stretch – the side ponds may be used if the paddle gear is intact. The A51, A4091 and the A453 cross the canal, while the A5 runs through Fazeley.

Fazeley Junction
Now tastefully restored with good moorings and a canalside seat made from a balance beam. Access to the pub is easy, and Chadwicks Stores, by the crossroads, is recommended.

Tamworth
Staffs. EC Wed. MD Sat. PO, tel, stores, garage, station, cinema. Tamworth was originally a Saxon town, and although only earthworks survive from this period, the town has much more quality and style than the industry that surrounds it. It is built predominantly of grey-black stone which is seen very effectively in the long railway viaduct to the east of the town centre. The castle is of Norman origin, but dates mostly from the time of Henry VIII; the town hall was built by Sir Thomas Guy, founder of Guy's Hospital, London. St Editha's church contains monuments and stained glass by William Morris.

Castle Museum Coins from the Tamworth mint of the Saxon and Norman periods. Also Roman antiquities and items of local interest.

BOATYARDS

BW Fazeley Yard 200yds west of the junction. R S W Slipway, moorings at the junction.

PUBS

Chequers Hotel Hopwas. (0827 53361). Canalside. Courage real ale; food, reductions for children. Garden.
Red Lion Hopwas. Canalside. Food.
Three Tuns Fazeley Junction. Manns real ale, bar food, garden. W
Peel Arms Market Street, Tamworth. Food, reductions for children.
Anchor Anchor Bridge. Glascote. Canalside. M & B real ale, garden, snacks.
Park Inn Bridge 74. Ind Coope (Burton) beer, food.

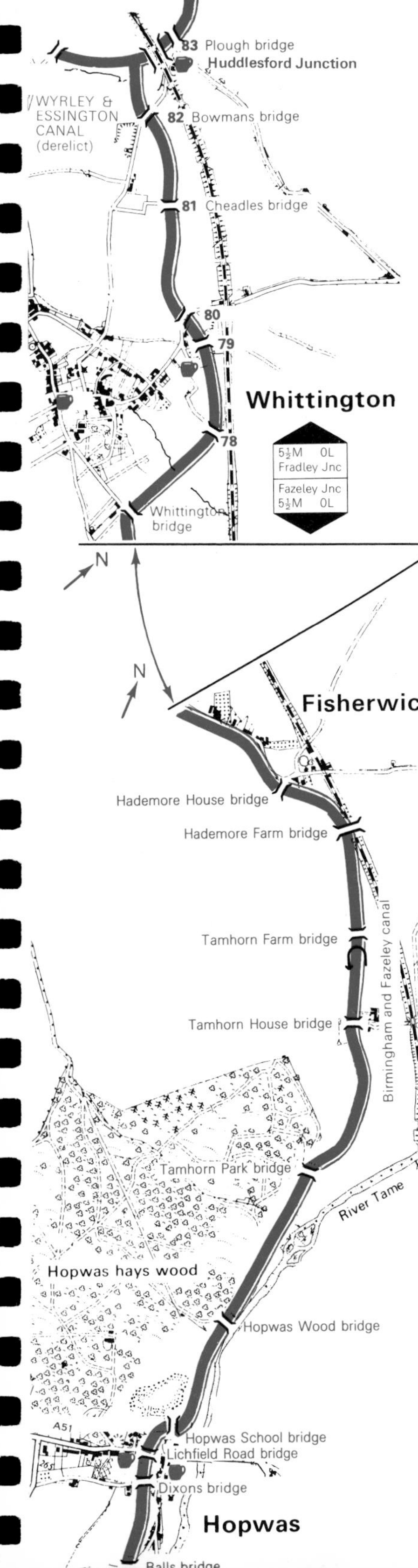

Whittington

Through open fields the canal follows the course of the River Tame very closely, passing below Hopwas. Beyond the village is a delightful wooded stretch that covers the side of the hill. Landing is forbidden because of the Whittington firing ranges. After the wood the canal continues in a side cut embankment with a view of Tamworth away to the east. It then wanders round Whittington, its course directed by the low hills on both sides. As it crosses Whittington Brook, the canal changes back from being the Birmingham & Fazeley to the Coventry; a note in the introduction to the Coventry Canal explains the reason. This also explains why the bridges are numbered again from here onwards. (Bridge 77 is at Fazeley Junction.) At Huddlesford the remains of the eastern end of the Wyrley and Essington Canal branches to the west. The railway joins the canal after Hopwas and follows it closely to Huddlesford: the A51 crosses at Hopwas.

Huddlesford
Staffs. PO box. A well-named hamlet cut in half by the railway line. At Huddlesford Junction the Wyrley & Essington Canal used to join the Coventry, but this end has long been abandoned: the first ¼ mile is used for moorings. The Wyrley & Essington was opened in 1792 to link Birmingham with Cannock Chase coalfield. It was extended to Huddlesford in 1797 to provide a more direct link with the Trent and the north east via Fradley Junction.
Whittington
Staffs. PO, tel, stores, garage. The only part of Whittington on the canal is a large housing estate. The village centre is further to the south, and is more attractive, held together by the large 19thC church with a conspicuous spire.
Fisherwick
Staffs. Tel. A small hamlet overlooking the canal.
Hopwas
Staffs. EC Wed. PO, tel, stores. Village built on the side of a hill at whose foot the canal and the River Tame run side by side. Set among trees above the village is the very unusual church, an early 20thC Arts and Crafts design. There is a wharf by Hopwas School Bridge. To the north is Hopwas Wood, a large area of planted and natural forest. Anyone walking should look out for the danger flags for Whittington firing ranges.

PUBS

Plough Plough Bridge (83). Ansells real ale, food, garden, mooring.
Bell Main Street, Whittington. (0543 432377). Meals *lunchtime and evening*.
Dog Inn Whittington. (0543 432252). Meals *lunchtime and evening*.
Swan Whittington. Food.

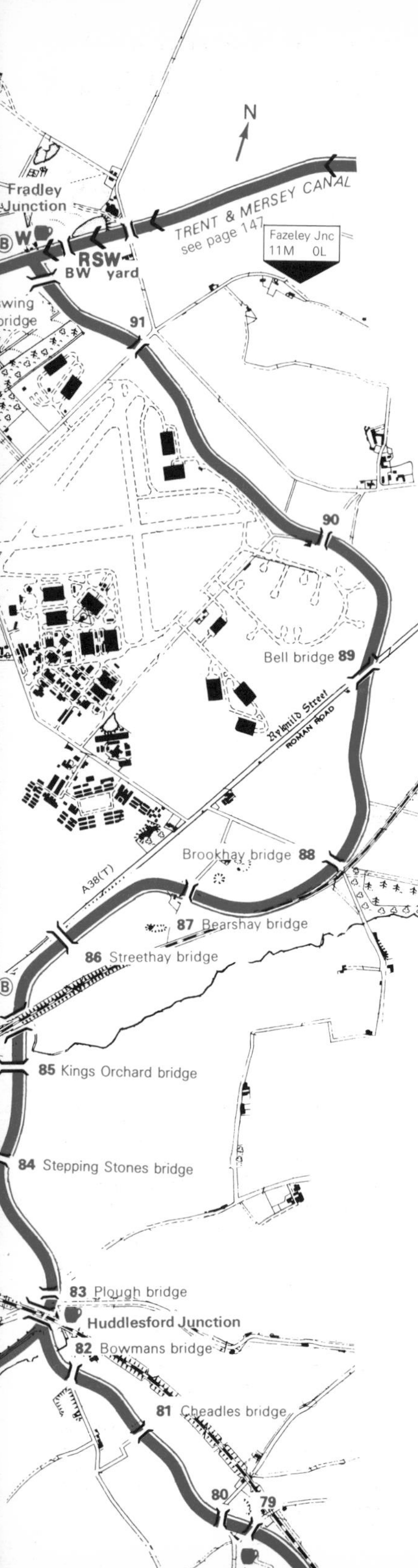

Fradley

The canal runs northwards through flat, open country towards Fradley Junction. Lichfield lies away to the west. After being crossed by the busy roar of the A38, a Roman road, the canal turns west, passing the perimeter of the disused airfield. There are no locks, but a swing bridge near the junction provides interest. At the junction the Coventry Canal meets the Trent & Mersey. There is a mooring at Bell Bridge, from which you can visit the garage and shop (*closed Sun afternoon*).

Fradley
Staffs. PO, tel, stores. A small village set to the east of the canal. It owed its prosperity to the airfield which is not used as such any more.

Fradley Junction
Staffs. PO box, tel, garage. The junction, a well-established canal centre, marks the northern end of the Coventry Canal. The Trent & Mersey runs west to Staffordshire, Shropshire and the North West, and east to Nottingham and the North East.

Lichfield
Staffs. PO, tel, stores, garage, cinema, station. 2 miles south west along the A38. Although not on the canal, Lichfield is well worth a visit. The town has a long history, its earliest charter being granted in 1387. The huge brown-stone cathedral, built in 1195–1325, is unique in that it has retained its three spires known as the 'Ladies of the Vale'. The west front has over 100 carved figures, many restored in the 19thC. The streets close by the cathedral and leading to the market square are the oldest, dating from the Tudor period. A fine 17thC house in the market square is the birthplace of Dr Johnson, now a museum. David Garrick and Joseph Addison came from Lichfield: so did Erasmus Darwin, the founder of the famous Lunar Society. Most of the 'Lunatics' (so called because they used to meet every full moon) were eminent men like Wedgwood, Boulton, Watt and Priestley. They met in Darwin's Lichfield house to discuss current scientific, philosophical and political affairs of mutual interest.

Art Gallery & Museum Bird Street. Local history and temporary art exhibitions displayed in the Norman castle. There is also the Staffordshire Regimental Museum.

BOATYARDS

BW Fradley Yard Fradley Junction. (0283 790236). [R][S][W] Overnight mooring, long-term mooring, toilets.

Swan Line Cruisers Fradley Junction. (0283 790332). [W][D] Pump-out (*not weekends*), gas, narrowboat hire, overnight mooring, dry dock, groceries, chandlery, books and maps, boat building, boat sales, engine sales and repairs. *Closed Sat afternoon and Sun in winter.*

Ⓑ **Lichfield Marina** Streethay Basin, Burton Road, Streethay, Lichfield. (0543 251981). [R] Overnight mooring, long-term mooring, winter storage, slipway, crane, chandlery, books and maps, boat sales, engine sales and repairs. *Closed Tue and weekend afternoons.*

PUBS

Swan Fradley Junction. Canalside. The focal point of the junction and justly famous. A fine public bar with a coal fire and pub games, a comfortable lounge for families, and a lively cellar bar. Ind Coope (Burton) real ale and bar meals (*not Sun*).

Plough Plough Bridge (83). Ansells real ale, food, garden, mooring.

GRAND UNION

LEICESTER SECTION AND THE SOAR NAVIGATION

Maximum dimensions

Norton Junction to Foxton Junction
Length: 72′
Beam: 7′
Headroom: 7′ 6″

Market Harborough to Leicester
Length: 72′
Beam: 10′
Headroom: 7′

Leicester West Bridge to River Trent
Length: 72′
Beam: 14′ 4″
Headroom: 7′ 6″

Mileage

NORTON JUNCTION to
Crick: 5
Welford arm: 15½
Market Harborough arm: 23¼
Blaby: 36
Leicester West Bridge: 41¼
Cossington Lock: 49
Barrow upon Soar: 53¼
Loughborough Basin: 57¼
Zouch Lock: 60½
RIVER TRENT: 66¼

Locks: 59

Manager:

(0509) 212729

The River Soar is a tributary of the River Trent and is approximately 40 miles long. It runs mainly through Leicestershire, rising at Smockington Hollow on the Warwickshire border. For most of the way from Aylestone (just south of Leicester) to the Trent, the Soar forms the Leicester section of the Grand Union Canal.

In 1634 Thomas Skipworth of Cotes attempted to make the River Soar 'portable for barges and boats up to the town of Leicester' by means of a grant from King Charles I in return for 10% of the profits. This scheme was a failure. But after several other attempts, prominent citizens of Loughborough secured an Act of Parliament in 1776, and the River Soar Navigation (Loughborough Canal) was opened two years later, bringing great prosperity to the town. The continuation of the navigation up to Leicester (the Leicester Canal) was built under an Act passed in 1791. Its opening was marked by the arrival in Leicester of two boats loaded with provisions from Gainsborough on the 21st of February 1794. The engineers concerned with construction of the Soar Navigation were John Smith and John May (Loughborough Canal) and William Jessop (Leicester Canal). With the completion of the Grand Junction Canal between Brentford and Braunston, a connection was soon established between this and the Soar Navigation, built to the narrow gauge, thwarting the Grand Junction's scheme for a system of wide canals.

The Loughborough Navigation was one of the most prosperous canals in England, by virtue of its position in relation to the Nottinghamshire–Derbyshire coalfield and the Erewash Canal. However, railway competition took its usual toll, and although trade revived when the Grand Union Canal purchased the Loughborough and Leicester Navigations in 1931, the improvement proved temporary. However, it is a pretty, rural river and is much enjoyed by those on pleasure craft.

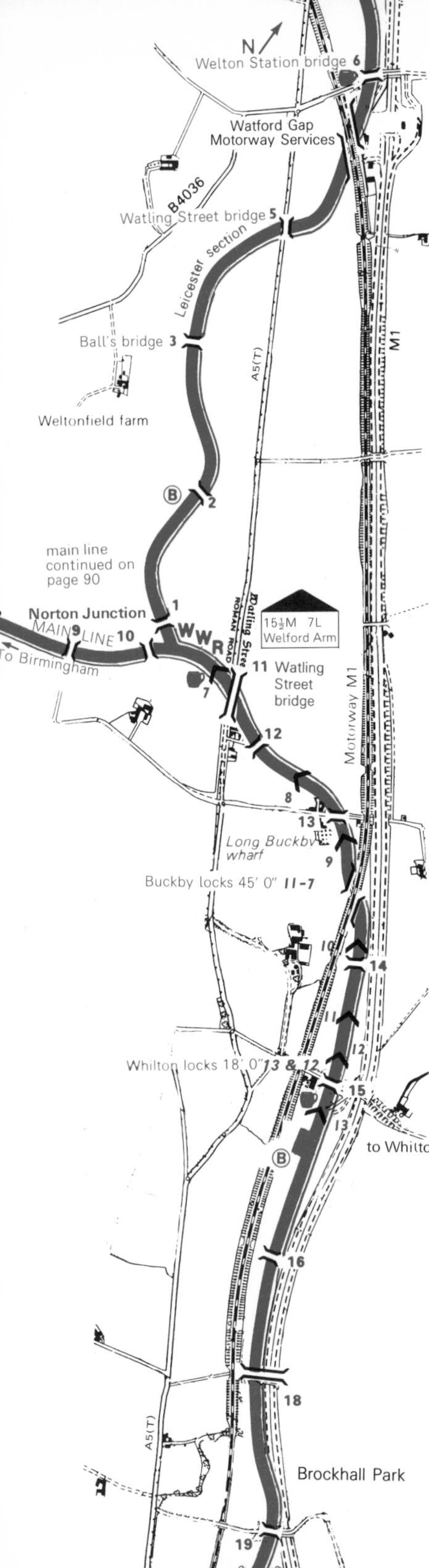

Norton Junction

Leaving Norton Junction there is a quiet, meandering mile through light woods and rolling fields before the motorway and railway take over; the canal passes the back door of the Watford Gap service area. The noise and bustle of the motorway and main railway line intrude, accentuating the sedate pace of those using the original of the three transport systems.

Buckby Wharf
Northants. PO box, tel, stores. A scattering of houses accompanies the canal through Buckby Locks. By the top lock, where the A5 crosses, there is a general store.

Whilton
Northants. PO, tel, stores. 1 mile east of the canal at the end of a road that goes nowhere. Whilton is quiet and unchanged, especially at the east end. There are several fine stone houses, including a pretty Georgian rectory. To the west is the site of Banaventa, a Roman settlement.

BOATYARDS

Ⓑ **Weltonfield Narrowboats** Weltonfield Farm, by bridge 2, Long Buckby. (0327 842282). S W *(not Sat)* D E Pump-out, gas, narrowboat hire, overnight mooring, long-term mooring, dry dock, chandlery, books and maps, boat building, boat sales, engine sales and repairs, boat lift, toilets.

Ⓑ **Whilton Marina** Whilton Locks, on the main line, Long Buckby. (0327 842577). S W P D E Gas, overnight mooring, winter storage, slipway, dry dock, groceries, chandlery, books and maps, boat sales, engine sales and repairs, toilets, shower.

PUBS

Stag's Head Watford Gap. (0923 703621). Canalside. Free house with lovely canalside rose garden.

New Inn Canalside, at Buckby Top Lock. Cosy alcoved free house, serving Marstons and Wilson's real ale and food. Next door is Gingers Canal Stores, for provisions and souvenirs.

Locks By bridge 15 and Whilton Marina. Large modern pub serving Charles Wells real ale and meals *lunchtime and evening*. Telephone kiosk outside.

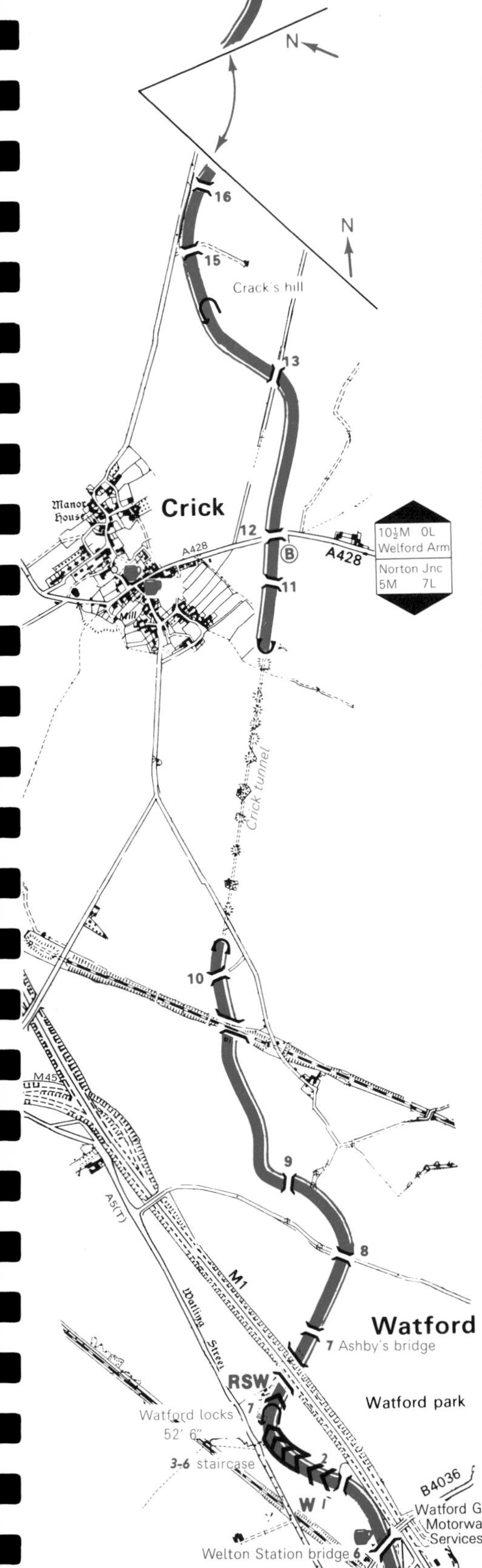

Crick

The Leicester line of the Grand Union is very attractive, quiet and in no hurry to reach Foxton. It wanders through rolling, hilly country, riverlike with constant changes of direction that guide it gently north eastwards. It avoids villages and civilisation generally; only the old wharves serve as a reminder of the canal's function. The slow course of the canal, its relative emptiness and its original plan combine to make it very narrow in places; reeds, overhanging trees and shallow banks quite often do not allow two boats to pass. After negotiating Watford Locks (last entry 19.15 in season) and reaching the summit level of 412ft there is nothing strenuous to look forward to, as this level continues for the next 22 miles. Four of these locks form a staircase – adopt a 'one up, one down' procedure, and use both ground and side paddles when going either up or down. Progress is slow and delays are likely if a queue builds up. At Watford the canal swings east away from the M1 for good. The locks and Crick Tunnel with its wooded approaches offer canal excitement to contrast with the quiet of the landscape. The A428 crosses east of Crick.

Crick
Northants. PO, tel, stores. Large village built round the junction of two roads. There are several attractive stone houses, and the large church has managed to escape restoration. It contains much decorative stonework and a circular Norman font.

Crick Tunnel
1528yds long, the tunnel was opened in 1814. All tunnels built in this area suffered great problems in construction. Quicksands caused the route of the tunnel to be changed and greatly affected work. Stephenson found similar difficulties when building the nearby Kilsby Tunnel for the London to Birmingham railway.

Watford
Northants. EC Sat. PO, tel, stores. Set in the middle of wooded parkland, Watford gives the impression of being a private village. The church and Watford Court dominate, and luckily the M1 has made no impact. The 13thC church contains some interesting monuments. The Court is partly 17thC although there are Victorian additions. The rich brown stone used throughout the village adds to the feeling of unity.

BOATYARDS

Ⓑ **Just Boats** The Wharf, Crick. (0788 822793). S W D Pump-out, gas, overnight mooring, long-term mooring, dry dock, toilets.

PUBS AND RESTAURANTS

Edwards By bridge 12, Crick. (0788 822517). Restaurant and coffee house. *Closed Sun eve and Mon.*

Red Lion Main Street, Crick. Wilson's and Ushers real ale in an attractive old pub, with low ceilings and coal fires. Meals *lunchtime and evening.*

Royal Oak Church Street, Crick. Wilson's real ale and snacks in a small cosy lounge. Games room.

Wheatsheaf Main Street, Crick. Recently refurbished pub dispensing Wilson's real ale. Food *lunchtime and evening*, games room, garden.

Yelvertoft

After skirting Crack's Hill, a curious tree-topped mound, the canal wanders to the east in a series of loops which cause it to miss both Yelvertoft and Winwick, the only villages in the section. Hills surround the course of the canal, encouraging its meandering. At one point it passes under the same road three times in under a mile. Occasional woods add to the pleasure of the isolation. After Winwick, a vague north-east course is resumed, passing the long abandoned village of Elkington. There are no locks, but a regular procession of brick arched bridges serves as a reminder that it is still a canal.

Yelvertoft
Northants. PO, tel, stores, garage. Set back from the canal, the village is built round a wide main street, terminated in the east by the church. Sadly, many of the original thatched roofs have been replaced.

Winwick
Northants. 1 mile south east bridge 23. A semi-deserted village, with many empty houses and a closed church. Many villages in this area are in a similar state, showing that this is really a forgotten part of England. Yet amidst the emptiness is the 16thC Manor House, built of richly decorated brick, with an ornamental Tudor gateway.

PUBS

Knightly Arms Yelvertoft. Popular village local serving Wilson's real ale along with snacks.

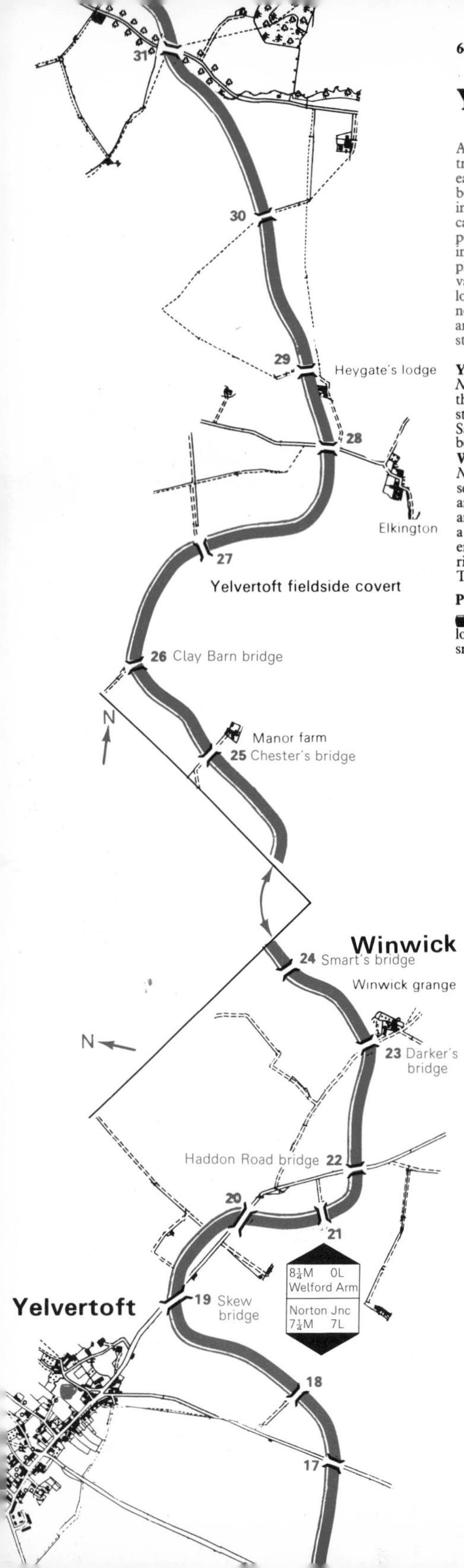

Welford

Continuing north east the canal wanders on through open fields, backed by wooded hills to the east. To the west there are splendid views over the Avon valley. The river passes under the canal before the Welford Arm. Beyond the valley the spires of South and North Kilworth churches can be seen for several miles. The Welford Arm, which was completed in 1814, branches away to the south east for 1½ miles linking the canal with the Welford and Sulby reservoirs, and reaches its terminus in a small basin; there is one shallow lock on the arm. Otherwise it is quiet and tree-lined, following closely the path of the Avon, whose source is just east of Welford. The arm was reopened to navigation in 1969, having been derelict for some years. The main line continues, entering the wooded cutting that announces Husbands Bosworth Tunnel. There are no locks, but many of the bridges are original, fine faded red brick, echoing the seclusion of the canal. The A427 crosses the canal east of North Kilworth, and the A50 passes through Welford.

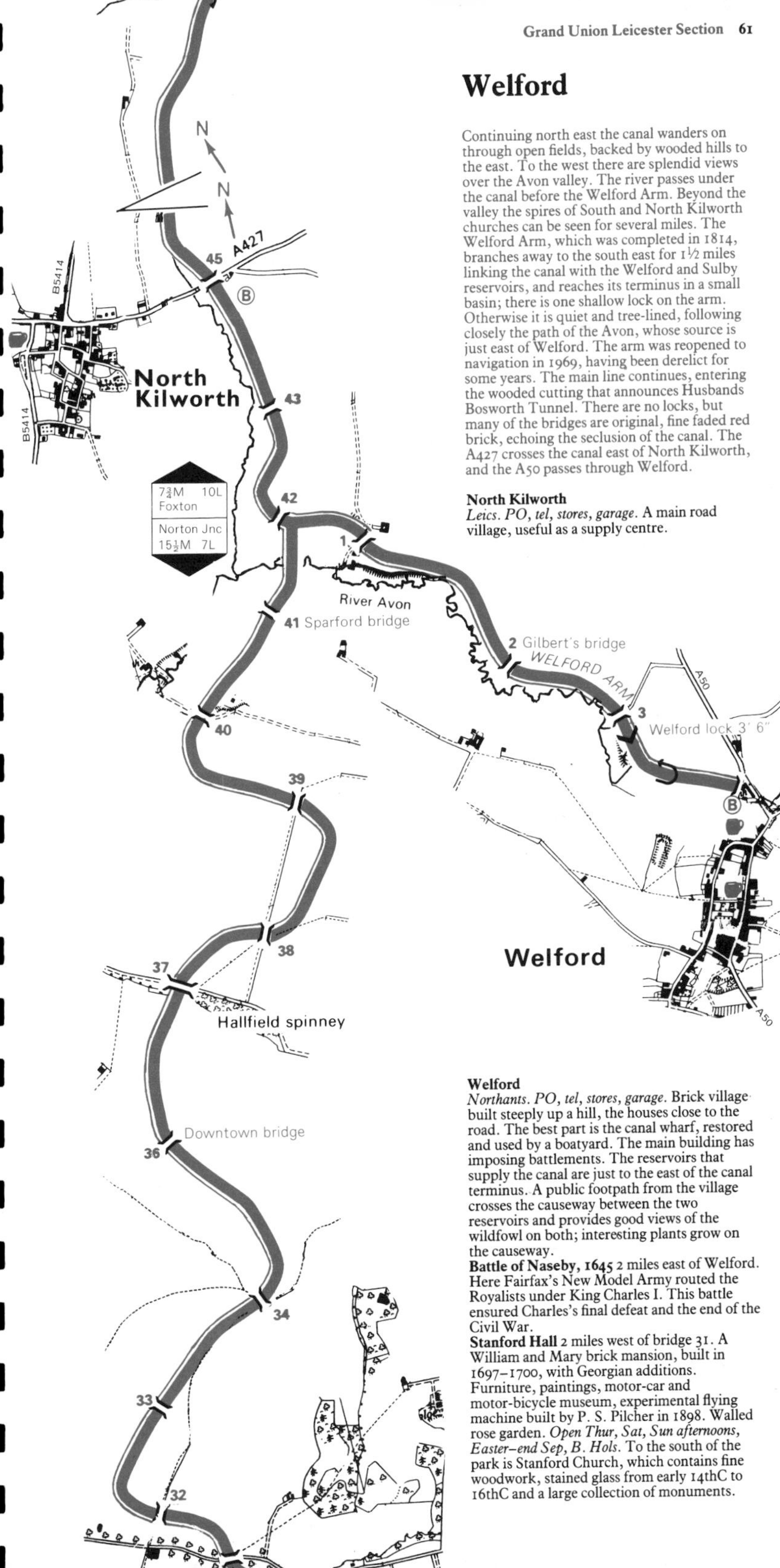

North Kilworth
Leics. PO, tel, stores, garage. A main road village, useful as a supply centre.

Welford
Northants. PO, tel, stores, garage. Brick village built steeply up a hill, the houses close to the road. The best part is the canal wharf, restored and used by a boatyard. The main building has imposing battlements. The reservoirs that supply the canal are just to the east of the canal terminus. A public footpath from the village crosses the causeway between the two reservoirs and provides good views of the wildfowl on both; interesting plants grow on the causeway.

Battle of Naseby, 1645 2 miles east of Welford. Here Fairfax's New Model Army routed the Royalists under King Charles I. This battle ensured Charles's final defeat and the end of the Civil War.

Stanford Hall 2 miles west of bridge 31. A William and Mary brick mansion, built in 1697–1700, with Georgian additions. Furniture, paintings, motor-car and motor-bicycle museum, experimental flying machine built by P. S. Pilcher in 1898. Walled rose garden. *Open Thur, Sat, Sun afternoons, Easter–end Sep, B. Hols.* To the south of the park is Stanford Church, which contains fine woodwork, stained glass from early 14thC to 16thC and a large collection of monuments.

BOATYARDS

Ⓑ **Black Prince Holidays** Canal Wharf, Welford. (0858 575580). [W] Boat building.
Ⓑ **North Kilworth Narrowboats** Kilworth Marina, North Kilworth. (0858 880484). By bridge 45. [R][S][W][D] Pump-out, gas, narrowboat hire, day hire boats, overnight mooring, long-term mooring (up to 26ft only), winter storage, slipway, dry dock, groceries, chandlery, books and maps, boat building, boat sales, engine sales and repairs, toilets, off-licence.

PUBS AND RESTAURANTS

Swan Inn Lutterworth Road, North Kilworth. Two-roomed local pub serving Ushers and Wilson's real ale. Open fire in the bar.
White Lion Lutterworth Road, North Kilworth. Large coaching inn offering Marstons real ale and *lunchtime* food. Garden.
Shoulder of Mutton High Street, Welford. Popular old village pub with paintings for sale in the lounge. Ushers and Wilson's real ale, meals *lunchtime and evening*, garden.
Swan High Street, Welford. One spacious bar where you can enjoy Marstons real ale and meals *lunchtime and evening*. Garden. Close to the canal basin.

Husbands Bosworth Tunnel. *Derek Pratt.*

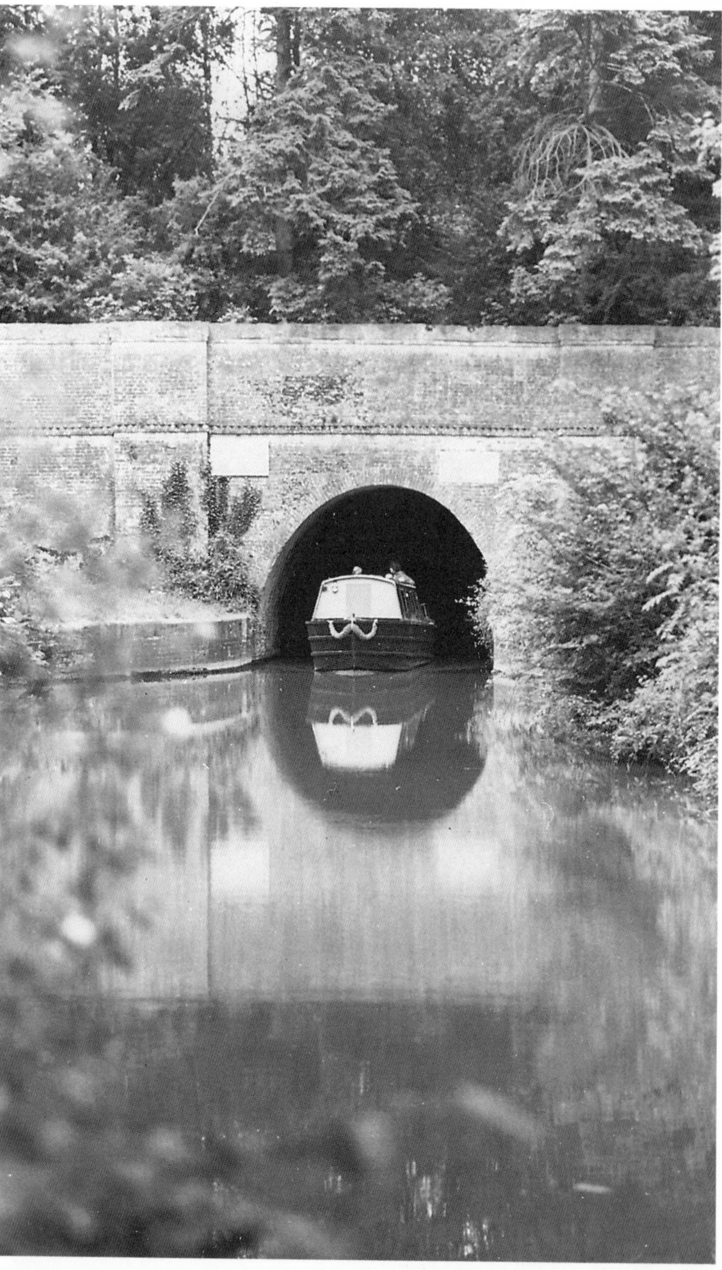

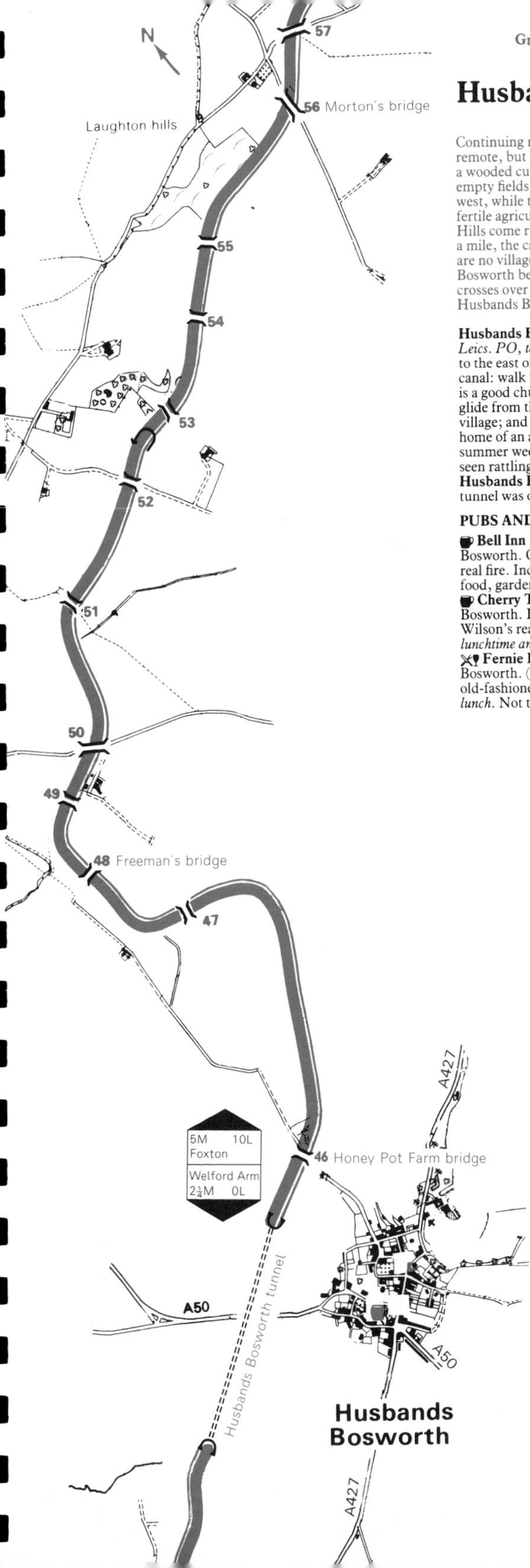

Husbands Bosworth

Continuing north east, the canal enters a remote, but attractive stretch. It wanders along a wooded cutting to the tunnel, then passes empty fields. Hills make a backdrop to the west, while to the east there are long views over fertile agricultural land. The wooded Laughton Hills come right down to the west bank for over a mile, the canal clinging to the hillside. There are no villages on the canal here, Husbands Bosworth being hidden by the tunnel. The A50 crosses over the tunnel and meets the A427 in Husbands Bosworth.

Husbands Bosworth
Leics. PO, tel, stores, garage. A pleasant village to the east of the canal tunnel. (Access from canal: walk up the lane from bridge 46.) There is a good church with a stumpy spire. Gliders glide from the little airfield just outside the village; and Husbands Bosworth is also the home of an annual steam engine rally, so on summer weekends strange vehicles can often be seen rattling along the main street.
Husbands Bosworth Tunnel 1166yds long, the tunnel was opened in 1813.

PUBS AND RESTAURANTS

Bell Inn Kilworth Road, Husbands Bosworth. Old, single-bar coaching inn with real fire. Ind Coope (Burton) real ale, *lunchtime* food, garden.

Cherry Tree High Street, Husbands Bosworth. Large basic pub serving Ushers and Wilson's real ale, and Bulmers real cider. Food *lunchtime and evening*, garden.

Fernie Lodge Berridges Lane, Husbands Bosworth. (0858 880551). Large pleasantly old-fashioned English restaurant. *Closed Sat lunch.* Not too expensive. Children's portions.

Foxton

The canal runs north east through fields to the top of Foxton Locks (*last entry 19.15 in season*). It then falls 75ft to join the 'Old Union' line to Leicester. At the bottom of the locks the 5¾ mile Market Harborough Arm branches off to the east and runs along the side of the hills which dominate the landscape to the south and cause the canal to meander extensively before reaching Market Harborough. To the north the fields fall away from the canal. It is a quiet, rural arm, with no villages, the canal becoming very river-like. It is lightly wooded in parts, with short cuttings hiding the landscape from view. Several examples of medieval ridge and furrow field patterns can be seen along the south bank, indicating the age of the countryside and its unchanged character. It is interesting to note the way the canal cuts across these ridges, especially near Gallow Hill. After passing Great Bowden Hall the hills rise to the south and the canal reaches Market Harborough Basin through suburban development. There are several old and very decayed brick arch bridges and also a swing bridge near Foxton. The cut leading to the site of the inclined plane is worth exploring. The A6 crosses the arm twice, and there is a station in Market Harborough.

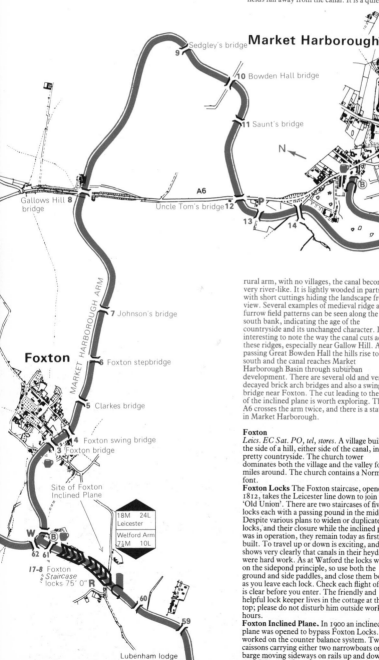

Foxton
Leics. EC Sat. PO, tel, stores. A village built on the side of a hill, either side of the canal, in pretty countryside. The church tower dominates both the village and the valley for miles around. The church contains a Norman font.

Foxton Locks The Foxton staircase, opened in 1812, takes the Leicester line down to join the 'Old Union'. There are two staircases of five locks each with a passing pound in the middle. Despite various plans to widen or duplicate the locks, and their closure while the inclined plane was in operation, they remain today as first built. To travel up or down is exciting, and shows very clearly that canals in their heyday were hard work. As at Watford the locks work on the sidepond principle, so use both the ground and side paddles, and close them both as you leave each lock. Check each flight of five is clear before you enter. The friendly and helpful lock keeper lives in the cottage at the top; please do not disturb him outside working hours.

Foxton Inclined Plane. In 1900 an inclined plane was opened to bypass Foxton Locks. It worked on the counter balance system. Two caissons carrying either two narrowboats or one barge moving sideways on rails up and down the plane. A steam driven winch pulling an endless cable was used to start the caissons moving. The journey time was reduced from 70 to 12 minutes. Mechanical problems and high running costs, plus the fact that the planned widening of the Watford flight never took place, soon made the plane a white elephant. In 1908 the Foxton Locks were reopened to traffic, and in 1911 the plane was closed to traffic. It was finally broken up in 1928, and the machinery sold for scrap. The cut leading to the bottom of the plane is still navigable, and the plane itself can still be traced, running at right angles to the east of the locks. It must have been a magnificent sight. The engine house has been re-constructed, an exploratory trail can be followed and there is a museum.

Market Harborough
Leics. EC Wed. MD Tue/Sat. PO, tel, stores, garage, banks, station. Established as a market town by 1203, Market Harborough still retains much of its rural elegance and local importance. The centre of the town is built round the church of St Dionysius which contains fine window tracery; however the most important and spectacular element is the spire, one of the finest in England. Visually it sets the scale for the whole town and holds it all together. The pleasure of the town centre is weakened by the presence of the A6, but the approach by canal is superb.

Archaeological & Historical Society Museum County Library, The Square. Contains the society's own collection and illustrates local life from the earliest times. Relics of the Battle of Naseby.

Parish Church of St Dionysius High Street. Built in the 14thC by Scropes and enlarged a century later. The broach spire and west tower are notable.

Old Grammar School High Street. Founded by Robert Smyth who was born here. It stands on wooden carved pillars, and behind the arches was held the ancient butter market. The building was used as the grammar school until 1892 and is now a meeting hall.

BOATYARDS

Ⓑ **Anglo-Welsh Canal Holidays** The Canal Basin, Leicester Road, Market Harborough. (0858 66910). R S W P D E Pump-out (*Mon–Fri*), narrowboat hire, slipway, gas, dry dock, boat building and repair, mooring, chandlery, toilets.

Ⓑ **Foxton Boat Services** Bottom Lock, Foxton. (0533 792285). R S W P D Pump-out, gas, narrowboat hire, day hire craft, overnight mooring, long-term mooring, slipway, crane, groceries, chandlery, books and maps, boat sales, engine sales, toilets, showers. Wet dock, *24hr* engine repairs.

BOAT TRIPS

Vagabond & Vixen (horse drawn) Canal trips for casual visitors on summer *Sundays and B. Hols* from Foxton bottom lock; available for charter by parties any other day (minimum 20 passengers, maximum 51). Ring (0533) 792285.

PUBS AND RESTAURANTS

Angel Hotel High Street, Market Harborough. Food.

Red Cow High Street, Market Harborough.

Six Packs Leicester Road, Market Harborough. Food.

Three Swans Hotel High Street, Market Harborough. Food.

Taylors Fish Restaurant 10 Adam & Eve Street, Market Harborough. (0858 63043). Jellied eels, pickled herrings, cockles followed by a wide variety of fresh fish. Take away, self service or waitress service. *L & D, closed Sun.*

Bridge 61 In the midst of Foxton Boat Services, a wonderful environment in which to enjoy Everards real ale and other guest beers.

Black Horse Foxton. Canalside. Food.

Shoulder of Mutton Main Street, Foxton.

Foxton Locks. *Derek Pratt.*

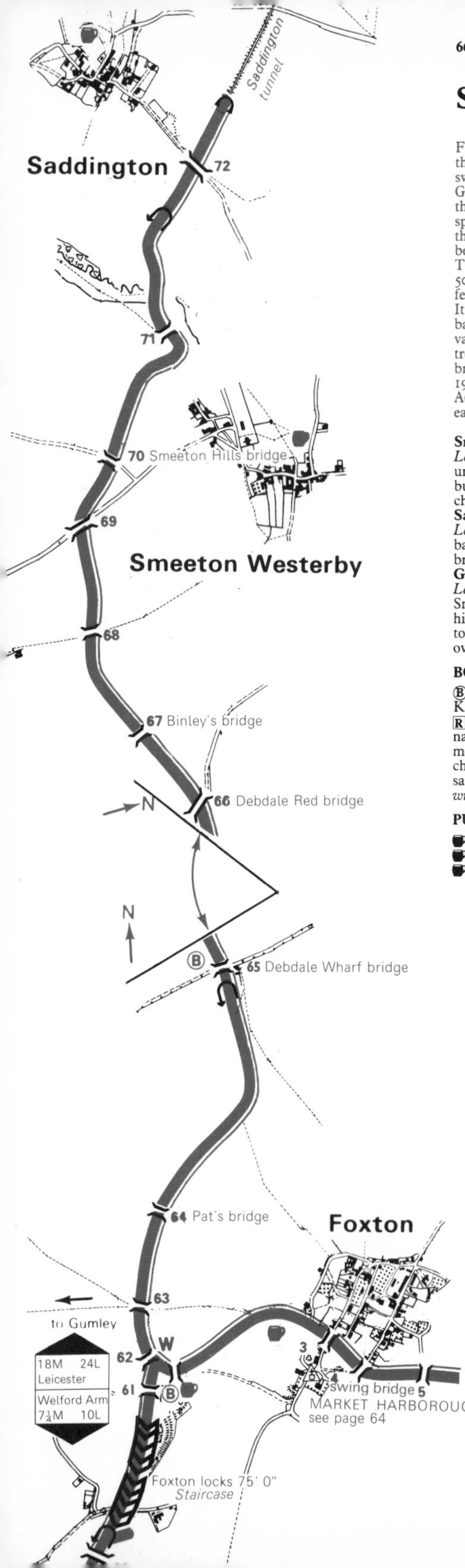

Smeeton Westerby

From Foxton the canal continues north, and then, following the contours of the valley, it swings north west towards Leicester. At first Gumley woods and hills dominate the canal to the west, while water meadows and pasture spread out to the east towards Foxton. Later, the hills close in on both sides, and the canal begins to twist and turn prior to Saddington Tunnel; Smeeton Hill, to the west, rises to over 500ft. Shortly before the tunnel an unnavigable feeder joins the canal to Saddington reservoir. It is a quiet, empty landscape, all villages set back from the canal, leaving it to pursue a vague course through open fields and occasional trees. No locks, and a curious mixture of bridges, some original, some rebuilt in the 19thC in blue brick, some more modern. The A6 and the railway pass beyond the hills to the east, parallel to the canal.

Smeeton Westerby
Leics. EC Wed. PO, tel, stores. The village undulates over the hills to the east of the canal, built along the sides of the main street. The church is Victorian, by Woodyer.
Saddington
Leics. EC Sat. PO, tel, stores. Small village set back from the canal, only the church tower breaking the skyline.
Gumley
Leics. PO box, tel. ½ mile west bridge 63. Small village scattered among trees, set on a hillside high above the canal. The Italianate tower of Gumley Hall rises above the trees, overlooking the valley.

BOATYARDS

Ⓑ **Ian Goode Narrowboats** Debdale Wharf, Kibworth. (0533 793034 or office 0536 771336). R S W D Pump-out (*Mar–Oct only*), gas, narrowboat hire, overnight mooring, long-term mooring, winter storage, crane, dry dock, chandlery, books and maps, boat building, boat sales, engine sales and repairs, toilets. *Closed winter weekends.*

PUBS

- **Queens Head** Saddington.
- **Kings Head** Smeeton Westerby.
- **Bell** Gumley.

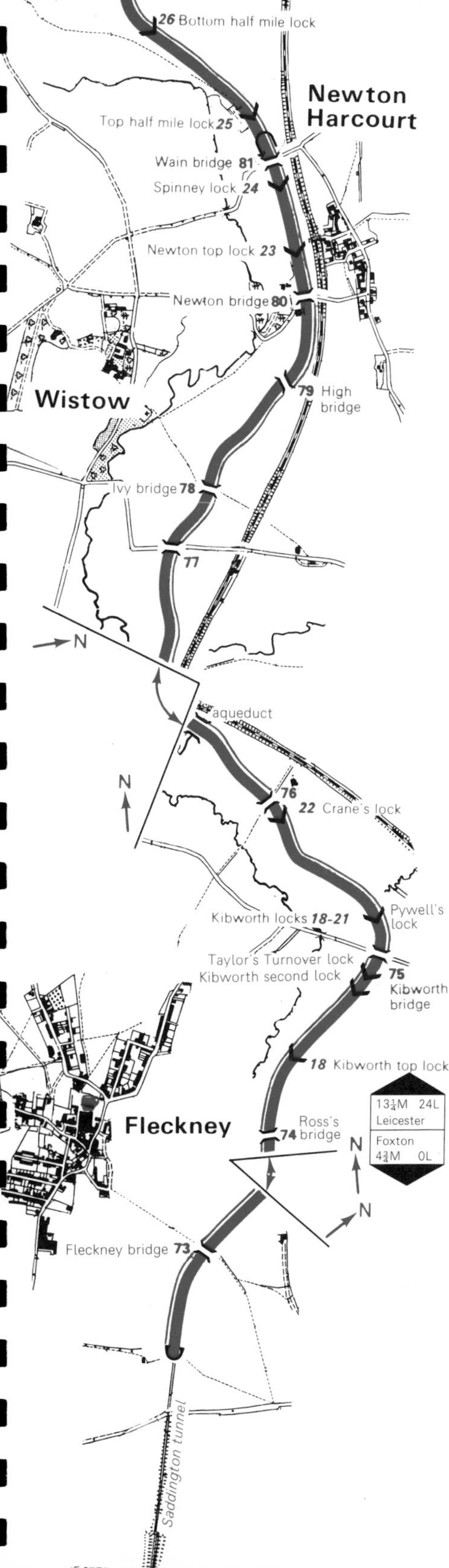

Fleckney

The canal passes through Saddington Tunnel and turns briefly north east before returning to its original course. It remains quiet and remote, although the peace is periodically shattered by the presence of the railway to the east which at times runs almost along the towpath. The hills give way after the tunnel to open fields and woods which give fine views to the west, especially across Wistow Park. The canal is often river-like and very shallow in places. Newton Harcourt breaks the rule of this canal by being beside it, the other villages keep their distance. The tunnel, the bridges, and the locks which begin the descent to Leicester provide plenty of canal interest although the amount of rubbish in the cut begins to increase. The A6 and the main railway slowly encroach on the canal to the east.

Newton Harcourt
Leics. EC Sat. PO, stores. Scattered village bisected by the railway in a cutting. This hides most of it from the canal, which sees only the church and manor, set pleasantly among trees. The church tower is 13thC, the rest Victorian. The canalside position is its best feature. The Hall is 17thC, with later rebuilding; it has a fine gateway. Newton Harcourt is a well-known Leicester beauty spot, popular on *Sunday afternoons.*

Wistow
Leics. For a while the canal runs through woods and parkland to the west adjoining Wistow Park. Wistow itself has a church and a Hall, the church with Norman work but mostly 18thC, including fine monuments. The Hall is Jacobean in principle but was largely rebuilt in the 19thC.

Fleckney
Leics. EC Wed. PO, tel, stores. An industrial village just 10 minutes' walk from the canal. Very useful for its supermarket, fish and chip shop and Chinese take-away.

Saddington Tunnel 880yds long, the tunnel was completed in 1797, after great difficulties owing to its being built crooked. Naturalists enthuse about the bats that nowadays live in the tunnel.

PUBS

Old Crown Fleckney. Good food and real ale in this friendly village pub.
Unfortunately there are no pubs in Newton Harcourt.

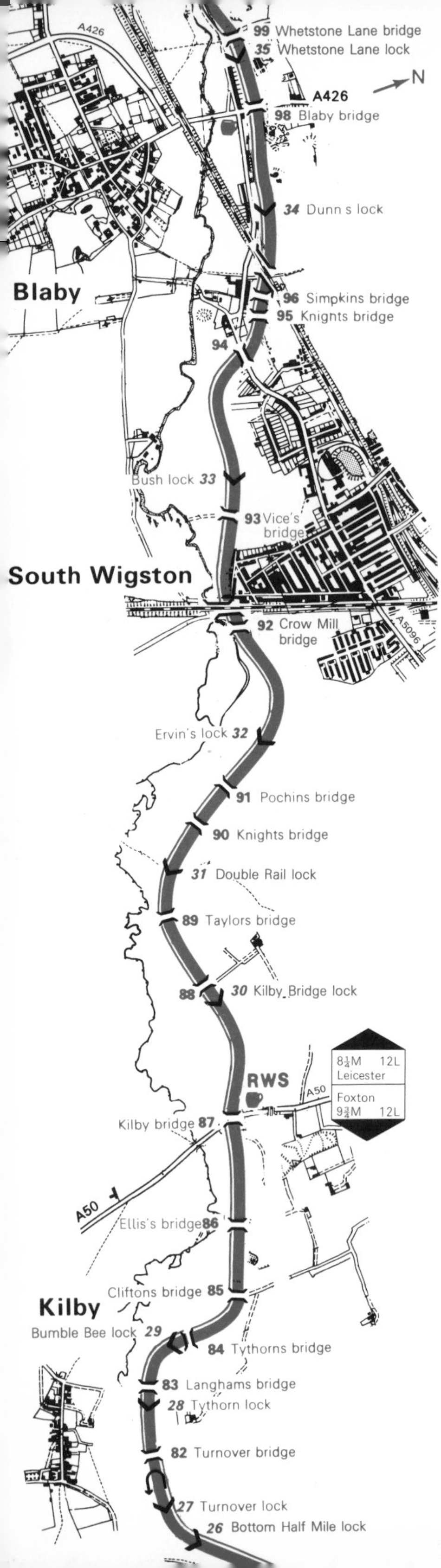

Wigston

The canal follows the north-westerly course of the River Sence, bounded by low hills to east and west. Still remote, until Kilby Bridge where indications of the town of Leicester begin with distant views of housing estates and factories. By the disused rail bridge at South Wigston the town seems to take over. There is no shortage of facilities. The locks continuing the steady fall, give the stretch its individuality. The A50 crosses at Kilby Bridge, the A426 at Blaby, and the railway keeps the canal company to the east.

Blaby
Leics. PO, tel, stores, garage. The church is partly 14thC, with a fine 18thC gallery unsuited to the Blaby of today. The County Arms, a monumental 1930s roadhouse by the A426 bridge, is more in keeping.
South Wigston
Leics. PO, tel, stores, garage. Wigston is now a part of Leicester but traces of its earlier independence can still be found. Much of the handsome church dates from the 14thC, especially the interior, while the cottages in Spa Lane with their long strips of upper window indicate an old Leicester industry, stocking making. At Wigston Parva there is a tiny Norman church and a monument to the Roman town of Veronae. Unfortunately only housing estates and a school can be seen from the canal, but exploration is worthwhile.
Kilby Bridge
Leics. PO, tel, garage.

BOATYARDS

BW Kilby Bridge Yard Kilby Bridge. (0533 882795). R S W

PUBS

County Arms Blaby. Enormous Beefeater Steak House.
Black Horse Blaby.
George Blaby.
Navigation Kilby Bridge. Lively saloon and tiny public bar with inglenook, coal fire and brasses. Ind Coope (Burton) real ale.

Aylestone

Following the River Sence to its junction with the Soar, the canal swings wide round Glen Parva and then flows north into Leicester along the Soar valley. After Glen Parva the buildings suddenly cease, and there follows a mile of very pleasant rural canal, lightly wooded to the east, and the extensive water meadows of the Soar to the west. The river and canal flow side by side separated only by the towpath; inevitably in winter this causes flooding, and so anyone intending to navigate this stretch out of season should check the state of the water before proceeding. Only the pylons and the distant views of Braunstone and Aylestone reveal the closeness of Leicester. The canal and the Soar meet by the gasworks where there is a huge weir; care is needed during times of flood. The canal enters Leicester along a pleasant cutting. A variety of buildings line the banks and there is a fine canalside walk under the ornamental bridges that lead straight into the town centre by West Bridge. These factors combine to make the canal entry to Leicester outstanding among large towns. The A46 and A426 run parallel to the canal, but the railway which follows it, the old Great Central line, is now closed.

Navigational note
Canal and River Soar meet just above Freeman's Meadow Lock, where there is an enormous unprotected weir. Care is needed, especially in time of flood. KEEP WELL OVER TO THE TOWPATH SIDE.

Aylestone
Leics. PO, tel, stores, garage. A Leicester suburb coming down to the east bank of the canal. The church contains an interesting stained-glass window of 1930. To the west of the canal the Soar is crossed by an old stone packhorse bridge of eight low arches, perhaps dating from the 15thC.

Glen Parva
Leics. PO, tel, stores, garage. Suburb of Leicester inseparable now from the main town. Curiously enough there was a Saxon cemetery in the town from which 6thC grave ornaments have been excavated.

PUBS

Country Arms Blaby, by bridge 98. Enormous Steak House.

Leicester

For almost all of its journey through the city of Leicester, the navigation pursues a course quite separate from the river, the navigation having been rebuilt towards the end of the 19thC as part of Leicester's flood prevention scheme. The City Council still has to maintain all the works, including three locks. For ½ mile south of West Bridge, the navigation, a section known locally as 'The Straight', is like a formal avenue, tree-lined and crossed by several ornamental iron bridges, but where it curves under the old Great Central railway the navigation begins to follow a less public course through the nether regions of Leicester. A combination of locks, derelict canal basins, tall factory buildings and a substantial stretch of parkland adds up to a stretch of urban canal that offers a greater variety of interest than exists in most other cities. At Belgrave Lock the canal joins the Soar, which proceeds to meander carelessly through the city's outskirts. Fortunately the broad margin of water meadows succeeds in keeping these at arm's length for most of the way. As is the case with all large towns, if you moor at an unprotected site make sure your boat is well locked if you leave it unattended.

Navigational note
It is worth remembering that the River Soar floods frequently in winter, so boaters travelling out of season should enquire about the navigational conditions in advance in order to avert the risk of running aground in the middle of a water meadow.

Thurmaston
Leics. PO, tel, stores, garage. This unexciting suburb stretches along the Roman road, the old Fosse Way, now bypassed by a dual carriageway. However the opportunity thus afforded to Thurmaston has not been exploited. Evidence of Roman habitation was discovered in 1955, when excavation of an Anglo Saxon cemetery brought to light 95 urns dating from 50 years after Julius Caesar's invasion.

Leicester
EC Mon. MD Wed, Fri, Sat. All services. A prosperous city with a thriving university. Fortunes were founded on the hosiery and the boot and shoe trades, but now a variety of light industries flourish in Leicester. There are a great deal of things to see, for this was the Roman town of Ratae, and there is plenty of evidence of the Roman buildings, plus a castle that dates from 1088, with the delightful church of St Mary de Castro next to it. The travel agent Thomas Cook started business in Leicester; in 1841 he organised the first publicly advertised excursion by train. It was a great success, and Cook made the organising of such trips a regular occupation. Leicester has a particularly good selection of museums, and it is fortunate that most of these are near the Grand Union Canal that flows through the centre of the city. The large shopping centre is to the east of West Bridge.

Leicester Abbey Abbey Park. All that remains of the abbey is a mansion built from the ruins and the old stone wall surrounding the grounds. Cardinal Wolsey was buried here in 1530. *Open daily.*

Leicester Museum & Art Gallery New Walk. Italian, Spanish and Flemish old masters. 18th–20thC English paintings. Also French Impressionists and German Expressionists, ceramics, silver, archives and geology.

Newarke Houses Museum. The social history of the area from 1500 to the present day. Locally made clocks and a clockmaker's workshop. Also shows the history of the hosiery, costume and lace industries.

Belgrave Hall Thurcaston Road. Small Queen Anne house and garden. Good collection of early 18th and 19thC furniture. Also stables, coaches and agricultural exhibits.

Jewry Wall & Museum of Archaeology Great Central Street. Leicester was once a Roman capital named Ratae Coritanorum. The Jewry Wall, a small portion of which remains, may have been part of a basilica or baths. Two Roman mosaic pavements can be seen in situ.

Guildhall Guildhall Lane. Contains fine oak panelling and an elaborately carved chimney-piece dated 1637.
Magazine The Newarke. The museum of the Leicester Regiment, honoured in the old stone gateway to the Newarke.
Museum of Technology in the Abbey Lane Pumping Station, Corporation Road. A new museum of mechanical exhibits, including four 19thC beam engines (which operate on certain weekends), hosiery machinery, a transport collection and an 84 ton steam shovel.
Tourist Information St Martin's Walk. (0533 511300).

BOATYARDS

Ⓑ **Leicester Marina** Old Bridge, Thurcaston Road. (0533 62194). W D S Pump-out, gas, mooring, slipway, chandlery, boat building and repairs, toilets, winter storage. Trip boat for charter.

PUBS AND RESTAURANTS

Joiners Arms Sanvey Gate, Leicester. South east of North Bridge. Banks' real ale.
Richmond Arms King Richards Road, Leicester. West of West Bridge.
Princess Charlotte Oxford Street. East of bridge 1.
Sir Robert Peel Jarrom Street. East of bridge 1, behind the Infirmary. Everards real ale.
Joe Rigatoni St Martins Square, Leicester. (0533 533977). Stylish pizza and pasta house offering good value meals. *L & D, closed Sun.*
Salad Days London Road, Leicester. (0533 550212). Café offering all home-cooked food. Very good value. *Open daily to 19.30, Sat to 14.30.*
Water Margin 76–78 High Street, Leicester (0533 624937). Reasonably priced and good Chinese food. *L & D.*

Paired working boats in Thurmaston Lock. *David Perrott.*

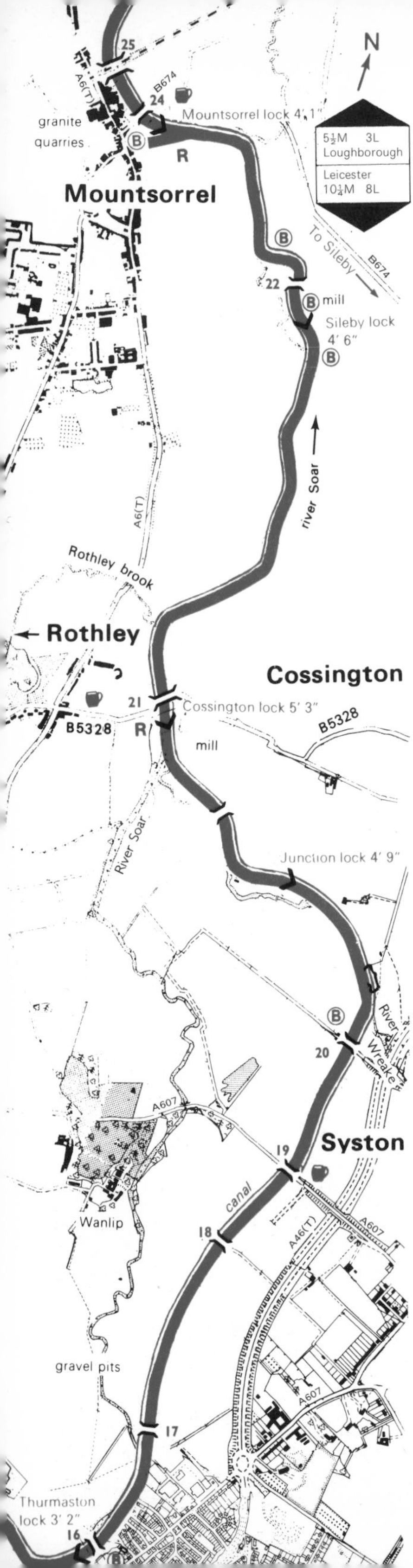

Mountsorrel

North of Thurmaston the canal leaves the river and heads north through an area scarred by busy gravel workings where loads are often carried to the ready mix concrete plant at Syston by *paired narrowboats*. Keep a look out for them, and give them priority. North of the Hope & Anchor pub more natural surroundings reappear, unspoilt by the nearby dual carriageway. Just beyond the boatyard, the River Wreake flows in from the north east; the name of the nearby boatyard and the next lock hints at the significance of this little river. The River Soar rejoins the canal by Cossington Lock. The mill here is many centuries old and is now a restaurant. The villages of Cossington and Rothley are one mile away from Cossington Lock, on opposite sides of the Soar. The Rothley Brook joins the canal north of the lock. The river continues northwards, flanked by low green hills on the west side and pleasant water meadows on the other. At Sileby Lock is another water mill. There has been a mill here since 1608 and the present building has been restored as a private residence. From here it is a short distance to Mountsorrel. The lock here is very much a waterways showplace and the boatyards and the lockside pub make it a busy one.

Mountsorrel

Leics. PO, tel, stores, garage, bank. It is but a few yards from the lock here to the centre of the village where the facilities in the long main street include a cheese shop, a saddler and a launderette. The A6 thunders through the village, but fails to destroy the dignity of the old buildings lining the road. The old covered market cross still survives. The church and the vicarage face each other over this village street; the generous dimensions of the vicarage and its elegant façade have more appeal than the rather plain church. In the hills that rise steeply behind the village are the extensive quarries that supply the well-known Mountsorrel granite, distinguished by its pinkish tinge. The stone is crushed there and used for road chippings.

Cossington

Leics. PO, tel. A mile east of Cossington Lock, this is a pretty village with wide, well-kept grass verges and plenty of trees. Although there is much new building, it mixes well with the old. The church is set apart among trees. Much rebuilt in Mountsorrel granite, it contains excellent Victorian stained glass.

Rothley

Leics. PO, tel, stores, garage. Lies in the valley of the Rothley Brook which runs to the south of the village and through the grounds of Rothley Temple, once a preceptory for the Knights Templar. The 13thC chapel with a figure of a Knight Templar still remains beside the Elizabethan house, once the home of the Babington family, and the birthplace of the poet, historian and dramatist Lord Macaulay. It is now an hotel. The Norman church in Rothley village is built mainly of granite, the massive tower, nave and aisles being subsequent additions. In the churchyard is a tall Anglo-Saxon cross, thought to be over 1000 years old.

The Wreake Navigation & the Oakham Canal

This waterway was opened in 1795 as a broadlocked river navigation from the canal north of Syston to Melton Mowbray, 15 miles away to the east. Beyond Melton the Oakham Canal extended the navigation as far as Oakham, in Rutland. When the railways were built the two waterways could not compete and the Oakham Canal was closed as early as 1846. More than a century later, some lengths still hold water; in other places the former canal bed is only a faint depression. The general course of the canal, which follows the contours of the land, can be traced on a 1in O.S. map. It is interesting to note how the railway follows a similar, but more direct, course. The Wreake Navigation was closed to traffic in 1877. The old navigation works are easily recognisable and the remains of the first lock can be found under ½ mile from its junction with the canal.

BOATYARDS

Ⓑ **Sileby Boatyard** Mountsorrel Lane, Sileby. (0509 813404). [R][S][WD][E] Pump-out, gas, overnight mooring, long-term mooring, winter storage, slipway, crane, groceries, chandlery, books and maps, boat building, boat sales, engine sales and repairs, toilets.
Ⓑ **Soar Valley Boatyard** Sileby Road, Mountsorrel. (0533 302642). Chandlery (also clothing), moorings, boat and engine sales.
Ⓑ **L. R. Harris & Son** Old Junction Boatyard, Meadow Lane, Syston. (0533 692135). [R][S][WD] Gas, chandlery, slipway, winter storage, boat sales and repairs, boat building, inboard and outboard engines sales and repairs. Welding specialists. *Open daily*.
Ⓑ **Nimbus Narrowboats** (Mill Lane Boatyard), Thurmaston. (0533 693069). [R][S][WD] Pump-out, slipway, gas, boat sales, overnight mooring, chandlery, books and maps, boat sales, engine repairs, toilets, showers.

PUBS

Waterside Inn Mountsorrel Lock. Comfortable pub serving Everards real ale, bar snacks, restaurant meals, *daily except Sat lunch and Sun dinner*.
Dog & Gun Mountsorrel. Two-room local with a homely atmosphere. Bass and M & B real ale.
Free Trade Inn Cossington Road, Sileby. Everards real ale in a thatched pub of great character.
✕ **Red Lion** Rothley, at crossroads up the hill west of Cossington Lock. Ind Coope (Burton) real ale, restaurant meals, *daily except Sun dinner*.
Royal Oak Cossington.
Hope & Anchor Syston. Canalside: good moorings.
Bakers Arms Syston.

The River Soar near Loughborough. *Derek Pratt*.

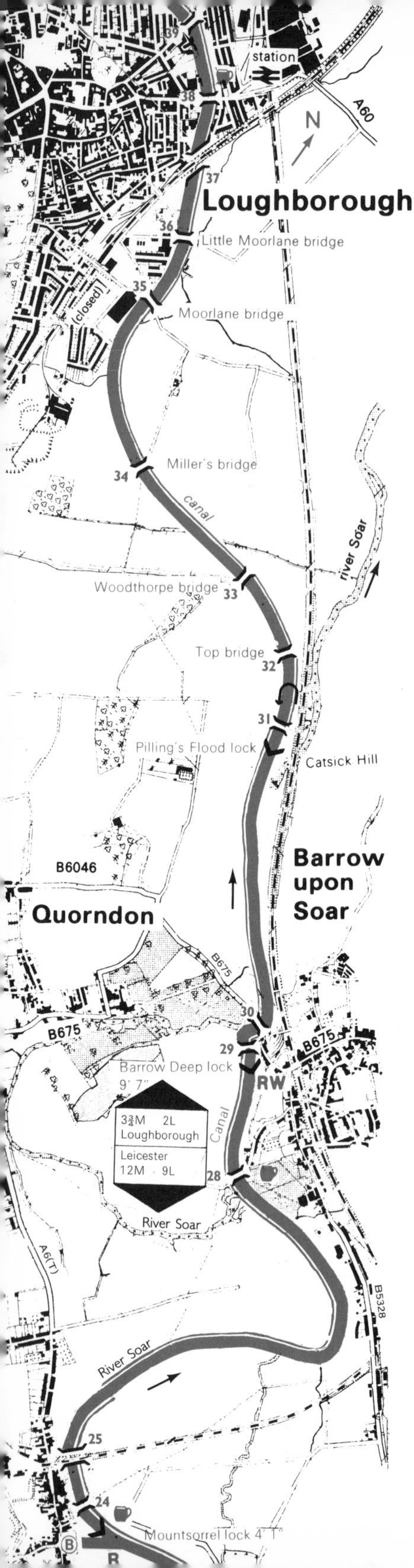

Loughborough

Leaving Mountsorrel Lock the navigation first passes under a red brick railway bridge, dated 1860 in bold figures; trucks containing Mountsorrel granite pass over this bridge on their way from the quarry to the main line. 300yds north of it are the remains of another, much smaller, bridge; this used to carry the towpath across the river. The canal crosses the valley, reaching the pretty village of Barrow upon Soar. A bridge and a canalside pub introduce a short section of canal that bypasses a wide meander of the River Soar. Before the canal rejoins the river its level is changed by a very deep lock; beyond it, the river reappears at the old five-arched bridge. Beyond, there follows a superb wooded stretch for nearly a mile, terminated by Pillings Flood Lock: boats heading downstream should keep left to avoid the weir. Since this is a flood lock, all the gates are usually open and one may pass straight through into the long canal section which enters the northern outskirts of Loughborough. The pleasant landscape is soon replaced by the lengthy back wall of an engineering works. The canal then passes under the old Great Central Railway and circles Loughborough to a T-junction. This marks the end of the Leicester Navigation and the start of the Loughborough Navigation, which completes the remaining nine miles to the River Trent.

Navigational note
There are flood warning lights at Barrow Deep, Bishop Meadow and Redhill Locks – do not pass if red light shows.

Loughborough
Leics. EC Wed. MD Thur, Sat. A busy industrial town famed for church bells which have been cast by John Taylor & Co for over a century. More important to the town's prosperity are the Brush companies, part of the Hawker Siddeley Group, who in the last 70 years have produced mechanical equipment like horse-buses, fuse links, rolling stock and a vast number of diesel locomotives for British Rail. But it is the bells by which Loughborough is known and remembered, for Taylor's bells ring in churches throughout England and abroad. (One of their largest bells is Great Paul, in St Paul's Cathedral, London.) The town's War Memorial is a Carillon Tower, the only municipal grand carillon in the country.

Barrow upon Soar
Leics. PO, tel, stores, garage, bank. Most of the village is on the hill on the far side of the railway cutting, but the prettiest part is down by the river, where the old stone bridge, the canal lock, the overhanging trees and the mêlée of small boats draw many visitors on a *summer Sunday afternoon*.

PUBS

Boat Meadow Lane, Loughborough. Canalside, at bridge east of junction. Unspoilt pub serving Marstons real ale.

Duke of York Nottingham Road, Loughborough. Canalside, at the bridge near the station. Bass real ale. Grocer and fish and chips nearby.

Navigation Mill Lane, Barrow upon Soar. Shipstone's, Marstons and John Smith real ale in a fine canalside pub. *Lunchtime* food (*not Sun*). Garden.

Soar Bridge Inn Barrow upon Soar. Near the river bridge. Everards real ale in a wood-panelled pub, which serves food. Petrol nearby.

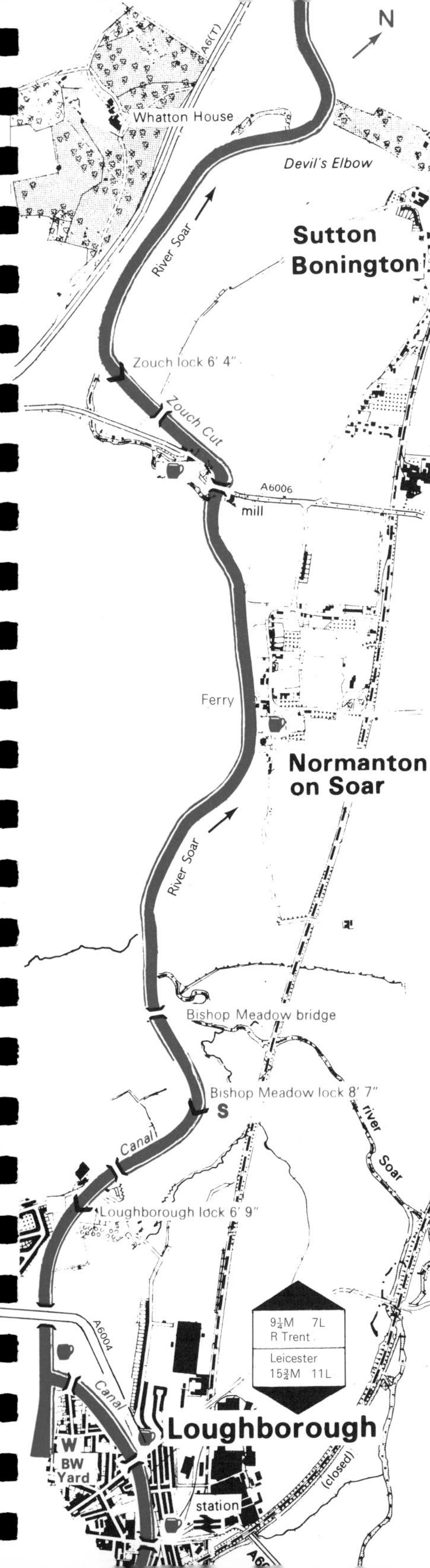

Normanton on Soar

The Loughborough Navigation has the same physical characteristics as the Leicester Navigation. It continues the fall towards the Trent with the same pattern of meandering river reaches and the occasional canal cut, with locks bypassing the weirs. In spite of the entrance of streams along the way, the River Soar does not seem to get any wider. Leaving Loughborough Wharf, the navigation follows a fairly straight and open course out into the country. Two locks bring it eventually back into the river, and from this point to its junction with the Trent, the Soar forms the county boundary between Leicestershire on the west side and Nottinghamshire on the east. Normanton on Soar is visible some way away because of its prominent church steeple; on approaching, one finds the church is only a matter of yards from the river bank. However the inhabitants of Normanton guard their waterfront jealously, making it extremely difficult to get ashore. Even the formal garden of the riverside pub displays a selection of notices strictly prohibiting the mooring of boats out of licensing hours. Below Normanton is the settlement of Zouch which, although tattier than Normanton, has a certain weary and less conventional charm, easier access and more facilities. Below Zouch Lock the A6 reappears and follows the side of the hill; the river is well shielded from this road by trees, but these are powerless against the multiple tracks of vast pylons which stalk along the valley here. At Devil's Elbow boats heading downstream should keep right to stay in the main navigation channel. The village of Sutton Bonington to the east is identified by its church spire.

Navigational note
Boaters are reminded that this is basically a river navigation, liable to flood in wet weather. Keep well clear of the weirs. If the warning light at Bishop Meadow Lock shows red – do not pass.

Whatton House
Visible from the river near the Devil's Elbow, this mansion was built about 1802, damaged by fire and restored in 1876. Its fine 25-acre gardens are *open summer Sun afternoons.*

Normanton on Soar
Notts. PO, tel. A quiet and carefully preserved village with wide grass verges and some discreetly pretty buildings, notably the post office, which is a black-and-white-timbered building with a thatched roof and steep gable ends, unusual in this part of the country. The cruciform church has a central tower and spire, rare in so small a church. On the east wall of the nave there are some excellent stone carvings; the centre one is an elaborate coat of arms with a quizzical lion in the middle. The plain glass windows make the church enjoyably light. A ferry here once again links Nottinghamshire to Leicestershire. A ramshackle array of small chalets line the riverbank.

BOATYARDS

Ⓑ **BW Loughborough Yard.** (0509 212729). W

PUBS

Rose & Crown Zouch. Canalside. Manns real ale, good food, a friendly atmosphere and convivial host. Patrons may moor at the attractive garden.

Plough Normanton. (0509 842228). Large old riverside pub with a garden where Tetley's and Ind Coope (Burton) real ale can be enjoyed.

Albion Inn. Unlikely looking canalside pub north of Loughborough serving Shipstone's, Banks', Hoskins & Oldfield, Ward and Lloyds real ales.

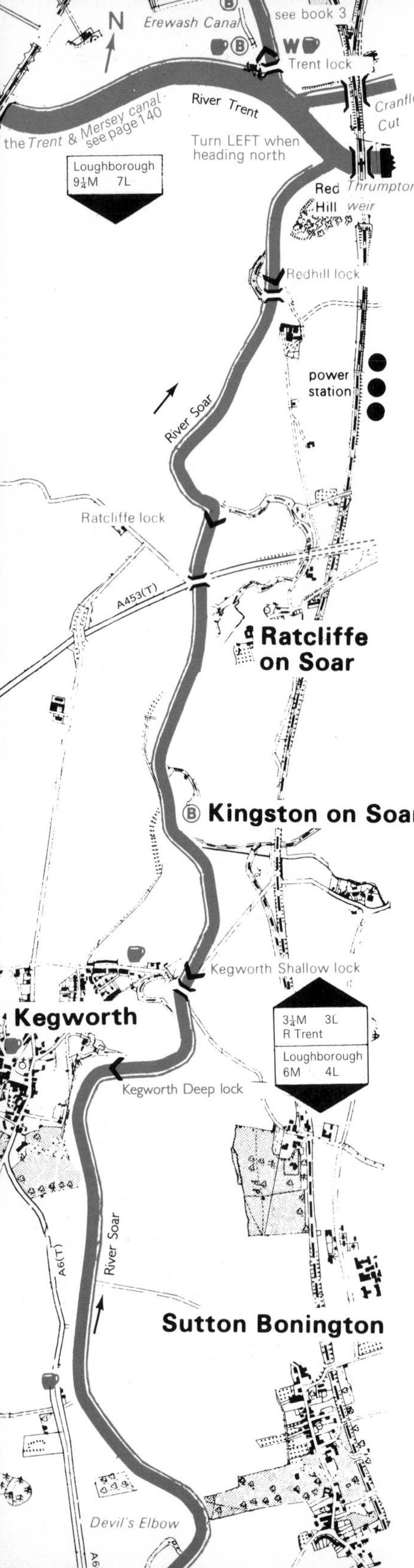

Kegworth

This is yet another stretch of pleasant meandering river. At the point where the A6 and the Soar almost touch there is a riverside pub and the headquarters of the Soar Boating Club. North of the pub a willow-lined reach leads to a stone mansion with spreading lawns where the channel divides. To the left (nearer Kegworth) is a maze of shallow and weedy backwaters, weirs and a water mill; boats should keep to the right for Kegworth Deep Lock where a new lock has been constructed beside the old as part of a flood prevention scheme. After another sharp swing to the north the channel divides again, and northbound boats should once more bear right for Kegworth Shallow Lock – this is a flood lock and so all four gates are usually open. There is a pub near here and a home bakery up the road. From this lock to the Trent the navigation is somewhat more isolated, but two notable landmarks are the spire of Ratcliffe on Soar church and the eight cooling towers and vast chimney of the Ratcliffe Power Station that totally dominates the landscape for miles around. The navigation skirts round the west side of Red Hill. The last lock here has beautifully kept lawns and a well-painted bridge – on which are shown the flood levels for 1955 and 1960 explaining the necessity for the flood prevention works. Milk, eggs and bread are available here. A few hundred yards below Red Hill Lock the Soar flows into the River Trent and loses its identity in this much bigger waterway.

Navigational note
Boats negotiating the junction of the rivers Soar and Trent should keep well away from Thrumpton Weir, which is just east (downstream) of the big iron railway bridge. Navigators are reminded that the main line of the Trent Navigation is the Cranfleet Cut. This begins 200yds upstream of the mouth of the Soar, hard by the large, wooden building which houses one of the many sailing clubs on the Trent. The entrance to the Erewash Canal is also here, marked by a lock and a cluster of buildings. If the warning light at Redhill Lock shows red – do not pass.

Ratcliffe on Soar
Notts. PO, tel, stores. A tiny village with a spired church dating from the 13thC. The interior of the nave is pleasantly uncluttered and rather spartan. There is no stained glass to darken it, and the white-washed walls accentuate the bold and ancient arches. In the chancel, on the other hand, there is a profusion of stone effigies and wall memorials, many of them to the Sacheverell family.

Kingston on Soar
Notts. PO, tel, stores. Situated east of the railway embankment, this is a small quiet estate village which looks much as it must have done 50 years ago. The church, still very much the focus of the village, is a pretty building of 1900, incorporating earlier fragments; there are some fine tombs.

Kegworth
Leics. PO, tel, stores, bank. Kegworth has an attractive situation up on a wooded hill that is crowned by the church spire, but although it is close to the river, access is easy only from Kegworth Shallow Lock; the walk into the village is not really rewarding, although the late Decorated church has a fine angel roof. The M1 motorway runs just west of the village.

BOATYARDS

Ⓑ **Kegworth Marine** Kingston Lane, Kegworth. (0509 672300). WD Day hire narrowboats, long-term mooring, slipway, boat building.

PUBS

Anchor Kegworth. Near Shallow Lock. Bass and Worthington real ale and food.

White House Riverside, south of Kegworth. Bass real ale and good food.

Cap & Stocking Borough Street, Kegworth. Bass and M & B real ale served from the jug. Food *lunchtime and evening* and an open fire in this traditional pub.

LLANGOLLEN CANAL

Maximum dimensions

Length: 72′
Beam: 6′ 10″
Headroom: 7′

Manager:

(0691) 622549

Mileage

Hurleston Junction (S.U. main line) to
Frankton Junction: 29
Pontcysyllte Aqueduct: 40
Llangollen: 44½
Llantisilio: 46

Locks: 21

In 1791 a plan was published for a canal from the Mersey to the Severn, to pass through Chester, the iron and coalfields around Ruabon, Ellesmere and Shrewsbury. There were to be branches to the limestone quarries at Llanymynech, and to the Chester Canal via Whitchurch. The new terminus on the Mersey was to be at the little fishing village of Netherpool, known after 1796 as Ellesmere Port. After extensive arguments about routes, the company received its Act in 1793. William Jessop was appointed engineer, and work began. By 1796 the Wirral line from Chester to Ellesmere Port was open, and was immediately successful, carrying goods and passengers (in express 'fly-boats') to Liverpool. The same year, the Llanymynech Branch was completed. The company continued to expand and build inwards, but failed to make the vital connections with the Dee and the Severn; the line south to Shrewsbury never got further than Weston, and the line northwards to Chester stopped at Pontcysyllte. By 1806 the Ellesmere company had opened 68 miles of canal, which included lines from Hurleston on the Chester Canal to Plas Kynaston via Frankton, and from Chester to Ellesmere Port; there were branches to Llanymynech, Whitchurch, Prees and Ellesmere, and a navigable feeder to Llangollen; the two great aqueducts at Chirk and Pontcysyllte were complete. However it was a totally self-contained system, its only outlet being via the old Chester Canal at Hurleston. Despite this, the Ellesmere Canal was profitable; it serviced a widespread local network, and gave an outlet to Liverpool (via the River Mersey) for the iron-works and the coalfields that were grouped at the centre of the system. This profitability was dependent upon good relations with the Chester Company. An attempted take-over in 1804 failed, but in 1813 the inevitable merger took place, and the Ellesmere & Chester Canal Company was formed. Today the Llangollen Canal is perhaps the most popular cruising canal in the country and as a result can be very crowded during the summer months. Those who cruise out of the peak season, or avoid the mid-week rush to Llangollen, will enjoy it more.

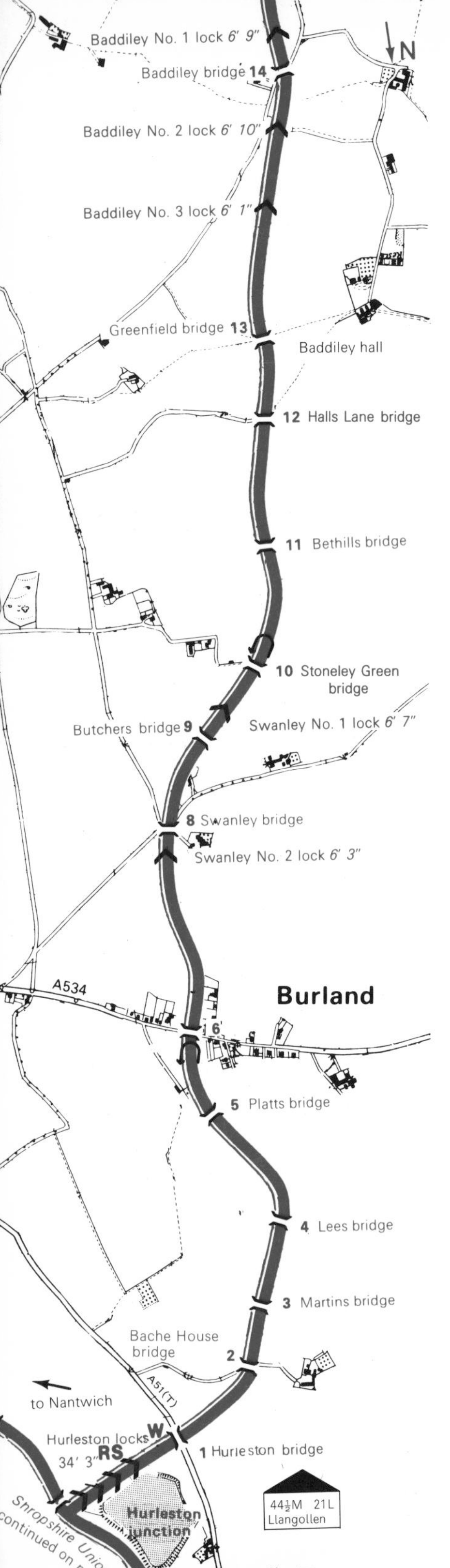

Shropshire Union canal continued on page 11

Hurleston

The Llangollen rapidly establishes its character as a quiet and pretty canal. Considering the spectacular scenery further west, it is hardly surprising that this is the most popular cruising waterway in the country – so much so, in fact, that in the height of the summer up to 400 boats a week use the canal. Leaving Hurleston, the canal runs through a very shallow valley past the hamlet of Burland to Swanley Locks. There is an old canalside house at Swanley Bridge (8) with a beautiful garden and weeping willows overhanging the water. The next three locks encountered are Baddiley Locks (note the unusual paddle gear at lock no 2); the tall Georgian house surrounded by trees to the west of the bottom lock is Baddiley Hall.

Navigational note
The Llangollen Canal is fed directly by the River Dee at Llantisilio, and there is a noticeable flow of water from west to east. Navigators should allow more time for journeys to Llangollen – *against the flow*.

Burland
Ches. Tel, stores, garage. A straggling settlement by the canal, useful as a supply centre; the general store here is open every day.

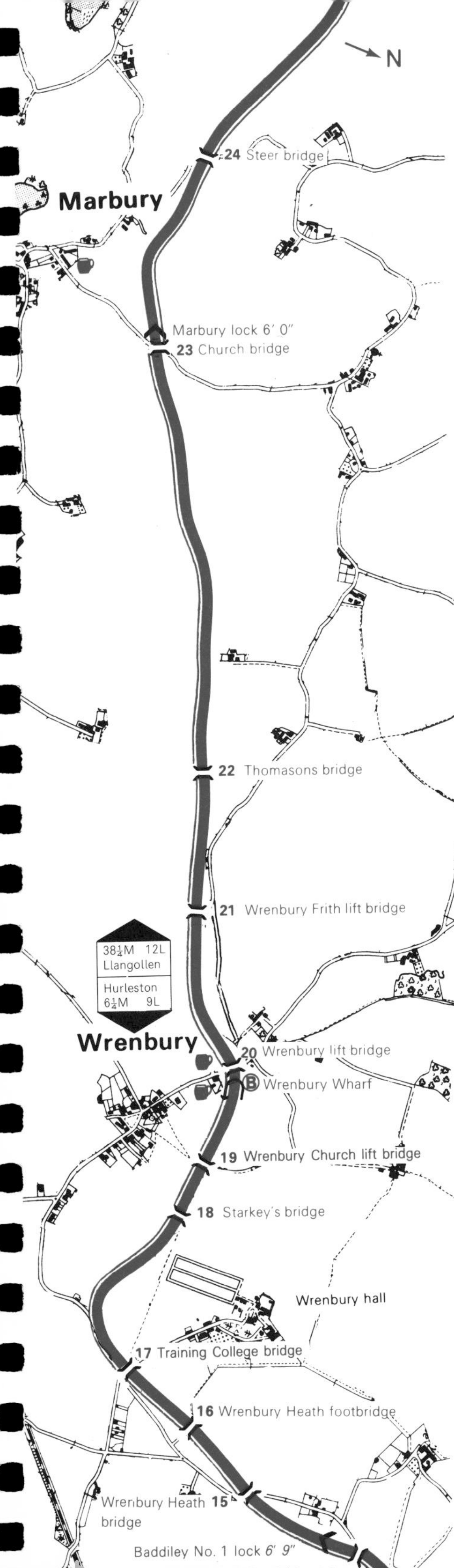

Wrenbury

The canal moves past Wrenbury Hall, formerly the home of Sir John Stapleton Cotton (one of Wellington's generals) and now a college, towards Wrenbury. The old farmhouse west of bridges 14 and 15 sells local honey, cheese, eggs, milk, etc. Wrenbury Wharf is a delightful spot. There are some fine warehouses and a former mill here, and a nearby pub, all grouped around the hydraulically operated lift bridge. Beyond the wharf, the soft green Cheshire countryside leads to Marbury Lock. The tall obelisk visible to the south is in distant Combermere Park.

Marbury
Ches. Tel. An enchanting village ½ mile south of Marbury Lock. Centred on an old farm, the village boasts several other old and timbered buildings. The church is a gem, and its setting is unrivalled: it stands on top of a little hill that overlooks a beautiful mere. The church grounds contain not just a graveyard but a garden, and the interior is correspondingly attractive and interesting. The sympathetically restored rectory stands next door.

Wrenbury
Ches. PO, tel, stores, garage, station. A quiet village ¼ mile from the wharf. There are some thatched cottages and a large church. It is refreshing to find a railway station still operating today in a village as small as this. The line goes from Crewe to Shrewsbury.

St Margaret's Church Overlooking the village green, this is a large, battlemented church with an early 16thC west tower and 18thC chancel and pulpit. The interior is very light and airy and contains a number of fine monuments of the last century, as well as several brasses.

BOATYARDS

Ⓑ **English County Cruises** Wrenbury, in the old mill by bridge 20. (0270 780544). R S W D E Pump-out, gas, narrowboat hire, overnight mooring, long-term mooring, winter storage, crane, dry dock, chandlery, books and maps, boat building, engine repairs, toilets, showers, gifts.

PUBS

Swan Marbury. Greenall Whitley beers in a handsome black-and-white pub with colourful window boxes and comfortable bars, facing a green. Small garden. Snacks.

Cotton Arms near Wrenbury Lift Bridge. Greenall Whitley beers. Snacks, children's room.

Dusty Miller Wrenbury. Large pub in a handsome converted 19thC mill. Robinson's real ale, meals and snacks. Canalside garden and rose garden.

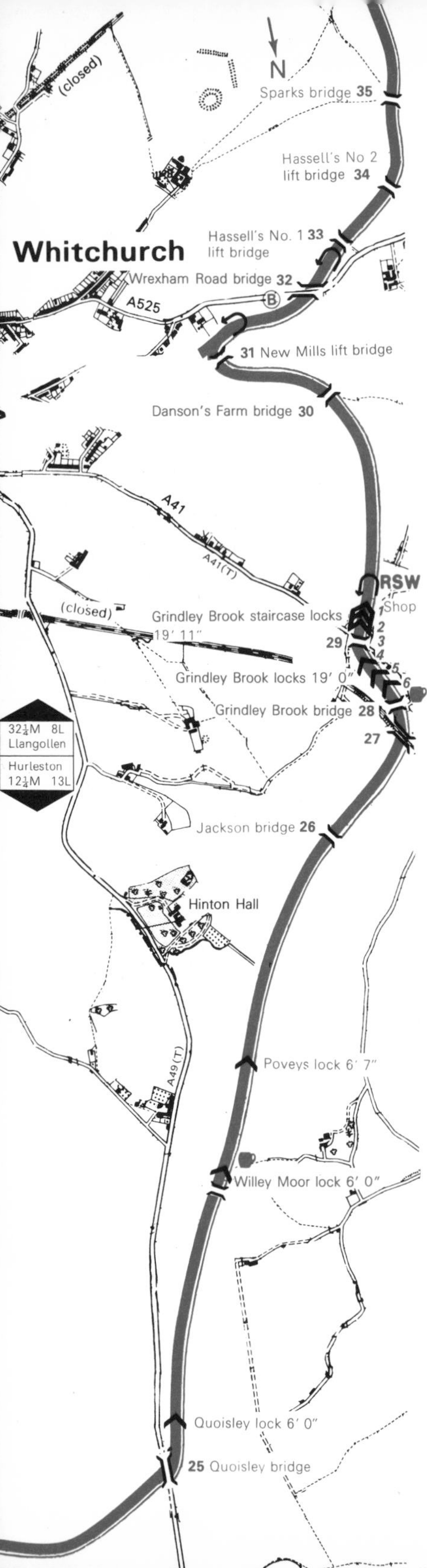

Grindley Brook

The canal continues to rise through a series of isolated locks as the sides of the valley begin to encroach on either side. One of them, Willey Moor, has a restaurant beside it. Hinton Hall, a large Victorian building, is shrouded in trees on the side of a hill. At the end of a straight stretch a massive railway embankment precedes a sharp bend to the bottom of the six locks at Grindley Brook; care should be exercised on the approach to the locks, and any boats stopping to visit the garage, shop or pub nearby should remain below the railway embankment. The first three locks are followed at the A41 bridge by three 'staircase' locks. Anyone requiring assistance or advice should look for the lock keeper, whose unusual house is at the top lock. There is a convenient store selling fresh vegetables, meat, provisions and souvenirs beside the staircase locks, and a cottage at the top lock where home-made pies can be bought. Another cottage to the south also offers home-cooked food. The canal now swerves round the side of a hill near Whitchurch: the first of a spattering of lift bridges marks the entrance to the long-abandoned Whitchurch Arm, now the subject of detailed restoration schemes.

Whitchurch
Shropshire. EC Wed. MD Fri. PO, tel, stores, garage, bank, station. A very fine town with some beautiful old houses of all periods in the centre. The streets are narrow and there is much to discover by wandering around. The striking church of St Alkmund on the hill was built in 1713, after the old church, called the Norman White Church – hence the name of the town – 'fell ye 31 of July 1711'. Oxford Canal connoisseurs will recognise its similarity to the magnificent church of the same vintage at Banbury. It has very big windows: indeed the whole church is on a grand scale. There are plenty of splendid pubs in the town, but unfortunately none near the canal.

BOATYARDS

Ⓑ **Viking Afloat** Wrexham Road, Whitchurch. (0948 2012). S W D Pump-out, gas, narrowboat hire, chandlery, provisions, overnight mooring, gifts, books and maps, boat sales, engine repairs, toilet, showers. Telephone. Also camping.

PUBS

Black Bear Whitchurch. Greenall Whitley beers. Booked meals in pub; pies etc.
Red Cow Whitchurch. (0948 4681). Sandwiches and pies.
White Bear Whitchurch. (0948 2638). Food. B&B.
Horse & Jockey Grindley Brook, near bottom lock. Greenall Whitley beers, garden, bar meals and snacks.
Willeymoor Lock Bar and restaurant for grills. Children welcome.

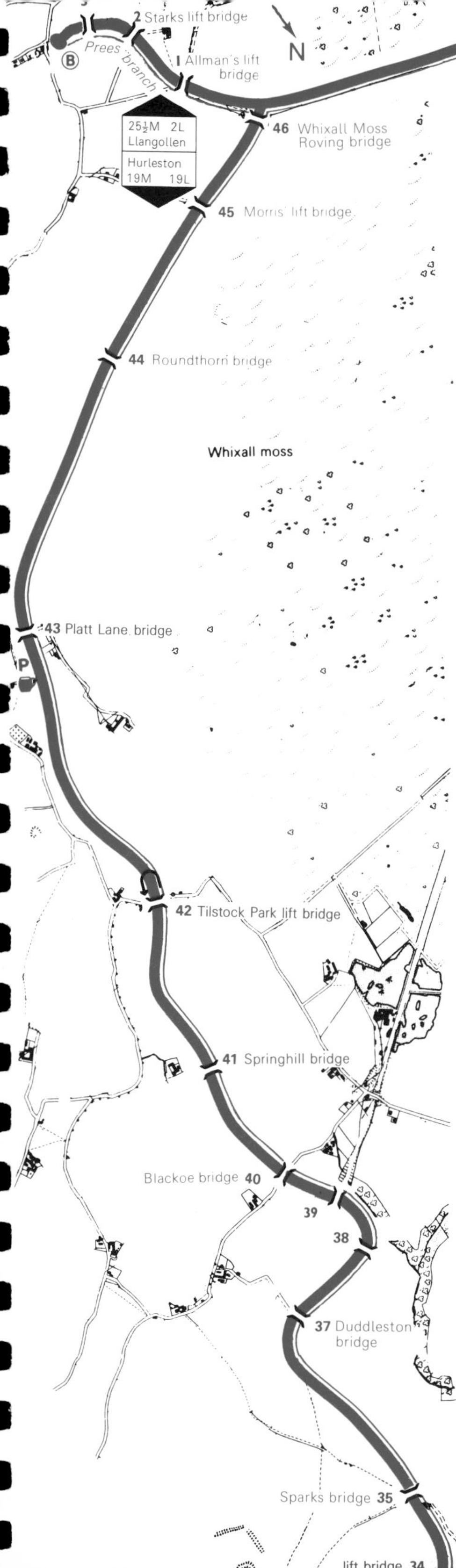

Whixall Moss

The canal now winds round the side of a succession of low hills as it begins to traverse a very remote and underpopulated area, passing no villages for miles but many farms and hundreds of healthy-looking cows. At Platt Lane the navigation straightens out and is carried on an embankment across the strange area of Whixall Moss, where peat cutting is still carried on. A solitary lift bridge interrupts the long straight, then there is a junction with the Prees Branch, which leads past two lift bridges to a marina. The main line veers off to the north west along another straight embankment, this time accompanied by woodlands, passing the border between England and Wales.

Prees Branch
Sometimes known as the Edstaston Branch, this arm curves round to Quina Brook. (It never did reach Prees.) The arm's principal value in recent years lay in the clay pits just over a mile from the junction: the clay from here was used until a few years ago for repairing the 'puddle' in local canals. The arm has been disused for some years, but the first ½ mile has been dredged and reopened to give access to a new marina constructed in the old clay pit. It is a very pleasant canal arm with two splendid old lift bridges – one of which is a rare skewed bridge. Naturalists find interesting plant communities along the unrestored section of the branch: enquiries may be made to the Nature Conservancy at the address given below.

Whixall Moss
A raised bog rich in flora and insect fauna – including mosquitoes! Like other meres and bogs in the area, Whixall Moss came into existence at the end of the Ice Age, as huge blocks of ice were left behind when the remainder of the ice cap melted and drained off into what is now the Severn valley. The peat surface remains, in spite of constant cutting of the peat for garden use. Naturalists can obtain information regarding access, etc, from the Regional Officer (Midlands), Nature Conservancy, Attingham Park, Shrewsbury, Shropshire.

Platt Lane
Shropshire. Tel, store. South east of bridge 43. A tiny settlement on the edge of the Moss with an equally tiny village store.

BOATYARDS

Ⓑ **Whixall Marina** At the end of the Prees Branch. (094872 420). R S W D E Pump-out, gas, overnight mooring, long-term mooring, winter storage, slipway, dry dock, chandlery, books and maps, boat building, boat and engine sales, engine repairs, toilets, showers, grocery shop, gift shop.

PUBS

Waggoners Platt Lane, Whixall. Basic Greenall Whitley pub, with a garden.

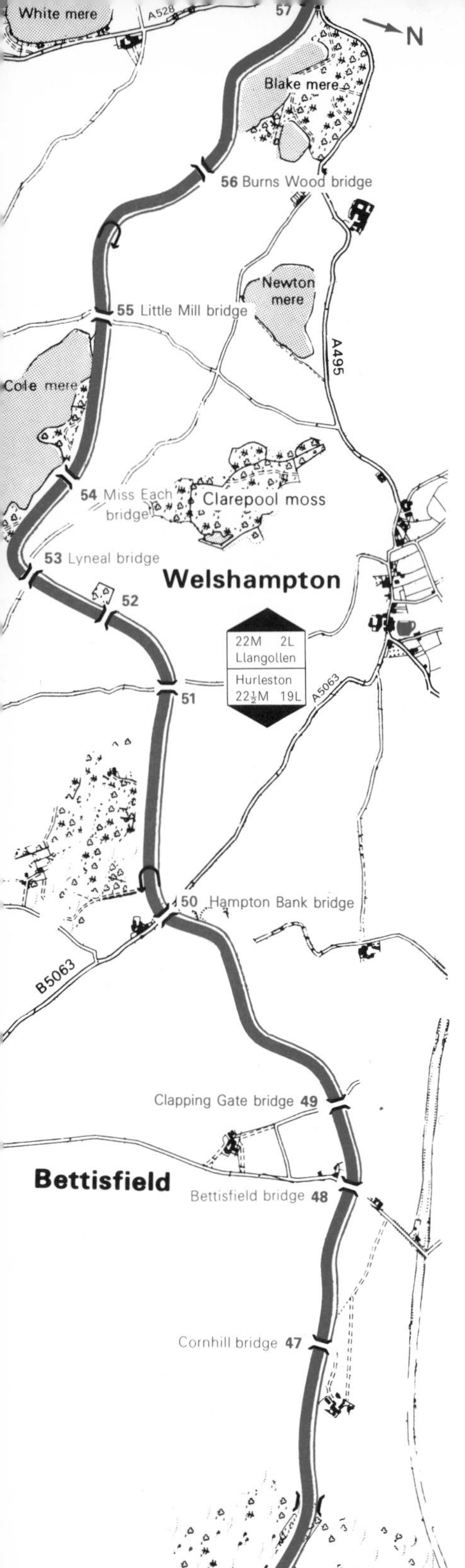

Bettisfield

Leaving Whixall Moss, the canal passes Bettisfield (where there are facilities including D and pump-out) and begins to wind this way and that, passing into Wales and out again. Soon the open countryside gives way to the hilly wooded landscape that precedes Ellesmere and contains several beautiful meres. The canal skirts first Cole Mere, which is below and mostly hidden from it by tall trees; there is a delightful timbered cottage at the west end. Then the navigation runs right beside Blake Mere: this is a charming little lake, surrounded by steep and thickly wooded hills. It is inhabited by many fish, and also ducks and other wild birds. One plunges immediately afterwards into the 87yd Ellesmere Tunnel and out into the open parkland beyond.

Welshampton
Shropshire. PO, tel, stores, garage. 1 mile west of bridge 50, the village contains the only pub since Platt Lane.

Bettisfield
Clwyd. PO, tel, stores (off-licence). There is little life in Bettisfield now: the pub and railway have closed and the station has become a private house. The church occupies a good position on the hill – it is a pretty Victorian building.

PUBS

Sun Welshampton. Greenall Whitley pub with a garden.

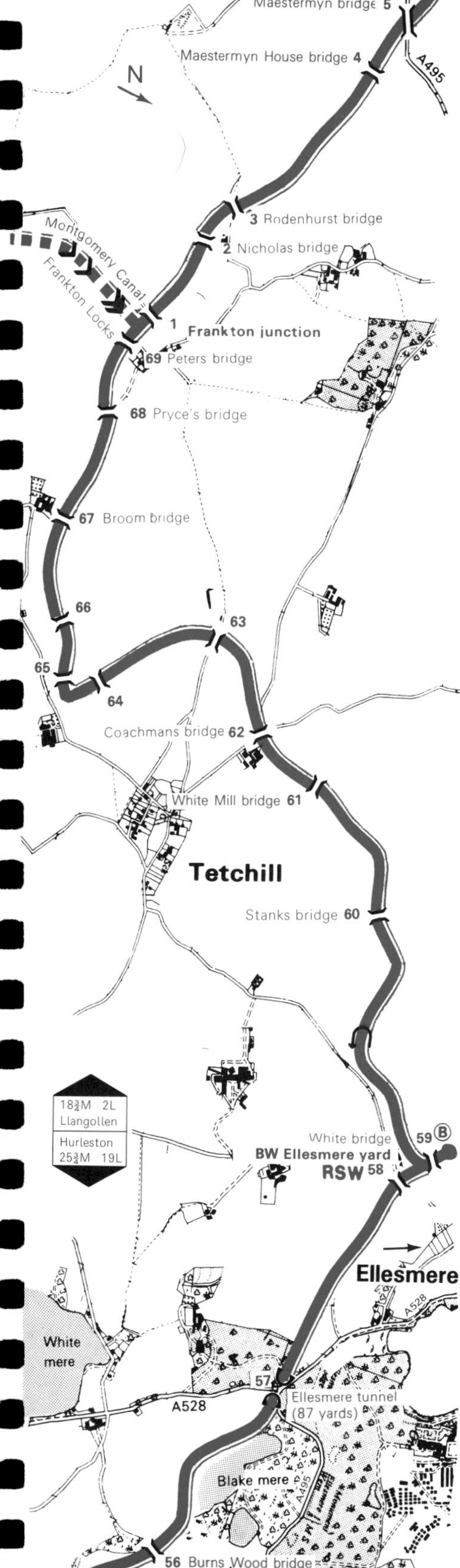

Ellesmere

Leaving Blake Mere and the tunnel, one soon arrives at Ellesmere. The town itself is reached via a short arm. Old warehouses and a small canalside crane testify to the canal trading that used to be carried on from here. The main line of the canal to Llangollen bears round sharply to the south west at the junction: the fine old buildings here house the BW maintenance yard with facilities for pleasure boats. Within the yard is 'Beech House', once the canal company's office. Beyond the yard, the country once again becomes quiet and entirely rural, while the canal's course becomes very winding. Frankton Junction is where boats used to branch off down the old Montgomery Canal south to Newtown. West of this junction, the bridge numbering on the Llangollen Canal starts again, because originally the Llangollen was only a branch of the Montgomery line.

The Montgomery Canal
When the Ellesmere Canal plans were published, they inspired a separate company to plan a canal from Newtown northwards to join the Llanymynech Branch of the Ellesmere Canal at Carreghofa. The canal was authorised in 1793, and by 1797 the line was open from Carreghofa to Garthmyl. The Montgomery Canal was mainly agricultural; apart from the limestone, it existed to serve the farms and villages through which it passed, and so was never really able to make a profit. The lack of capital and income greatly delayed the completion of the western extension to Newtown, which was not finally opened until 1821, having been financed by a separate company. The canal was never reopened after a breach about two miles beyond Frankton Junction in 1936. Parts of the canal have, however, been restored. At present it is an excellent cross-country walk and a good day out can be had at Welshpool, where *narrowboat Alt* provides a static exhibition, gifts and refreshments (0938 553271) and *narrowboat Llinos* is available for trips. These are run *daily during the summer* and last 1¼ hours (0938 553271). Day boats and canoes can be hired here and there is an excellent museum in the warehouse. Powis Castle is close by and there are some excellent pubs in the town.

Tetchill
Shropshire. PO, tel, stores, garage. A small farming village, quiet and unpretentious.

Ellesmere
Shropshire. EC Thur. PO, tel, stores, garage, bank. This handsome 18thC market town with its narrow winding streets is an attractive place to visit. There are many tall red brick houses and several terraces of old cottages. It takes its name from the large and beautiful mere beside it.

St Mary's Church Standing on a hill overlooking the mere, the general appearance of this large red-stone church is Victorian, belying its medieval origins. It contains a medieval chest hewn out of a solid block of oak, many fine effigies and a beautiful 15thC font.

BOATYARDS

BW Ellesmere Yard at junction with Ellesmere Arm. R S W Dry dock for hire.
Ⓑ **Maestermyn Marine** see next page.

PUBS AND RESTAURANTS

Millies 1 Birch Road, Ellesmere. (0691 623689). Half a mile from bridge 58 in a 16thC building. Imaginative and reasonably priced food in this restaurant and wine bar. *Open L & D in summer (not L Sun & Wed).*

Nightingales Restaurant 8 Market Street, Ellesmere. (0691 622863). A friendly and intimate restaurant with a full and varied à la carte menu. *Dinner only from 19.00 Mon–Sat.*

Bridgewater Arms Hotel Ellesmere. (0691 622647). Restaurant: *lunches and dinners daily.*

Swan Ellesmere. Greenall Whitley beers.

White Hart Ellesmere. A very old timbered building where Border real ale is available. Food, garden.

Narrowboat Inn by bridge 5. Real ale, snacks and canalside garden.

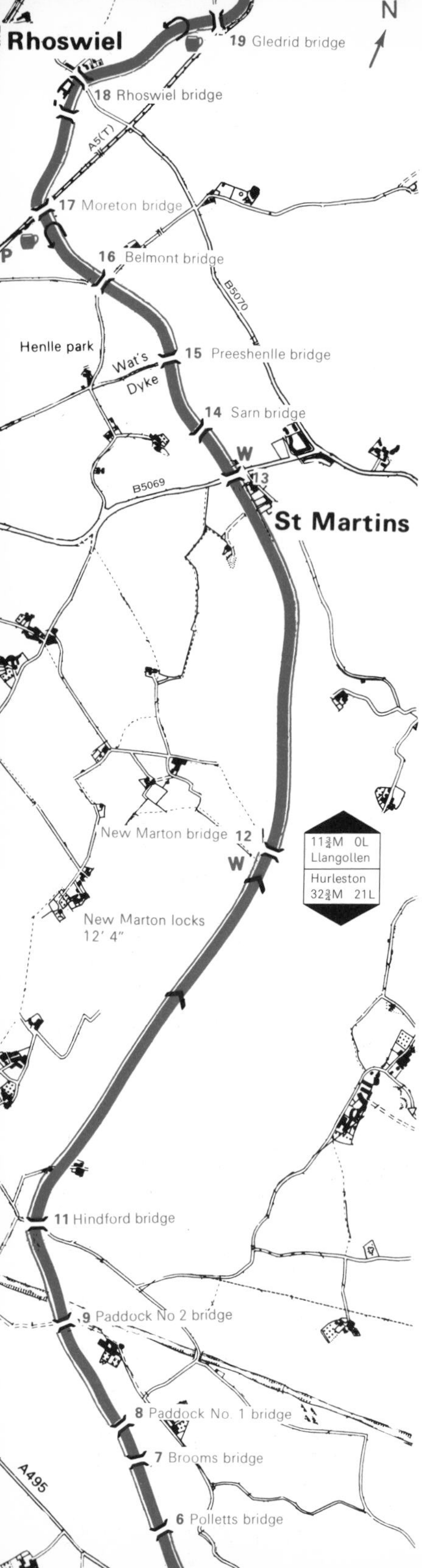

Henlle Park

The navigation continues to run west and north through quiet, green countryside. At Hindford Bridge there is a pub and restaurant. Beyond, the canal climbs through the two New Marton Locks – the last to be encountered on the way to Llangollen. There is a shop, run by the lock keeper, at the top lock. By bridge 13 you can watch pots being made, and buy them if you wish. Gradually the land becomes hillier as one passes Wat's Dyke and Henlle Park. The A5 joins the navigation near Chirk Bank.

Rhoswiel
Shropshire. PO, tel, stores. A tiny mining village on the Welsh border; the canal runs through it in a slight cutting.

BOATYARDS

Ⓑ **Maestermyn Marine** Ellesmere Road, Whittington. (0691 62424). R S W D Pump-out, gas, narrowboat hire, slipway, chandlery, boat sales and repairs, provisions, off-licence, overnight mooring.

PUBS AND RESTAURANTS

Lion by bridge 17. Snacks.
Jack Myttons by bridge 11. (0691 662327). Meals, snacks, provisions, craft shop. Children welcome. Gas, overnight mooring.
New Inn Gledrid, Chirk. (0691 773250). Canalside, at bridge 19 and on A5 road. Banks' real ale. Restaurant: *lunches and dinners daily.* Children welcome.

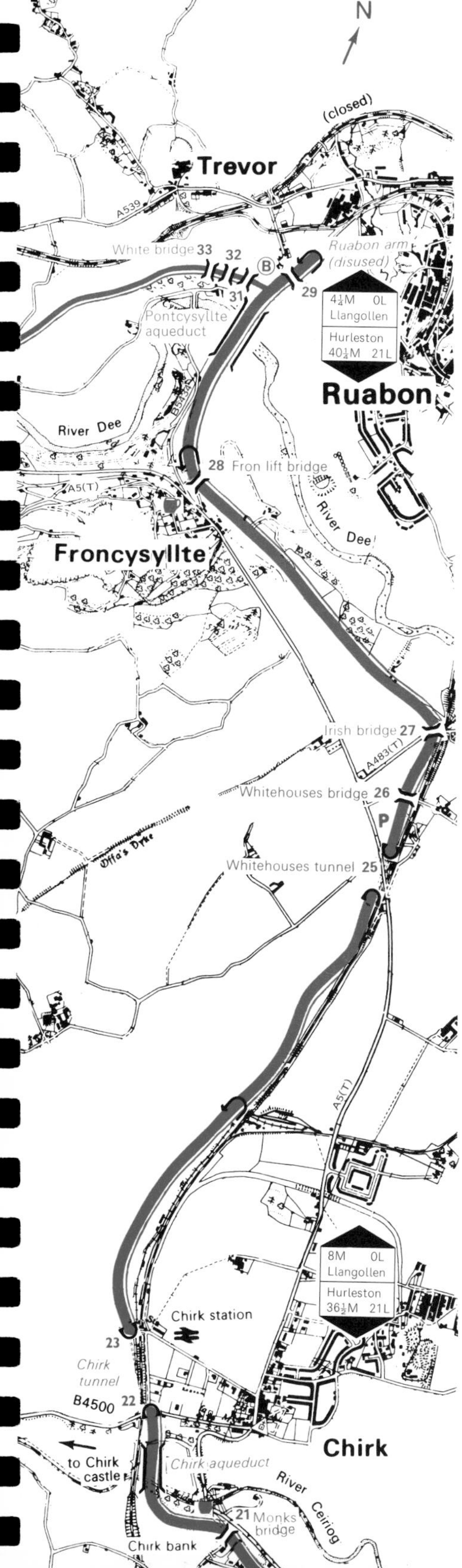

Chirk and Pontcysyllte

One soon begins to realise why this canal is so famous. The approach of the Welsh mountains drives the navigation into a side cutting half way up the side of a hill. Passing Chirk Bank, one rounds a corner and suddenly finds oneself on Chirk Aqueduct – an impressive structure by any canal enthusiast's standards, but slightly overshadowed by the railway viaduct alongside. At the end of the aqueduct the canal enters a tunnel immediately. At the north end of the tunnel a strong smell of chocolate betrays a canalside cocoa factory; Chirk station is conveniently nearby. A long wooded cutting follows, then the railway reappears alongside. Another, shorter tunnel at Whitehouses is negotiated before the canal meets the valley of the River Dee. Here the railway charges off to the north on a magnificent viaduct, while the canal clings to the hillside. By now the scenery is superb and the views excellent. But more is yet to come! Passing the village of Froncysyllte (*PO, tel, stores*), the canal launches out into this deep valley on a massive embankment, then crosses the River Dee on the breathtaking Pontcysyllte Aqueduct. At the north end of the aqueduct there is a boatyard and a tricky 90-degree turn. From this point to Llangollen the canal is very narrow and is not recommended for boats drawing more than 21in. The short arm towards Ruabon was originally projected as the canal's main line towards Chester and the Mersey. (The dry dock at the Trevor Junction dates from this time.) The line from Trevor to Llantisilio was envisaged purely as a navigable feeder. However the idea of a direct line to Chester was soon dropped and a connection made instead with the Chester Canal at Hurleston Junction. There are moorings and a turning place in the restored basins beyond Anglo-Welsh Canal Holidays.

Navigational notes
1 The canal now becomes very shallow, accentuating the flow 'downstream'. Just go slowly and revel in the Welsh scenery.
2 Do not enter Pontcysyllte Aqueduct if a boat is approaching from the opposite direction.

Pontcysyllte Aqueduct
Easily the most famous and most spectacular feature on the whole canal system, this aqueduct cannot fail to astonish the visitor. Apart from its great height of 120ft above the River Dee and its length of over 1000ft, the excitement to be derived from crossing this structure by boat is partly due to the fact that, while the towpath side is safely fenced off with iron railings, the offside is completely unprotected from about 12in above the water level. The safest way for children to enjoy the great aqueduct is inside the boat. The aqueduct was built by Thomas Telford, and is generally reckoned to be one of his most brilliant and most successful works. The concept of laying a cast iron trough along the top of a row of stone piers was entirely new, and entirely Telford's: he realised that such a high crossing of the Dee valley was inevitable if time- and water-wasting locks were to be avoided, and it was obvious to the canal company that a conventional brick or stone aqueduct would be quite unsuitable. His plan for the aqueduct was greeted at first with derision; but the work went ahead, was completed in 10 years and opened in 1805. One can hardly imagine the utter amazement felt by people of that time as they witnessed boats moving easily across this tall, beautiful and unique structure. Today, the aqueduct remains as built, apart from recent renewals of balustrading and the towpath structure. The masonry is apparently in prime condition (note the very thin masonry joints), and the dovetailed joints in the iron trough hardly leak at all. The cast-iron side plates of the trough are all wedge-shaped, like the stones in a masonry arch. It is, without doubt, a masterpiece.
Chirk
Clwyd. EC Thur. PO, tel, stores, garage, bank, station. An unassuming place whose 18thC village centre is full of A5 traffic. Most of Chirk is in Wales but a few houses on the south side

are in England, including the Bridge Inn.
Chirk Castle 1 mile west of Chirk Tunnel. Built in 1295 as a Marcher Fortress, it has been the home of the Myddelton family since 1595. The dungeon under the west range remains as built, the interior rooms are richly decorated and the entrance gates are a remarkable example of wrought-iron work, made in 1721. There are traces of Offa's Dyke within the park. *Open Tue, Wed, Thur and Sun afternoons in summer, also B. Hol Mon.* Light lunches and teas.

Chirk and Whitehouses Tunnels
Neither of these tunnels is wide enough for two boats to pass – although each tunnel has a towing path running through it. Chirk Tunnel is 459yds long. Whitehouses Tunnel is 191yds.

Chirk Aqueduct
Opened in 1801, this is a splendidly massive brick and stone aqueduct carrying the canal in a narrow cast iron trough from England into Wales. The River Ceiriog flows 70ft below, and the great railway viaduct is beside and a little higher than the aqueduct.

BOATYARDS

Ⓑ **Anglo-Welsh Canal Holidays** Canal Wharf, Trevor, Llangollen. (0978 821749). In the Ruabon Arm. R S W D E Pump-out, gas, narrowboat hire. Dry dock. Sale and repair of diesel engines. Local shops, tel, toilet. *Services available Mon–Fri.*

BOAT TRIPS

Ribbon Plate Restaurant Boats *Eirlys* operates from Trevor and *Erianfa* from Ellesmere. Both are licensed restaurant boats carrying up to 50 people. *Ribbon Plate* operates from Trevor, and carries 10–12 people. Please book on (0978) 823215.

PUBS AND RESTAURANTS

Mill Inn Trevor, near Anglo-Welsh.

Aqueduct Froncysyllte. Border beers and snacks.

Britannia Froncysyllte. Border beers and snacks.

Hand Hotel Church Street, Chirk. (0691 773472). Border beers. Restaurant: *lunches and dinners (except Sun evening).*

Bridge Chirk Bank. 'Last pub in England', on the A5 downhill from bridge 21. Banks' real ale. Sandwiches etc.

Pontcysyllte Aqueduct. *Derek Pratt.*

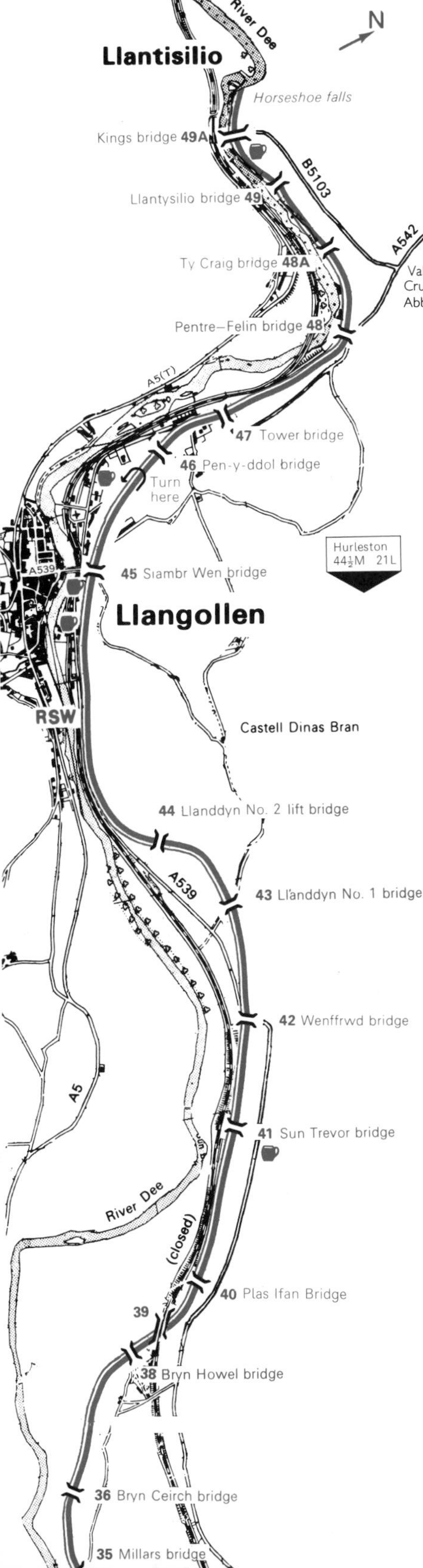

Vale of Llangollen

This is another stretch of very great beauty. All the way to Llangollen the navigation sidles along the tree-covered mountains, with views down into the Vale of Llangollen. In places the mountainside is very steep, making the canal so narrow that only one boat can negotiate the channel at a time. The scene of several major breaches between 1982–85, repairs have cost a breathtaking £5 million over the 10-mile stretch between Chirk and Llangollen. The canal passes high above the town, but it doesn't stop there: the tiny channel continues as a feeder to weave up the valley to Llantisilio. At this delightful spot the Horseshoe Falls (in fact a large semi-circular weir built by Telford across the River Dee) provide the water which is constantly passed from the river through a sluice and meter into the canal. Then it flows past Llangollen and the aqueducts, right back down to Hurleston reservoir – to the tune of six million gallons a day.

Navigational note
There is **no** turning point west of the winding hole at Llangollen, so boats longer than about 10ft should not venture up the feeder. However the towpath is in excellent shape and it makes a very enjoyable walk. There are good temporary moorings and other facilities at Llangollen.

Llantisilio
Clwyd. The village is set on a steep hillside among trees that overlook the Horseshoe Falls. The Victorian church is of interest: parts of the interior are taken from the nearby Valle Crucis Abbey, and the south window still contains 16thC glass.
Valle Crucis Abbey 1½ miles north west of the town. Picturesque ruins of the Cistercian abbey founded in 1201 by Madoc, Lord of Powys. The abbey fell into neglect after the Dissolution of the Monasteries in 1539.
Eliseg's Pillar ¼ mile north of the abbey. Erected in 18thC to commemorate Eliseg, who built the fortress on the top of Dinas Bran.
Llangollen
Clwyd. EC Thur, MD Tue. PO, tel, stores, garage, bank. Renowned for its International Musical Eisteddfod every July, it is in one of the finest stretches of the Dee valley. The canal runs along the hillside overlooking the town, which is built steeply along the fast flowing river. The centre of the town is on the south side of the 14thC bridge across the Dee, and contains many stone-built Victorian buildings. Great centre for pony trekking and other outdoor pursuits, especially climbing and walking. The parish church of St Collen in Church Street is a fine 13thC building, enlarged in 1865 and containing a superb carved oak ceiling. One place well worth a visit is the Llangollen Pottery in Regent Street, where the pottery is all hand-made and hand-decorated – a fascinating sight. The railway line is closed, although a railway society has some steam locomotives which run along a ¾ mile restored section on *summer Suns*. The Tourist Information office is in Parade Street.
Plas Newydd On southern outskirts of town. An attractive black-and-white-timbered house which, from 1779–1831, was the home of the eccentric Lady Eleanor Butler and Miss Sarah Ponsonby, known as the 'Ladies of Llangollen'. Their visitors, who included Browning, Tennyson, Walter Scott and Wordsworth, presented them with antique curios, which are now on display in the elaborately panelled rooms. Part of the 12-acre grounds is a public park. *Open daily May–Sep.*
Castell Dinas Bran ½ mile north of canal. The ruins of the castle built for Eliseg, Prince of Powys, are conspicuous from boats approaching the town, and stand on a 1100ft mountain accessible to energetic walkers from various points along the canal, including bridge 45. It was once an important fortress, defending Wales from the English. From the summit there is a glorious view of the district.

BOAT TRIPS AND EXHIBITION

The Wharf, Llangollen. (0978 860702). Fine museum of canal history. *Open daily in summer*. Horse-drawn boat trips to Pentrefelin, public trips and private charter – ring for details.

PUBS AND RESTAURANTS

Chain Bridge Hotel near Horseshoe Falls. Meals and residential.
Royal Hotel Llangollen. (0978 860202). Meals and residential.
Royal Oak Llangollen. Pub in a very old barn.
Jenny Jones On A542, 300yds west of bridge 45. Spacious beamy pub serving real ale and bar food. Garden.
Bridge End Below bridge 45. (0978 860634). Large and comfortable pub serving Robinson's real ale, bar snacks and meals in the Tudor Grill. Wonderful taxidermist shop next door.
Caesars (0978 860133). Tiny restaurant on south side of the bridge over the river. Limited menu based on fresh produce. Only eight tables so booking is essential. *Dinner only. Closed Sun.*
Gales 18 Bridge Street, Llangollen. (0978 860089). Tasteful wine bar with simple but excellent food. *Closed Sun. No children allowed in after 20.00.*
Sarah Ponsonby On the A539 east of bridge 45. (0978 861119). Thomas Greenall Original real ale, bar and restaurant food. Garden, play area, children welcome. Handy for the Llangollen moorings.
Sun Trevor Above bridge 41. Beautifully situated pub with exceptional views. Brasses, beams and fine inglenook with a cosy curved settle. Castle Eden real ale, food. Garden, telephone outside.

A beautifully wooded stretch of the Llangollen Canal near Ellesmere Tunnel. *Derek Pratt.*

NORTH OXFORD
AND GRAND UNION (NORTON JUNCTION TO BRAUNSTON TURN)

Maximum dimensions

Length: 70′
Beam: 7′
Headroom: 7′

Mileage

BRAUNSTON TURN to:
Hillmorton Bottom Lock: 7½
Rugby Wharf Arm: 10¼
Stretton Stop: 15¾
HAWKESBURY JUNCTION (Coventry Canal): 22¾

Locks: 4

Manager:

(0926) 812882

The Oxford was one of the earliest and for many years one of the most important canals in southern England. It was authorised in 1769, when the Coventry Canal was in the offing, and was intended to fetch coal southwards from the Warwickshire coalfield to Banbury and Oxford, at the same time giving access to the River Thames. James Brindley was appointed engineer; he built a winding contour canal 91 miles long that soon began to look thoroughly out-dated and inefficient for the carriage of goods. Brindley died in 1772, and was replaced by Samuel Simcock; he completed the line from Longford, where a junction was made with the Coventry Canal, to Banbury in 1778. After a long pause, the canal was finally brought into Oxford in 1790, and thereafter through traffic flowed constantly along this important new trade route.

In 1800, however, the Grand Junction Canal opened (excepting the tunnel at Blisworth) from London to Braunston, and the Warwick & Napton and Warwick & Birmingham Canals completed the new short route from London to Birmingham. This had the natural – and intended – effect of drawing traffic off the Oxford Canal, especially south of Napton Junction; but the Oxford company protected itself very effectively against this powerful opposition by charging outrageously high rates for their 5½-mile stretch between Braunston and Napton that had become part of the new London–Birmingham through route. Thus the Oxford maintained its revenue and very high dividends for many years to come.

By the late 1820s, however, the Oxford Canal had become conspicuously out of date with its extravagant winding course; and under the threat of various schemes for big new canals which, if built, would render the Oxford Canal almost redundant, the company decided to modernise the northern part of their navigation. Tremendous engineering works were therefore carried out which completely changed the face of the canal north of Braunston. Aqueducts, massive embankments and deep cuttings were built, carrying the canal in great sweeps through the countryside and cutting almost 14 miles off the original 36 miles between Braunston Junction and the Coventry Canal. Much of the old main line suddenly became a series of loops and branches leading nowhere and crossed by elegant new towpath bridges inscribed 'Horseley Ironworks 1828'.

This very expensive programme was well worthwhile. Although toll rates, and thus revenue, began to fall because of keen competition from the railways, dividends were kept at a high level for years; indeed a respectable profit was still shown right through to the 20thC.

This part of the Oxford Canal, along with the Grand Union between Norton Junction and Braunston Turn, is included to complete the popular Grand Union (Leicester section), River Soar, Trent & Mersey, Coventry, and North Oxford cruising circuit.

Norton to Braunston

From Norton Junction to Braunston the canal runs westward through hills and wooded country. At first there are good views to the north and north east, with the embankment carrying the Leicester line branching away to the north. The canal then runs into a wooded cutting which leads to Braunston Tunnel. A similar cutting follows the tunnel, and then the landscape opens out although the hills stay present on either side. There is an excellent canal shop by lock 1, where fresh fruit and vegetables, provisions, canal crafts and chandlery can be obtained. Long rows of moored craft, including many narrowboats, flank the canal, and there is a fine selection of old buildings. A large marina with many beautifully restored buildings situated on an arm to the south meets every boating need; note also the iron side-bridge and the 18thC dry dock. The arm in fact was part of the old route of the Oxford Canal before it was shortened by building a large embankment (Braunston Puddle Banks) across the Leam valley to Braunston Turn. The entrance to this arm was thus the original Braunston Junction.

Braunston
Northants. PO, tel, stores, launderette. Set up on a hill to the north of the canal, so that the spire of Braunston church dominates the valley for miles around. The village is really a long main street, with houses of all periods that give the feeling of a spacious market town. A very well known canal centre, it is no less significant today than when the Oxford and Grand Junction canals were first connected here.

Braunston Tunnel
Opened in 1796, to bore through the Northamptonshire heights, the tunnel is 2042yds long. Its construction was hindered by quicksands, and a mistake in direction has given it a slight 'S' bend.
Two boats of 7ft beam can pass in this tunnel, but wide beam boats must get permission from BW on (0788) 890666 to arrange a passage.

Welton
Northants. PO, tel, stores. The village climbs up the side of a steep hill, which makes it compact and attractive, especially round the church.

BOATYARDS

Braunston Boats Bottom Lock, Braunston. (0788 891079). WD Pump-out, gas, narrowboat hire, long-term mooring.

Braunston Marina The Wharf, Braunston. (0788 891373). Under the fine bridge dated 1834. RSWD Gas, pump-out, overnight mooring, long-term mooring, winter storage, dry dock, wet dock, chandlery, boat building, engineering – all services. Toilets.

Union Canal Carriers Canalside, Braunston. (0788 890784). SD Pump-out, gas, narrowboat hire, overnight mooring by arrangement, long-term mooring, books and maps, boat building, boat sales, engine sales and repairs. *24hr* breakdown service (ring 0788 812156 *evenings*).

PUBS AND RESTAURANTS

Boatman Braunston. (0788 891313). Once the Rose & Castle, now a comfortable and friendly modern hotel/restaurant/pub. Ruddles and Webster's real ale, bar meals (vast helpings) and candlelit dinners. Children's room, canalside garden with swings and overnight mooring for patrons.

Old Plough High Street, Braunston. Popular village pub of character, with games/family room. Ansells and Ind Coope (Burton) real ale, good food *lunchtime and evening*. Garden.

Wheatsheaf The Green, Braunston. Locals' pub with a warm atmosphere. Wilson's real ale, food *lunchtime and evening*, garden.

Admiral Nelson By lock 3, Little Braunston. Dating from 1730 and originally a farmhouse, this building still retains much of its traditional charm. Warmed by a log fire in winter, there is home cooked food *lunchtime and evening every day*. Breakfast, morning coffee and afternoon teas are also available during the *summer*. Good choice of real ale, and Northamptonshire skittles for amusement. Canalside garden.

Braunston
Braunston Turn
To Birmingham
North Oxford Canal
22¾M 4L Hawkesbury
Little Braunston
6-1 Braunston locks 35' 6"
Braunston tunnel
A361
A45(T)

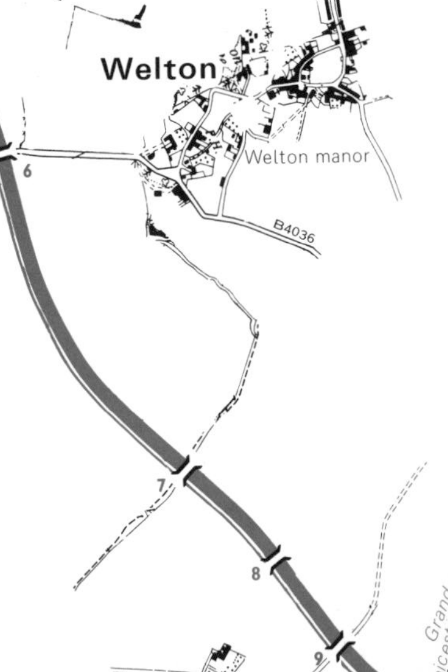

Grand Union Leicester section
see page 58
Norton Junction
A5(T)
4¼M 6L Braunston
To Blisworth

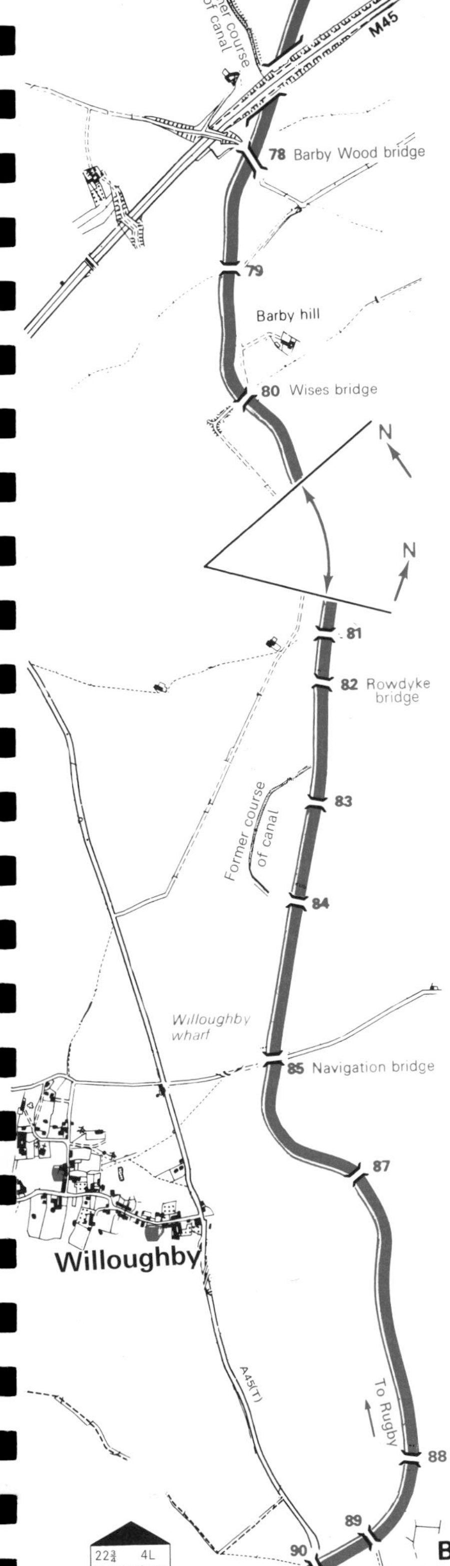

Willoughby

North west from Braunston the canal runs through wide open country, backed by bare hills to the east. At bridge 87 the medieval ridge and furrow patterns are in evidence. Skirting round Barby Hill, the canal swings north east towards Hillmorton and Rugby. The railway and the A45 run to the west of the canal, and the M45 crosses after Barby Hill.

Willoughby
Warwicks. PO, tel, stores, garage, transport café. Mellow red-brick village to which new buildings have been unobtrusively added. The small church is dominated by a fine 18thC rectory.

BOATYARDS

The Boat Shop. (0788 891310). Crafts and gifts on board a boat moored at Braunston Turn.

PUBS

Rose Inn Willoughby.

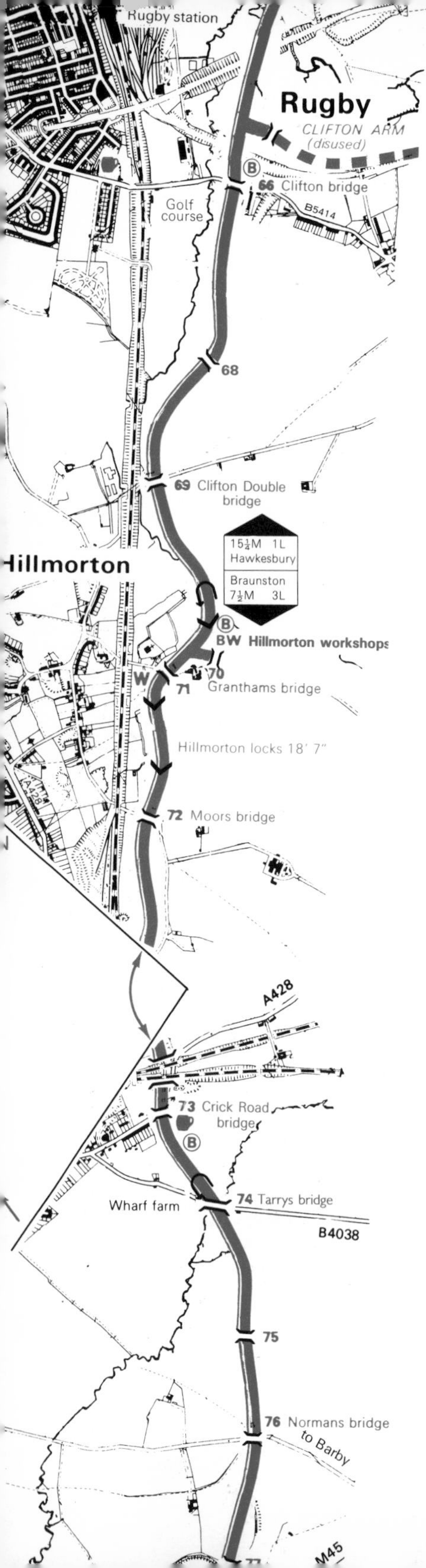

Hillmorton

After running north east for 2 miles, the canal swings in a wide arc round Rugby. To the east the radio masts dominate the landscape. The canal descends Hillmorton Locks, a flight of three paired narrow locks, and passes the attractively sited BW maintenance yard and hire craft base. There is an excellent all-purpose grocer's shop at bridge 71. The railway accompanies the canal through Hillmorton and the A428 crosses south of the town. The little brick footbridge at the bottom locks is a delight to the eye.

Hillmorton
Warwicks. PO, tel, stores, garage. Its church dates from c1300, but there have been additions as late as the 18thC. There is an interesting medieval cross in the centre of the village, but the independence this implies has long since been swallowed up by Rugby.

BOATYARDS

BW Hillmorton Yard The Lock, Brindley Road, Hillmorton. (0788 561386). R S W Dry dock.

Ⓑ **Clifton Cruisers** Clifton Wharf, Vicarage Hill, Clifton on Dunsmore. (0788 543570). R W D Pump-out, gas, narrowboat hire, long-term mooring, groceries, chandlery, books and maps, boat building, engine repairs, off-licence, gifts.

Ⓑ **Rugby Boatbuilders** (Inland Marine Leisure) Hillmorton Wharf, Crick Road, Rugby. (0788 544438). S W D Steel narrowboats built, repaired or fitted out. Engines overhauled. Narrowboat hire, pump-out, gas, dry dock, mooring, chandlery, toilets, gift shop. *Closed winter weekends.*

PUBS

Clifton Inn Clifton Road, Rugby. South of bridge 66. Popular locals' pub with mock Tudor façade. Pleasant lounge, basic bar and leaded windows. Ansells and Ind Coope (Burton) real ale, snacks, garden.

Stag & Pheasant School Street, Hillmorton. Good basic pub offering Ansells real ale and snacks.

Old Royal Oak Canalside at bridge 73. A substantial brick pub with a very tidy garden. Sam Smith's and Youngers real ale, meals *lunchtime and evening.*

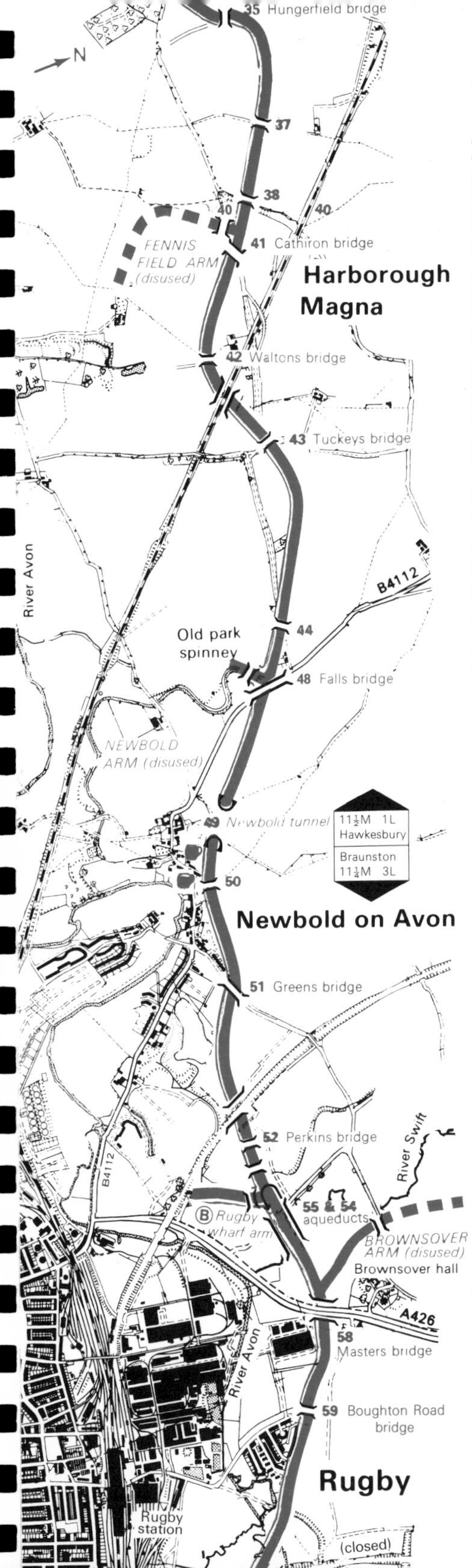

Rugby

Continuing the swing round Rugby, the canal enters a side cut embankment whose tall towpath hedge hides the town from view. There are shops to the south of bridge 59 and a picnic area below bridge 58. The River Avon is crossed by an aqueduct, and the Rugby Arm branches to the west; there is a boatyard on the arm. A short open stretch and then another deep cutting take the canal to Newbold, where the short tunnel and thickly-wooded cutting lead the canal into open countryside. The iron bridges over the various arms reveal the course of the old canal. The B4112 accompanies it through Newbold.

Harborough Magna
Warwicks. PO, tel, stores. Quiet red-brick village 1 mile to the north of the canal from bridges 43 or 48. The 14thC church has many Victorian additions, including an interesting stained-glass window.

Newbold on Avon
Warwicks. PO, tel, stores, garage, fish & chips, launderette. A pleasant village with an interesting 15thC church and attractive cottages. At the wharf near the tunnel mouth are two pubs right next door to each other: why not try both?

Newbold Tunnel
This 250yd long tunnel was built during the shortening of the Oxford Canal in the 1820s. The old route was at right angles to the new, and the old tunnel mouth can be seen from the south by Newbold church. The new tunnel was cut wide enough to allow for a towpath on both sides, a luxury at that date.

Rugby
Warwicks. EC Wed. MD Mon/Fri/Sat. PO, tel, stores, garage, station, theatre, cinema, leisure centre. A settlement for 2000 years, which has grown in turn as an agricultural centre, market town (since 1255), seat of learning and railway centre. More recently the heavy electrical industry has become established here. St Andrew's parish church dates from the 14thC, but in 1879 Butterfield added a nave and a tower, making it probably the only church in England to have a double peal of bells. Butterfield's work is also much in evidence in Rugby school, which also gave its name to rugby football. A granite plaque commemorating the 'exploit of William Webb Ellis' in 1823 which gave birth to the game can be seen in the grounds. Nearby in St Matthew's Street are the James Gilbert Museum of Rugby Football and the Tourist Information Centre at Rugby Library, where the Exhibition Gallery and Museum have regular displays. There is a pedestrianised shopping centre, a leisure centre and an open market with a town crier. Look out for Miranda's Shop in Chapel Street, reputedly the oldest building in the town. The Monday livestock market is one of the largest in the area. Information boards and town maps will be found near bridges 30, 50 and 66.

Tourist Information Centre Rugby Library, St Matthew's Street, Rugby. (0788 71813).

BOATYARDS

Ⓑ **Willow Wren Hire Cruisers** Rugby Wharf, off Consul Road, Leicester Road, Rugby. (0788 562183). R S W D Pump-out, narrowboat hire, overnight mooring, long-term mooring, wet dock, books and maps. *Closed Sun & Mon.*

PUBS

Old Lion Harborough Magna, on the B4112. Quiet lounge with beamed ceiling and giant handpumps for mature drinkers, separate lounge for the younger set. Ansells real ale, food *lunchtime and evening*, garden, games room.

Boat Newbold Wharf. One long room with cosy alcoves and a fire. Davenports real ale and Westons real cider, food *lunchtime and evening*, garden.

Barley Mow Main Street, Newbold. Canalside pub with two small bars and pleasant garden. M & B real ale and *lunchtime* food.

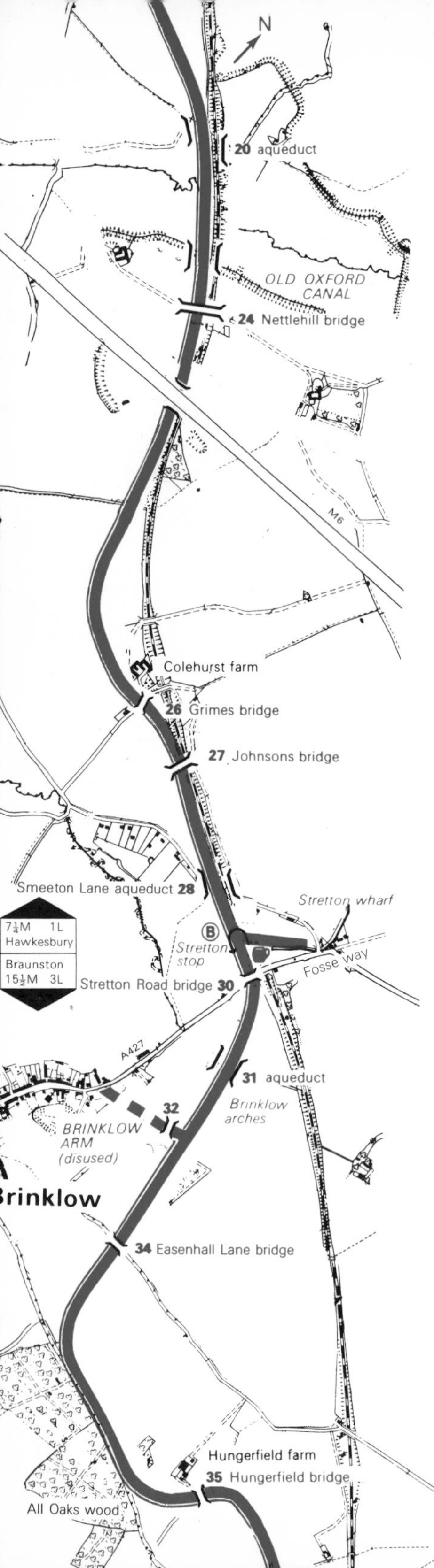

Brinklow

Continuing north west, the canal runs through fine farming land, and passes All Oaks Wood, where good moorings have been provided. By Brinklow the canal passes over an embankment, which was originally an aqueduct; the arches have long been filled in. Brinklow Arm to the west is unnavigable. The long embankment continues through Stretton Stop and past Stretton Arm, used for mooring. Open, rolling fields follow, and then the canal enters a deep cutting, spanned by the new motorway. The M6 cuts through this stretch, and has greatly altered the landscape. The elegant iron bridges that occur periodically mark the course of the old Oxford Canal, prior to the 1829 shortening. The railway follows the canal to the east. The A4114 crosses through Brinklow.

Brinklow
Warwicks. PO, tel, stores, garage. A spacious pre-industrial village built along a wide main street, the A4114. The church is alongside the earthworks that mark the site of the castle built to defend the Fosse Way, and is unusual in having a distinctly sloping floor.

BOATYARDS

Ⓑ **Rose Narrowboats** Brinklow Marina, Stretton Stop, Rugby. (0788 832449). [R][S][W][P][D][E] Pump-out, gas, narrowboat hire, day hire craft, overnight mooring, long-term mooring, slipway, groceries, chandlery, books and maps, boat building and painting, boat sales, engine sales and repairs. Gift shop, art gallery, pottery.

PUBS

Railway Canalside at Stretton Stop. Davenports and Marstons real ale in an open-plan lounge. *Lunchtime* food.

White Lion Broad Street, Brinklow. A local pub where the folk club meets on *Friday*. Plush lounge, old fashioned bar. M & B real ale, snacks, garden, games room.

✕ **Bulls Head** Broad Street, Brinklow. (0788 832355). Whitbread real ale in a large Family Diner establishment. Restaurant meals *lunchtime and evening*.

Raven Broad Street, Brinklow. A good pub at the top of the village, with bar billiards and Ansells and Ind Coope (Burton) real ale. Extensive range of bar meals, *lunchtime and evening*. Garden with livestock.

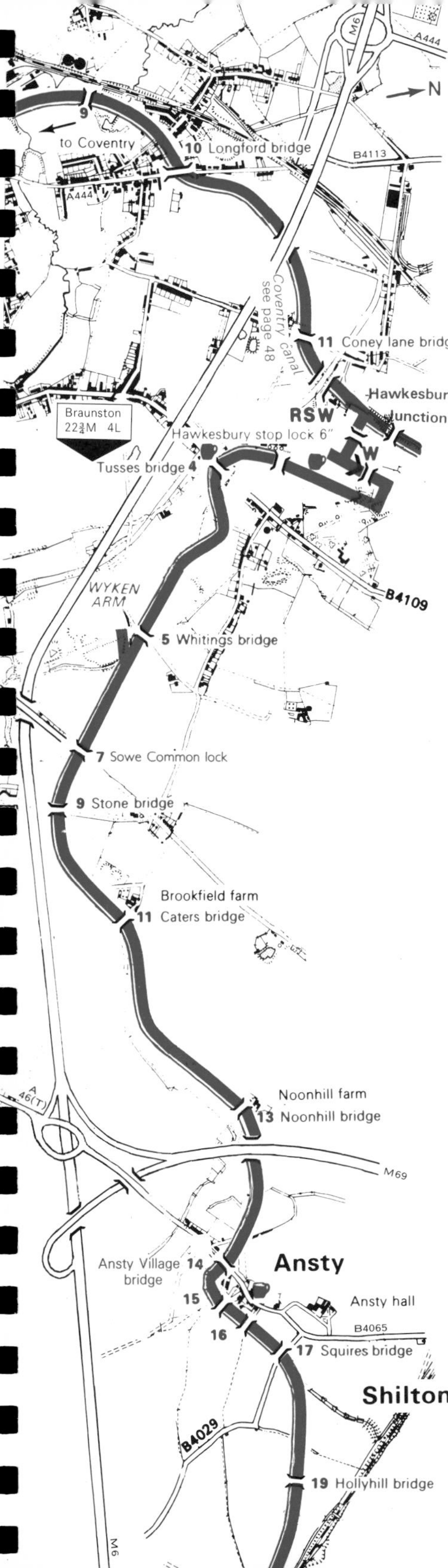

Shilton

Continuing north west, the canal leaves the cutting and crosses a long embankment, which is shared by the railway. The open landscape continues to Ansty, although the motorway is never far away. After the village the first signs of Coventry appear, with views of pylons and housing estates. The new Wyken Colliery Arm leaves to the west: it was built to replace the old one eaten up by the motorway which comes alongside the canal at this point. Sharp bends then lead to the stop lock before Hawkesbury Junction, the end of the Oxford Canal where it joins the Coventry. The last stretch of the Oxford is characterised by the 1820s shortenings, the straight cuttings and embankments obviously date from this period, while the cast-iron bridges mark the old route. The railway turns away before Ansty.

Ansty
Warwicks. PO, tel, stores, garage. Tiny village that grew up along the canal, now disturbed by the A46. To the north are the church and Hall together; the Hall is mostly 18thC. This area has been much altered by motorway construction.
Shilton
Warwicks. PO, tel, stores, garage. ½ mile north of bridge 17. Main road village left bewildered by the railway and the A46.

PUBS

Greyhound Hawkesbury Junction. Canalside. M & B real ale in a listed canalside building. Food.
Elephant & Castle Canalside, by bridge 4. M & B beers, food.
Old Crown Aldermans Green Road. A cosy pub with carved woodwork, beams, brasses, and snug settees, south of Tusses Bridge (4). Ruddles real ale, food *lunchtime and evening*, garden. Children allowed in if you are eating.
Crown Inn Ansty. Tiny snug, low ceilings and real fires – M & B real ale, food *lunchtime and evening.*
Crown Church Road, Shilton. Good traditional locals' pub with bench seats. Ansells real ale.

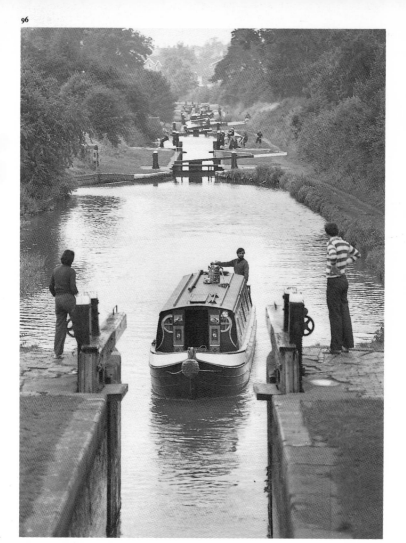

Audlem Locks, Shropshire Union Canal. *Derek Pratt.*

SHROPSHIRE UNION

Maximum dimensions

Autherley to Nantwich, and Middlewich Branch
Length: 72′
Beam: 7′
Headroom: 8′
Nantwich to Ellesmere Port
Length: 72′
Beam: 13′ 3″
Headroom: 8′

Manager:

Autherley Junction to Audlem Bottom Lock: (0785) 74253
Audlem Bottom Lock to Ellesmere Port and the Middlewich Branch: (0606) 40566

Mileage

AUTHERLEY JUNCTION (Staffs & Worcs Canal) to Norbury: 15½
Market Drayton: 27
HURLESTON JUNCTION (Llangollen Canal): 40¾
Barbridge Junction (Middlewich Branch): 42
Chester Junction with Dee Branch: 58
ELLESMERE PORT JUNCTION with Manchester Ship Canal: 66½

Locks: 47

Middlewich Branch
Middlewich (Trent & Mersey Canal) to Barbridge Junction: 10

Locks: 4

The Chester Canal

In 1772 an enabling Act was passed for a canal from the River Dee in Chester to join the Trent & Mersey Canal at Middlewich, with a spur to Nantwich. The building of the Trent & Mersey was the cause of this new venture, for it was seen as a threat to the future of the River Dee Navigation and the port of Chester. The new canal was designed to bolster Chester as an alternative port to Liverpool, and so was planned as a barge canal, with locks 80ft by 14ft 9in. Work started in Chester in the middle of 1772 and progressed very slowly. There were engineering and financial problems, and the main line of the new canal was altered to terminate at a basin and warehouses just outside Nantwich: the proposed line to Middlewich was now to be a branch. The Nantwich–Chester link was completed in 1779, but the spur to Middlewich was not built until 54 years later. When the Nantwich–Chester Canal was finished, arguments with the Dee River Company delayed the building of the river lock. By this time competition with the Trent & Mersey was out of the question. Although regular freight and fast passenger services were run, the canal was wholly uneconomic and in 1787 the company collapsed. In 1790 it was revived and the canal repaired, for the directors saw the publication of the plans of the Ellesmere Canal as their last chance to complete the line to Middlewich.

The Birmingham & Liverpool Junction Canal

The future prosperity of the Ellesmere & Chester was limited by the lack of an outlet to the south, without which its trade could never be more than local. So the company was much cheered by the plans for the Birmingham & Liverpool Junction Canal which received its Act in 1825. The line from Nantwich to Autherley, on the Staffordshire & Worcestershire Canal, would give a direct link between Liverpool and the Midlands, and thus with the canal network as a whole. After serious engineering difficulties the canal was opened in 1835, shortly after the opening of the long-planned branch from the Chester Canal to the Trent & Mersey at Middlewich, providing access to Manchester and the Potteries. Railway competition was close at hand by this date, and so the Birmingham & Liverpool Junction and Ellesmere & Chester companies worked closely together to preserve their profits. Ellesmere Port was greatly enlarged, and by 1840 steam haulage was in use on the Wirral line and on the Mersey itself. In 1845 the two companies merged, and then shortly after were reformed as the Shropshire Union Railways & Canal Company.

The Shropshire Union

The Shropshire Union Railways & Canal Company was formed under the shadow of railway expansion. Its initial plans were to build railways instead of canals, on the principle that it would halve the construction costs to lay a railway along the bed of an existing canal. By 1849 this plan had been abandoned, for the slow development of railways in Wales had shown the company that canals could still be profitable. Throughout the mid 19thC the Shropshire Union network remained profitable, and did not experience the steady decline of other major canal systems. The London & North Western Railway Company was a major shareholder in the Shropshire Union, and they were very happy to let the canals remain as they provided the company with a significant tentacle into Great Western Railway territory. As a result the Shropshire Union was allowed to expand steadily; in 1870 the company owned 213 narrowboats, and in 1889 there were 395. By 1902 this fleet had increased to 450 boats. A few branches were threatened with closure on the grounds of unprofitability, but none were carried out.

The flourishing trade continued until the 1914–18 war, which started a pattern of regular heavy losses from which the company was never able to recover. In 1921 the company gave up canal carrying, and sold most of its fleet of boats to private operators. Locks were closed at weekends, and standards of maintenance began to slip. In 1922 the Shropshire Union Company was bought out by the London & North Western Railway, which then was swallowed in turn by the newly-formed London Midland & Scottish Railway. Despite these changes the network remained open, although trade declined rapidly. Many traders were driven away by the lack of maintenance, which meant that most boats could only operate half empty. In 1936 a breach occurred on the Montgomery Canal 1 mile south of Frankton Junction; the company set out to repair the damage and then changed their minds. (The Weston line had been similarly abandoned after a breach in 1917.) With trade at a standstill there were no complaints, and in 1944 an Act was passed making closure official. This Act also officially abandoned 175 miles of the old Shropshire Union network. Out of this mass closure only the main line and the Middlewich Branch remained, although the Llangollen Branch (see page 77) luckily also escaped closure, being originally retained as a water supply channel. The Montgomery Canal also survives, partially restored.

The Shropshire Union Canal. *Derek Pratt.*

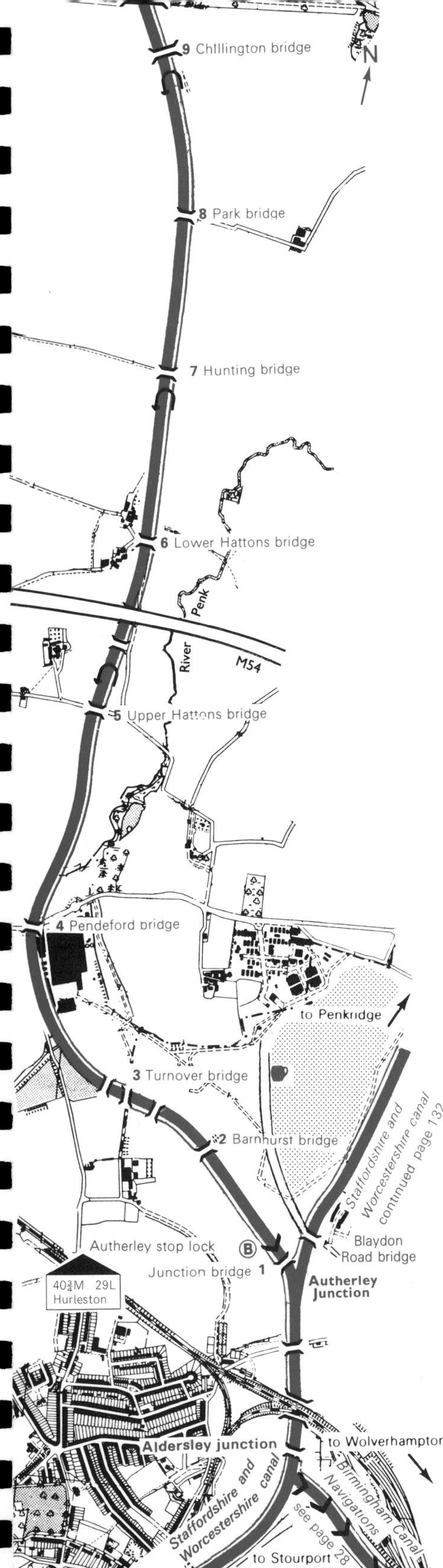

Autherley Junction

The Shropshire Union Canal leaves the Staffordshire & Worcester Canal at Autherley Junction, and runs straight along the side of the former Wolverhampton Aerodrome at Pendeford, now covered with houses. Passing the Wolverhampton Boat Club (visiting boaters welcome), the canal soon enters a short cutting, which is through rock, and narrow in places. Emerging briefly into the green and quiet countryside that is found along the whole length of this navigation, the canal plunges into a deep, long cutting that is typical of this particular stretch. There are picnic sites by bridges 2 and 3.

Navigational note
The canal is very narrow south of bridges 5 and 6, and between bridges 8 and 9.

Autherley Junction
An important and busy canal junction, where in 1830 Thomas Telford brought his Birmingham & Liverpool Junction Canal (now part of the Shropshire Union system) to join the much older Staffordshire & Worcestershire Canal (built by James Brindley and opened in 1772). There is a former canal toll office here, also a boatyard and a boatclub. The stop lock has a fall of only about 6in: it was insisted upon by the Staffs & Worcs Company to prevent the newer canal 'stealing' water from them. Autherley Junction is sometimes confused with Aldersley Junction, ½ mile to the south, where the Birmingham Canal Navigations join the Staffs & Worcs Canal from the east after falling through the Wolverhampton flight of 21 locks.

BOATYARDS

Ⓑ **Water Travel** Autherley Junction, Oxley Moor Road, Wolverhampton. (0902 782371). R S W D E Pump-out, gas, narrowboat hire, overnight mooring, long-term mooring, winter storage, slipway, chandlery, provisions, books and maps, boat building, boat sales, engine repairs, licensed club house, telephone, toilet.

PUBS

Pendulum North west of Blaydon Road Bridge. Food *lunchtime and evening*. Massive Safeway supermarket next door.

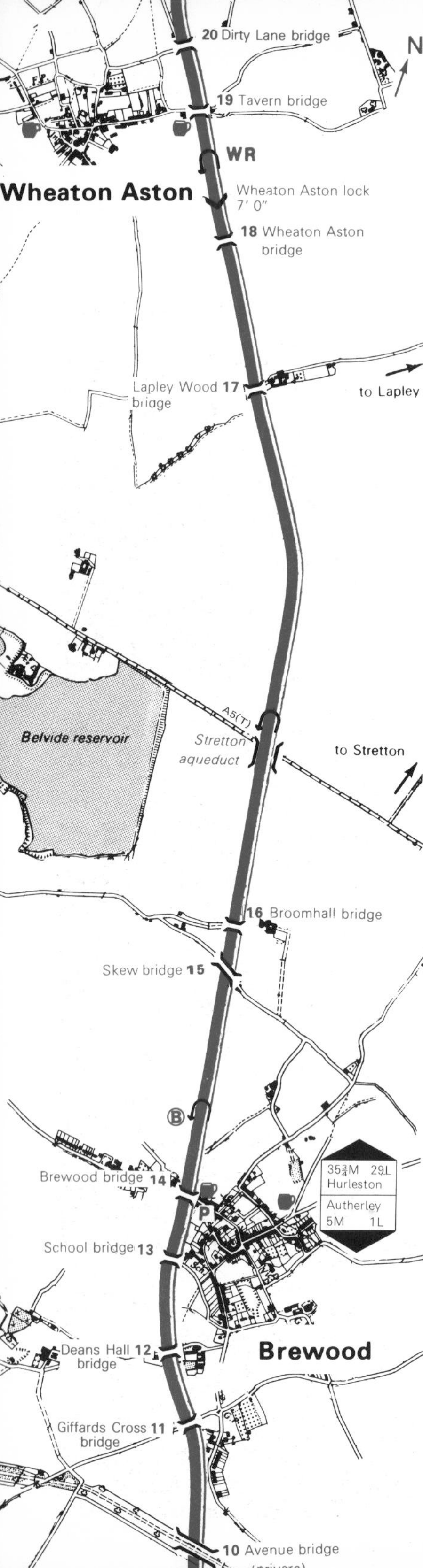

Brewood

Leaving the balustraded Avenue Bridge (10), which leads westward to Chillington Hall, the canal curves in a bold cutting past the village of Brewood (moorings by bridge 14) and its attractive wharf – and moves north west along a very straight embankment. The head bank of the big Belvide reservoir can be seen on the west side; its feeder stream enters the canal just south of Stretton Aqueduct. This solid but elegant cast-iron structure carries the canal over the A5. Crossing the aqueduct by boat tends to give the canal traveller an air of great superiority over the teeming motorists below. After another long wooded cutting the canal reaches Wheaton Aston Lock. This lock marks the end of the long 'pound' from Autherley and the beginning of the 17-mile level that lasts almost to Market Drayton. Reasonably priced diesel can be obtained by bridge 19.

Wheaton Aston
Staffs. PO, tel, stores, garage. Overrun by new housing. The village green around the church (rebuilt in 1857) is a memento of a more pleasant past. The garage beside the canal can repair boat engines and also sells chandlery; while at the lock cottage local hand-painted canal ware may be bought.
Lapley
Staffs. ¾ mile north east of bridge 17. The central tower of the church dominates the village. It is an interesting building with fine Norman windows, an old Dutch font and traces of medieval paintings on the nave wall. The church as we see it now was completed in the 15thC.
Stretton
Staffs. 1 mile north east of Stretton Aqueduct off the A5. The church was rebuilt in the 19thC but retains its original chancel and fragments of medieval glass in the east window.
Stretton Hall Built in 1620 to designs by Inigo Jones. Most interesting features are the vast fireplace with steps up to it for chimney sweep boys, and the remarkable staircase suspended by chains from the roof. The house is private.
Belvide Reservoir A large nature reserve open to naturalists. The Royal Society for the Protection of Birds is developing the reserve to include displays and hides, enabling enthusiasts to have a greater opportunity to observe the many species of birds. There is only private club fishing and no sailing on the reservoir, so as to preserve the bird sanctuary.
Brewood
Staffs. EC Wed. PO, tel, stores, bank, garage. The name (pronounced 'Brood') derives from Celtic 'Bre' meaning 'hill', thus giving 'wood on the hill'. It originally consisted of a Roman fort on Beacon Hill to defend Watling Street but is now a beautiful, quiet village with some extremely attractive Georgian houses in groups. The village church is a tall, elegant building which has been greatly restored but still contains a 16thC font and several 16thC effigies and 17thC monuments commemorating the Giffard family of Chillington Hall.
Chillington Hall 1½ miles west of the canal, south west of Brewood, this has been the home of the Giffard family since the 18thC. The existing hall was built in the 18thC, and the wooded park in which it stands was designed by 'Capability Brown'. The hall is approached by an avenue of trees, at the eastern end of which is Giffard's Cross. This is said to mark the spot where Sir John Giffard in 1513 shot a wild panther with his crossbow, thus saving the lives of a woman and her child. The panther, a gift from a friendly Oriental, had escaped from its cage. *Open Thur afternoons, May–Aug.*

BOATYARDS

Ⓑ **Countrywide Cruisers** The Wharf, Brewood. (0902 850166). Just north of bridge 14. R S W D Pump-out, narrowboat hire, gas, long-term mooring, winter storage, slipway, books and maps, boat building, engine repairs, toilet, gifts.

PUBS

Hartley Arms Canalside at Tavern Bridge, Wheaton Aston. Modern pub dispensing Banks' real ale. Food *lunchtime and evening*. Garden.

Coach & Horses Wheaton Aston. An old coaching inn in the village. Banks' real ale and snacks.

Three Stirrups Brewood. Food, garden, children's room.

Bridge Inn By bridge 14, Brewood. Basic, busy and friendly canalside pub offering Ansells real ale and *lunchtime* snacks. Garden.

Lion Hotel Stafford Street, Brewood. Three minutes' walk from bridge 14. Large and cheerful lounge where you can enjoy Bass and M & B Springfield real ale. Bar food *lunchtime and evening*, children allowed in *up to 20.00* if taking a meal.

Swan Hotel Market Square, Brewood. Three minutes' walk from bridge 14 to this smart old pub with open fires. Bass real ale and *lunchtime* bar food.

The elegant balustraded Avenue Bridge near Brewood. Shropshire Union Canal. *Derek Pratt*.

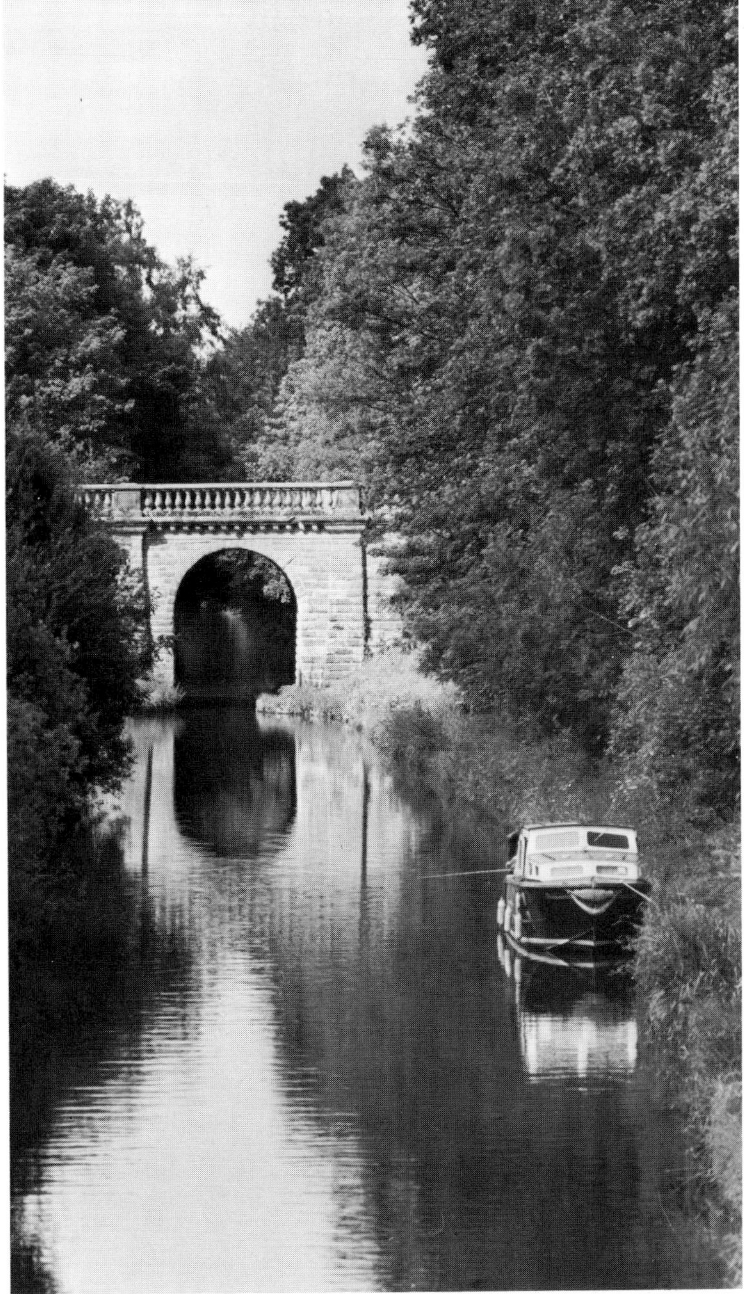

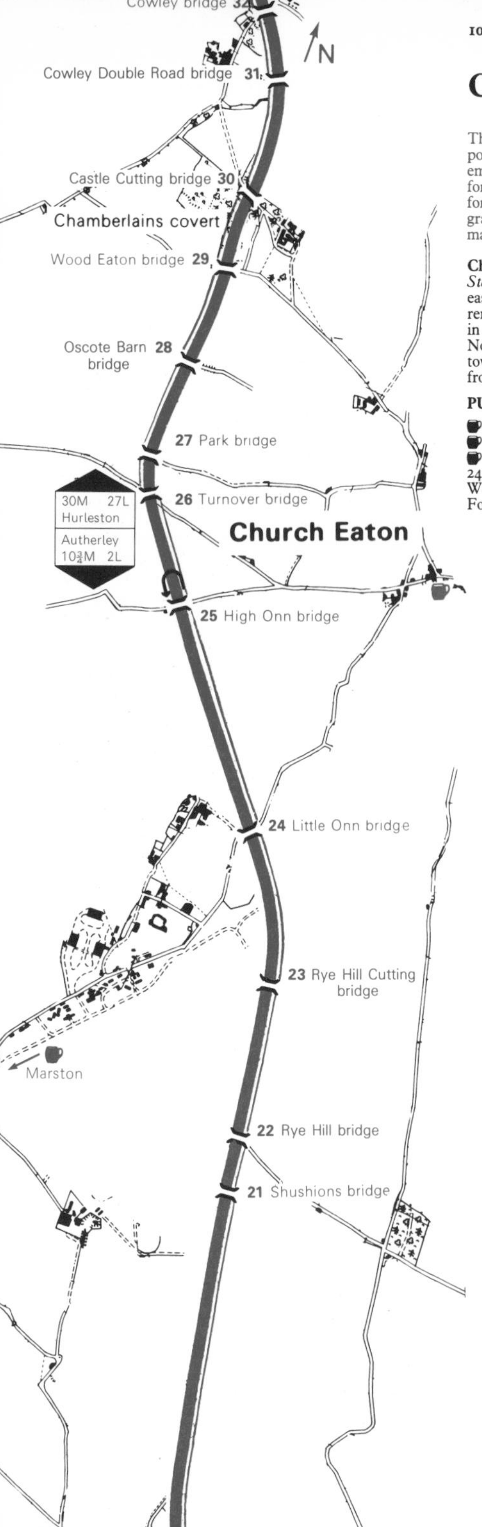

Church Eaton

The canal now proceeds along the very long pound, alternately in cuttings and on embankments. Both offer interest; the cuttings for their rich vegetation, and the embankments for the excellent views over quiet, unspoilt grazing land. The garage at Wheaton Aston has marine diesel and can also supply gas.

Church Eaton
Staffs. EC Wed. PO, tel, stores. 1 mile north east of bridge 25. Parts of the old village remain, especially at the end of the village street in the vicinity of the fine church: St Editha's, a Norman structure with the spire added to the tower in the 15thC. The east window dates from about 1400 and almost fills the wall.

PUBS

Royal Oak Church Eaton.
Swan Church Eaton.
Fox Marston. 1 mile south west of bridge 24. Country pub with a wide range of real ale – Woods, Lloyds, Wadworths and Ruddles. Food *lunchtime and evening (not Sun)*, garden.

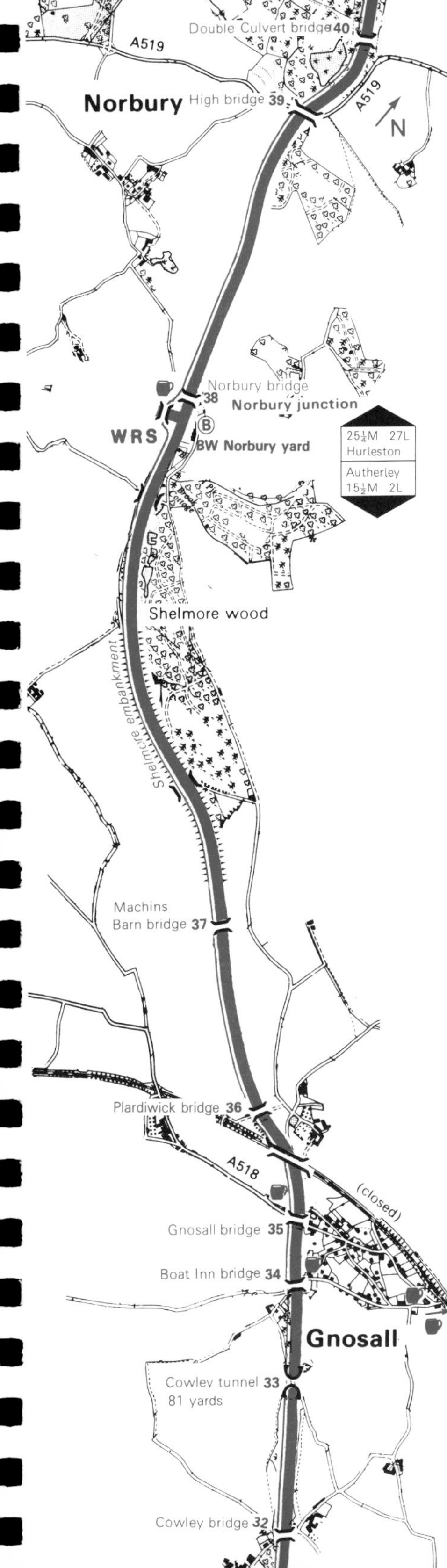

Norbury Junction

The canal now enters the very deep and almost vertical cutting that terminates in Cowley Tunnel. North of the tunnel is Gnosall where there are moorings between bridge 35 and the tunnel; shortly after this, the canal moves round the side of Shelmore Wood and crosses the mighty Shelmore Embankment before reaching Norbury Junction, where the Newport Branch used to lock down from the main line. North of here is the long Grub Street cutting which features the well-known High Bridge with a masonry strut, carrying a short telegraph pole, built across its tall arch.

Norbury Junction
This was once the outlet for the Shrewsbury, Newport and Trench branches on to the rest of the Shropshire Union Canal system. There was a long flight of locks from the junction down to Newport, but these are now closed.
Shelmore Embankment
The construction of this great embankment, 1 mile long, just south of Norbury Junction, was the source of endless grief and expense to the Birmingham & Liverpool Junction Canal Company in general and to Thomas Telford, their engineer, in particular. It was an enormous task anyway to shift the millions of cubic feet of earth to build the bank; but while the contractors struggled to complete it, the bank slipped and collapsed time and again. By early 1834, Shelmore Embankment was the only unfinished section of the whole canal. It was not until 1835, after 5½ years' solid work on it and well after Telford's death, that the embankment was completed by William Cubitt and the B&LJ Canal was opened as a through route. There are flood gates at each end, to close off the channel in case of a breach. These were closed each night during World War II as a precaution against bombing.
Gnosall
Staffs. PO, tel, garage, stores, east of bridge 35. The main feature of interest in the village is the church of St Laurence, a mile east of the canal. It is a 15thC building with original Norman tower arches. The east window has fine decorated tracery framing modern stained glass.
Cowley Tunnel
This short tunnel was originally intended to be much longer – 700yds – but most of it was opened out at an early stage in construction (during the early 1830s) because of dangerous faults in the rock, and now only 81yds remain. The tunnel is unlined, and to the south of it a very steep narrow cutting through solid rock stretches a considerable distance – an awe-inspiring sight.

BOATYARDS

BW Norbury Yard Norbury Junction, Woodseaves. (078 574 253). R S W *48hr* mooring.
Ⓑ **Shropshire Union Cruisers (Dartline)** Norbury Junction, Woodseaves. (078 574 292). R W D Pump-out, gas, narrowboat hire, day hire craft, overnight mooring, long-term mooring, slipway, dry dock, wet dock, groceries, chandlery, books and maps, boat and engine repairs, toilets. Café *open summer weekends.*

BOAT TRIPS

Summer cream tea cruises on *Hanley* for up to 46 people. Ring (078 574) 292.

PUBS

Junction Inn Canalside, at Norbury Junction. Superbly situated canal pub. The clock on the bar is from a U-boat. Banks' and McEwans real ale, food *lunchtime and evening.* Garden, children's room.
Navigation Canalside, at bridge 35.
Royal Oak Gnosall, in the village by the railway bridge. Basic bar, comfortable lounge, where you can enjoy Ansells and Ind Coope (Burton) real ale. Snacks, garden.
Boat Boat Inn Bridge. Comfortable canalside pub with bar billiards, Marstons real ale and food *lunchtime and evening.* Garden.
Horns Gnosall. In the village, beyond the railway bridge. M & B and Bass real ale, *lunchtime* food.

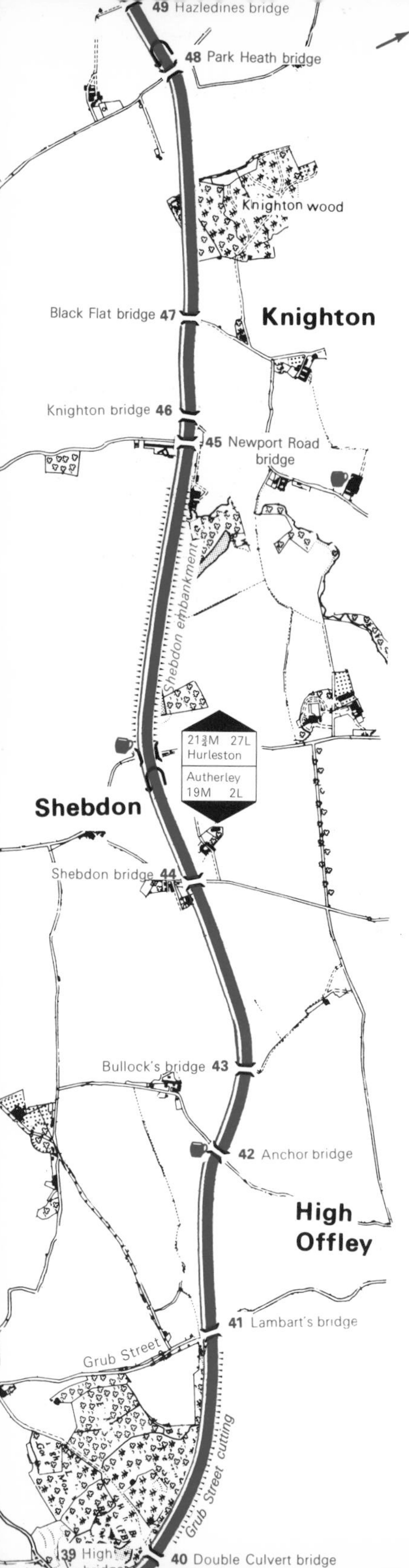

Shebdon

The canal moves out of Grub Street cutting through the unusual double-arched bridge, containing a small telegraph pole and, passing the village of High Offley on a hill to the north, continues in a north-westerly direction through the quiet open farmland that always accompanies this canal. Along this stretch are two canalside pubs – both amaze the traveller by their very survival, situated as they are on quiet roads and an even quieter canal. The great Shebdon Embankment is heralded by an aqueduct; at the far end is a large ex-chocolate factory (now producing only dried milk), whose goods used to be carried to and from Bournville (on the Worcester & Birmingham Canal) by canal boat. Knighton post office, stores and telephone are by bridge 45.

High Offley
Staffs. Tel. Hill-top farming village, scattered round a large 15thC church. Good views in all directions.

PUBS

Haberdashers Arms Knighton, ½ mile north east of bridge 45. A tiny Banks' real ale pub, headquarters of the local Potato Club. Garden.

Wharf Inn Canalside, below Shebdon Embankment. Friendly pub offering Burtonwood real ale and good value meals, *lunchtime and evening*. Garden. Also sells groceries and serves breakfast.

Anchor Canalside, at Anchor Bridge (42). An unspoilt hostelry with an open fire, where you can enjoy Ansells, Marstons and Wadworths real ales. Snacks, garden. *Open lunchtime and evening Mar–Oct. Closed lunchtime in winter.*

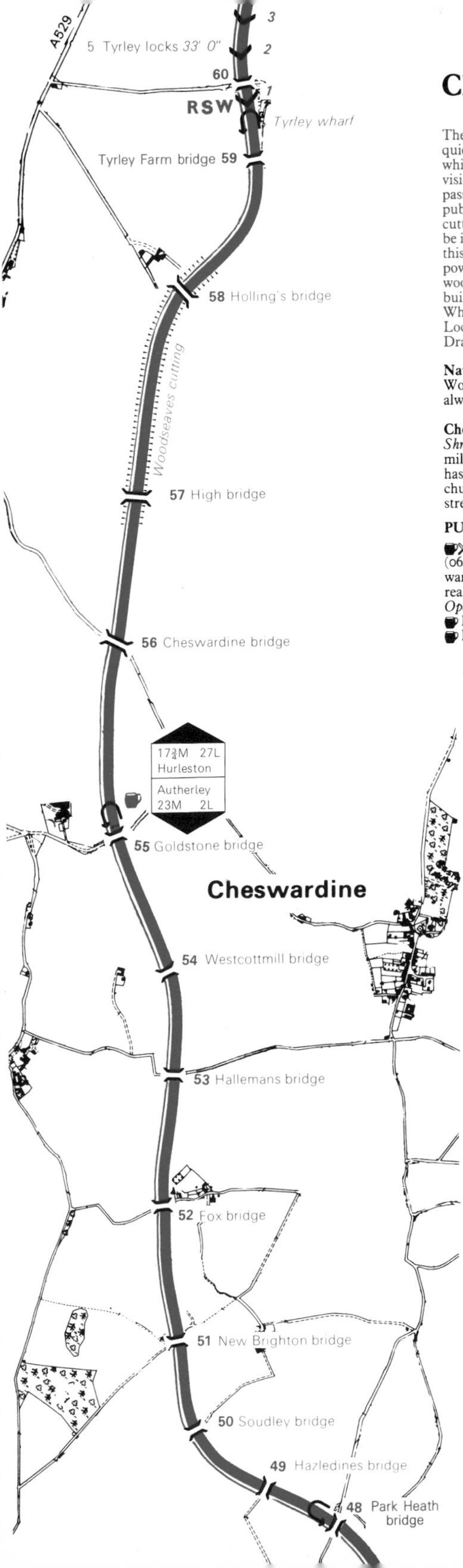

Cheswardine

The canal continues north west through the quiet, empty landscape. Hills rise to the right, while the massive bulk of the Wrekin is clearly visible to the south west, 15 miles away. After passing Goldstone Wharf, with its thriving pub, the canal plunges into the very deep rock cutting near Woodseaves. One can hardly fail to be impressed by the magnitude of a work like this, cut as it was entirely by men without powered machines. At the north end of this wooded cutting is the delightful group of buildings (dated 1840) comprising Tyrley Wharf. Good moorings here. The five Tyrley Locks now begin the fall towards Market Drayton.

Navigational note
Woodseaves cutting is very narrow; there is not always room to pass another craft.

Cheswardine
Shropshire. PO, tel, stores, garage. Situated 1 mile up a long hill east of bridge 55, the village has a traditional, well-knit feeling about it. The church is sited on a rise overlooking the village street. It contains some good 19thC glass.

PUBS

Wharf Tavern Canalside, at bridge 55. (063 086 226). Once a coal wharf and warehouse, now a popular canal venue. Ansells real ale, bar meals and Grill Room. Garden. *Opens 12.00.*
Fox & Hounds Cheswardine.
Red Lion Cheswardine.

A529
5 Tyrley locks 33' 0"
3
2
1
60
RSW
Tyrley wharf
Tyrley Farm bridge 59
58 Holling's bridge
Woodseaves cutting
57 High bridge
56 Cheswardine bridge
17¾M 27L
Hurleston
Autherley
23M 2L
55 Goldstone bridge
Cheswardine
54 Westcottmill bridge
53 Hallemans bridge
52 Fox bridge
51 New Brighton bridge
50 Soudley bridge
49 Hazledines bridge
48 Park Heath bridge

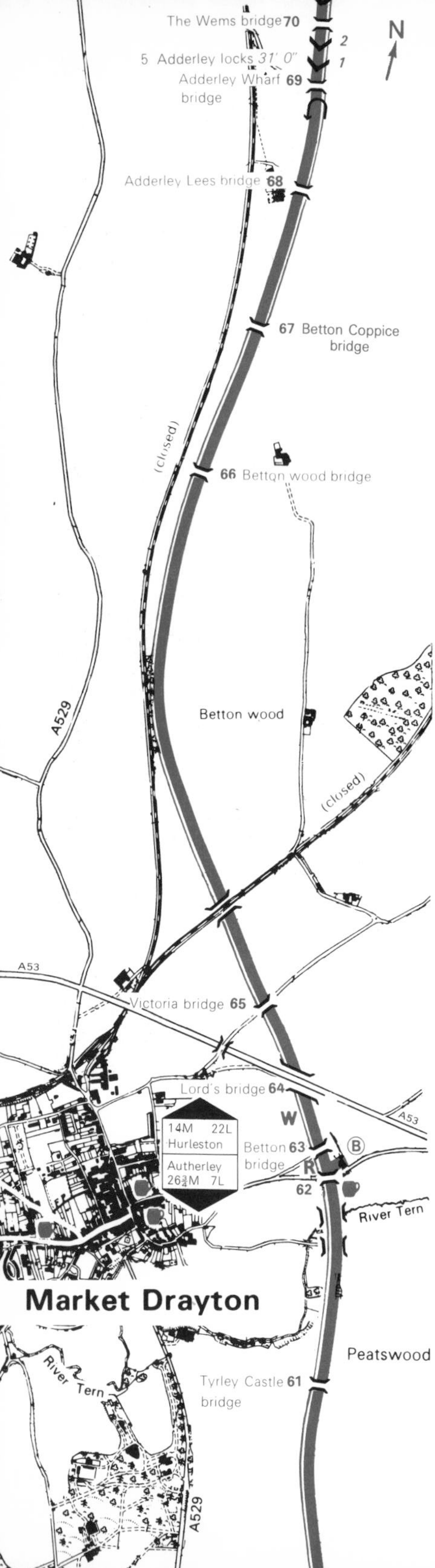

Market Drayton

The canal continues to fall through Tyrley Locks, which in places are almost roofed over by trees, then crosses a minor road and the River Tern via aqueducts, and arrives at Market Drayton. There are two large boatyards here, so there are always many boats about and great care is needed in navigation. North of Market Drayton the canal regains its peaceful isolation, passing through a pleasant wooded cutting (which is alleged by the superstitious to shelter a vociferous ghost) before arriving at the five Adderley Locks, winners in 1980 of the 'best kept lock' competition. Coal and logs are available from Ortons, Victoria Wharf, Market Drayton. (0630 2472).

Market Drayton
Shropshire. EC Thur. MD Wed. PO, tel, stores, garage, banks, launderette. On the west bank of the canal, it is the market centre for the surrounding district, and is a very attractive town with some splendid old buildings. It was destroyed by fire in 1651, but fortunately picturesque black-and-white timberframing was again used for the rebuilding, the best of which is the National Westminster Bank in the market square and the adjacent Sandbrook Vaults (1653) in Shropshire Street. The parish church of St Mary is large and well-sited overlooking the Tern valley and dates from the 12thC. The Corbet Arms Hotel is a fine centre-piece to the main square. The town now claims to be the home of gingerbread – there are three bakeries producing their own and the original Billingtons which was sold at a weekly market in the Buttercross.

BOATYARDS

Ⓑ **Holidays Afloat** The Boatyard, Market Drayton. (0630 652641). Gas, narrowboat hire, long-term mooring, winter storage, slipway, chandlery, boat building, engine repairs, fishing tackle. *Closed Sun.*

BOAT TRIPS

Adventures Afloat provide an upmarket 'camping boat' for day or week-long cruises. Ring (0630) 652641.

PUBS AND RESTAURANTS

Talbot Canalside at bridge 62.
Coach & Horses Shropshire Street, Market Drayton. A small 18thC local – note the chimney breast in the lounge. Open fire, Marstons real ale, garden.
✕ **Corbet Arms Hotel** High Street, Market Drayton. (0630 2037). A Georgian coaching inn with a very forward lady ghost in room 7. M & B Springfield real ale, bar meals, restaurant (*L & D*), snacks.
Crown Queen Street, Market Drayton. Dating from 1651, this pub has four small rooms, one with a kitchen range. Marstons real ale, *lunchtime* food, snacks.
Many other good real ale pubs in Market Drayton.

Tyrley Locks, Shropshire Union Canal. *Derek Pratt.*

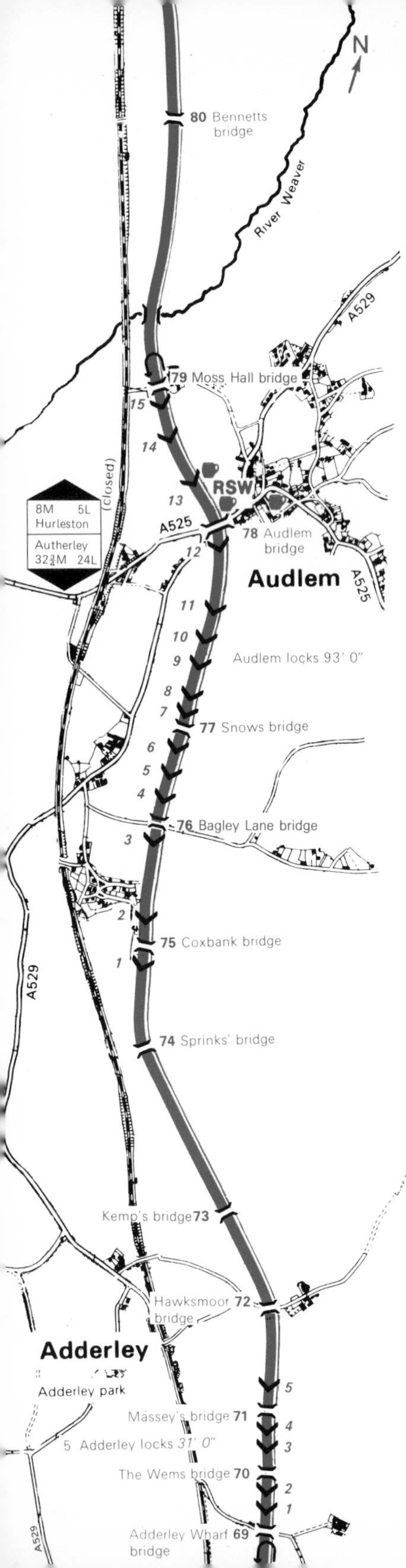

Audlem

Adderley Locks, the middle of the three main groups of locks between Autherley and Nantwich, are shortly followed by the 15 locks in the Audlem flight, lowering the canal by over 90ft to the dairylands of southern Cheshire. The locks are close together, well maintained, and provide over two hours' energetic navigating. There is an attractive cottage at the top lock, the wharf has a craft shop, and there are two pubs near bridge 78, along with a general store. The bottom of the locks is marked by a well restored canal stable and just to the north a minor aqueduct over the tiny River Weaver.

Audlem
Ches. PO, tel, stores, garage, bank. Some pleasant houses are grouped around the church in this expanding and well-kept canalside village. The massive shape of the 15thC church seems to spill down from its hillock in battlemented layers. The colonnaded structure at its foot was once a butter market. The mellow old buildings on the canal wharf have been well renovated and there are good moorings by the old wharf crane. Wholefoods available by Audlem Bridge.

Adderley
Shropshire. PO, tel, stores, garage. A rather under-populated village, bisected by the now closed railway and flanked by the large Shavington and Adderley Parks. The unusual church, set by itself, was rebuilt of red sandstone in 1801 in neo-classical style. In 1958 a large portion of the church was closed to reduce maintenance costs, including the tower dated 1712, the transepts and the chancel. As a result the much smaller interior is better suited to contemporary needs and feels more like a large formal drawing room than a church.

Shavington Hall Adderley. An impressive red-brick house dating from 1685 with 19thC additions and alterations. A fine park surrounds the house, which is not open to the public.

PUBS

Bridge Canalside at Audlem Bridge. A friendly traditional pub with a children's room. Enjoy a pint of Marstons real ale here, and food *lunchtime and evening*. Garden. Gas is available from Moseleys hardware shop, which backs onto the canal between here and the craft shop.

Shroppie Fly The Wharf, Audlem. This converted warehouse serves M & B Springfield real ale from a bar built like a narrowboat, complete with cratch. Food *lunchtime and evening*, garden.

Lord Combermere The Square, Audlem. Handy for those who fancy a pint of McEwans real ale. Garden, children's room.

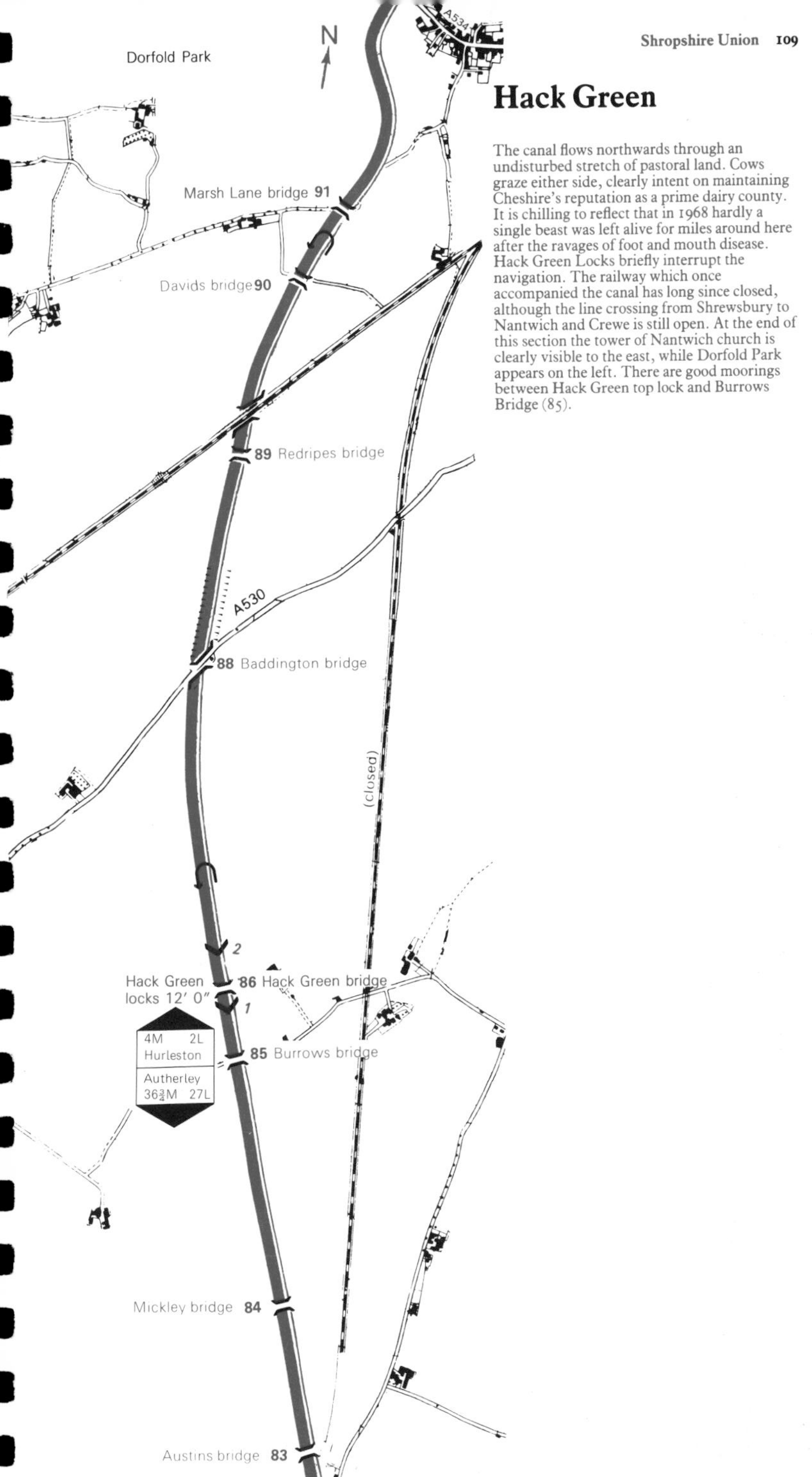

Hack Green

The canal flows northwards through an undisturbed stretch of pastoral land. Cows graze either side, clearly intent on maintaining Cheshire's reputation as a prime dairy county. It is chilling to reflect that in 1968 hardly a single beast was left alive for miles around here after the ravages of foot and mouth disease. Hack Green Locks briefly interrupt the navigation. The railway which once accompanied the canal has long since closed, although the line crossing from Shrewsbury to Nantwich and Crewe is still open. At the end of this section the tower of Nantwich church is clearly visible to the east, while Dorfold Park appears on the left. There are good moorings between Hack Green top lock and Burrows Bridge (85).

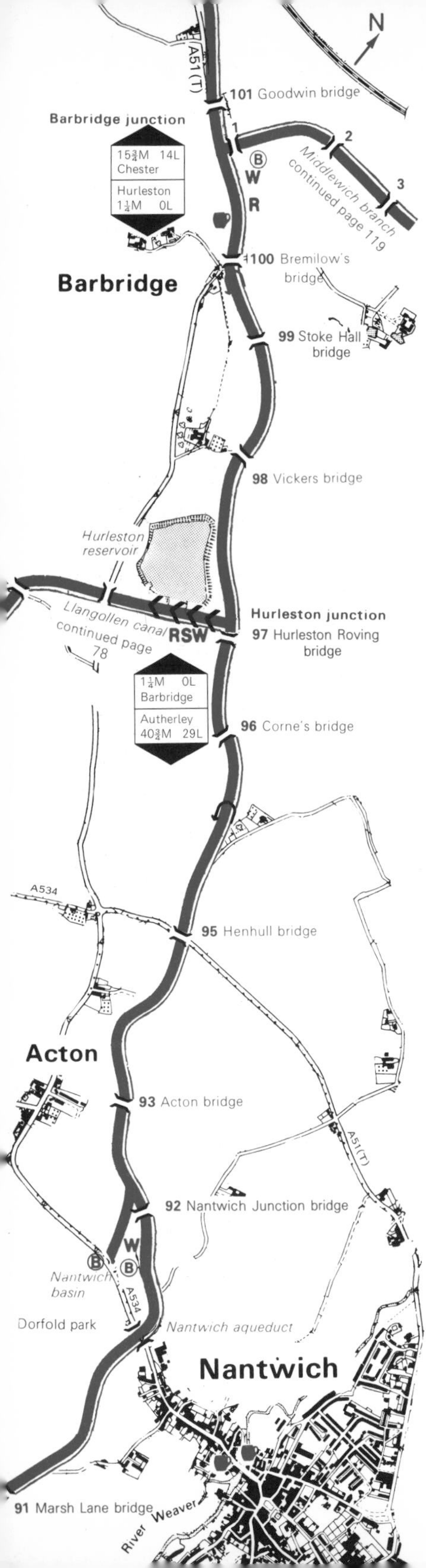

Nantwich

Swinging round Dorfold Park on a long embankment, the canal crosses the Nantwich–Chester road on a fine cast-iron aqueduct and soon reaches an oblique canal junction at Nantwich Basin: this is where Telford's narrow Birmingham & Liverpool Junction Canal joins the older Chester Canal. The stop-gates to be seen at each end of the embankment are a precaution against flooding in the event of a breach or damage to the aqueduct. The wide bridgehole at the next and all subsequent bridges reveals the difference in gauge of the two canals. The Chester Canal's width is complemented by its sweeping course, as it curves gracefully round the hillside to Hurleston Junction. Here the Llangollen Canal branches off up four narrow locks on its way to North Wales (see page 78). Meanwhile the main line of the Shropshire Union soon reaches Barbridge (*PO, tel, stores, garage*) where there is a junction with the Middlewich Branch. This branch (see page 119) connects the Shropshire Union system to the Trent & Mersey Canal.

Navigational note
If you are heading southwards and wish to take on water at bridge 92, slow down well in advance. The water point is immediately south of the bridge.

Acton
Ches. PO, tel, stores. A small village with a large church of red stone and an old pub with a mounting block outside.
Dorfold Hall ¼ mile south west of Nantwich Basin. Built by Ralph Wilbraham in 1616, this beautiful Jacobean house is approached along an avenue of trees. The panelled rooms contain fine furnishings and family portraits. *Open Mon afternoons May–Sep.*
Nantwich Basin
A busy, canal basin, once the terminus of the isolated Chester Canal from Nantwich to Ellesmere Port. When the B & LJ Canal was first authorised in 1826, Telford intended to bring it from Hack Green across Dorfold Park and straight into Nantwich Basin; but the owner of the park refused to allow it and forced the company to build the long embankment right round the park and the iron aqueduct over the main road. This proved a difficult and costly diversion since, as at Shelmore, the embankment repeatedly collapsed. Today the old canalside cheese warehouses have been skilfully restored by BW and there are two boatyards and a boat club based here.
Nantwich
Ches. EC Wed. MD Thur, Sat. All services.
A very fine old town, prosperous since Roman times because of its salt springs, which made it the country's main salt-mining centre until the 19thC. The town was devastated by fire in 1583 but rebuilt in fine Tudor style. Many of the half-timbered houses still remain: two especially interesting buildings on the road into town from the basin are the Cheshire Cat Inn and a tiny cottage built in 1502 and restored in 1971. On London Road are the Tollemache Almshouses built in 1638 by Sir Edmund Wright, who became Lord Mayor of London in 1641.
Church of St Mary Church Lane. Focal point of the town centre, it is a large and magnificent red sandstone church which stands behind its former graveyard, now an open green. It dates from the 14thC though it was greatly restored in 1885. It has an unusual octagonal tower and the vaulted chancel contains 20 ornate 14thC choir stalls with canopies.

BOATYARDS

Ⓑ **Barbridge Marina** Wardle, Nantwich. (027 073 682). R S W Gas, overnight mooring, long-term mooring, winter storage, slipway, chandlery, books and maps, boat building, boat and engine sales, engine repairs, toilet.

Breakdown call out – ring Mick Sivewright on 027 073 621. *Closed Tue & Wed in winter.*
Ⓑ **British Waterways Hire Cruiser Base** Basin End, Nantwich. (0270 625122). R S W D Pump-out, gas, narrowboat hire, overnight mooring (*not weekends*), dry dock, chandlery, books and maps, toilet, servicing and repairs, engine repairs, day boat hire, off licence.
Ⓑ **Simolda** Basin End, Nantwich. (0270 624075). On the canal, between bridge 92 and the aqueduct. W (close by) Pump-out, narrowboat hire, boat building, boat sales, gantry.

PUBS AND RESTAURANTS

Barbridge Inn Chester Road, Barbridge. A busy, attractive countryside pub, offering Boddingtons real ale. Children's room, garden. Meals *lunchtime and evening*.
Oddfellows Arms Welsh Row, Nantwich. A pub with many nooks and crannies. Tetley's real ale, meals *lunchtime and evening*, garden.
Wilbraham Arms Welsh Row, Nantwich. Comfortable pub with an elegant frontage. John Smith real ale, food *lunchtime and evening*, children's room.
Churche's Mansion 150 Hospital Street, Nantwich. (0270 625933). A fine Elizabethan merchant's house, built in 1577 with an oak-panelled interior. The fixed price lunch is remarkably good value, washed down with Hyde's real ale or real lemonade. *L & D.*

Shropshire Union Canal at Beeston. *Derek Pratt.*

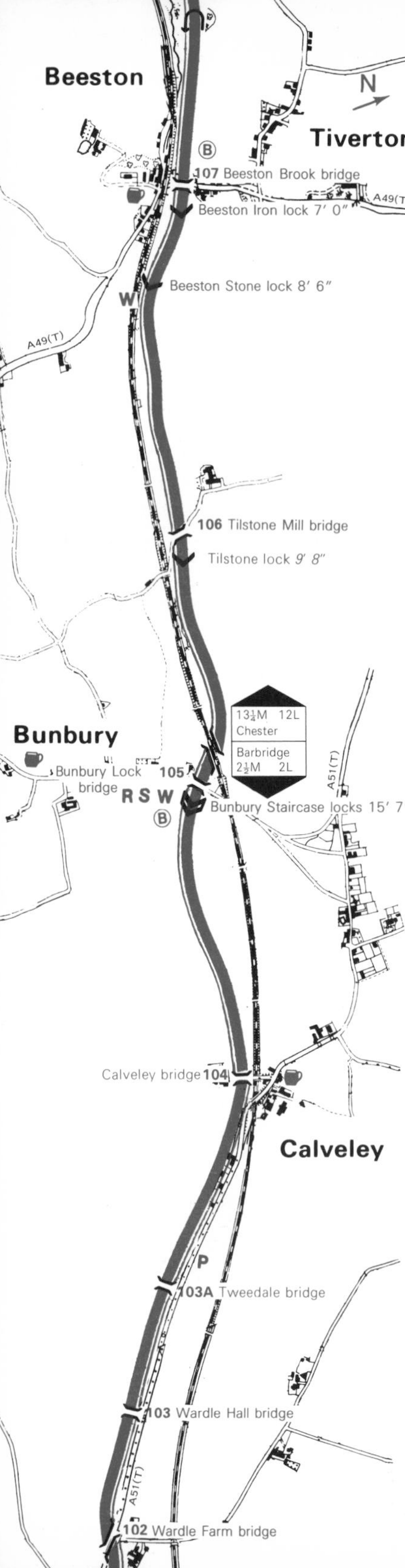

Bunbury

The canal moves almost westwards now alongside a busy main road, passing an enormous radar scanner. At Calveley, large modern cheese warehouses remind the traveller that Cheshire cheese is not merely local produce but a major export. Here the towpath changes sides and the Crewe–Holyhead railway joins the canal. At Bunbury Wharf two staircase locks require thought before action: they are also 14ft wide, like all subsequent locks between here and Chester. There is a fine range of stables beside Bunbury Locks, now used as a boatyard, and a former warehouse beside the bridge which still displays the Shropshire Union Railways & Canal Company's name on its gable wall. There are good moorings, with [W], between bridge 105 and the railway. Beyond the wharf, wooded hills crowd in on the canal, which flows like a river through a narrow valley. There are occasional views to the west of the ruined Beeston Castle on its isolated hill. An old water mill beside the very pretty Tilstone Lock is now used as an outdoor activities base by the local Scout group. At Beeston two contrasting lock-chambers are encountered: one is made of stone, the other of cast-iron flanged plates to overcome running sand below it. The water point at the stone lock is in the lockside lobby. There were once similar lobbies at all locks on the SU main line: only three now survive. Up the hill to the north of the two locks is Tiverton. (*PO, tel, stores, garage.*) There is a convenient café to the south of bridge 107, *open seven days a week (also groceries)* and by the Iron Lock a shop sells crafts and jams.

Bunbury
Ches. EC Wed, Sat. PO, tel, stores, garage, bank. A mile south west of Bunbury Locks, the village is bigger than it looks at first, being virtually split into three sections. The attractive part is nearest, around the church. This is an outstanding building: supremely light, airy and spacious, it stands as a fine monument to workmanship of the 14th and 15thC, and represents a powerful contrast to the unimaginative architecture that characterises so many modern buildings. The ornamental tomb in the sanctuary contains the body of Sir George Beeston: he is said to have commanded one of the English ships against the Spanish Armada, at the remarkable age of 88.

Calveley
Ches. Tel, stores, garage. This rather insignificant village has been practically overwhelmed by the canal, road and railway that carve their respective ways through it. Old wharf buildings now house a canal shop.

BOATYARDS

Ⓑ **Chas Hardern** Beeston Castle Wharf (close to bridge 107), nr Tarporley. (0829 732595). [R][S][W][D] Pump-out, gas, narrowboat hire, overnight mooring, crane, chandlery, books and maps, boat and engine repairs, gifts.

Ⓑ **Dartline Cruisers** The Canal Wharf, Bunbury. (0829 260638). [R][S][W][D] Pump-out, gas, narrowboat hire, day hire craft, overnight mooring, long-term mooring, chandlery, provisions, books and maps, boat building, boat and engine sales and repairs, toilet.

PUBS AND RESTAURANTS

Wild Boar Motor Lodge Inn Beeston. (0884 260309). Restaurant in a large Tudor building.

Beeston Castle Hotel. Beeston. (0884 260234). Restaurant. *Closed Tue.*

Nags Head Bunbury.

Dysart Arms Bunbury, by the church.

Tollemache Arms ½ mile north east of Bunbury Wharf. (0829 260289). Food.

Davenport Arms Calveley, near the wharf. (0829 260430). Greenalls real ale in a smart, friendly pub five minutes from the canal. Home-made bar food *lunchtime and evening*, restaurant meals (*L & D*) and garden.

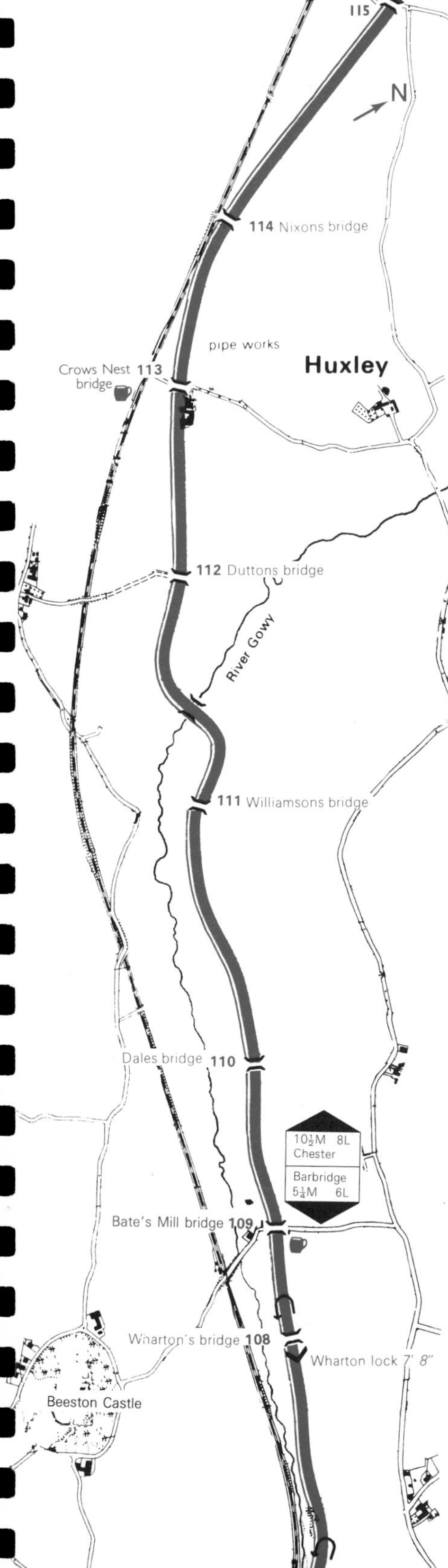

Bate's Mill

Leaving Beeston, the canal moves out of the narrow valley into more open countryside. From Wharton Lock an excellent view is obtained of the massive bulk of Beeston Castle, a landmark which can be seen from places up to 30 miles away. As one moves westward, the romantic-looking turrets of neighbouring Peckforton Castle come into view, revealing the long ridge of hills of which Beeston Castle forms the eastern end. The countryside here is flat and quiet, and packed with cows and buttercups. The railway accompanies the canal for some of the way: so does the tiny River Gowy, which fed the old Bate's Mill. There is a pipe works near Crow's Nest Bridge.

Beeston Castle The impressive ruins of a 13thC castle built by the Earl of Chester. Situated on top of a steep hill dominating the surrounding countryside, it was in an ideal, almost unassailable position. From the castle, one may have a remarkable view of the Cheshire Plain, and one can see the well in the courtyard. It is 360ft deep. *Open Mon to Sat and Sun afternoons.*

PUBS

Aldersey Arms Hotel 200yds south west of Crow's Nest Bridge. Food.
Shady Oak Canalside, at Bate's Mill Bridge. (0829 733159). Food.

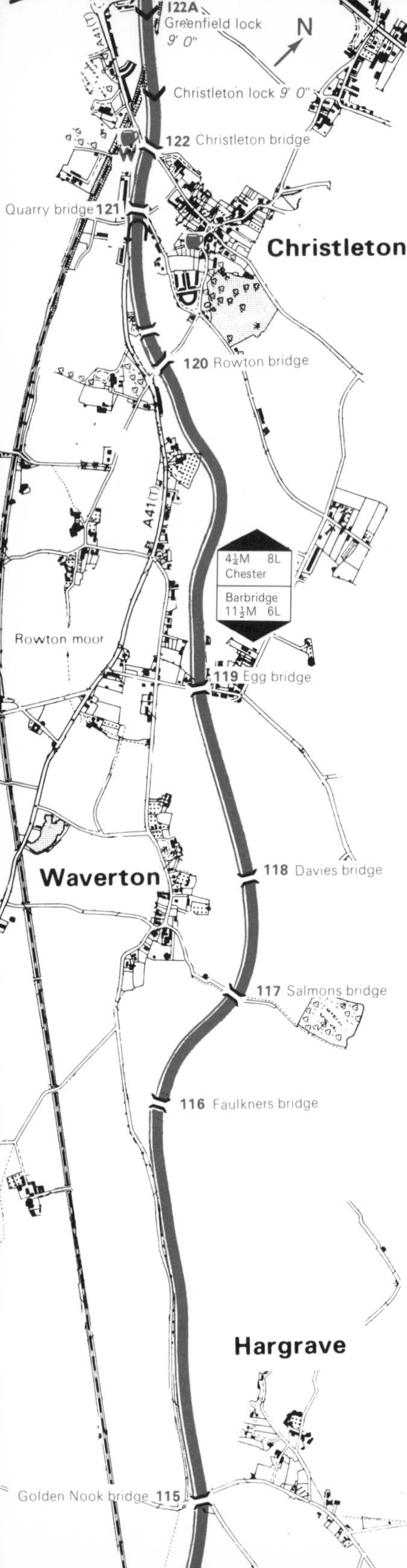

Christleton

The canal continues through the flat but very green landscape of the Cheshire Plain past Waverton with its conspicuous church tower and, past a fine brick mill by Egg Bridge, along through the unprepossessing Rowton Moor to the delightful village of Christleton. Here the towers and chimneys of Chester come into view and the railway dives under the canal in a short tunnel. The canal is badly silted between bridge 115 and Christleton Lock. Mooring is possible by Ye Old Trooper pub. Just south of here is a general store in an attractive canal warehouse – it is *open every day*.

Christleton
Ches. PO, tel, stores. A very pleasant village near the canal, well worth visiting. The village green is still very much the centre of the village: church and pub are beside it, as are several well-kept elegant houses. It is refreshing to find a village so near to a big town that has so defiantly retained its identity.
Battle of Rowton Moor. It was here, 3 miles from Chester, that one of the last major battles of the Civil War took place in 1645. The Parliamentarians completely routed the Royalists who, still under fierce attack, retreated to Chester. It is said that King Charles I watched the defeat from the walls of Chester, but it is more probable that he saw only the final stages under the walls of the city. Charles fled, leaving 800 prisoners and 600 dead and wounded.
Waverton
Ches. PO, tel, stores. The sturdy church tower carries a pleasing, modest spire. Inside the church, which was greatly restored by the Victorians, the low aisle arches lend a certain cosiness to the building.

PUBS

Ring o'Bells Christleton. A busy local serving Bass real ale.
Old Trooper Christleton Bridge. (0244 335784). A Beefeater pub/restaurant (*L & D*) serving Boddingtons real ale. Garden.

Chester

This is a most interesting and unusual stretch of canal. Leaving Christleton, the canal drops down into the ancient city of Chester through five locks: none of these have top gate paddles, and they all take rather long to fill. The canal goes straight through the middle of the town and is very much open to view. Passing a large lead works – with its tall chimney and 'shot tower' – and a great variety of bridges, the navigation approaches the old city and suddenly curves round into a very steep rock cutting: the city wall is high up on one side. King Charles' Tower stands on the wall. Soon the Northgate Locks (a staircase) are reached: at the bottom is a sharp right turn to Tower Wharf, a good place to tie up for the night. There is a boatyard at the head of the arm leading down into the River Dee.

Chester
Ches. EC Wed. MD Tue, Thur. All services. There is a wealth of things to see in this Roman city, which is the sort of place that is enjoyable to walk round even in the rain. It is in fact an excellent town to see on foot, because of the amazing survival of almost all the old city wall. This provides Chester with its best and rarest feature – one can walk right round the city on this superb footpath, over the old city gates and past the defensive turrets, including King Charles' Tower above the canal, which contains an exhibition depicting the Civil War. Chester is in fact the only city in England with its walls still complete in their 2-mile circuit. Portions of the original Roman work still remain, but in the Middle Ages several gates and towers were added, one of which – the Eastgate – has, since 1897, carried an elaborate clock to commemorate Queen Victoria's Diamond Jubilee. Other splendid features are the race course – the Roodee – (just outside the city wall and therefore well inside the modern town) where Chester Races are held each year in *May, Jul and Sep* – it can easily be overlooked for free from the road that runs above and beside it; the superb old cathedral; the bold new theatre; the 'Rows' – unique double-tier medieval shopping streets; and the immense number of old and fascinating buildings throughout the town, such as Leche House, God's Providence House and Bishop Lloyd's Palace in Watergate Street.
Chester Cathedral Northgate Street. A magnificent building of dark red stone on the site of a 10thC minster. In 1092 the Earl of Chester and St Anselm founded a Benedictine abbey, which was dissolved in 1540, but in the following year it was made a cathedral and the seat of a bishop. The monastery buildings still remain: in the cathedral the 14thC choir stalls with their intricate carvings depict the Tree of Jesse showing the genealogy of Christ.
Abbey Square Outside the cathedral, opposite the Victorian town hall, the square is entered through a massive gateway built in 1377, where the 'Chester Mystery Plays' were performed.
Church of St John the Baptist St John's Street. Impressive 12thC church that was built on the site of an earlier Saxon church. The nave contains fine examples of austere Norman pillars and arcades. The ruins of the choir at the east end still remain, as well as those of the tower which collapsed in 1573.
Chester Castle Grosvenor Road. The original timber structure c1069 was replaced by stone walls and towers by Henry III. Unfortunately in 1789 the defensive walls were removed to make way for the incongruous Thomas Harrison group of buildings, which include the Grand Entrance and Assize Courts. The main part of the castle is occupied by troops of the Cheshire Regiment, but the 13thC Agricola Tower is open to the public. The county archives, which include numerous documents relating to the canal, are kept here.
Museum of the Cheshire Regiment Situated inside the tower of the Castle, it contains relics of many wars, including maps, plans, photographs and standards.
Grosvenor Museum Grosvenor Street, Chester. (0244 21616). Exhibits the archaeology and natural history of Chester.

Fine collection of Anglo-Saxon coins. *Closed Sun morning.*
Stanley Palace Watergate Street, Chester. Beautifully timbered house built in 1591 as the town house of the Stanleys, Earls of Derby. It was restored in 1935 and is now used as the headquarters of the English-Speaking Union.
Northgate Locks
Hewn out of solid rock, these three staircase locks lower the canal by 33ft, an impressive feat of engineering and a suitable complement to the deep rock cutting nearby. The locks are now sandwiched between a large new flyover and a low railway bridge.
The Dee Branch
This branch into the tidal River Dee runs through three wide locks from the boatyard near Tower Wharf. There used to be a large basin below the second lock, but this has now been filled in. The bottom lock and bridge are new, having been built to replace an old single-tracked swing bridge on a main road. There is a very sharp bend into the branch from Tower Wharf. Anyone wishing to take a boat into the River Dee *must* give *24hrs* notice to BW on (0244) 390372 during office hours. (The bottom lock has to be kept padlocked to prevent silting up at high water.) It is practicable to enter or leave the River Dee at this point only for four hours either side of high water, since there is insufficient water at the entrance for the rest of the time.

BOATYARDS

Ⓑ **David Jones Boatbuilders** Upper Cambrian View, Chester. (0244 376363). At junction with Dee Branch. Shipwrights, wood and steel boats built, all repairs and specialise in antique boats. *Open Mon–Fri, weekends by appt.*
Ⓑ **BW Chester Yard** Tower Wharf, Chester. (0244 390372). R W Dry dock and slipway.

PUBS

Albion Albion Street, Chester. City centre pub of great character, serving *lunchtime* food and Greenall Whitley real ale. Open fire, children allowed in if you are eating.
Bouverie Arms Garden Lane, near Tower Wharf, Chester. Greenall Whitley real ale, garden and *lunchtime* food in a pub near the moorings.
Bull & Stirrup Upper Northgate Street, Chester. Boddingtons and Higsons real ale in a handsome pub. The lounge bar has two video screens, but you can escape these in the public bar. Food *lunchtime and evening.*
Olde Custom House Watergate Street, Chester. An old pub opposite the original Customs House. Marstons and Border real ale, and *lunchtime* food.

The Boat Museum at Ellesmere Port: a good reason to venture north of Chester. *Derek Pratt.*

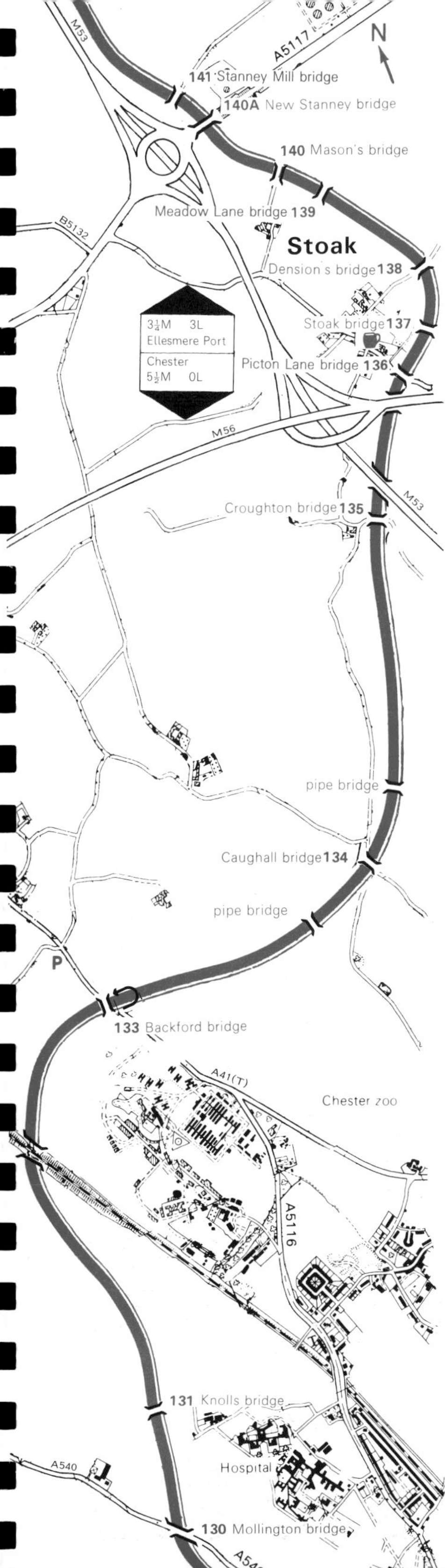

The Wirral

Sweeping northwards along the lockfree pound from Chester to the Mersey, the canal enters open country for the last time as it crosses the Wirral. The handsome stone railway viaduct over the navigation carries the Chester–Birkenhead line; here one turns briefly eastwards, passing along a shallow, green and peaceful valley. Chester Zoo is only ½ mile south of the cast-iron Caughall Bridge. Stoak (or Stoke – alternative spellings) is now surrounded by canal and motorway. The church is conspicuous from the navigation; north of the village, the distant oil refineries and chimneys herald the industrial activity along Merseyside.

Stoak
Ches. Tel. There is little of interest in this scattered village except a pleasant country pub and a small, pretty church.
Chester Zoo Chester. (0244 380280). ½ mile south of Caughall Bridge (134). Wide variety of animals, shown as much as possible without bars and fences, enhanced by attractive flower gardens and its own miniature canal. Largest elephant house in the world. *Open daily 10.00–dusk. Closed Xmas.*

PUBS

Bunbury Arms Stoak. Food, garden.

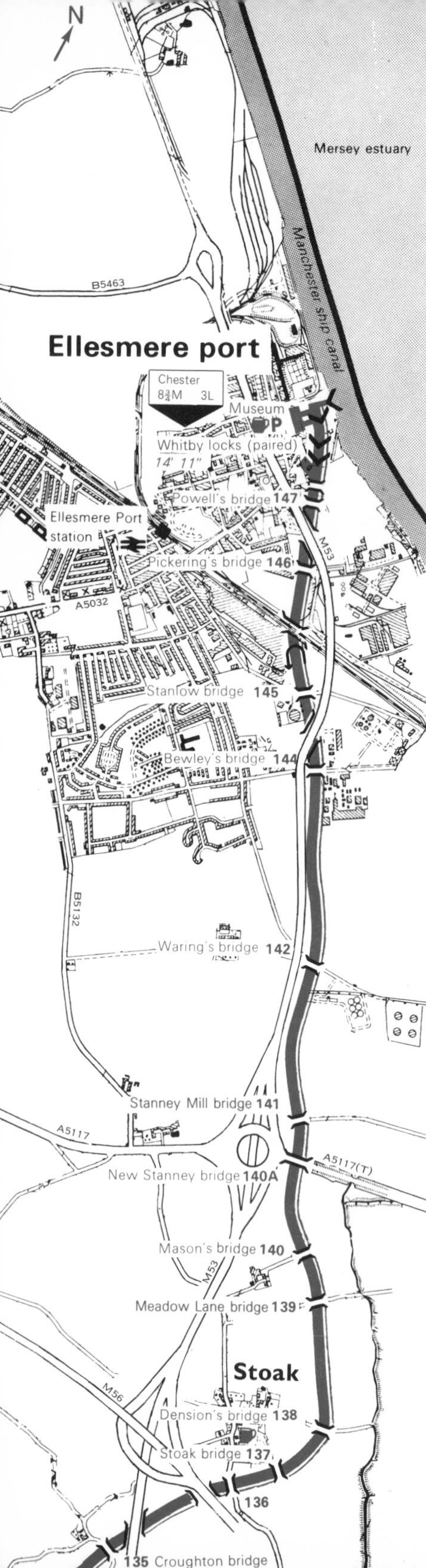

Ellesmere Port

The canal now rapidly enters an area of large-scale industries, crossed and re-crossed by the new Wirral motorway. Oil refineries and chemical works seem to predominate in a gaunt, manmade landscape in which the canal is completely forgotten and shunned by industry which it fostered long ago. The docks and basins of the port itself, where the Shropshire Union Canal meets the Manchester Ship Canal, are – or were – very extensive. Telford's famous warehouses in which the narrowboats and barges were loaded and discharged under cover were regrettably set alight by local hooligans and had to be demolished in the interests of safety. But now part of the old dock complex is the home of the Boat Museum, a large sub-aqua centre and the new headquarters of the British Sub-Aqua Club, making the journey beyond Chester well worthwhile. There is still access for boats from the Shropshire Union through several wide locks down into the Manchester Ship Canal. But no pleasure boat may enter the Ship Canal without previously seeking permission from the Manchester Ship Canal Company (061-872 2411 ex 2348). Boat owners should remember that amongst other conditions the company, before considering granting entry to pleasure boats, insists that every boat should carry conventional navigation lights, an anchor and cable, at least 50 fathoms of rope, and third party insurance cover worth at least £50,000.

Ellesmere Port
Ches. EC Wed. MD Fri. All services. An industrial town of little interest apart from the fine Victorian railway station.
The Boat Museum (051-355 5017). Established in the old Ellesmere Port basins. Exhibits, models and photos trace the development of the canal system from early times to its heyday in the 19thC. Vessels on display in the basin include narrowboats, a tunnel tug, a weedcutter plus some larger vessels. Restored period cottages. An exciting and expanding venture, not to be missed. *Open 10.00–17.00. Closed Xmas day and Boxing day.* Admission charge.
Stanlow Abbey Beside the Mersey, 1½ miles east of the canal on Stanlow Point. Remains of the Cistercian abbey founded in 1178 by John, Baron of Halton. Now isolated by the Ship Canal.

BOAT TRIPS

Arranged from the Boat Museum on *Narrowboat Centaur*.

PUBS

- **Bulls Head** Ellesmere Port.
- **Horse & Jockey** Ellesmere Port.
- **Bunbury Arms** Stoak. Food, garden.

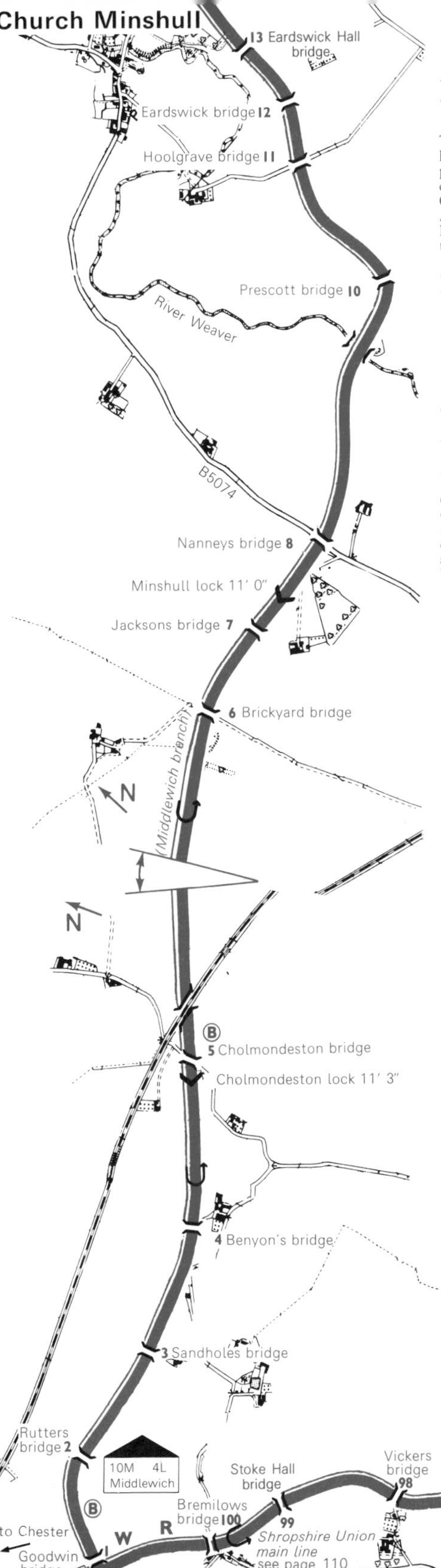

Barbridge

This attractive and under-rated link canal leaves the main line at Barbridge Junction, passing a boatyard and heading east through quiet and remote countryside. By Cholmondeston Lock there is a huge marina. After passing another lock, the canal crosses the River Weaver on an aqueduct as it approaches the village of Church Minshull.

Church Minshull
Ches. PO, tel, stores, garage. An old and mellow village beside the River Weaver. The notable 18thC church in the centre of the village is the subject of a Preservation Order. It is certainly the core of this most attractive place – and next to it is an old country pub.

BOATYARDS

Ⓑ **Venetian Marine** Cholmondeston Lock, Nantwich. (027 073 251). R S W D Gas, overnight mooring, long-term mooring, slipway, dry dock, groceries, chandlery, books and maps, boat sales, engine sales and repairs, toilets.

Ⓑ **Barbridge Marina** Wardle, Nantwich. (027 073 682). R S W Gas, overnight mooring, long-term mooring, winter storage, slipway, chandlery, books and maps, boat building, boat and engine repairs and sales, toilet. *24hr* breakdown service.

PUBS

Kings Arms Barbridge. Canalside, at Bremilow's Bridge.

Jolly Tar Barbridge Junction.

Badgers Arms Church Minshull. Food.

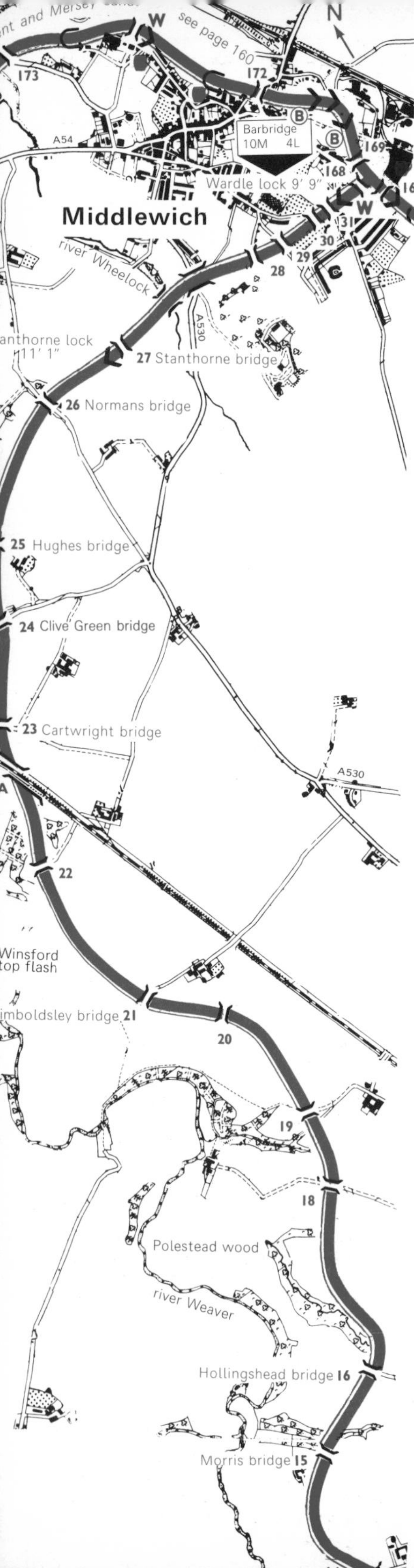

Middlewich

This is a quiet stretch of canal passing through rich farmland interspersed with woods. There are superb views to the west over the River Weaver and Winsford Top Flash. At bridge 22A the main London–Glasgow electric railway line makes a noisy crossing. The canal then descends through two locks to Middlewich, where it joins the Trent & Mersey. This last 20yds of the Middlewich Branch used to belong to the Trent & Mersey, and the bridge over the entrance to the branch is grandiosely inscribed 'Wardle Canal 1829'. There are good moorings at the boatyard to the left of the junction.

Middlewich
Ches. EC Wed. PO, tel, stores, bank, garage. A town that since Roman times has been dedicated to salt extraction. Most of the salt produced here goes to various chemical industries. Subsidence from salt extraction has prevented redevelopment for many years, but a big renewal scheme is now in progress. The canalside area is a haven of peace below the busy streets. Tourist Information is by bridge 172.
St Michael's Church A handsome medieval church which was a place of refuge for the Royalists during the Civil War. It has a fine interior with richly carved woodwork.

BOATYARDS

Ⓑ **Andersen Boats** Wych House Lane, Middlewich. (060 684 3668). Pump-out, gas, narrowboat hire.
Ⓑ **Middlewich Narrowboats** Canal Terrace, Lewin Street, Middlewich. (060 684 2460). R S W D Pump-out, gas, narrowboat hire, overnight mooring, long-term mooring, dry dock, groceries, chandlery, books and maps, boat building, engine repairs, boat painting, toilets. *Closed Jan and Feb.* Have a look at the beautifully decorated house and garden round the back.

PUBS

Big Lock Middlewich. Canalside. Food.
Newton Brewery Inn Canalside above big lock. Garden.
Kings Lock Middlewich. Canalside. Fish and chips opposite.

STOURBRIDGE

Maximum dimensions

Length: 70′
Beam: 7′
Headroom: 6′

Mileage

STOURTON JUNCTION to
Wordsley Junction: 2
Stourbridge: 3¼
BLACK DELPH bottom lock: 5¼

Locks: 20

Manager:

021-456 2723

The Stourbridge and Dudley Canals are to some extent inseparable, being part of the same grand scheme to link the Dudley coal mines with the Stourbridge glass works, and with the Severn Navigation by means of the Staffs & Worcs Canal. The Acts for the two canals were passed on the same day in 1776. Well supported by local glass masters, the Stourbridge Canal was soon under way, with Thomas Dadford as engineer. From a junction with the Staffs & Worcs at Stourton, the canal ran to Stourbridge. There was a 2-mile branch to the feeder reservoirs on Pensnett Chase, with 16 rising locks, and another level branch ran to Black Delph, where it met the Dudley Canal.

Combined with the Dudley Canal, the Stourbridge was soon profitable, and it was not long before the two companies were seeking to increase their revenue. They decided to try to capture some of the rich traffic on the Birmingham Canal. A joint proposal for a junction with the Birmingham Canal line via the Dudley Tunnel was authorised in 1785, and the through route was opened in 1792. Although the two companies worked so closely together, they resisted the temptation to amalgamate, relying on their mutual dependence to sort out any problems. Although the Dudley Canal became part of the BCN system the central position of the Stourbridge made it a very profitable undertaking, and throughout the early years of the 19thC the trade steadily increased. Even the opening of the rival Worcester & Birmingham Canal in 1815 did not affect the profits. Revenues were further increased in 1840 when the Stourbridge Extension Canal, later GWR-owned, was opened to capture the coal trade from the Shut End collieries.

In the middle of the 19thC, railway competition began to affect the canal, first from the Oxford Worcester & Wolverhampton Railway, and later from the Great Western Railway. Revenues began their inevitable decline, but the Stourbridge was able to maintain its profits, and thus its independence until nationalisation in 1948, although by then it was in the same run down state as most canals in Britain. Commercial traffic died away, and by the 1950s the canal was no longer usable.

In 1964 the Staffs & Worcs Canal Society and the BWB decided to restore the 16 locks, and reopen the line between Birmingham and the Severn. Using volunteer labour provided by the Society and money and know-how provided by BWB, work slowly progressed, and in 1967 the Stourbridge Canal was reopened to traffic. Recently the town arm has been reopened, and the terminus is being developed.

Stourbridge

The Stourbridge Canal leaves the Staffs & Worcs at Stourton Junction. From the junction the canal runs east and starts at once the climb towards Birmingham. Two locks are followed by the A449 bridge, where the towpath turns over to the north bank on a separate iron split bridge. The waterside gardens of Stewponey village accompany the canal through two more locks and then pretty wooded countryside surrounds it all the way to Wordsley Junction. Only the occasional bridge breaks the rural seclusion, and these carry little traffic. The canal approaches Wordsley Junction over a small aqueduct where the Stourbridge Town Arm branches off to the south immediately beyond the roving bridge, a structure as old as the canal itself. The short diversion along the arm is well worth making, with interest soon provided at Coalbourne Brook Bridge, where the old arch can still be seen amidst later additions. This bridge once carried the Kinver Light Railway (see page 128 under Stewponey Wharf) to the Fish Inn just a short distance east of here. As the canal makes a sharp turn into Stourbridge, Ironworks Wharf can be seen, overlooked by Riverside House, built for the ironmaster. The arm ends by the very fine Bonded Warehouse building, restored as the headquarters of the Stourbridge Navigation Trust. Built around 1790, it was enlarged in 1849. The ground floor used to be open, to facilitate unloading from the narrowboats which used to trade here. On the other side of Canal Street are the former offices of the Stourbridge Navigation Company. A pub and a Chinese take-away are close at hand, and the town centre is a few minutes' walk to the south. The main line goes straight on, starting immediately the climb up 16 locks. Wordsley lies to the north and Amblecote to the south of the flight, but the two places are barely distinguishable. There is easy access to the towns from the bridges that interrupt the flight. The surroundings become steadily more industrial and there are many traces of the role played by the canal in the Stourbridge glass industry. Beyond lock 13 the canal passes the Redhouse Glassworks (Stuart Crystal). Tidy moorings have been provided for those who wish to visit the museum in the restored bottle kiln. By lock 12 stands a superb timber warehouse known as 'Dadford's Shed', enclosed by a short arm. A handsome row of brick cottages can be seen by the next two locks, which are known as 'the staircase', although they are not actually built in that way. The Dock off-licence and general stores will be found here. At the top of the flight (BW key needed for the top lock) the main line swings away to the south east under a bridge – straight ahead is the Fens Branch, which leads to Pensnett reservoir (or Fens Pools). This is a feeder for the canal. The towpath stays on the north for the branch, but turns over to the south bank on the main line. It swings south round Brierley Hill, and then a more open landscape flanks the canal in the last stage of its journey. After passing under the last bridge Delph bottom lock comes into sight, and here the Stourbridge Canal ends. The excellent pub and water point make this a good place to stop before tackling 'The Nine Locks' – a name which has survived since 1850 when the flight was rebuilt as the EIGHT locks we see today. Remains of the original locks can still be seen in places, to the east. Near the top stands a row of canal stables, restored as a museum and interpretive centre for the Delph Locks

Conservation Area. Beyond the site of the Round Oak Steelworks the canal continues to Park Head Junction (see page 33).

Brierley Hill
West Midlands. All shops and services. A Black Country town founded on coal, iron and limestone, where no less than 12 pit pumping engines (known as 'whimseys') once kept the mines drier than they would otherwise have been. Of course the mines are no more, and redevelopment has wrought extensive changes. There are a great many pubs, notwithstanding the decline since 1843, when it was recorded that there was one for every 143 head of population, who found refuge from their daily task in ale and good company. The 18thC Victorian church, when first built, had the poet Thomas Moss appointed as perpetual curate. His most notable work was a sentimental piece called 'The Beggar', which adorned many Victorian drawing rooms and was mentioned by Dickens in 'Nicholas Nickleby'.
Redhouse Glassworks Working Museum Stuart & Sons, Wordsley, Stourbridge. (0384 71161). By Glassworks Bridge on the Stourbridge Sixteen. The elegant brick cone, one of only four surviving in the country, stands 100ft high right by the canal. Built 1788–94 it replaced earlier buildings on the same site, and housed a furnace around which the glassmaking activities took place. Although still undergoing restoration, visitors can see glassmaking and cutting in progress, and visit the Stuart Crystal shop. There are also factory tours. *Open every day.* Free. Café, and good moorings.
Thomas Webb Crystal is situated up the hill in Amblecote, with **Webb Corbett Crystal** close to the terminus of the Stourbridge Town Arm.
Broadfield House Glass Museum Barnet Lane, Kingswinford. (0384 273011). 1 mile north west of Glasshouse Bridge, off the A491. The history of glassmaking in the locality. *Open afternoons Tue–Fri & Sun, and all day Sat.*

Stourbridge
Worcs. EC Thur. MD Fri/Sat. All services. Although the origins of Stourbridge go back to the Middle Ages, there is little trace of this today. It is almost entirely a 19thC town, reflecting the great expansion of the glass industry during that period. There is one 18thC church, St Thomas's, and a great variety of Victorian ones, none of which is remarkable.

PUBS

Waterloo 200yds north west of Delph top lock. Banks' real ale, bar snacks in a small main road pub.
Bell Canalside at the bottom of Delph Locks. A fine renovated local serving Holts real ale and *lunchtime* snacks. *PO & tel* next door. W close by.
Old Bush Moor Street, Brierley Hill. By Farmer's Bridge. Plain, friendly canalside pub offering Hansons real ale and snacks at *lunchtime.*
Sampson & Lion By lock 5 on the Stourbridge Sixteen. An old canal pub where the boatmen's horses were once stabled. Bar food, games room, garden. Children welcome.
Bird in Hand John Street, opposite Stuart Crystal. Hansons real ale in a handsome local. Fish and chips just down the road.
Vine Glassworks Bridge. Banks' real ale in a main road pub. Bar food *Mon–Sat.*
Mooring End of the Stourbridge Town Arm. Real ale, bar meals, garden. Chinese take-away next door, Wordsley Crystal Shop opposite.
Royal Oak 200yds north of Stourbridge basin. Large road house dispensing Banks' real ale and food.
Old Crispin Inn Church Street, Stourbridge. A terraced pub offering Marstons, Hook Norton and Cotleigh real ale along with excellent home-cooked food *lunchtime and evening (not Sun eve).*

The Stourbridge Sixteen. *David Perrott.*

STAFFORDSHIRE & WORCESTERSHIRE

Maximum dimensions

Length: 72′
Beam: 7′
Headroom: 6′ 6″

Manager:

Stourport to Gailey: (0785) 74253
Gailey to Great Haywood: (0283) 790236

Mileage

STOURPORT to:
Kidderminster Lock: 4½
Wolverley Lock: 6
STOURTON JUNCTION: 12¼
Swindon: 16¾
Bratch Locks: 19
ALDERSLEY JUNCTION: 25
AUTHERLEY JUNCTION: 25½
GREAT HAYWOOD JUNCTION: 46

Locks: 43

Construction of this navigation was begun immediately after that of the Trent & Mersey, to effect the joining of the rivers Trent, Mersey and Severn. After this, only the line down to the Thames was necessary to complete the skeleton outline of England's narrow canal network.

Engineered by James Brindley, the Staffs & Worcs was opened throughout in 1772, at a cost of rather over £100,000. It stretched 46 miles from Great Haywood on the Trent & Mersey to the River Severn, which it joined at what became the bustling canal town of Stourport. The canal was an immediate success. It was well placed to bring goods from the Potteries down to Gloucester, Bristol and the West Country; while the Birmingham Canal, which joined it halfway along at Aldersley Junction, fed manufactured goods northwards from the Black Country to the Potteries via Great Haywood. Stourport has always been the focal point of the canal, for the town owed its birth and rapid growth during the late 18thC to the advent of the canal. It was here that the cargoes were transferred from narrowboats into Severn Trows for shipment down the estuary to Bristol and the south west.

The Staffordshire & Worcestershire Canal soon found itself facing strong competition. In 1815 the Worcester & Birmingham Canal opened, offering a more direct but heavily locked canal link between Birmingham and the Severn. The Staffs & Worcs answered this threat by gradually extending the opening times of the locks, until by 1830 they were open 24 hours a day. When the Birmingham & Liverpool Junction Canal was opened from Autherley to Nantwich in 1835, traffic bound for Merseyside from Birmingham naturally began to use this more direct, modern canal, and the Staffs & Worcs lost a great deal of traffic over its length from Autherley to Great Haywood. Most of the traffic now passed along only the ½-mile stretch of the Staffs & Worcs Canal between Autherley and Aldersley Junctions. This was, however, enough for the company, who levied absurdly high tolls for this tiny length. The B & LJ company therefore cooperated with the Birmingham Canal company in 1836 to promote in Parliament a Bill for the 'Tettenhall & Autherley Canal and Aqueduct'. This remarkable project was to be a canal 'flyover', going from the Birmingham Canal right over the profiteering Staffs & Worcs and locking down into the Birmingham & Liverpool Junction Canal. In the face of this serious threat to bypass its canal altogether, the Staffs & Worcs company gave way and reduced its tolls to a level acceptable to the other two companies. In later years the device was used twice more to force concessions out of the Staffs & Worcs.

In spite of this setback, the Staffs & Worcs maintained a good profit, and high dividends were paid throughout the rest of the 19thC. When the new railway companies appeared in the West Midlands, the canal company would have nothing to do with them; but from the 1860s onwards, railway competition began to bite, and the company's profits began to slip. Several modernisation schemes came to nothing, and the canal's trade declined. Like the other narrow canals, the Staffordshire & Worcestershire faded into obscurity as a significant transport route by the middle of this century, although the old canal company proudly retained total independence until it was nationalised in 1947. Now the canal is used almost exclusively by pleasure craft – and it is certainly a most delightful canal for cruising and walking, especially in the southern reaches in the sandstone area.

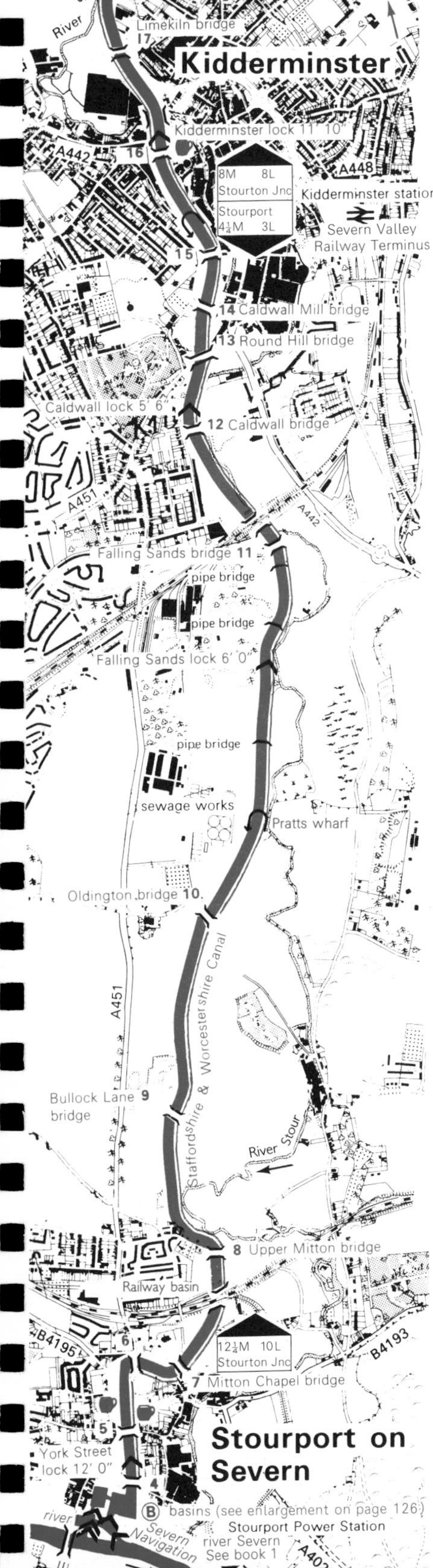

Stourport and Kidderminster

This canal is, without doubt, one of the prettiest waterways in England and the locks and basins at Stourport have an intriguing combination of all kinds of engineering features and fine buildings. The famous clock tower looks out over all. There are two sets of locks here, narrow and broad – *they are open 08.00–13.00, 13.30–16.00*. The narrow locks are those most commonly in use, and they are in a staircase – the lock keeper is usually around to help if you have difficulties. *For an enlarged map of the Stourport Basin area see page 126.* To reach the Staffs & Worcs Canal itself, boats should proceed to the eastern corner of the upper basins, pass under the bridge and climb the deep lock at York Street. There is a useful shop and off-licence by the lock. Above the lock are good temporary moorings, opposite a boatyard which has carefully preserved and utilised the old canal buildings. Although it is still in the middle of Stourport, the canal has already acquired a secluded, unspoilt character, flanked by discreet houses and walls and accompanied by a rural towpath. The navigation seems to creep through the town, twisting along past the big disused Milton Railway Basin at a railway bridge and emerging quickly into the country. It follows the west side of a little valley, the steep slopes rising sharply from the water. The River Stour approaches and at Pratt's Wharf the towpath rises over an almost unrecognisably overgrown lock that once joined the canal to the Stour. This river used to be navigable from here for 1¼ miles down to the Wilden Ironworks. The sweet smell from an adjacent sewage works spurs the traveller on towards Kidderminster and suddenly the canal's surroundings change, for the hillside on the west bank becomes a dramatic cliff of crumbling red rock rising sheer from the canal. This is the southern end of a geological feature that stretches almost to Wombourn, 15 miles away. Falling Sands (BW key required) and Caldwall Locks both enjoy delightful situations at the foot of the sandstone, and both have split iron bridges of a type usually associated with the Stratford-on-Avon Canal. Beyond Falling Sands Bridge look out for steam trains on the viaduct, now that the Severn Valley Railway (0299 403816) has extended to Kidderminster station. Kidderminster is now reached, and the canal's course through the centre of it is truly private, passing along a corridor of high walls, factories and warehouses that clearly date from the arrival of the canal in Kidderminster. As the buildings mount up, the navigation narrows until it escapes by diving into a short tunnel, at the end of which is a deep lock. One surfaces to find a very different scene: this is open townscape, with traffic all around, shopping streets close by and a church just ahead, on a rise. There are good moorings here, by the gardens, and the old wharf crane, with easy access to the town. Nearby is a statue of Richard Baxter, the 17thC thinker who 'advocated unity and comprehension' in religion. Just above Kidderminster Lock, the River Stour appears: the canal crosses it on an aqueduct. Continuing northwards, the canal curves away to leave the town centre behind, passing now more modern and less picturesque industrial works.

Kidderminster
Worcs. EC Wed. MD Thur, Sat. Kidderminster exists above all for carpet weaving. The industry was first introduced here in 1735, when the town was already a prosperous cloth manufacturing centre, and today there are many factories in Kidderminster involved in the production of carpets. Born here in 1793 was Rowland Hill, who founded the Penny Post in 1840: his statue in front of the head post office commemorates his 'creative mind and patient energy'. From the canal, one sees little but the older industrial side of Kidderminster, which is not without interest. The best place for access to the town is from Kidderminster Lock; the public baths are conveniently beside bridge 15. There is a fine selection of pubs and the

centre of the town is quite quiet thanks to an inner ring road which leaves it virtually vehicle free. This road unfortunately passes the door of the impressive, dark church of St Mary, cutting it off completely from Church Street, in which Kidderminster's few Georgian houses are situated.

Kidderminster Museum & Art Gallery Market Street. Collection of archaeological finds and exhibits of local interest. Small permanent art collection, including some Brangwyn etchings. (There is much more to see at the Worcestershire County Museum in Hartlebury Castle. *See below.*) *Closed Sun.*

Stourport-on-Severn
Worcs. EC Wed. PO, tel, stores, garage, bank. When the engineer James Brindley surveyed the line for the Staffordshire & Worcestershire Canal in the early 1760s, he chose to meet the River Severn at the hamlet of Lower Milton, 4 miles downstream of Bewdley where the little River Stour flowed into the Severn. Basins and locks were built for the boats, warehouses for the cargoes and cottages for the workmen. The canal company even built in 1788 the great Tontine Hotel beside the locks. The hamlet soon earned the name of Stourport, becoming a busy and wealthy town. The two basins were expanded to five (one has since been filled in) and the locks were duplicated. Nowadays, plenty remains of Stourport's former glory, for the basins are always full of boats (there is a boat club and boatyards). The delightful clock tower still functions, a canal maintenance yard carries on in the old workshops by the locks, and the Tontine Hotel still has a licence. Mart Lane (on the north-east side of the basins) is worth a look – the original 18thC terrace of workmen's cottages still stands. Numbers 2, 3 and 4 are listed as ancient monuments. In contrast with the basin area, the town of Stourport is not interesting, and although it was built on account of the canal, the town has no relationship at all with the basins now. It seems to have grown up away from the canal.

Hartlebury Castle Hartlebury. 2 miles east of Stourport on the B4193 (0299 250410). The home of the Bishops of Worcester, this castle was built in the 15thC, virtually destroyed in 1646 and rebuilt in the 18thC. *Open 1st Sun in month, B. Hol weekends, Wed afternoon in summer.*

The Worcester County Museum Housed in part of the castle. It shows the story of the archaeology, geology, crafts and industries of the county. *Open afternoons Mar–Nov; 11.00–17.00 B. Hols. Closed Sat.*

BOATYARDS

Ⓑ **Severn Valley Cruisers** York Street Boatyard, Stourport. (029 93 71165). R S WD Pump-out, gas, narrowboat hire, overnight mooring, long-term mooring, winter storage, slipway, crane, dry dock, chandlery, books and maps, boat building, boat sales, engine sales and repairs, toilets. Boat shop in Mart Lane.

Ⓑ **Stroudwater Cruisers** Engine Lane, Stourport. (029 93 77222). R S WD Pump-out, narrowboat hire, overnight mooring, long-term mooring, winter storage, books and maps, boat building, boat and engine repairs, boat sales, crane, toilet.

BOAT TRIPS

Severn Steamship Company (029 93 71177). Regular day trips to Worcester from Stourport Bridge, also private charter for parties, discos and schools. Up to 199 persons.

PUBS AND RESTAURANTS

Bridge Inn Mill Street, Kidderminster. East of bridge 16. Snacks.

Bay Horse Market Street, Kidderminster. Banks' real ale, snacks.

Horn & Trumpet Kidderminster. Close to the 'church' moorings. Real ale, food.

Boars Head Worcester Street, Kidderminster. Banks' real ale, *lunchtime* food, snacks.

Green Man & Still Oxford Street, Kidderminster. M & B real ale.

Bird in Hand Stourport. Canalside, south of the railway bridge. Whitbread real ale, garden.

Black Star Stourport. Canalside, by bridge 5. Marstons real ale, snacks.

Lord Nelson York Street, Stourport. M & B real ale.

Bell Stourport, by York Street Lock. Hansons real ale, food, garden.

Tontine Hotel Stourport Basin. Banks' real ale and food (*lunchtime Mon–Sat*) in a very large pub built by the canal company in 1788.

Old Crown Stourport, by the Severn Bridge. Banks' real ale.

Severn Tandoori 11 Bridge Street, Stourport. (029 93 3090). A very good, reasonably priced, comfortable and smart restaurant. *L & D.* Take-away service.

STOURPORT BASINS

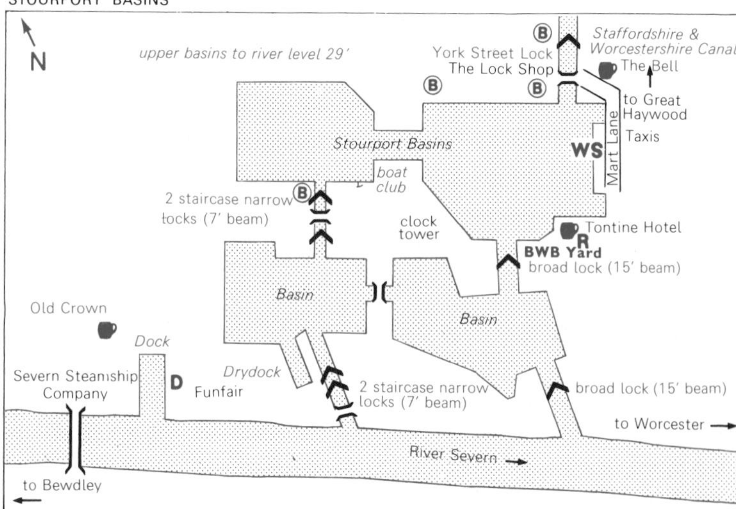

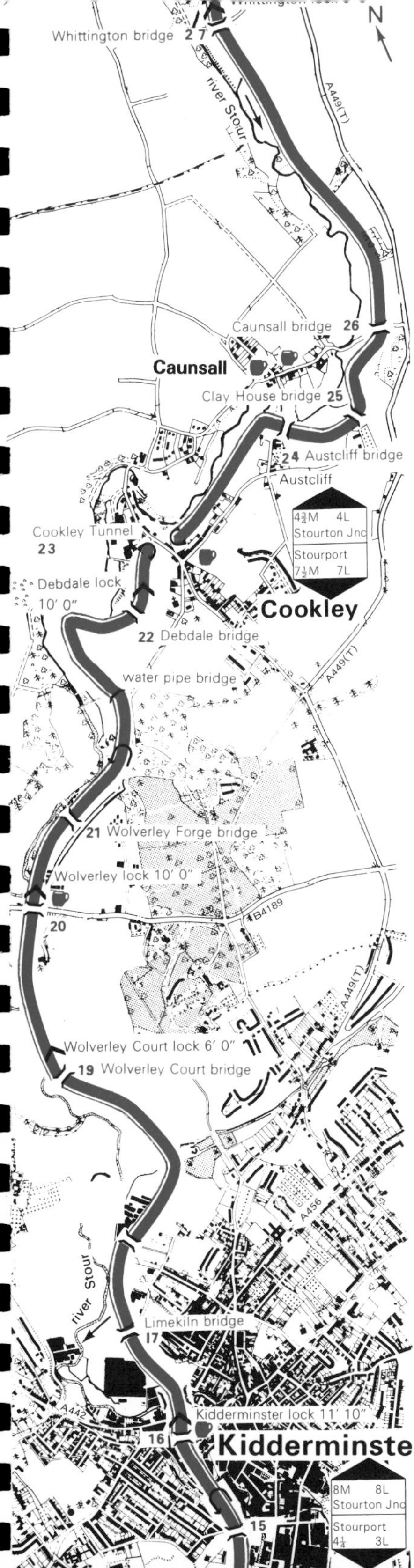

Wolverley

This is another delightful stretch of waterway. Leaving Kidderminster, the navigation moves into an area of quiet watermeadows created by the little River Stour, which is now on the west side. Past an isolated lock, the village of Wolverley on the other side of the valley is given away by its unusual Italianate church standing on a large outcrop of rock. The approach to the deep Wolverley Lock is lined by trees. There is a pub beside the lock, and good moorings above and below it. Beyond here, the course of the canal becomes really tortuous and narrow as it proceeds up the narrow, thickly wooded valley, forced into endless diversions by the steep cliffs of friable red sandstone. Vegetation of all kinds clings to these cliffs, giving the impression of jungle foliage. At one point the navigation opens out, becoming momentarily like a normal canal; but soon the rocks and trees encroach again, returning the waterway to its previous constricted width. An impressive promontory of rock compels the canal to double back on itself in a great horse-shoe sweep that takes it round to the pretty Debdale Lock. A doorway reveals a cavern cut into the solid rock here; this was used as an overnight stable for towing horses. Beyond Cookley Tunnel, the steep rocks along the right bank used to culminate in a remarkable geological feature where Austcliff Rock overhung the canal. It was recently removed when it became unstable. Thick woods here keep the nearby A449 road at bay. Across the River Stour, ¼ mile west of bridge 26, is the small settlement of Caunsall. There are farms here, and two pubs, but little else.

Cookley
Worcs. PO, tel, stores, garage, fish & chips. The village is set well above the canal, which passes underneath it in a tunnel. Although it has an attractive situation, Cookley is not a particularly pretty village, and there is little to visit. There is a big steel works near the canal, where the biggest bulldozer wheel in the world was made. Down in the valley, near the River Stour, there are the older, more attractive cottages of the village. And clearly visible are the entrances to caves in the cliff face. To reach Cookley from the canal, it is best to moor west of the tunnel, then walk up the path to the village.

Wolverley
Worcs. PO, tel, stores. 400yds north west of bridge 20. A very unusual and pretty village on the west side of the Stour valley. The church is predominant, a dark red structure built in 1772 in a precise Italianate style. It stands on a sandstone rock so steep that the building has to be approached by a zigzag path cut through the constantly eroded sandstone. Most of the village is clustered just to the north of the church, near the little-used but dignified stone buildings of the old grammar school. The school was endowed in 1629, but most of the buildings date from 1820. Around it is the bulk of this small village, where gardens make the most of the brook that flows through. There is an attractive pub in the centre, and another, with spacious gardens, up the hill. Wolverley is a village certainly worth visiting – it is easily accessible from Wolverley Lock.

PUBS

Portelet Inn Caunsall, ¼ mile west of bridge 26. Banks', Hoskins and Oldfield real ale, excellent and reasonably priced food in a friendly, comfortable pub with a terrace. Well worth the walk from the canal.

Anchor Caunsall, ¼ mile west of bridge 26. Snacks, telephone outside.

Bulls Head Cookley. Up the hill from the tunnel, near the shops. Banks' real ale in a popular local. Food *lunchtime and evening*, garden.

Lock Canalside at Wolverley Lock. Banks' real ale and food at *lunchtime (not Sun)*. Lockside terrace.

Queens Head Wolverley, near the old school. Banks' real ale, terrace.

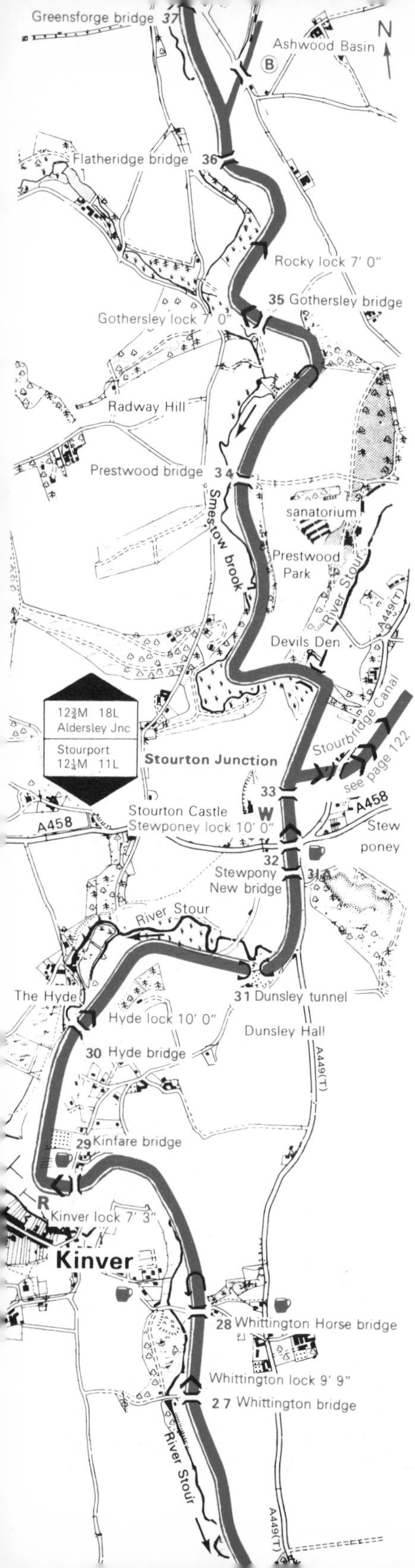

Kinver

Between bridges 26 and 27 the canal passes from Worcestershire into Staffordshire, but the surroundings of this remarkable waterway do not change: it continues through secluded woodlands, the rocky hillside on the east bank steepening as the valley narrows again. The nearby main road remains unnoticed, while the canal reaches Whittington Lock which has a pretty lock cottage beside it and a seat made from an old balance beam and dedicated to Jim Robbins, Chairman of the Staffs & Worcs Canal Society 1964–67. The bridge at the lock tail is typical of this navigation, its parapet curving fluently round and down to the lower water level. A couple of hundred yards north is another delightful scene, where on either side of the canal a few cottages, pretty gardens and moored boats face the waterway and the low bridge. Then really tall, steep hills appear on the east bank, rising to over 250ft. Three isolated cottages cling to the hill in a clearing among the trees. The canal leaves this damp, mossy area and bends round to Kinver Lock. There is a pub here, and a road, leading round to the village, which is behind the bold modern (1939) waterworks. This pumps from the vast underground lake that lies deep below the great sandstone ridge stretching from Kidderminster to Wombourn. Beyond Hyde lock, the canal wanders along the edge of woods on the east side of the valley, where in one place the sandstone, eroded away, is supported on brick pillars – it then passes through the charmingly diminutive (25yds long) Dunsley Tunnel, a rough-hewn bore with overhanging foliage at each end. The next lock is at Stewponey, where Stourton Castle stands just over the river. The Stourbridge Canal leaves at Stourton Junction, north of the wharf; the first of the many locks that carry the canal up towards Dudley and the Birmingham Canal Navigations is just a few yards away. (*See page 122.*) Beyond Stourton Junction, a 90-degree bend to the left takes the canal to an aqueduct over the River Stour: this river now disappears to the north east and is not seen again. Its place near the canal is taken by the little Smestow Brook as far as Swindon. At the far end of the aqueduct is a curious narrow boathouse (known as the Devil's Den) cut into the rock. Prestwood Park is concealed in the woods above the east bank. The hall is now a hospital: it used to be the home of the Foleys, a family of Black Country ironmasters. Beyond Prestwood Bridge (34), now sensitively rebuilt in red brick, to the original design, the canal continues through Gothersley and Rocky Locks, reaching eventually a fork: the narrow entrance on the right leads into the very long Ashwood Basin, where there is a boatyard.

Ashwood Basin
This used to be a railway-connected basin owned by the National Coal Board. After the line was closed, the basin was disused for some years; but now it provides a pleasant mooring site for a large number of pleasure boats. There is a boatyard and a boatclub here. A road is carried over the basin by a small viaduct.

Stewponey Wharf
An interesting wharf at the head of Stewponey Lock with a restored octagonal toll office. Near the wharf can be seen the long-abandoned track of the Kinver Valley Light Railway, which used to run from Stourbridge to Kinver. From Stewponey to Kinver it followed a route close to the canal. Note also the fine circular weir by the refurbished lock. Just across the river from the wharf is the impressive bulk of Stourton Castle, while in the opposite direction – but shielded by trees – is a fast main road, a built-up area and a large roadhouse serving food. There is a telephone box and a small grocery hard by. A petrol station is not far away.

Stourton Castle Just a few yards west of Stewponey Wharf, this building is a curious mixture of building styles and materials. The castle is notable as the birthplace of Cardinal Pole in 1500. A friend of Mary Tudor, Pole became Archbishop of Canterbury in her reign after Cranmer had been burned at the stake. The castle is private.

Kinver

Staffs. PO, tel, stores, garage, bank, launderette. Kinver clearly has a reputation as a very pretty village. It is surrounded by tall hills and consists of a long main street of reasonably attractive houses, but its chief glory is its situation – it nestles among tall wooded hills, a position that must strike the visitor as remarkable for a village so close to the industries and unexciting geographical features of the West Midlands. Kinver Edge (National Trust property), west of the village, is a tremendous ridge covered in gorse and heather, and for anyone prepared to toil up to the top from the valley it provides a splendid view of the Cotswold and Malvern Hills. Kinver church is near the Edge, and is reached by a steep zigzag road. The church overlooks the village and contains several things of interest, including plaques recording the Charter granted by Charles I in 1629 and the Charter granted by Ethelbad in 736, giving '10 cessapis of land to my general Cyniberte for a religious house'.

BOATYARDS

Ⓑ **Ashwood Marina** Kingswinford. (0384 295535). R S W D Gas, overnight mooring, long-term mooring, winter storage, slipway, crane, chandlery, books and maps, boat building, boat and engine sales and repairs, toilets, showers, licensed club and restaurant. *Closed Fri.*

PUBS AND RESTAURANTS

Stewponey & Foley Arms Overlooking Stewponey Lock. Cold buffet *lunchtime Mon–Fri*, grill room and Banks' real ale in a massive road house.

Vine By Kinver Lock. Food, garden.

Ye Old White Hart Kinver.

Whittington (0384 872110) 300yds east of bridge 28, along a footpath. Dating from 1300, this building has an impressive history. It was the home of Dick Whittington's grandfather, and much later of Lady Jane Grey, whose ghost is sometimes encountered. There are also priest holes and a tunnel to the nearby Whittington Hall. Restaurant and wine bar.

The picturesque Bratch Locks. *David Perrott.*

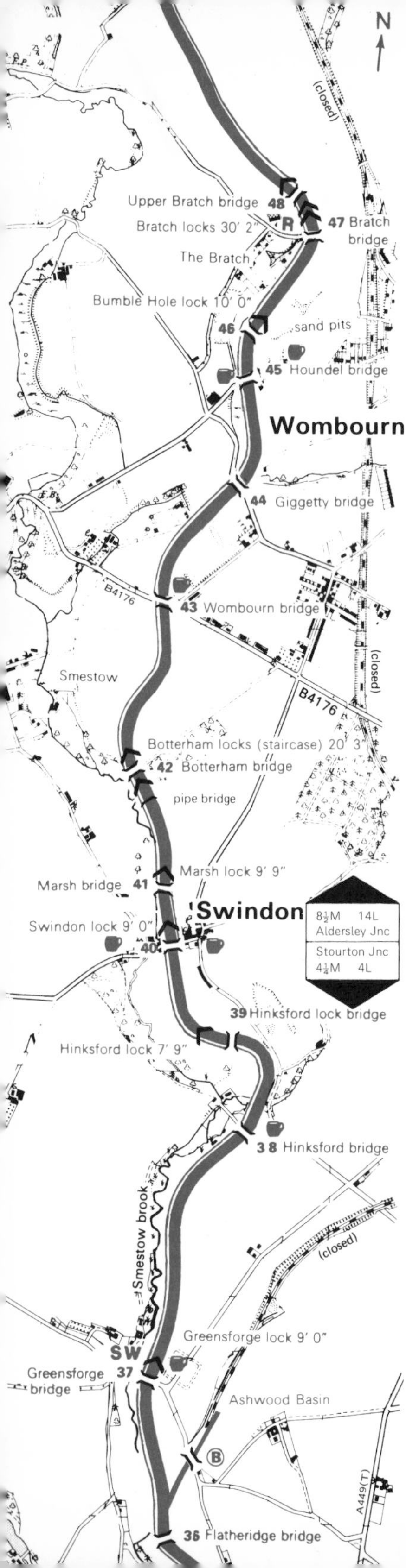

The Bratch

North of Rocky Lock, the outcrops of sandstone are seen less frequently, the countryside becoming flatter and more regular. However the locks do not disappear, for the canal continues the steady rise up the small valley of the Smestow Brook through southern Staffordshire towards Wolverhampton. At Greensforge Lock there is an attractive pub, and another of the pretty, circular weirs that are found, often hidden behind a wall or a hedge, at many of the locks along this delightful canal. Another wooded, rocky section leads again to more open country. At Hinksford there is a residential caravan site down in the valley, and another pub near bridge 38, with a public telephone outside. On through the isolated Hinksford Lock, the navigation bends round to Swindon where the canal is flanked by the tidy gardens of new houses. There are four locks hereabouts, Botterham being a two-step staircase with a bridge crossing in the middle. North of here, the canal begins to lose its rural character as it encounters the modern outskirts of Wombourn, passing under a new bridge that, happily, retains the original cast-iron name plates. There is a pub by this bridge (43) and a few shops not far to the north east of the next one (44). Yet another pub is at the next bridge (45); beyond it is Bumble Hole Lock. The three Bratch Locks are next, raising the canal level by over 30ft. From the top, one may enjoy a good view back down the valley, with the spire of Wombourn Church backed by the great ridge of the Orton Hills to the east. Leaving the Bratch, the canal wanders through open farmland parallel to a long-closed railway, arriving at the pleasantly situated Awbridge Lock.

Bratch Locks
With their octagonal toll office, attractive situation and very unusual layout, these three locks are well known among students of canal engineering and architecture. At first sight they appear curiously illogical, with an impossibly short pound between the bottom of one lock and the top gate of the next; but the secret of their operation is the side ponds hidden behind the towpath hedge and the culverts that connect these to the intermediate pounds. In fact, to work through these locks, boaters should simply treat each one as a separate lock like any other on the canal. *However, it is especially important when locking through to close the gates and paddles of each lock before operating the paddles of the next.* Busy in summer.

Wombourn
Staffs. PO, tel, stores. An attractive village much expanded by housing developments.

Swindon
Staffs. PO, tel, store, fish & chips. A small village, once a mixture of farming and industry. The 19thC ironworks has been demolished, replaced by a housing estate.

BOATYARDS

Ⓑ **Wombourne Canal Services** Giggetty Wharf, bridge 44, Wombourne. (0902 892242). 🅆 Pump-out, chandlery, repairs, engine sales. *24hr* emergency call out.

PUBS

Mount Pleasant Near bridge 45. Food, garden. Bass and M & B real ale.

Round Oak Canalside, at bridge 45. M & B Springfield real ale. Food *lunchtime Mon–Sat.* Garden. Note the old post box set into the wall.

Waggon & Horses Near the canal at bridge 43, on B4176. Hansons real ale, *lunchtime* food, garden.

Green Man 100yds west of bridge 40. An old local, serving Banks' real ale and snacks.

Old Bush Inn Swindon village, 150yds east of bridge 40. Hansons real ale in a homely pub. Shops and post office opposite.

Bush Hinksford, 100yds north east of bridge 38. Garden.

Navigation Greensforge. Canalside, at the lock. Snacks and Wem real ale.

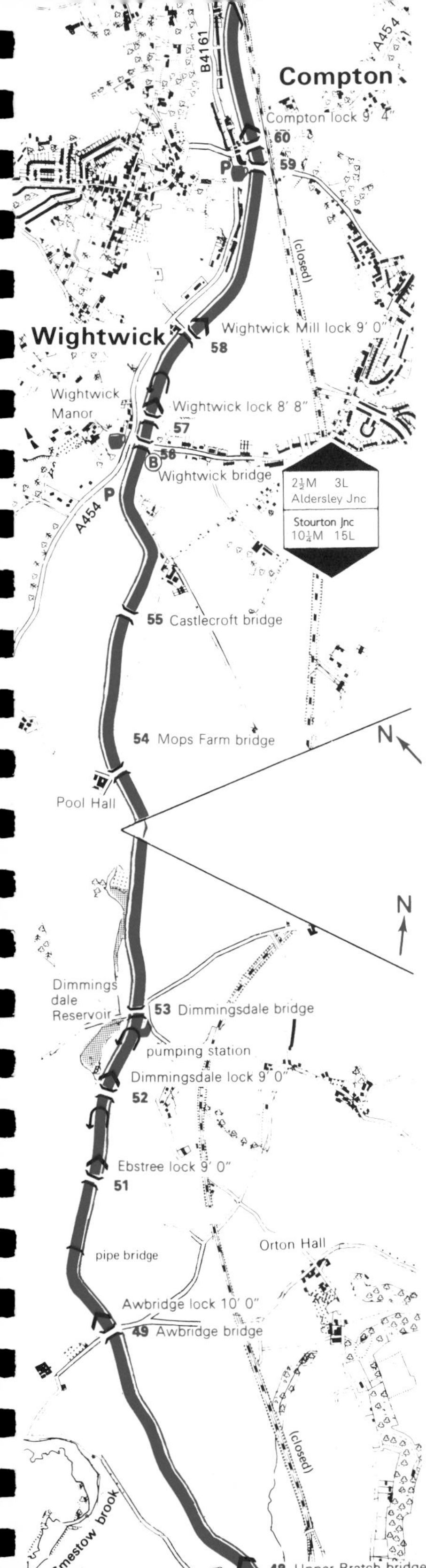

Dimmingsdale

North of Wombourn, the countryside becomes less interesting. Although it is still quiet, and remote from roads and railways, the canal is pestered by overhead power lines for a mile as it rises through Awbridge, Ebstree and Dimmingsdale Locks. By bridge 53, an arm provides moorings for a fine array of traditionally painted working boats, amidst overhanging trees. Just above the bridge here, a derelict yard spills its refuse onto the towpath, but things quickly improve as the pretty lakes to the west close in. These are in fact canal-feeding reservoirs, of considerable interest to fishermen. Ahead, the hills of Wightwick overlook the navigation as it approaches a shallow valley and a busy main road. This valley – in places an artificial cutting – contains the canal right through to the flatter land at Autherley. Houses, mostly modern, are never far away, although the canal manages to preserve intact its rural character all the way through what are in effect the western outskirts of Wolverhampton. Compton Lock marks the end of the 31-lock climb from the River Severn at Stourport, a rise of 294ft. From here northwards, a 10-mile level pound takes the Staffs & Worcs on to Gailey, where the first of 12 locks begins the fall towards the Trent & Mersey Canal.

Compton
Staffs. PO, tel, stores, launderette. A busy but uninteresting village with a modern shopping centre and some pubs. The canal lock was the first that James Brindley built on the Staffs & Worcs in the late 1760s, but unfortunately the cottage here has been demolished. However the nearby coal wharf still handles coal, although of course the waterway is no longer used for this trade – nor for any other.

Wightwick
Staffs. (pronounced 'Wittick'). Once a village, now a suburb. But there is a hill and plenty of trees, and in spite of the busy A454 it is a pleasant scene around the canal bridge and the old country pub.

Wightwick Manor *National Trust property.* 300yds north west of bridge 56, across the A454 and up the hill. Built between 1887 and 1893, the manor has an exterior that embodies many of the idiosyncrasies of the time. Inside, it is furnished with original wallpapers and fabrics by Morris and various contributions by the Pre-Raphaelites. This certainly makes a change from the usual venerable stone or timbered buildings that are open to the public. *Open afternoons on Thur, Sat and B. Hol weekends. Closed Feb.*

PUBS

Oddfellows Hall Compton, 50yds west of bridge 59. Banks' real ale, food, garden.

Swan Compton, near the Oddfellows. Banks' real ale.

Mermaid Wightwick. 50yds north west of bridge 56.

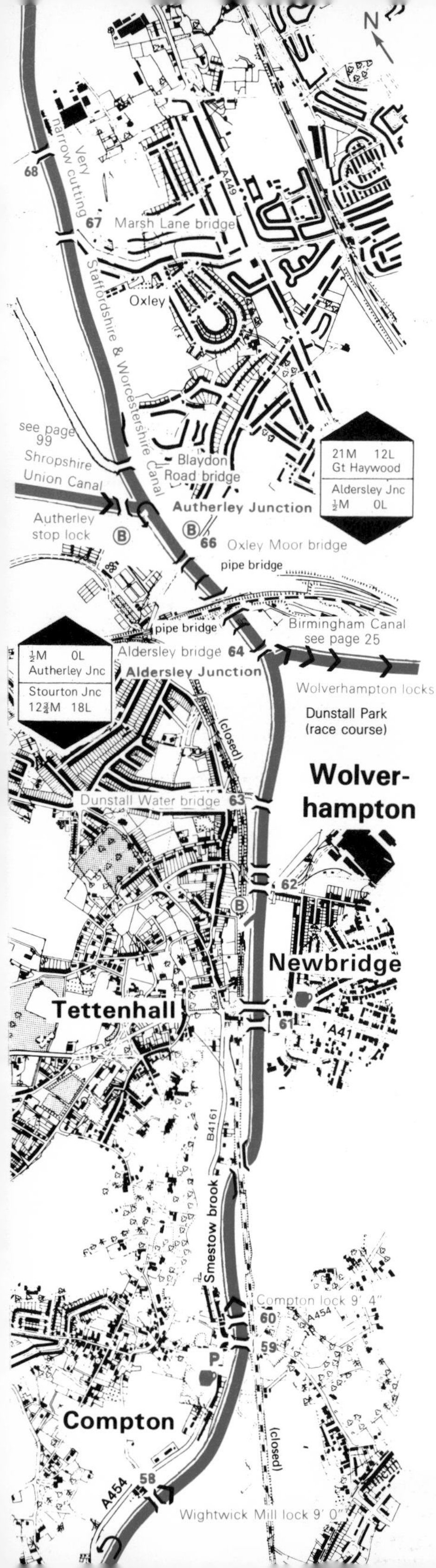

Aldersley & Autherley Junctions

The canal continues along the pleasant cutting through the Wolverhampton outskirts, passing under the big iron bridge that carries a closed railway. Trees on either side shield the navigation from the houses of Tettenhall. A large concrete road bridge at Newbridge Wharf dwarfs the nearby original brick-arched bridge and reminds the traveller of the hurly-burly world on either side of this quiet corridor of green. It is, however, an excellent place to stop for supplies. The shop here is *open 06.00–22.00*. Several boating centres are passed, then the trees of Dunstall Park appear on the right, followed by Aldersley Junction. At this secluded place the bottom of the 21 Wolverhampton locks brings the main line of the Birmingham Canal into the Staffordshire & Worcestershire Canal. There is a towpath 'roving' bridge at the junction; past it is a criss-cross of railway and pipe bridges, then the cutting eases away and the canal goes under a road bridge, emerging at last in a rather flat, open landscape, with housing estates to the east. The big white bridge on the towpath side marks Autherley Junction: the stop lock here is at the entrance to the Shropshire Union main line. There is a large boatyard north of the stop lock, and extensive BW moorings. Straight ahead at Autherley is the continuation of the Staffs & Worcs to the Trent & Mersey Canal at Great Haywood Junction.

Tettenhall

Staffs. PO, tel, stores, garage, pub and other facilities are conveniently placed by bridge 61. A comfortable residential suburb of Wolverhampton (the city centre is a mere 2 miles to the south east). There is little to see, but the battlemented tower of the Norman church is worth a look – it is 300yds north of bridge 61. The church was burnt down in 1950, only the tower surviving the conflagration. The new church, built in 1955, contains some interesting stained glass.

BOATYARDS

Ⓑ **Water Travel** Autherley Junction, Oxley Moor Road, Wolverhampton. (0902 782371). R S W D E Pump-out, gas, narrowboat hire, overnight mooring, long-term mooring, slipway, chandlery, provisions, books and maps, boat building, boat and engine repairs, boat sales, licensed club house, telephone, toilet.

Ⓑ **Oxley Moor Stop** South of Autherley Junction. W D Pump-out, mooring, provisions, gifts, teas.

Ⓑ **Double Pennant Boatyard** Hordern Road, Wolverhampton. (0902 752771). W D Gas, overnight mooring, slipway, chandlery, books and maps, boat and engine sales and repairs, toilet.

Ⓑ **Wolverhampton Passenger Boat Services** Newbridge Wharf, bridge 61. (0902 757494). W Pump-out, overnight mooring, gifts, repairs. (Excellent licensed shop close by. *Open 06.00–22.00*).

PUBS

Newbridge Tettenhall. (0902 754911). 50yds east of bridge 61. Meals.

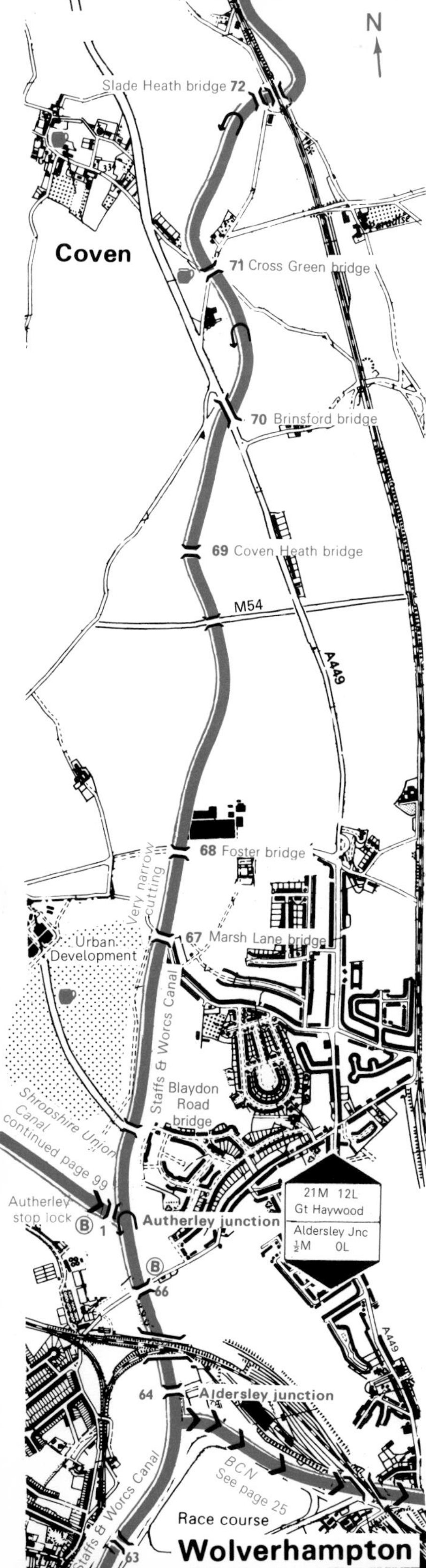

Coven

Leaving Autherley and the junction with the Shropshire Union Canal (see page 99), the Staffs & Worcs runs through a very narrow cutting through rock: there is room for only one boat here, so a good lookout should be kept for oncoming craft. Soon the navigation leaves behind the suburbs of Wolverhampton and enters pleasant farmland. The bridges need care: although the bridgeholes are reasonably wide, the actual arches are rather low. The age of this canal shows itself in its extremely twisting course after passing the railway bridge. There are few real centres of population along this stretch, which comprises largely former heathland.

Coven
Staffs. PO, tel, stores, garage, fish & chips. The only true village on this section, Coven lies beyond a dual carriageway north west of Cross Green Bridge. There are a large number of shops, including a launderette.
Autherley Junction
A busy canal junction with a full range of boating facilities.

BOATYARDS

Ⓑ **Water Travel** Autherley Junction, Oxley Moor Road, Wolverhampton. (0902 782371). R S W D E Pump-out, gas, narrowboat hire, overnight mooring, long-term mooring, slipway, chandlery, provisions, books and maps, boat building, boat and engine repairs, boat sales, licensed club house, telephone, toilet.

PUBS

Rainbow Inn Coven. Fairly new village pub serving Ansells real ale and food. Terrace.

Anchor Inn (0902 790466). Canalside by Cross Green Bridge. Good moorings. Ansells real ale, garden, steak bar. Large roadhouse popular with young people.

Pendulum North west of Blaydon Road Bridge. Food *lunchtime and evening*.

Aldersley Part of Wolverhampton Stadium. Bar snacks.

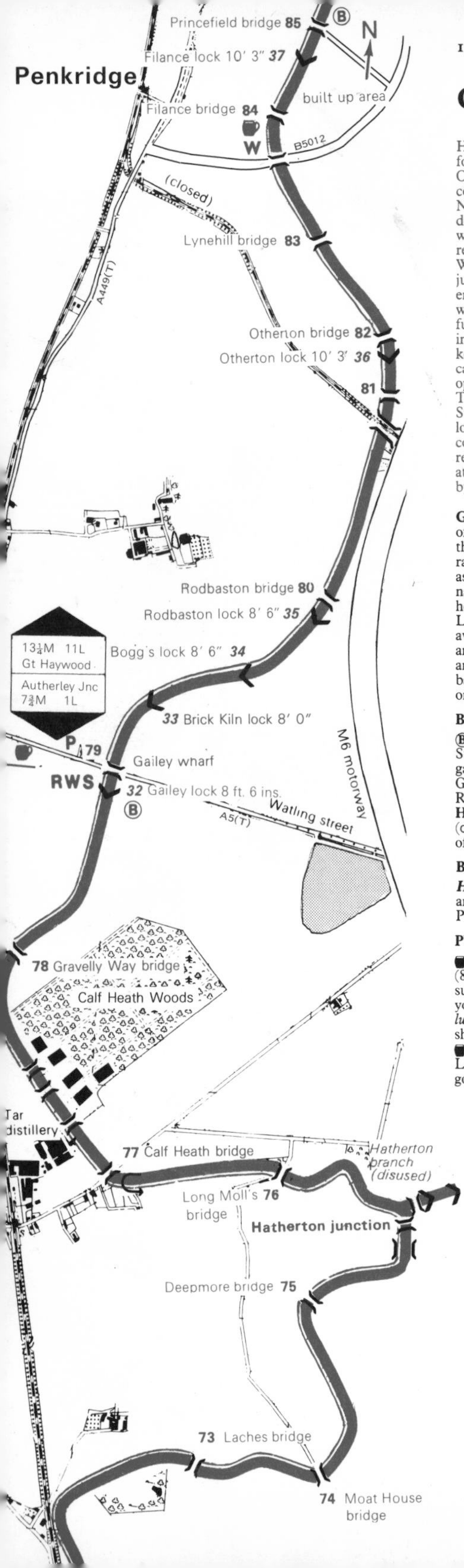

Gailey Wharf

Hatherton Junction marks the entrance of the former Hatherton Branch of the Staffs & Worcs Canal into the main line. This branch used to connect with the Birmingham Canal Navigations. The branch is closed above the derelict second lock, although the channel, with the hulks of three wooden narrowboats, remains as a feeder for the Staffordshire & Worcestershire Canal. There is a marina at the junction. Not far away, a chemical works is encountered astride the canal in what used to be woodlands. Gailey Wharf is about a mile further north: it is a small canal settlement that includes a post office and a large, round toll keeper's watchtower now containing a useful canal shop. The picturesque Wharf Cottage opposite has been restored as a bijou residence. The canal itself disappears under Watling Street and falls rapidly through another five locks towards Penkridge. The M6 motorway comes alongside for ½ mile, screening the reservoirs which feed the canal. These are very attractive locks: many of them are accompanied by little brick bridges.

Gailey and Calf Heath reservoirs ½ mile east of Gailey Wharf, either side of the M6. The three are feeder reservoirs for the canal though rarely drawn on. The public has access to them as nature reserves to study the wide variety of natural life, especially the long-established heronry which is thriving on an island in Gailey Lower reservoir. In the Gailey Upper, fishing is available to the public from the riparian owner and in Gailey Lower a limited number of angling tickets are available on a season ticket basis each year from BW. There is club sailing on two of the reservoirs.

BOATYARDS

Ⓑ **Gailey Marine** The Wharf, Watling Street, Standeford. (0902 790612). [R][S][W] Pump-out, gas, narrowboat hire, boat building, boat sales. Gifts and provisions opposite in The Roundhouse.
Hatherton Marina At Hatherton Junction. (0902 790570). [W][D] Gas, pump-out, off-licence, shop, restaurant, moorings.

BOAT TRIPS

Hatherton Belle is a 45-seater boat with disco and licensed bar. Public trips *B. Hols & Sun.* Private hire. Details (0902) 790570.

PUBS

Cross Keys Canalside, at Filance Bridge (84). Once a lonely canal pub, now it is surrounded by housing estates. Popular with young people, it serves M & B real ale and food *lunchtime and evening*. There is a useful Spar shop 100yds north, on the estate. [W]
Spread Eagle ½ mile west of Gailey Wharf. Large road house serving Banks' real ale and good *lunchtime* food. Garden.

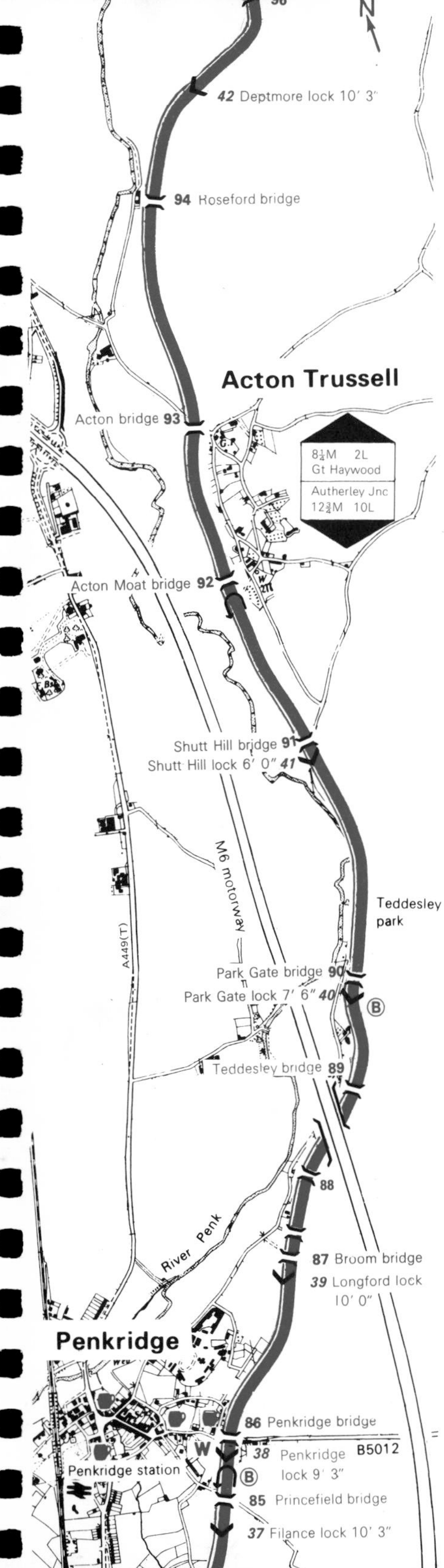

Penkridge

The navigation now passes through Penkridge and is soon approached by the little River Penk: the two water courses share the valley for the next few miles. Apart from the noise of the motorway, this is a quiet and pleasant valley: there are plenty of trees, a handful of locks and the large Teddesley Park alongside the canal. At Acton Trussell the M6 roars off to the north west and the canal moves along to the blissful isolation that surrounds Deptmore Lock. There is an inhabited lock cottage here; the residents' easiest means of access to the rest of the world is by boat to Radford Bridge.

Acton Trussell
Staffs. PO, tel, stores. A village overwhelmed by modern housing: much the best way to see it is from the canal. The 15thC church stands to the south, overlooking the navigation.
Teddesley Park On the east bank of the canal. The Hall, once the family seat of the Littletons, was used during the last war as a prisoner-of-war camp, but has since been demolished. Its extensive wooded estate still remains.
Penkridge
Staffs. EC Wed, MD Mon. PO, tel, stores, coffee house, garage, bank, station. Above Penkridge Lock is a good place to tie up in this village which is relatively old. It is bisected by a trunk road, but luckily most of the village lies to the east of this road. The church is tall and sombre, and looks well kept. Early English – mostly 12thC, but restored in the 1880s. There is a fine Dutch 18thC wrought iron screen, and the tower is believed to date from about 1500.

BOATYARDS

Ⓑ **Teddesley Boat Company** Park Gate Lock, Teddesley Road, Penkridge. (078 571 4692). R S W D Pump-out, gas, narrowboat hire, long-term mooring, winter storage, crane, chandlery, books and maps, boat building, boat and engine sales and repairs. *Closed winter Sun.*
Ⓑ **Bijou Line** Penkridge Wharf, Cannock Road, Penkridge. (078 571 2732). R S W D E Pump-out, gas, narrowboat hire, overnight mooring (by arrangement), long-term mooring, books and maps, boat sales, engine repairs, fitting out, gifts.

PUBS

The Moat House Bridge 92, Acton Trussell. Very attractive Banks' real ale pub with a conservatory and garden. Nice moorings.
Boat Canalside, by Penkridge Lock. Mellow red-brick pub with plenty of brass in the homely bars. Ind Coope (Burton) and Ansells real ale. Food *lunchtime and evening until 20.30.*
Star Market Place, Penkridge. A very fine old pub, tastefully renovated. Banks' real ale, food *lunchtime and evening.* Garden.
White Hart Wolverhampton Road, Penkridge. (078 571 2242). This historic former coaching inn has an impressive frontage. M & B real ale, meals *lunchtime and evening,* garden.
Railway Wolverhampton Road, Penkridge. (078 571 2685). Ansells, Tetley's and Ind Coope (Burton) real ales are available in this pleasant main road pub. Food *lunchtime and evening,* garden.

07885 714178

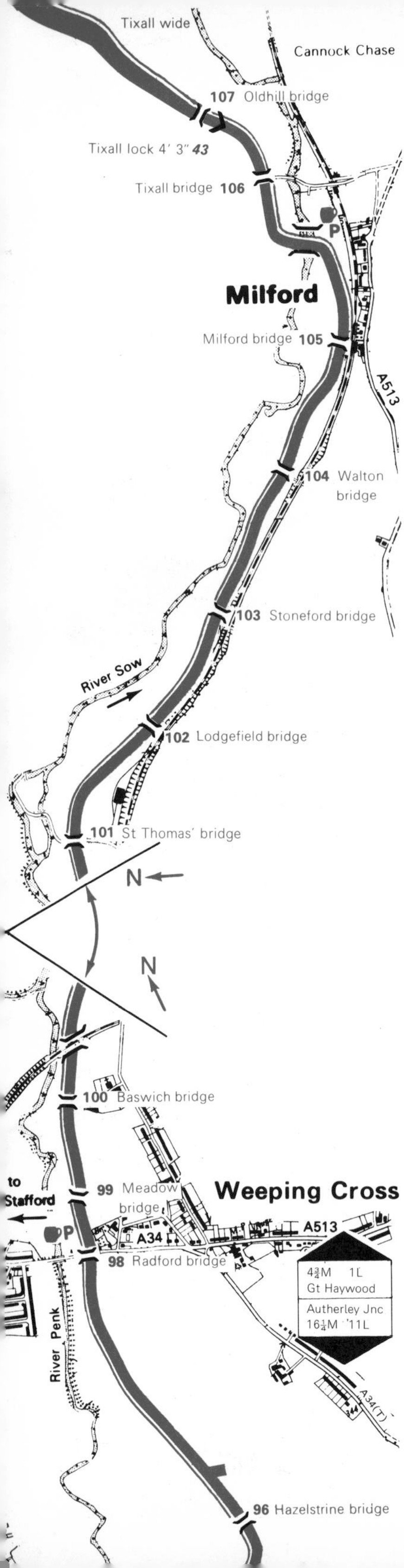

Sow Valley

Flowing north along the shallow Penk valley, the canal soon reaches Radford Bridge, the nearest point to Stafford (about 1½ miles to the centre of town – there is a frequent bus service). A mile north of here the canal bends around to the south east and follows the pretty valley of the River Sow. At Milford the navigation crosses the Sow via an aqueduct – an early structure by James Brindley, carried heavily on low brick arches. Tixall Lock offers some interesting views in all directions: the castellated entrance to Shugborough Railway Tunnel at the foot of the thick woods of Cannock Chase and the distant outline of Tixall Gatehouse.

Milford
Staffs. PO, tel, stores, garage. The village straggles parallel and close to the canal but access is obstructed by the busy railway: it is best reached from Tixall Bridge (106). Milford is an estate village on the fringes of Cannock Chase; there is a great big green near the pub. Milford Hall is hidden by trees.
The Stafford Branch
Just west of bridge 101 are the remains of the lock that used to take a branch off the Staffs & Worcs to Stafford. The branch, 1 mile long, was unusual in that it was not a canal but the canalised course of the River Sow, which joins the River Penk just by the former lock (Baswich Lock). The branch has not been used for years.
Stafford
Staffs. EC Wed, MD Tue, Fri, Sat. All services. This town is well worth visiting, since there is here a remarkable wealth of fine old buildings – including even the main post office. The Market Square survives, its best feature being the National Westminster Bank. There is a handsome City Hall complex of ornamental Italianate buildings, c1880. The robust-looking gaol stands nearby; and the church of St Mary's stands in very pleasing and spacious grounds. There are some pretty back alleys: Church Lane contains a splendid-looking eating house, and at the bottom of the lane a fruiterer's shop is in a thatched cottage built in 1610. All this in the middle of a town as large as Stafford is truly rewarding.
Art Gallery The Green, Stafford. (0785 57303). On first floor of Stafford Central Library. Contemporary art, crafts and photography. Craft shop. *Closed Sun and Mon.*

PUBS

Trumpet Canalside, at Radford Bridge. (0785 42825). A friendly pub and restaurant serving Bass real ale. Meals *lunchtime and evening*. Large garden with playground. Barbecues in summer. Good moorings.
Barley Mow Milford Common. (0785 661079). Pub/steak bar with a small hamburger bar next door.

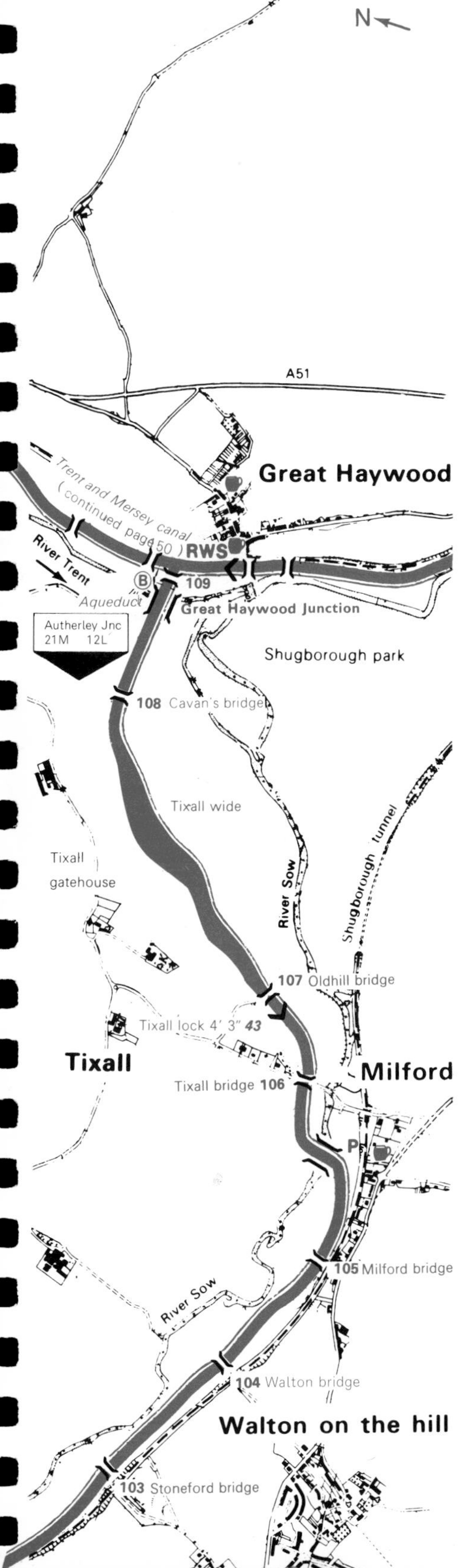

Tixall

The canal now quickly completes its journey to the Trent & Mersey Canal at Great Haywood. It is a length of waterway quite unlike any other. Proceeding along this very charming valley, the navigation enters Tixall Wide – an amazing and delightful stretch of water more resembling a lake than a canal, and navigable to the edges. The Wide is noted for its kingfisher population. Up on the hill to the north is the equally remarkable Tixall Gatehouse, while woods across the valley conceal Shugborough Hall. The River Trent is met, on its way south from Stoke-on-Trent, and crossed on an aqueduct. There is a wharf and towpath bridge across Haywood Junction. Fresh produce can be purchased at the farm here, and gifts are sold in the old canal toll booth.

Great Haywood
Staffs. PO, tel, stores. Centre of the Great Haywood and Shugborough Conservation Area, the village is not particularly beautiful but is closely connected in many ways to Shugborough Park, to which it is physically linked by the very old Shugborough Bridge, where the crystal clear waters of the River Sow join the Trent on its way down from Stoke. Haywood Lock is beautifully situated between this packhorse bridge (which is an Ancient Monument) and the unusually decorative railway bridge that leads into Trent Lane. The lane consists of completely symmetrical and very handsome terraced cottages: they were built by the Ansons to house the people evicted from the former Shugborough village. There is an interesting-looking Roman Catholic church in Great Haywood: the other curious feature concerns the Anglican church. About 100yds south of Haywood Lock is an iron bridge over the canal. This bridge, which now leads nowhere, used to carry a private road from Shugborough Hall which crossed both the river and the canal on its way to the church just east of the railway. This was important to the Ansons, since the packhorse bridge just upstream is not wide enough for a horse and carriage, and so until the iron bridge was built the family had to *walk* the 300yds to church on Sunday mornings! Gas, coal and logs available from Brian's shop.

Shugborough Hall *National Trust property.* Walk south along the road from bridge 106 to the A513 at Milford Common. The main entrance is on your left (access is easier from the Trent & Mersey, see page 150). The present house dates from 1693, but was substantially altered by James Stuart around 1760 and by Samuel Wyatt around the turn of the 18thC. It was at this time that the old village of Shugborough was bought up and demolished by the Anson family so that they should enjoy more privacy and space in their park. Family fortunes fluctuated greatly for the Ansons, the Earl of Lichfield's family; eventually crippling death duties in the 1960s brought about the transfer of the estate to the National Trust. The Trust have leased the property to Staffordshire County Council who now manage the whole estate. The house has been restored at great expense. There are some magnificent rooms and many treasures inside.

Museum of Staffordshire Life This excellent establishment, which is effectively Staffordshire's county museum, is housed in the old stables adjacent to Shugborough Hall. Open since 1966, it is superbly laid out and contains all sorts of exhibits concerned with old country life in Staffordshire. Amongst other things it contains an old fashioned laundry, the old gun-room and the old estate brew-house, all completely equipped. Part of the stables contains harness, carts, coaches and motor cars. There is an industrial annexe up the road, containing a collection of preserved steam locomotives and some industrial machinery. *House, grounds and museum open Mar–Oct 10.30–17.30 Tue–Fri & B. Hol Mon, Sat & Sun afternoons only.*

Shugborough Park There are some remarkable sights in the large park, that encircles the Hall. Thomas Anson, who inherited the estate in 1720, enlisted in 1744 the help of his famous brother, Admiral George Anson, to beautify and improve the house and the park. And in

1762 he commissioned James Stuart, a neo-Grecian architect, to embellish the park. 'Athenian' Stuart set to with a will, and the spectacular results of his work can be seen scattered round the park. The stone monuments that he built have deservedly extravagant names like the 'Tower of the Winds', the 'Lanthorn of Demosthenes' etc.

Tixall

Staffs. PO, tel, stores. A quiet and unspoilt hamlet facing the wooded slopes of Cannock Chase. Just to the east are the stables and the Gatehouse of the long-vanished Tixall Hall. This massive square Elizabethan building is fully four storeys high and restored for holiday lets! It stands alone in a field; one can only wonder at the size of the former hall with a gatehouse as huge as this. It is clearly visible from the canal: indeed Tixall Wide may have been made to resemble a 'broad' purely because it was in full view of the Gatehouse and the Hall.

BOATYARDS

Ⓑ **Anglo Welsh Waterways Holidays** The Canal Wharf, Mill Lane, Great Haywood. (0889 881711). R S W D Pump-out (*Mon–Fri*), gas, narrowboat hire, long-term mooring, books and maps, minor engine repairs, toilet.

PUBS & RESTAURANTS

Clifford Arms Great Haywood. (0889 881321). Friendly village local. Bass real ale, bar food *Fri, Sat & Sun only*. Garden.

Fox & Hounds Great Haywood. (0889 881252). Plush village pub serving Ansells and Tetley's real ale, and food *lunchtime and evening*. Garden.

The Lockhouse Restaurant Trent Lane, Great Haywood. (0889 881294). Morning and afternoon tea, coffee and cakes, hot and cold carvery at *lunchtime* and home-cooked English food in the *evening*. *Open 10.00–21.00 daily, but not Sun eve.*

Barley Mow Milford Common. (0889 661079). Pub/steak bar with a small hamburger bar next door.

A distinctive Trent & Mersey Canal milepost. *David Perrott.*

TRENT & MERSEY

Maximum dimensions

Derwent Mouth to Burton upon Trent
Length: 72′
Beam: 13′ 6″
Headroom: 7′
Burton upon Trent to Great Haywood
Length: 72′
Beam: 7′
Headroom: 6′ 3″
Great Haywood to Middlewich
Length: 72′
Beam: 7′
Headroom: 5′ 9″
Middlewich to Anderton
Length: 72′
Beam: 14′ 6″
Headroom: 7′
Anderton to Preston Brook
Length: 72′
Beam: 7′
Headroom: 7′

Manager:

Derwent Mouth to Trentham: (0283) 790236
Trentham to Preston Brook: (0606) 40566

Mileage

DERWENT MOUTH to
Swarkestone Lock: 7
Willington: 12¼
Horninglow Wharf: 16½
Barton Turn: 21¼
Fradley, junction with Coventry Canal: 26¼
Great Haywood, junction with Staffs & Worcs Canal: 39
Stone: 48½
Stoke Top Lock, junction with Caldon Canal: 58
Harding's Wood, junction with Macclesfield Canal: 63¾
King's Lock, Middlewich, junction with Middlewich Branch: 76¼
Anderton Lift, for River Weaver: 86½
PRESTON BROOK north end of tunnel and Bridgewater Canal: 93½

Locks: 76

This early canal was originally conceived partly as a roundabout link between the ports of Liverpool and Hull, while passing through the busy area of the Potteries and mid-Cheshire, and terminating either in the River Weaver or in the Mersey. One of its prime movers was the famous potter Josiah Wedgwood (1730–1795). Like the Duke of Bridgewater a few years previously, he saw the obvious enormous advantages to his – and others' – industry of cheap, safe and rapid transport which a navigation would offer compared with packhorse carriage (the only alternative then available). Wedgwood was greatly assisted in the promotion of the canal by his friends, notably Thomas Bentley and Erasmus Darwin. Pamphlets were published, influential support was marshalled; and in 1766 the Trent & Mersey Canal Act was passed by Parliament, authorising the building of a navigation from the River Trent at Shardlow to Runcorn Gap, where it would join the proposed extension of the Bridgewater Canal from Manchester.

The ageing James Brindley was appointed engineer of the new canal. Construction began at once and much public interest was excited in this remarkable project, especially in the great 2900yd tunnel under Harecastle Hill.

Once opened in 1777 the Trent & Mersey Canal was a great success, attracting much trade in all kinds of commodities. Vast tonnages of china clay and flints for the pottery industry were brought by sea from Devon and Cornwall, then transhipped into canal boats on the Mersey and brought straight to the factories around Burslem, taking finished goods away again. Everyone near the canal benefited: much lower freight costs meant cheaper goods, healthier industries and more jobs. Agriculture gained greatly from the new supply of water, and of stable manure from the cities.

The Trent & Mersey soon earned its other name (suggested by Brindley) as the Grand Trunk Canal – in the 93 miles between Derwent Mouth and Preston Brook, the Trent & Mersey gained connection with no fewer than nine other canals or significant branches.

By the 1820s the Trent & Mersey was so busy that the narrow and slowly-sinking tunnel at Harecastle had become a serious bottleneck for traffic. Thomas Telford was called in; he recommended building a second tunnel beside Brindley's old one. His recommendation was eventually accepted by the company, and a tremendous burst of energy saw the whole tunnel completed in under three years, in 1827. A much-needed towpath was included in this new tunnel.

Although the Trent & Mersey was taken over in 1845 by the new North Staffordshire Railway Company, the canal flourished until the Great War as a most important trading route. Today there is practically no trade at all along the canal, but it is assured (by statute) of a future as a pleasure cruising waterway. There used to be four tunnels on the Trent & Mersey apart from the pair at Harecastle. One of these was at Armitage, a 130yd bore through solid rock. But mining subsidence began to affect the tunnel, and during 1971–2 it was opened out and a road bridge built to carry the main road (A513) that crosses at this point.

Look out for the handsome cast-iron mile posts – 59 of them are original, 34 are replacements, identical except for the caster's mark 'T & MCS 1977'.

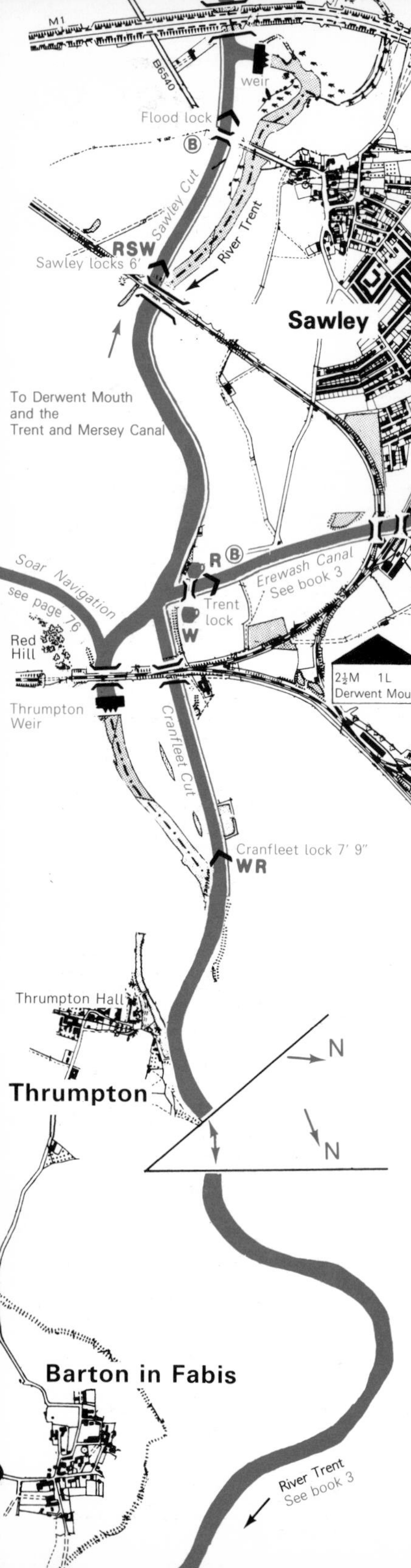

River Trent

The Trent & Mersey Canal begins at Derwent Mouth, some 2½ miles upstream of the point where the Soar Navigation enters the River Trent at a complicated waterways junction. Navigators leaving the Soar and heading towards the Trent & Mersey should turn LEFT (west) thus avoiding Thrumpton Weir, which lies beyond the large railway bridge. The entrances to the Cranfleet Cut and Erewash Canal (Trent Lock) are passed, both lying to the right, while continuing upstream to the railway bridge where the paired Sawley Locks (power-operated, by the keeper) will be seen at the entrance to the Sawley Cut. The flood lock is usually open, but should it need operating, be sure to leave a paddle open at each end after you have passed through. Keep to the LEFT when travelling upstream, or to the RIGHT when travelling downstream, to avoid another large weir by the M1 motorway bridge.

Trent Lock
A busy and unusual boating centre at the southern terminus of the Erewash Canal. There is a boatyard and two pubs here.

Sawley
Notts. PO, tel, stores, garage, fish & chips. The tall church spire attracts one across the river to Sawley, and in this respect the promise is fulfilled, for the medieval church is very beautiful and is approached by a formal avenue of lime trees leading to the 600-year-old doorway. But otherwise Sawley is an uninteresting main road village on the outskirts of Long Eaton.

Sawley Cut
In addition to a large marina and a well-patronised BW mooring site, the Derby Motor Boat Club has a base on the Sawley Cut where well over 100 boats are kept. All kinds of boats are represented here: canal boats, river boats and even sea-going boats. It is certainly no place to be passing through on a summer Sunday late-afternoon, for there will be scores of craft queuing up to pass through the locks after spending the weekend downstream. There are windlasses for sale at Sawley Lock, as well as the more conventional facilities.

BOATYARDS

Ⓑ **Sawley Marina** Trent Lock, Long Eaton. (0602 734278). R S W P D E Pump-out, day hire boats, overnight mooring, long-term mooring, winter storage, slipways, crane, dry dock, chandlery, books and maps, boat building, boat sales, engine sales and repairs, toilets, showers, café. (Maintains a watch on marine VHF.)

Ⓑ **Davisons** Trent Lock, Long Eaton. (0602 734278). Boat building, engine repairs. *Closed Sat & Sun.*

PUBS AND RESTAURANTS

Steamboat Inn Trent Lock, on the Erewash Canal. (0602 732606). Built by the canal company in 1791, when it was called the Erewash Navigation Inn, it is now a busy and popular venue. The bars have been handsomely restored and decorated with suitably nautical objects and real ale is served. Bar and restaurant meals *lunchtime and evening*. Garden, playground, children welcome.

Navigation Inn Trent Lock. Large popular pub with a fine riverside garden. Horne's real ale and *lunchtime* food.

Harrington Arms Sawley. Hardy & Hanson real ale.

White Lion Sawley. Ind Coope (Burton) real ale. Children welcome.

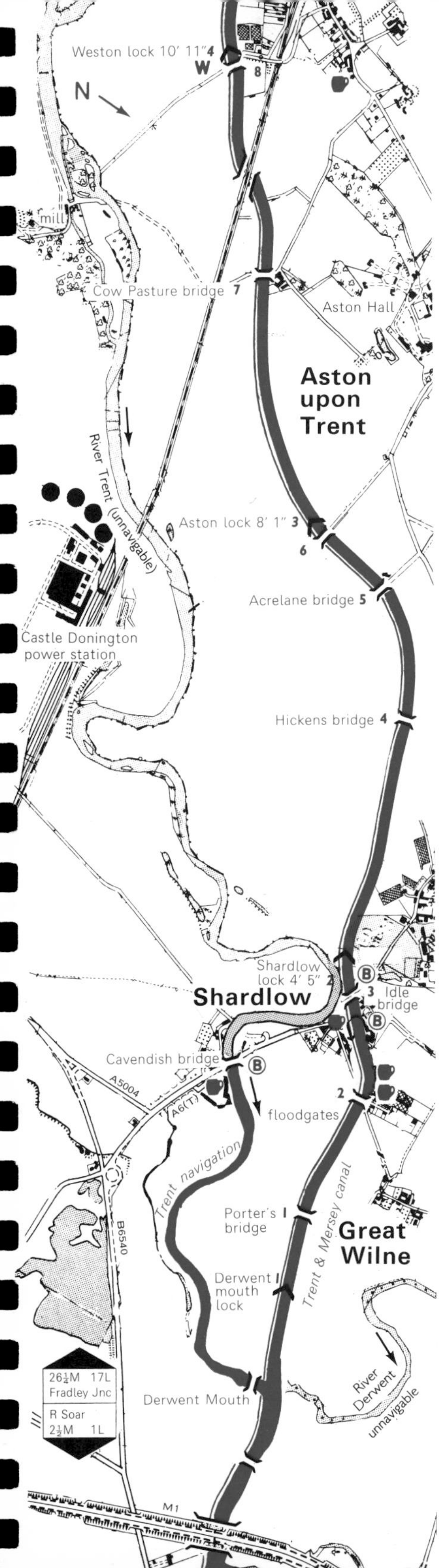

Shardlow

The Trent & Mersey Canal begins at Derwent Mouth, a 'crosswater' formed by the junction of the canal, the River Derwent and the River Trent. The Trent is navigable virtually to Shardlow (turn left under the concrete footbridge) thus making it possible to visit this remarkable village by either canal or river. The Derwent, although attractive, is not navigable. The first canal lock, Derwent Mouth Lock, is overlooked by a big shady chestnut tree, beyond which is Shardlow, one of the most interesting 'canal villages' on the whole inland waterway network. The Trent & Mersey Canal is very much the main street of Shardlow, and so one has an excellent view of the place from a boat. On the side of the little brick arch bridge at Aston Lock is a keystone inscribed 'J.C. 1770'. The letters could possibly refer to Josiah Clowes, an early canal trader and engineer, but the date establishes this canal bridge as among the oldest in the country.

Navigational note
Those heading towards the River Trent should not pass Shardlow floodgates if the warning light shows red.

Aston upon Trent
Derbs. PO, tel, stores, petrol. A pleasant village nearly a mile from the canal and, despite its name, over a mile from the river. (Access by a footpath from Aston Lock.) The sturdy stone church dates from the 12thC to the 15thC. Inside are fine monuments and good Victorian stained glass.

Shardlow
Derbs. PO, tel, stores, garage. Few canal travellers will want to pass through Shardlow without stopping. It is a magnificent example of a small canal port in a prime state of preservation. Everywhere there are living examples of large-scale canal architecture, as well as old-established necessities like canal pubs and a boatbuilding yard. By the lock is the biggest and best of these buildings – the 18thC Trent Mill, which has a large central arch for boats to enter and unload. Restored in 1979 as a canal centre, it retains all its original proud elegance. Other buildings in Shardlow are built in this handsome but functional style. To the north of the village is an 18thC stone-fronted hall.

BOATYARDS

Ⓑ **Valley Cruises** Hoskins Wharf, London Road, Shardlow. (0332 799019). In the restored Trent Corn Mill, just below Shardlow Lock. [W][D] Pump-out, gas, narrowboat hire, overnight mooring, books and maps, gift shop.
Ⓑ **Dobson's Boatyard** The Wharf, Shardlow. (0332 792271). On the canal. [R][S][W][D] Pump-out, gas, overnight mooring, long-term mooring, winter storage, slipway, chandlery, books and maps, boat building, boat and engine sales, engine repairs, toilets, wet dock.
Ⓑ **Shardlow Marina** On the River Trent. (0332 792832). [R][S][W] Pump-out, overnight mooring, long-term mooring, winter storage, slipway, chandlery, books and maps, boat building, boat and engine sales, engine repairs, toilets, showers, licensed club house and restaurant.

BOAT TRIPS

60-seater trip boat *Aquarius* available for charter, ring (0332) 792285 for details.

PUBS AND RESTAURANTS

Malt Shovel Aston. Ind Coope (Burton) real ale.
Canal Tavern Hoskins Wharf. Food.
Navigation By bridge 3, Shardlow. Davenports real ale, food.
Malt Shovel Shardlow. Superb old (1779) canalside pub, with small beamed bars and collection of beer mugs. Marstons real ale and good bar food. Garden.
New Inn Shardlow, next to the Malt Shovel. Bass Charrington real ale.
Lady in Grey Shardlow. (0332 792331). Elegant restaurant/hotel. The 'lady' is a ghost.
Old Crown Cavendish Bridge. Bass real ale in a riverside pub.

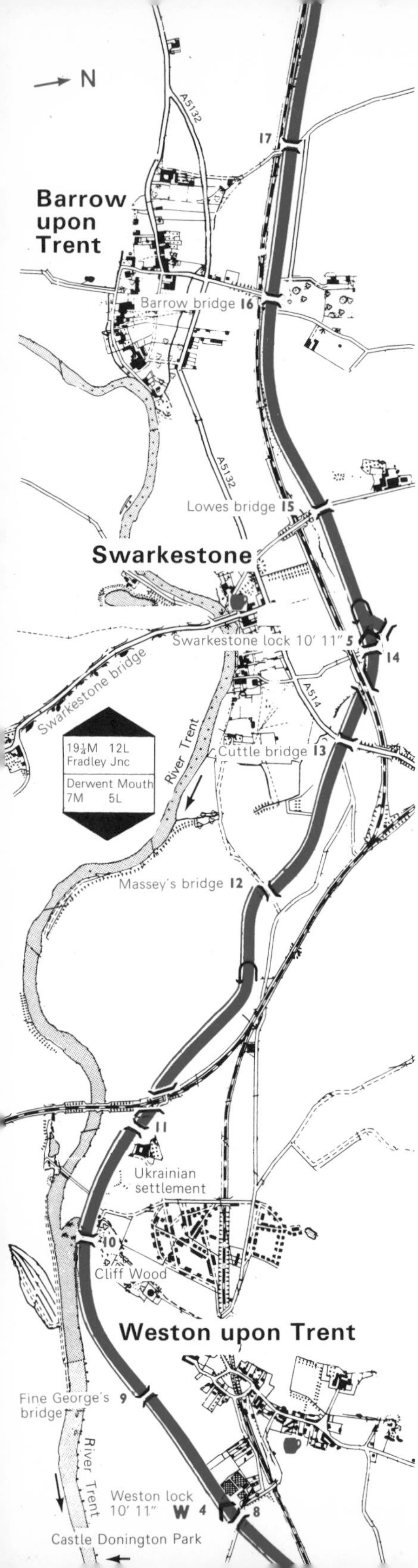

Swarkestone Junction

The village of Weston upon Trent is near Weston Lock. The wooden lock balance beams of the bottom gates, impeded by the bridge, are of necessity short; but they are massively wide – 22in square at the end. One may enjoy a pleasant walk by going down the lane south east from the lock to the river opposite King's Mills. The church and the rectory stand to the north of the village, on a hill with a fine view of the Trent valley. There are two enormous copper beech trees in front of the rectory. Leaving Weston, the canal passes a thickly wooded hillside – anyone who goes ashore at bridge 10 and walks up the hill is in for a surprise, for as likely as not a group of men will be found in front of a house arguing volubly – *in Russian*. For this is a farming settlement run by and for expatriate Ukrainians. The colony has been established here since the war and is entirely self-supporting. At Swarkestone Lock there is a short arm, used for moorings, all that remains of the Derby Canal. The old toll house at the junction has however found a new role as the headquarters of the Swarkestone Boat Club. The lock here is very deep, with a fall of almost 11ft. As with the other deep locks, it has very low top gates which incorporate substantial paddles. The River Trent continues its course to the south of the canal, and can be seen at intervals through the hedges and trees. The countryside is green and pleasant, with only the occasional freight train rumbling by to disturb the peace.

Barrow upon Trent
Derbs. PO, tel, stores. A small, quiet village severed from the canal by the busy A514. A lane from the church leads down to the river. Until recently the old hall stood next to the church, very much the focus of the village. But now bright modern houses stand in its place and the surviving lodge house looks uncomfortably irrelevant. Opposite is a mellow terrace of old workmen's cottages; these would also have served the hall.

Swarkestone
Derbs. PO, tel, stores. The main feature of Swarkestone is the 18thC five-arched stone bridge over the main channel of the River Trent. An elevated causeway then carries the road on stone arches all the way across the Trent's flood plain to the village of Stanton by Bridge. Away from the river, Swarkestone seems a rather tired village. The small church is tucked away in the back lanes; it contains interesting monuments of the Harpur family. In a field nearby are the few remains of Sir Richard Harpur's Tudor mansion, a barn, a gateway and a summer house.

Weston upon Trent
Derbs. PO, tel, stores. A scattered village that is in fact not very close to the Trent. The isolated church is splendidly situated beside woods on top of a hill, its sturdy tower crowned by a short 14thC spire. Inside are fine aisle windows of the same period. The lock gardens make the approach from the canal particularly attractive.

PUBS

Ragley Boat Stop New pub 300yds west of bridge 17. Marstons and Ind Coope (Burton) real ale.

Crew & Harpur Swarkestone, by the river bridge. Bass real ale and food.

Plough Weston upon Trent.

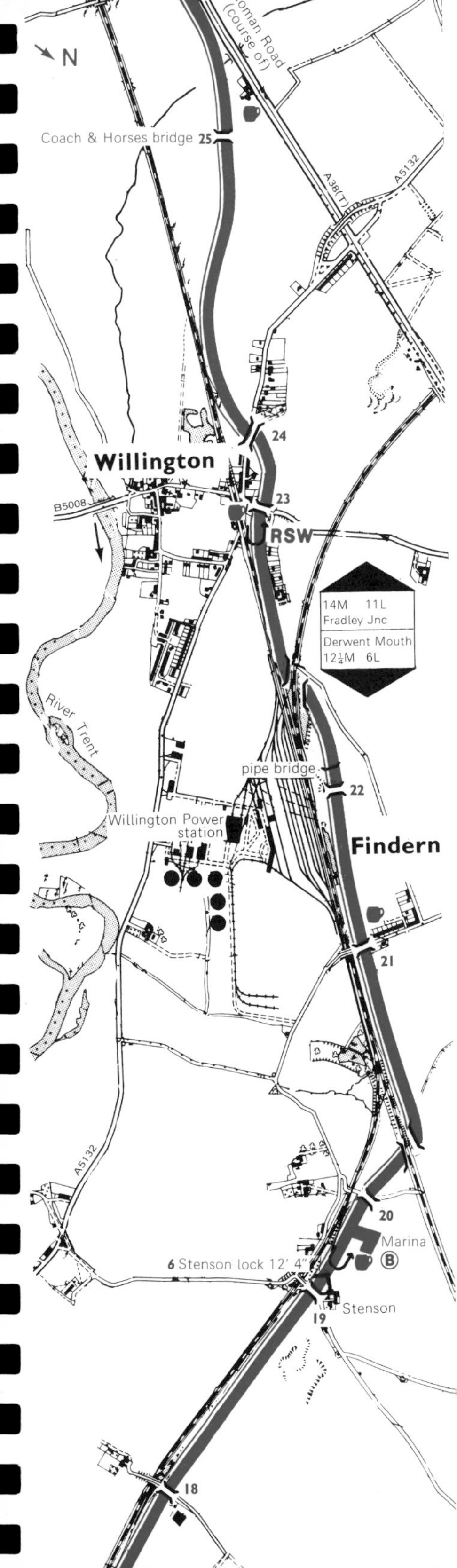

Stenson Lock

The canal passes through bridge 18, which is an unusual one – although the decking is a new concrete one, the old brick abutments have been retained and the concrete girders have been so laid that they seem to float above the abutments. The old cast-iron bridge number-plate has been cemented back into the concrete. Just by the bridge is Arleston House, an attractive old building with ground floor walls of stone and the upper tiers of brick. Stenson Lock is the last of the wide locks until Middlewich – it has a massive fall of 12ft 4in. Stenson is a small farming centre, always a popular mooring spot and now benefiting from the large marina to the north. After passing through a railway bridge, the canal changes course and heads off in a south-easterly direction for Burton upon Trent. The village of Findern is up a hill to the north, while to the south is the large Willington Power Station. Willington village has fine moorings by landscaped gardens, a sanitary station and a choice of three pubs, making it an excellent overnight stop. The A38 and the busy railway line now converge on the canal and escort it almost to Alrewas.

Repton
Derbs. 1½ miles south east of Willington (over the River Trent) is Repton, one of the oldest towns in England. It was once the capital of Mercia and the crypt below St Wystan's Church was built in the 10thC. One of the finest examples of Saxon architecture in the country, this crypt was completely forgotten until the end of the 18thC when a man fell into it while digging a grave. Repton public school dates from 1551 and there is much of historical interest in the school and the town.
Willington
Derbs. PO, tel, stores, fish & chips. The railway bisects by an embankment this busy little village, which has three pubs, all huddled together.
Findern
Derbs. PO, tel, stores, fish & chips. A small, quiet village where Jedekiah Strutt, the inventor of the ribbed stocking frame, served a seven-year apprenticeship with the local wheelwright. Until several years ago the village green was no more than a waste patch used by cars as a short cut and a parking place. When suggestions were made to turn it into a formal cross roads, the indignant Women's Institute galvanised the villagers into actually uprooting all traces of tarmac from the green and turfing the whole area properly. With the spired Victorian church beside it, the green is nowadays an ideal place for a summer snooze. A pub is nearby.

BOATYARDS

Ⓑ **Midland Canal Centre** Stenson Marina. (0283 701933). R S W D Pump-out, gas, narrowboat hire, overnight mooring, long-term mooring, winter storage, slipway, dry dock, chandlery, books and maps, boat building, boat and engine sales, engine repairs, toilets, gift shop.

PUBS

Every Arms On A38 west of bridge 25 (but access only from bridge 26 to avoid crossing private land). Cold snacks.
Green Man Willington. Bass real ale.
Rising Sun Willington. Food. Marstons real ale.
Green Dragon Willington. Ind Coope (Burton) real ale. Food, garden.
All three pubs at Willington are near bridge 23.
Greyhound Findern. Canalside, at bridge 21. Ind Coope (Burton) real ale. Large garden for children, and outside bar (sometimes). Many moored boats here.
Bubble Inn Alongside Stenson Lock and Marina, this pub in a converted barn serves Ind Coope (Burton) real ale and food.

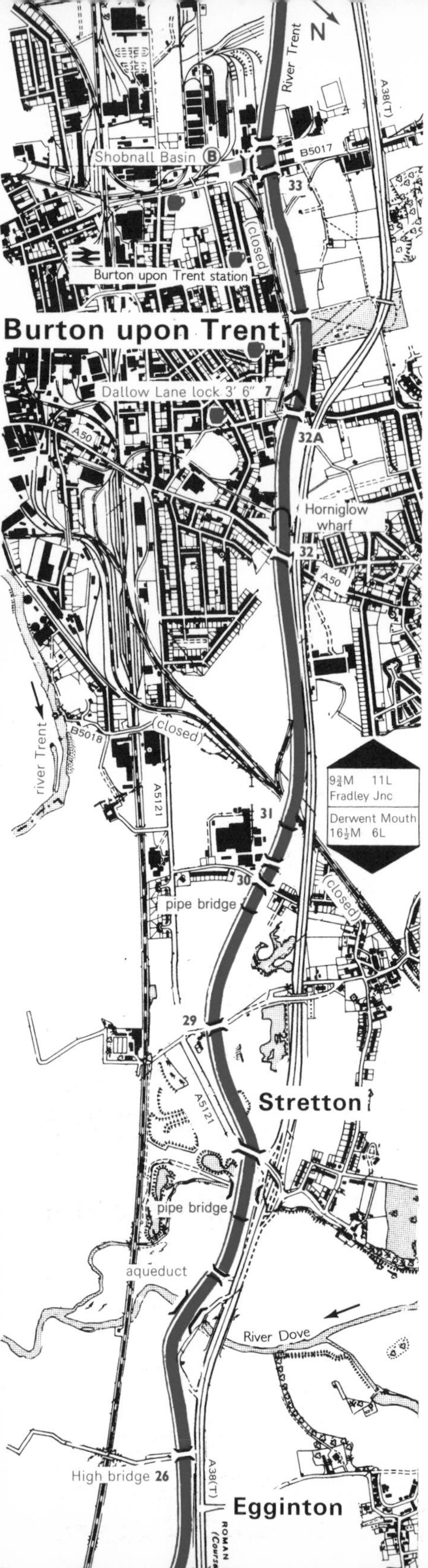

Burton upon Trent

A nine-arched stone aqueduct carries the canal over the River Dove, beside a handsome five-arched bridge, no longer in use. Factories and car parks herald the outskirts of Burton upon Trent. The canal passes along one side of Burton, without entering the town. Much of the old canalside architecture has been demolished and there is little of interest to see by the canal. The lovely smell of malt and hops is strongest to the west of the town, where the canal passes between the Marstons and Bass breweries. Dallow Lane Lock is the first of the narrow locks, an altogether easier job of work than the wider ones to the east. Shobnall Basin is now used by a boatyard, and secure moorings may be available from which to explore the town.

Burton upon Trent
Staffs. EC Wed. MD Thur, Sat. All services. Known widely for its brewing industry, which originated here in the 13thC, when the monks at Burton Abbey discovered that an excellent beer could be brewed from the town's waters, because of their high gypsum content. In 1708 the first full-scale brewery was established, and by mid-century ale was being exported, two customers being Peter the Great and the Empress Catherine of Russia. At one time there were 31 breweries producing three million barrels of ale: alas now only a handful remain. Perhaps the most widely known of Burton's products is IPA, India Pale Ale. Originally intended for export, it was released on the home market by underwriters after being salvaged when a boat carrying a cargo to India sank. The advent of the railways had an enormous effect on the street geography of Burton, for gradually a great network of railways took shape, connecting with each other and with the main line. These branches were mostly constructed at street level, and until recent years it was common for road traffic to be held up by endless goods trains chugging all over the town. Little of this system remains. The east side of the town is bounded by the River Trent, on the other side of which are pleasant hills. Near the site of the old abbey is an unusual bridge; it is an iron trestle footbridge stretching for over ¼ mile across the watermeadows. The main shopping centre lies to the east of the railway station.
Museum and Art Gallery Guild Street, Burton upon Trent. Exhibits largely devoted to local history. Extensive collection of British and foreign birds. *Closed Sun.*
The Bass Museum Horninglow Street, ¾ mile from Horninglow Basin. All aspects of brewing during the late 19thC. Also a preserved steam engine, café and shop. Conducted tours around the new brewery. *Open daily.* Admission charge.
Heritage Brewery Museum Anglesey Road, Burton upon Trent. (0283 69226). Established in the old Tiger Brewery, built in 1881 for Thomas Sykes when it was known as The Cripplegate Street Brewery, it remains substantially as built, a prime example of a typical 19thC brewery which is still functioning. *Open 10.00–16.00 Tue–Sat Easter–Mid Oct; 11.00–15.00 Sun May–Sep.* Charge.
Shobnall Basin
This is all that remains of the former Shobnall Branch, a canal which used to give the breweries the benefit of modern transport until the coming of railways. The old branch was in fact bought by the North Staffordshire Railway Company (along with the whole of the Trent & Mersey Canal), and replaced by a railway track, leaving just a short dock. The LMS Railway Company, which succeeded the North Staffordshire Company, used to deliver canal maintenance materials to Shobnall Basin to be collected by maintenance boats from Fradley Junction. Disused until recently, it has now been dredged and brought back to life as a boatyard. The dignified entrance bridge still remains. There even used to be a canal pub at this point.

Egginton
Derbs. PO, tel, stores. A quiet village lying off the A38. The church, set apart from the village, is pleasingly irregular from the outside, with a large chancel and squat tower. Unusual Tudor windows in the south wall make the inside very light.

BOATYARDS

Ⓑ **Jannel Cruisers** Shobnall Marina, Shobnall Road, Burton upon Trent. (0283 42718). In Shobnall Basin. [R][S][W][D] Pump-out, gas, narrowboat hire, overnight mooring, long-term mooring, winter storage, slipway, dry dock, chandlery, books and maps, boat building, boat sales, engine sales and repairs, toilets.

PUBS

In a town renowned for its beer, the following pubs are worth seeking out. The first four are closest to the canal:

Compasses Inn Wellington Street. Friendly local with an open fire, serving Ind Coope (Burton) real ale. Bar meals *lunchtime and evening*, garden.

Star & Garter Grange Street. Large welcoming pub with a children's room. Marstons real ale and *lunchtime* food.

Prince Arthur Shobnall Street. Local pub with a large lounge. Ind Coope (Burton) real ale, bar billiards.

Loaf & Cheese Waterloo Street. Bass real ale in a quiet local.

Duke of York Victoria Street. Superb unspoilt back street pub serving Marstons real ale.

Black Horse Moor Street. Marstons real ale in a cosy lounge bar. Home-made Stilton cheese with mussels is on the menu.

Roebuck Station Street. The brewery tap for Ind Coope.

Coopers Tavern Cross Street. Here the Bass real ale comes direct from the barrels in the brewery – there is no bar! Children allowed in until *20.00*.

Burton Bridge Brewery Bridge Street. Their own real ale, plus bar *lunches*.

Stenson Lock, Trent & Mersey Canal. *Derek Pratt.*

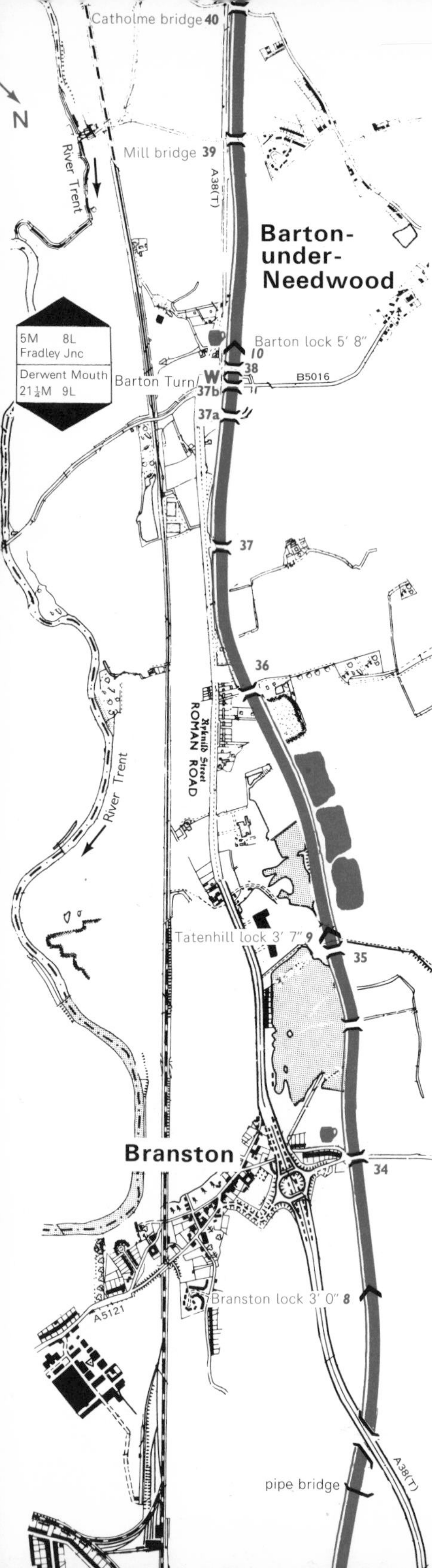

Barton Turn

The straight A38 runs beside the canal for several miles, depriving the navigator of any peace. The road is mostly a dual carriageway, and this contrasts massively with the narrow canal and its tiny old narrow bridges, many with a two-ton weight restriction. Up on the hills to the north west is the well-wooded Sinai Park – the moated 15thC house here, now a farm, used to be the summer home of the monks from Burton Abbey. At Branston Bridge is the only canalside pub for several miles in either direction – an excellent place to sample some of the best of Burton's produce. Beside Tatenhill Lock is an attractive cottage, and at the tail of the lock is yet another of the tiny narrow brick bridges that are such an engaging feature of this navigation. Above the lock is one of the many old cast-iron distance posts still surviving on this canal; they all show the mileage to Shardlow and Preston Brook, the two ends of the Trent & Mersey Canal. More are now being replaced, paid for by willing sponsors. After passing flooded gravel pits and negotiating the tiny brick arch of bridge 36, the canal and the A38, the old Roman road, come close together – thankfully the settlement of Barton Turn has been passed, leaving the main street (the old Roman road of Ryknild Street) wide and empty. One can enjoy working through the lock and visiting the pub unmolested by motor traffic. There is a telephone here, and a petrol station.

Barton-under-Needwood
Staffs. PO, tel, stores. Many years ago, when there were few roads and no canals in the Midlands, the only reasonable access to this village was by turning off the old Roman road, Ryknild Street; hence, probably, the name Barton Turn. The village is indeed worth turning off for, although unfortunately it is nearly a mile from the canal (bridges 38, 39 or 40). A pleasant footpath from Barton Lock takes one a quiet back way to the village, which is set on a slight hill. Its long main street has many attractive pubs. The church is battlemented and surrounded by a very tidy churchyard. Pleasantly uniform in style, it was built in the 16thC by John Taylor (Henry VIII's private secretary) on the site of his cottage birthplace. The former Royal forest of Needwood is to the north of the village.

Branston
Staffs. PO, tel, stores, garage, fish & chips. Although this is apparently the place where the famous pickle originated, it is a small, unexciting village, severed from the canal by the improvement of the A38, virtually to motorway standard. So the village has no sense of cohesion, and the canal traveller would have little reason to suspect its existence were it not for the map. Most of those on the canal will see no more than the excellent pub.

PUBS AND RESTAURANTS

Bell Barton-under-Needwood. (0283 712249). Restaurant (*closed Sun evenings and all day Mon*).

Three Horseshoes Barton-under-Needwood. Food.

Little Chef Canalside at Barton. (0283 716135). *Open 07.00–22.00 daily.*

Shoulder of Mutton Barton-under-Needwood.

Barton Turns Barton Turn, just opposite Barton Lock. Marstons beer.

Bridge Canalside, at Branston Bridge (34). Smart and cosy pub with an open fire on cold days. Marstons real ale served straight from the cask, and good food. Large sheltered garden. Frozen meals, bread, milk and sugar available to boaters, plus cycle hire (Burton upon Trent is 10 minutes' ride away).

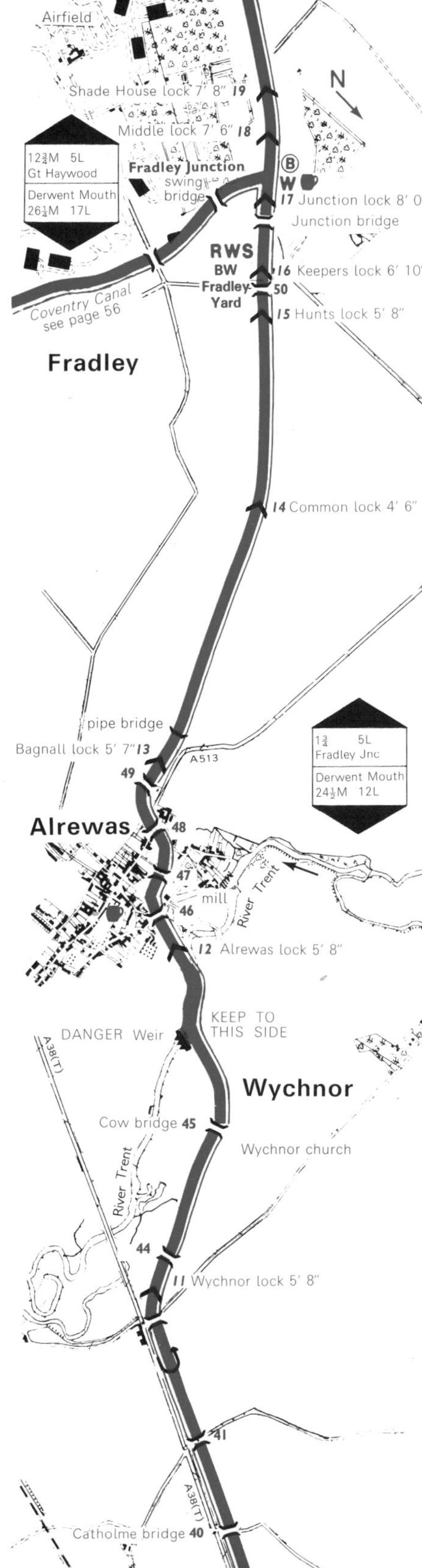

Fradley Junction

Boaters will be pleased to have reached Wychnor Lock – for here the A38 finally parts company with the canal, and some peace returns. To the west is the little 14thC Wychnor Church. It is a delightful scene, especially in the early morning or late afternoon: the cows grazing in the wide watermeadows or being herded across the wooded trestle bridge, the church with its small Elizabethan brick tower looking out over the swans, reeds and endless backwaters and side channels that run through the valley; and in the distance are the trees and church tower of Alrewas. All the way along here, little sluices and weirs carry water off the navigation down to the Trent; before Alrewas Lock the canal actually joins the River Trent – there is a large weir which should be given a wide berth. The towpath rises onto a trestle bridge, no doubt to keep the feet of boatmen leading horses dry in times of flood. **In times of flood great caution should be exercised along this stretch – keep well over to the towpath side at all times.** The canal winds through the pretty village of Alrewas, passing the old church (bell ringing practice Tuesday evening – beware of mooring close by at this time!), several thatched cottages and a brick bridge. The navigation then enters open country at Fradley, and its junction with the Coventry Canal.

Fradley Junction
A long-established canal centre where the Coventry Canal joins the Trent & Mersey. Like all the best focal points on the canals, it is concerned solely with the life of the canals, and has no relationship with local roads or even with the village of Fradley. The junction bristles with boats, for, apart from it being an inevitable meeting place for canal boats, there is a boatyard, a British Waterways maintenance yard, BW moorings, a boat club and a popular pub all in the middle of a five-lock flight.

Alrewas
Staffs. PO, tel, stores, garage, restaurant. Away from the A513, this is an attractive village whose rambling back lanes harbour some excellent timbered cottages. The canal's unruffled passage through the village gives the place a restful air, and the presence of the church and its pleasant churchyard adds to this impression. The River Trent touches the village (note the old mill building) and provides it with a fine background which is much appreciated by fishermen. The somewhat unusual name 'Alrewas', pronounced 'olrewus', is a corruption of the words 'Alder Wash' – a reference to the many alder trees which once grew in the often-flooded Trent valley and gave rise to the basket weaving for which the village was once famous.

Alrewas Church A spacious building of mainly 13thC and 14thC construction, notable for the unmatching nave arches (octagonal and quatrefoil) and the old leper window, which is now filled by modern stained glass.

BOATYARDS

BW Fradley Yard Fradley Junction. (0283 790236). [R][S][W] Overnight mooring, long-term mooring, toilets.

Ⓑ **Swan Line Cruisers** Fradley Junction, Burton upon Trent. (0283 790332). [W][D] Pump-out (*not weekends*), gas, narrowboat hire, overnight mooring, dry dock, groceries, chandlery, books and maps, boat building, boat sales, engine sales and repairs.

PUBS

Swan Fradley Junction. Canalside; the focus of the junction and justly famous. A fine public bar with a coal fire and pub games, a comfortable lounge used by families, and a lively cellar bar. Ind Coope (Burton) real ale and bar meals (*not Sun*).

Crown Alrewas, near bridge 46. Snacks.

George & Dragon High Street, Alrewas. (0283 790202). Marstons real ale, bar food and restaurant in an old village local. Garden.

William IV Alrewas. Marstons real ale, snacks.

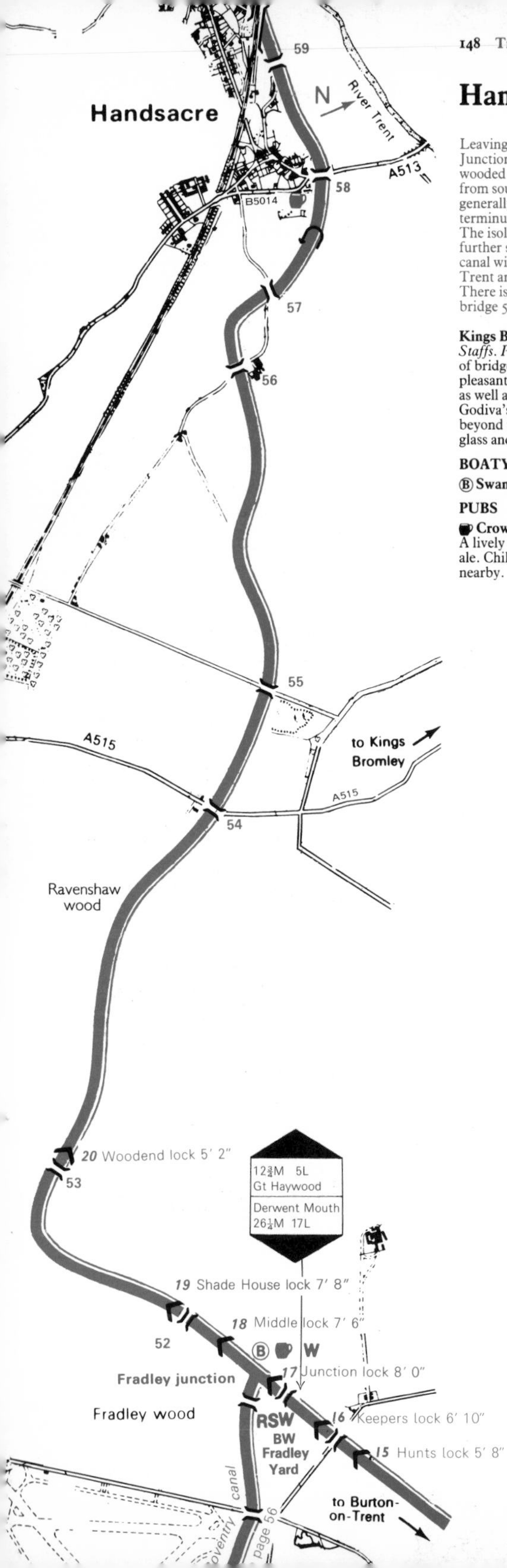

Handsacre

Leaving the Coventry Canal at Fradley Junction, the Trent & Mersey climbs past wooded heathland and abruptly changes course from south west to north west, a direction it generally maintains right through to its terminus at Preston Brook, over 67 miles away. The isolated Woodend Lock introduces a further stretch of woodland; beyond this the canal winds towards Armitage as the River Trent and the railway converge on either side. There is a useful general store 500yds south of bridge 59, and fish and chips near bridge 58.

Kings Bromley
Staffs. PO, tel, stores. A village 1½ miles north of bridge 54, along the A515. There are some pleasant houses and an old mill to be seen here, as well as what is reputed to have been Lady Godiva's early home. The Trent flows just beyond the church, which contains some old glass and a 17thC pulpit and font.

BOATYARDS

Ⓑ **Swan Line Cruisers.** *See page 147.*

PUBS

Crown Handsacre. Canalside, at bridge 58. A lively and welcoming pub serving Bass real ale. Children's room. Grocer and fish and chips nearby.

Handsacre
N
River Trent
A513
B5014
59
58
57
56
55
54
53
52
A515
to Kings Bromley
Ravenshaw wood
20 Woodend lock 5' 2"
12¾M 5L Gt Haywood
Derwent Mouth 26¼M 17L
19 Shade House lock 7' 8"
18 Middle lock 7' 6"
Ⓑ W
Fradley junction
17 Junction lock 8' 0"
Fradley wood
RSW
BW Fradley Yard
16 Keepers lock 6' 10"
15 Hunts lock 5' 8"
Coventry canal
page 56
to Burton-on-Trent

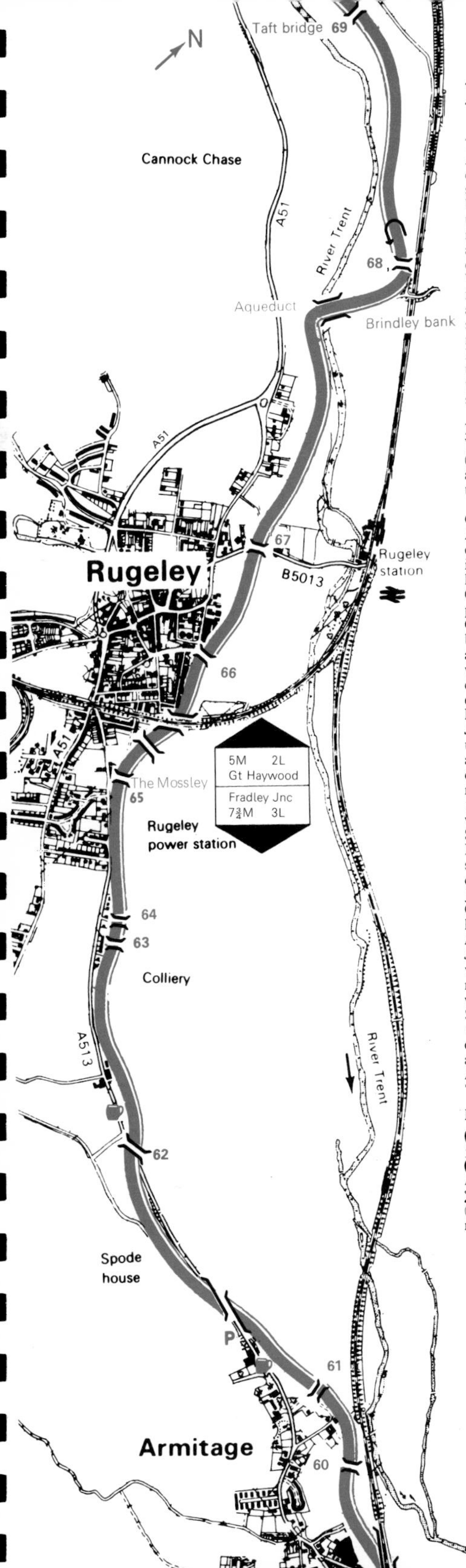

Rugeley

The canal now skirts Armitage, passing the Armitage pottery and church. Then the A513 crosses the canal on a new bridge where the short (130yds) Armitage Tunnel used to run before its roof was removed in 1971 to combat the subsidence effects of coal being mined nearby. There is a distinguished restaurant just across the road here, very much a rarity on canals in general and this area in particular. West of the tunnel stands Spode House, a former home of the pottery family. The towers and chimneys of the colliery and huge power station come into view; they take a long time to recede. There are now pleasant moorings at Rugeley, by the recreation ground, with the town centre only a short walk away. North of the town, the canal crosses the River Trent via a substantial aqueduct.

Navigational note
West of bridge 61 the canal is very narrow (following the removal of Armitage Tunnel), and wide enough for one boat only. Check that the canal is clear before proceeding.

Cannock Chase
An area of outstanding natural beauty and officially designated as such in 1949. The Chase is all that remains of what was once a Norman hunting ground known as the King's Forest of Cannock. Much of the existing forest has been planted and tended by the Forestry Commission, about 7000 acres of land having been acquired since 1920. Flora and fauna are abundant and include a herd of fallow deer whose ancestors have grazed in this area for centuries. Shugborough Park is at the north end of the Chase.

Rugeley
Staffs. PO, tel, stores, garage, banks, station. An unexciting place with a modern town centre and a dominating power station. There are two churches by bridge 67: one is a heap of 14thC ruins, the other is the parish church built in 1822 as a replacement. Cannock Chase rises west of the town.

Spode House Skirted by the canal. Spode House and Hawkesyard Priory stand side by side. The priory, which is only a small community now, was founded in 1897 by Josiah Spode's grandson and his niece Helen Gulson when they lived at Spode House. The latter is now used as a conference centre.

Armitage
Staffs. PO, tel, stores, garage. A main road village, whose church is interesting: it was rebuilt in the 19thC in a Saxon/Norman style, which makes it rather dark. The font is genuine Saxon, however, and the tower was built in 1690. The organ is 200 years old, and enormous: it came from Lichfield Cathedral and practically deafens the organist at Armitage. The town is widely known for its 'Armitage Ware' water closets.

PUBS AND RESTAURANTS

Ash Tree Canalside, at bridge 62. (0889 578314). A boat club is based here.
Plum Pudding Canalside, west of Armitage. (0543 490330). Food.
Old Farmhouse Restaurant Armitage. (0543 490353). A very popular English restaurant. *Closed Sun eve & Mon.*

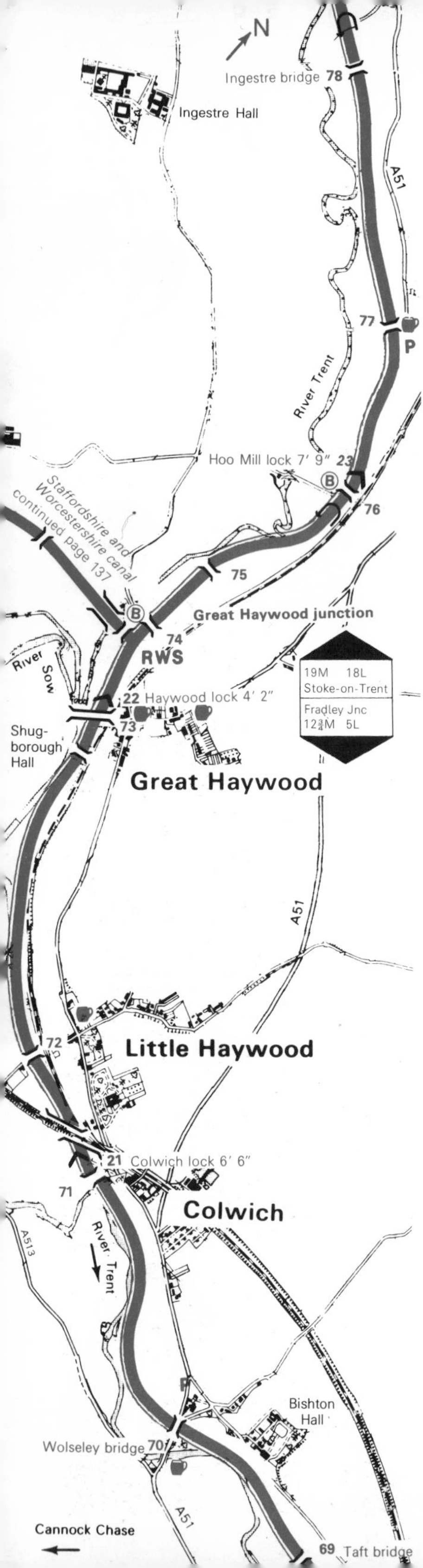

Great Haywood

One now enters an immensely attractive area that is full of interest. Accompanied by the River Trent, the canal moves up a narrowing valley bordered by green slopes on either side, Cannock Chase being clearly visible to the south. Wolseley Hall has gone, but Bishton Hall (now a school) still stands: its very elegant front faces the canal near Wolseley Bridge. Passing Colwich, an important railway junction, the canal reaches the perimeter of Shugborough Park: the impressive façade of the Hall can be seen across the parkland. At Great Haywood Junction the Staffs & Worcs Canal (see page 137) joins the Trent & Mersey from the west under a graceful towing path bridge – there is a useful boatyard here. Then the Trent valley becomes much broader and more open. Hoo Mill Lock is a busy spot: a boatyard stretches either side of it. North of the lock a busy road joins the hitherto quiet canal for a while. To the west is Ingestre Hall.

Great Haywood
Staffs. PO, tel, stores. Centre of the Great Haywood and Shugborough Conservation Area, the village is not particularly beautiful but is closely connected in many ways to Shugborough Park, to which it is physically linked by the very old Shugborough Bridge, where the crystal clear waters of the River Sow join the Trent on its way down from Stoke. Haywood Lock is beautifully situated between this packhorse bridge (which is an Ancient Monument) and the unusually decorative railway bridge that leads into Trent Lane. The lane consists of completely symmetrical and very handsome terraced cottages: they were built by the Ansons to house the people evicted from the former Shugborough village. There is an interesting-looking Roman Catholic church in Great Haywood: the other curious feature concerns the Anglican church. About 100yds south of Haywood Lock is an iron bridge over the canal. This bridge, which now leads nowhere, used to carry a private road from Shugborough Hall which crossed both the river and the canal on its way to the church just east of the railway. This was important to the Ansons, since the packhorse bridge just upstream is not wide enough for a horse and carriage, and so until the iron bridge was built the family had to *walk* the 300yds to church on Sunday mornings!
Shugborough Hall *National Trust property.* Entry to the Hall from the Trent & Mersey is just 5 minutes' walk from bridge 73 at Haywood Lock across the River Trent via the packhorse bridge. The present house dates from 1693, but was substantially altered by James Stuart around 1760 and by Samuel Wyatt around the turn of the 18thC. It was at this time that the old village of Shugborough was bought up and demolished by the Anson family so that they should enjoy more privacy and space in their park. Family fortunes fluctuated greatly for the Ansons, the Earl of Lichfield's family; eventually crippling death duties in the 1960s brought about the transfer of the estate to the National Trust. The Trust has leased the property to Staffordshire County Council who now manage the whole estate. The house has been restored at great expense. There are some magnificent rooms and many treasures inside.
Museum of Staffordshire Life This excellent establishment, which is effectively Staffordshire's county museum, is housed in the old stables adjacent to Shugborough Hall. Open since 1966, it is superbly laid out and contains all sorts of exhibits concerned with old country life in Staffordshire. Amongst other things it contains an old fashioned laundry, the old gun-room and the old estate brew-house, all completely equipped. Part of the stables contains harness, carts, coaches and motor cars. There is an industrial annexe up the road, containing a collection of preserved steam locomotives and some industrial machinery. *House, grounds and museum open Mar–Oct 10.30–17.30 Tue–Fri & B. Hol Mon, Sat & Sun afternoons only.*
Shugborough Park There are some remarkable sights in the large park that encircles the Hall. Thomas Anson, who inherited the estate in

1720, enlisted in 1744 the help of his famous brother, Admiral George Anson, to beautify and improve the house and the park. And in 1762 he commissioned James Stuart, a neo-Grecian architect, to embellish the park. 'Athenian' Stuart set to with a will, and the spectacular results of his work can be seen scattered round the park. The stone monuments that he built have deservedly extravagant names like the 'Tower of the Winds', the 'Lanthorn of Demosthenes' etc.

BOATYARDS

Ⓑ **Anglo-Welsh Waterways Holidays** The Canal Wharf, Mill Lane, Great Haywood. (0889 881711). [R][S][W][D] Pump-out (*Mon–Fri*), gas, narrrowboat hire, long-term mooring, books and maps, minor engine repairs, toilet.

PUBS AND RESTAURANTS

Coach & Horses Motel Near bridge 77. A comfortable pub with a skittle alley, usually offering at least eight real ales. Food *lunchtime and evening*, garden, children's room.

Clifford Arms Great Haywood. Friendly village local. Bass real ale, bar food *Fri, Sat & Sun only*. Garden.

Lockhouse Restaurant Trent Lane, Great Haywood. (0889 881294). Morning and afternoon tea, coffee and cakes, hot and cold carvery at *lunchtime* and home-cooked English food in the *evening*. Personally run, very friendly and handy for Anglo-Welsh visitors. Banks' real ale. *Open 10.00–21.00 daily, but not Sun eve.*

Fox & Hounds Great Haywood. Plush village pub serving Ansells and Tetley's real ale, and food *lunchtime and evening*. Garden.

Red Lion Little Haywood. Village local with a comfortable lounge. Ansells and Ind Coope (Burton) real ale, bar meals *lunchtime and evening*.

Wolseley Arms Wolseley Bridge (70). Comfortable pub which has Bass real ale. Bar meals *lunchtime and evening*, restaurant *open Tue–Sat*. Garden.

The Trent & Mersey near Great Haywood. *Derek Pratt.*

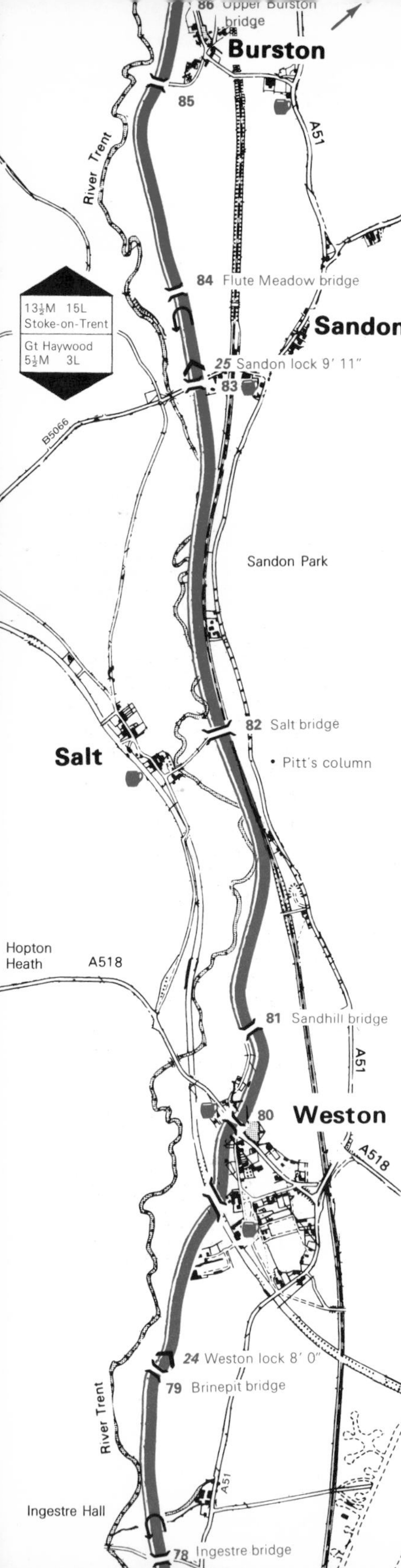

Sandon Park

Continuing up the Trent valley past Ingestre Hall and Park, the canal enjoys a length in which locks are few and far between. Weston (*PO, tel, stores*) is left behind and railway and main road converge as the valley narrows. The wooded Sandon Park rises steeply on the north bank; the canal passes now through quiet meadows to the little village of Burston.

Burston
Staffs. Tel. A hamlet apparently untouched by modern times, in spite of the proximity of three transport routes. Most of the village is set around the village pond. A very quiet place.
Sandon
Staffs. Tel. A small estate village clustered near the main gates to Sandon Park. The main road bisecting the place is enough to send any canal boatman scurrying back to the safety of the pretty Sandon Lock. There is a pub, however, opposite the park gates. All Saints Church, up the hill, is 13thC to 15thC with a Norman font and a 17thC wall painting.
Battle of Hopton Heath This was fought 1½ miles west of Weston. An inconclusive Civil War battle on the 19th March 1643, it reflected the strategic importance to both sides of Stafford, only 4 miles south west of the battlefield. In the engagement, 1800 Parliamentarians met 1200 Royalists (mostly cavalry). Supported by 'Roaring Meg' – a 29-pound cannon – the Royalists took the initiative, making several bold and effective cavalry charges against the enemy. However, the Roundheads' musketry fought back strongly, and after the Royalist leader (the Earl of Northampton) was killed, the Cavaliers weakened and fell back. Eventually both sides were exhausted and nightfall brought an end to the battle. Casualties – at under 200 – were surprisingly light, and neither side could claim a victory. The Cavaliers returned to Stafford, but two months later they lost the town for good to the Roundheads.
Ingestre Hall ½ mile south west of bridge 78. Originally a Tudor building, the Hall was rebuilt in neo-Gothic style following a disastrous fire in 1820. The house is surrounded by large attractive gardens. Now a residential arts centre open to visitors only on the *first Sat in Jul*.

PUBS

Greyhound Burston. 10-minutes walk up the lane from bridges 85 or 86. A thriving country pub, where Burtonwood real ale can be enjoyed with good food, *lunchtime and evening*. Garden.
Dog & Doublet Sandon. A refurbished former coaching inn, serving Ansells and Ind Coope (Burton) real ale. Bar food *lunchtime and evening*. Garden; children allowed into the function room.
Holly Bush Salt. Access from a stile near bridge 82; then walk up the lane.
Saracen's Head By bridge 80, Weston. Multi-roomed pub near the canal. Bass real ale, snacks, garden.
Woolpack The Village Green, Weston. M & B Springfield real ale, food *lunchtime and evening*, garden.

Stone

The 100-year-old tower of Aston Church is prominent as the canal continues up through the quiet water meadows of the Trent valley. Soon Stone is entered; below the bottom lock is a good place to tie up for the night – a fine old canal pub by the lockside, children's playground and shops are very close by. These locks are deeper than most on a narrow canal – their average rise is about 10ft. Just above the second lock is a boatyard and three dry docks: there is another boatyard a few yards further on. Lock 29 is accompanied by a little tunnel under the road for boat horses. The Stone Locks are followed by another flight of four, climbing up the valley to Meaford. The present Meaford Locks replaced an earlier staircase of three, the remains of which can be seen by lock 33. Here the electric railway line draws alongside.

Stone
Staffs. EC Wed, MD Tue, Thur, PO, tel, stores, garage, bank, station, cinema. A busy and pleasant town with excellent boating and shopping facilities. The old priory church began to fall down in 1749, so in 1753 an Act of Parliament was obtained to enable the parishioners to rebuild it. The new church (St Michael's in Lichfield Road) was consecrated in 1758, having cost £5000: it is a handsome building in open ground (no graves) on a slope at the east end of the town.

BOATYARDS

Ⓑ **Canal Cruising Co** Crown Street, Stone. (0785 812688). R S W D E Pump-out, gas, narrowboat hire, overnight mooring, slipway, dry dock, groceries, books and maps, boat building, boat sales and repairs, boat painting, engine sales and repairs.

Ⓑ **Stone Boatbuilding** Newcastle Road, Stone. (0785 812688). R S W D Pump-out, gas, long-term mooring, winter storage, slipway, crane, dry dock, chandlery, books and maps, boat building, boat sales, engine sales and repairs, toilets, showers.

Ⓑ **Staffordshire Narrowboats** The Wharf, Newcastle Road, Stone. (0785 816781). R S W D E Pump-out, gas, narrowboat hire, overnight mooring, long-term mooring, winter storage, slipway, chandlery, books and maps, boat building, engine sales and repairs, toilets.

PUBS

Rising Sun Newcastle Road, Stone. Canalside pub with a basic bar and a plush lounge. Bass real ale, *lunchtime* food, live jazz.

Swan Stafford Street, Stone. Traditional pub serving M & B Springfield real ale and snacks. Garden.

Crown & Anchor Station Road, Stone. Bass real ale and bar meals *lunchtime and evening* are available in this pub, which has a very plush lounge.

Stone Inn Radford Road, Stone. Pub decorated with old photographs of the Joules brewery. Bass and Stones real ale and *lunchtime* snacks.

Star Canalside, at Stone bottom lock. Bass and Stones real ale is served in this 13-room pub where apparently no two rooms are on the same level. Good bar food, children's room, patio. No winking lights or bleepers in the bar. An excellent traditional canal pub.

Pheasant Old Road, Stone. An original old Joules pub, now serving M & B Springfield and Bass real ale. Garden.

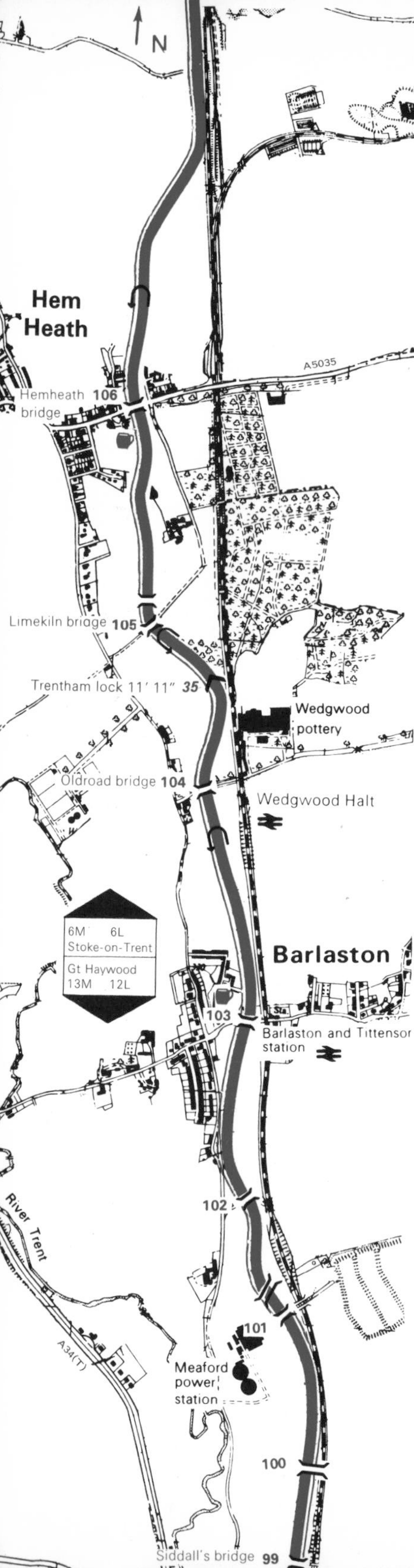

Barlaston

The valley widens out now and becomes flatter and less rural. Meaford Power Station and the railway flank the canal as it approaches straggling Barlaston. Just before Trentham Lock, where there are good moorings, is the Wedgwood pottery, set back from the canal. The factory is conveniently served by Wedgwood Halt. North of Hem Heath Bridge, where there is a useful shop in the petrol station, looms Stoke-on-Trent with its periphery of bleak industrial wastelands.

Trentham Gardens 1 mile west of bridge 106. The Hall, which was built by Barrie and which formerly belonged to the Duke of Sutherland, was demolished in 1909 except for the ballroom and orangery. Now used as a leisure centre, the place possesses formal Italian gardens and, among other facilities, a lake for fishing and boating, an open air swimming pool, and a miniature railway. Concerts are held in the ballroom.

Wedgwood Factory The Wedgwood Group is the largest china and earthenware manufacturer in the world. It was started in 1759 in Burslem by the famous Josiah Wedgwood, the 'Father of English Potters', who came from a small pottery family. By 1766 he was sufficiently prosperous to build a large new house and factory which he called Etruria – a name suggested by his close friend Dr Erasmus Darwin – and to use the canal, of which he was a promoter, for transport. It was here that he produced his famous Jasper unglazed stoneware with white classical portraits on the surface. He revolutionised pottery making with his many innovations and after his death in 1795 the company continued to expand. In the 1930s the Wedgwoods decided to build a new factory because mining subsidence had made Etruria unsuitable. The Etruria factory has unfortunately since been demolished but the large new factory began production in 1940 in Barlaston and is still the centre of the industry, with six electric tunnel ovens which produce none of the industrial smoke that is commonly associated with the Potteries. The Wedgwood Museum at Barlaston has a vast range of exhibits of Wedgwood pottery. The works is only a few yards from the canal, accessible from bridge 104. The Visitor Centre is *open daily*, and a small charge is made. There are demonstrations, a shop, a museum and refreshments (children under five are restricted to certain areas). Parties of 12 people and over must book (0782 204218). A stop here should be on every canal traveller's itinerary.

PUBS AND RESTAURANTS

Trentham Inn Near bridge 106. A large pub/steakhouse, serving food *lunchtime and evening*.

Plume of Feathers Station Road, Barlaston. A canalside estate pub with a bowling green. Bass real ale, food *lunchtime and evening*, garden.

Stoke-on-Trent

This is an industrial length of canal, passing right through Stoke-on-Trent with all its factories and warehouses. The signs of the pottery industry are everywhere. But the most remarkable manifestation of the industry is the 'bottle kilns' – the brick furnaces shaped like gigantic bottles about 30ft high that still stand, cold and disused now (but, happily, to be preserved), at the side of the canal. The Caldon Canal (see page 42) leaves the main line just above Stoke Top Lock. A statue of James Brindley, who built the T & M, was erected at the junction in 1989.

Stoke-on-Trent
Staffs. EC Thur, MD Wed, Fri, Sat. All services. The city was formed in 1910 from a federation of six towns (Burslem, Fenton, Hanley, Longton, Stoke and Tunstall) but became known as 'The Five Towns' in the novels of Arnold Bennett. The thriving pottery industries are the source of the city's great prosperity – one to visit is the famous Spode China works which is right in the centre of the town in Church Street. The Town Hall in Glebe Street, is an imposing and formal 19thC building. Opposite the Town Hall is the parish church of St Peter, a 19thC structure in Perpendicular style which contains a commemorative plaque to Josiah Wedgwood. The 1986 National Garden Festival was held on the site of the old Shelton steelworks, transforming the area into a large parkland of continuing benefit to residents and visitors alike. The actual city centre is Hanley.
City Museum and Art Gallery Bethesda Street, Hanley. (0782 202173). As one might expect, it contains one of the world's most outstanding collections of ceramics including work from Egypt, Persia, China, Greece and Rome. The historical development of pottery manufacture in Stoke-on-Trent is also traced from Roman times to the present day. *Open weekdays and Sun afternoons.*
Shirley's Bone Mill (0782 287577). By lock 39. This Victorian potter's miller's works was built in 1857 and ground bone, flint and stone for the pottery industry until closure in 1972. It has now been restored as part of an industrial complex incorporating a blacksmith's shop with working steam-powered machinery. Originally the raw materials and ground products were transported by canal via the short arm, and present day canal travellers will find plenty of moorings available. A statue of James Brindley, the builder of the Trent & Mersey Canal, was erected at the junction with the Caldon Canal in 1989. *Open for guided tours Wed–Sun, closed Mon & Tue.* Free.
Tourist Information Centre 1 Glebe Street, Stoke-on-Trent. (0782 411222). Access from bridge 113.

BOATYARDS

Ⓑ **Stoke Marina** Stoke-on-Trent. (0782 274099). R S W Toilets, showers.
Ⓑ **BW Etruria Yard** At junction with Caldon Canal. (0782 215597). R S W Toilet.
Dolphin Boats Near bridge 112, Stoke-on-Trent. (0782 49390). W Gas, overnight mooring, long-term mooring, winter storage, slipway, groceries, chandlery, books and maps, boat building and sales, engine sales and repairs. Breakdown service.

PUBS

Rose & Crown Etruria Road, east of bridge 117. A superb former Parkers Brewery showpiece pub with an open fire, serving Ansells, Ind Coope (Burton) and Tetley's real ale, home-cooked food *lunchtime*.
Rendezvous Etruria Road, west of bridge 117. A refurbished pub, formerly the Shelton. Tetley's real ale, wide range of *lunchtime* food.
China Gardens Canalside at the Marina, Etruria. (0782 260199). Large lounge, a grill restaurant and a special family room. Local celebrities are featured in their Etruria Hall of Fame. Bass real ale, *lunchtime* bar meals, garden with playground.
Bird in Hand Etruria Vale Road. Close to the junction, this is a popular canal pub. Ansells real ale, snacks, garden.

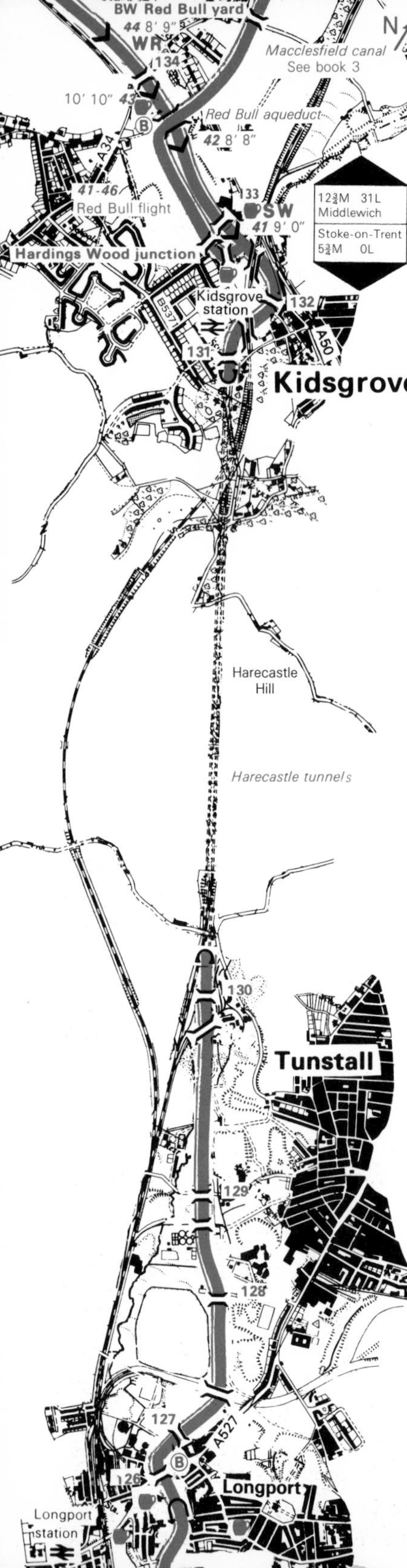

Harecastle Tunnel

The canal continues for a while through a heavily industrial area mostly connected with the pottery business and its needs. Before long the navigation abandons its very twisting course and makes a beeline for Harecastle Hill and the 2926yd tunnel through it. (The odd colour of the water here is caused by local ironstone strata.) Only one of the tunnels is navigable now. The tunnel is too long to see through, so no boat may proceed through it unless in accordance with the instructions given on the notice board or as authorised by the tunnel keeper. At the north end of the tunnel, the navigation passes Kidsgrove station and a useful coal yard: just beyond it is Harding's Wood Junction with the Macclesfield Canal where there are two pubs and a grocer. The Trent & Mersey proceeds to descend from the summit level through a flight of paired narrow locks. Just below the second lock, the Macclesfield Canal crosses the T & M on Red Bull Aqueduct. By now the industrial built-up area of the Potteries is being rapidly replaced by pleasant countryside.

Kidsgrove
Staffs. MD Tue. All services. Originally a big iron and coal producing town. Kidsgrove was much helped in its growing size and prosperity by the completion of the Trent & Mersey Canal, which gave the town an outlet for these goods. James Brindley is buried in the town in a churchyard at Newchapel.
St Saviour's Church Butt Lane. This building is unusual in looking quite unlike a church. Built in 1878, it was designed in black and white Tudor style.
The Three Harecastle Tunnels
There are altogether three parallel tunnels through Harecastle Hill. The first, built by James Brindley, was completed in 1777, after 11 years' work. To build a 9ft wide tunnel 1¾ miles long represented engineering on a scale quite unknown to the world at that time, and the world was duly impressed. Since there was no towpath in the tunnel the boats – which were of course all towed from the bank by horses in those days – had to be 'legged' through by men lying on the boat's cabin roof and propelling the boat by 'walking' along the tunnel roof. (The towing horse would have to be walked in the meantime over the top of the hill.) This very slow means of propulsion, combined with the great length of the narrow tunnel and the large amount of traffic on the navigation, made Harecastle a major bottleneck for canal boats. So in 1822 the Trent & Mersey Canal Company called in Thomas Telford, who recommended that a second tunnel be constructed alongside the first one. This was done: the new tunnel was completed in 1827, with a towpath (now removed), after only three years' work. Each tunnel then became one-way until in the 20thC Brindley's bore had sunk so much from mining subsidence that it had to be abandoned. An electric tug was introduced in 1914 to speed up traffic through Telford's tunnel; this service was continued until 1954. The third tunnel through Harecastle Hill was built years after the other two, and carried the Stoke–Kidsgrove railway line. It runs 40ft above the canal tunnels and is slightly shorter. This tunnel was closed in the 1960s: the railway line now goes round the hill and through a much shorter tunnel. Thus two out of the three Harecastle tunnels are disused.

Navigational note
Harecastle Tunnel Do not enter in an unpowered craft. With the complete removal of the towpath, headroom is no longer the great problem it used to be. A one-way system operates, but its operating schedule is liable to change from time to time. Follow the instructions given on the boards at each end or the instructions of the tunnel keeper.

BOATYARDS

Ⓑ **BW Red Bull Yard** North of bridge 134. (0782 785703). R W

Ⓑ **David Piper** Red Bull Basin, Church Lawton, Kidsgrove. (0782 784754). By Red Bull Aqueduct. W D Pump-out, gas, overnight mooring, long-term mooring, winter storage, slipway up to 60ft, chandlery, books and maps, boat building, boat sales, engine sales and repairs. Useful source of information regarding tunnel opening times.

Ⓑ **Stoke-on-Trent Boat Building** Longport Wharf, Longport, Stoke-on-Trent. (0782 813831). R S W D Pump-out, gas, overnight mooring, long-term mooring, winter storage, slipway, chandlery, books and maps, boat building and repairs, boat sales, engine sales and repairs, gift shop, toilet.

PUBS

Red Bull Canalside by the Red Bull flight. Robinson's real ale, food *lunchtime and evening*, garden.

Blue Bell At the junction with the Macclesfield Canal. Thoughtfully modernised pub serving Burtonwood, McEwans and Youngers real ale. *Lunchtime* food, snacks, garden.

Tavern Opposite the Blue Bell. Public bar with pool table and comfortable lounge. Tetley's real ale. *Lunchtime* food, snacks, garden.

Duke of Bridgewater Near bridge 126. The lounge is full of narrowboat relics.

Pack Horse Station Street, canalside at bridge 126. A lively pub dispensing Ansells and Ind Coope (Burton) real ale. HQ of local IWA and folk music club (*Fri*). Snacks, garden.

Railway Near Longport Railway Station. Excellent *lunchtime* buffet and Bass real ale. Garden.

Travellers Rest 239 Newcastle Street, Middleport. Here you can sink a pint of Titanic Premium Bitter, or Ansells Aylesbury or Ind Coope (Burton) real ale. Also Gaymers real cider. Folk music *lunchtime Sun*, jazz *Mon evening*. Food, snacks, garden.

Longport Wharf, Stoke-on-Trent: a traditional boat and butty prepare to leave. *David Perrott.*

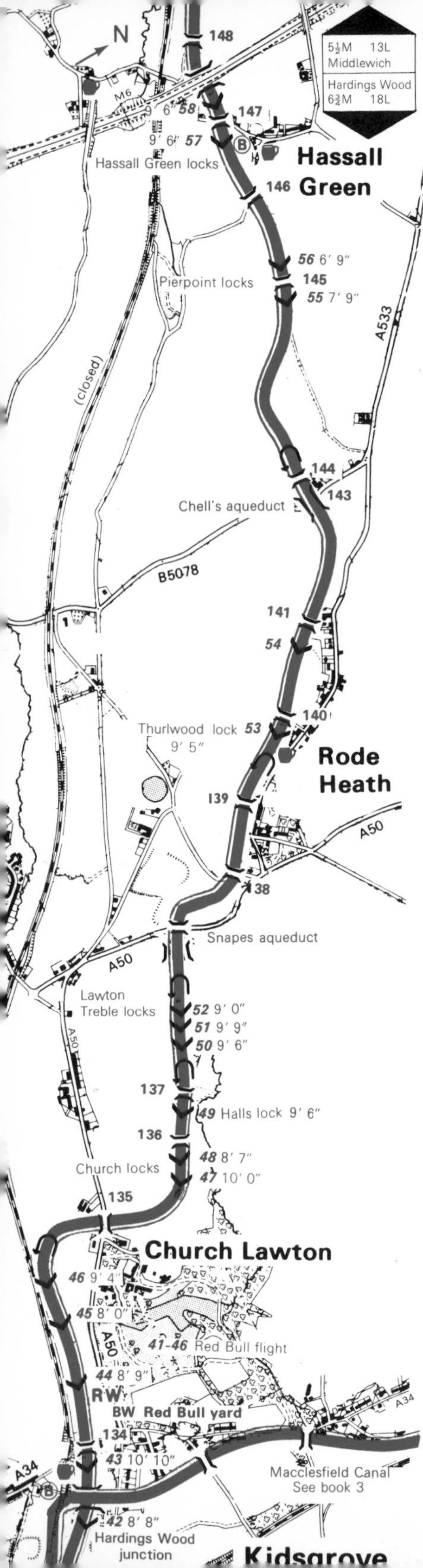

Rode Heath

Leaving behind the spire of Church Lawton, the canal continues to fall through a heavily locked stretch sometimes called 'heartbreak hill' but known to the old boatmen as the 'Cheshire Locks'. The countryside is entirely rural and pleasant, slightly hilly and wooded. Two minor aqueducts are encountered, but the locks are more interesting: they are all pairs of narrow locks, side by side. Some of the duplicate locks are unusable or even filled in, but many of them are in good condition, so navigators can choose whichever lock is set in their favour. The duplicate lock at Thurlwood, alongside the existing lock, used to be one of the strangest structures on the waterways network. Known as Thurlwood Steel Lock, it was built in 1957 to overcome subsidence caused by local brine pumping, and was a massive and complicated affair, with a huge steel superstructure. Unused for many years, it was dismantled in 1988. At Hassall Green a *PO, tel and stores* incorporating a canal shop and boatyard services can be found just by the new concrete bridge. The M6 motorway crosses noisily nearby.

Rode Heath
PO, tel, stores. A useful shopping area right by bridge 139.

BOATYARDS

Ⓑ **Vistra Marina** Hassall Green, Crewe. (0270 762266). S W D Pump-out, gas, long-term mooring, winter storage, groceries, books and maps, engine repairs. Also post office, general store, off-licence, gifts, café, paraffin, coal. Emergency repairs and boat fitting.

BOAT TRIPS

Shearwater Takes up to 12 people to Church Lawton and back. Restaurant and bar. Ring (0270) 762266.

PUBS

Romping Donkey Hassall Green. A pretty country pub, offering real ale, and bar meals and snacks *lunchtime and evening*. Children welcome, garden.

Broughton Arms Canalside at Rode Heath. Friendly and popular pub with good moorings. Snacks, garden.

Lawton Arms Knutsford Road, Church Lawton. A locals' pub dispensing Robinson's real ale. Garden. Busy at *lunchtime*.

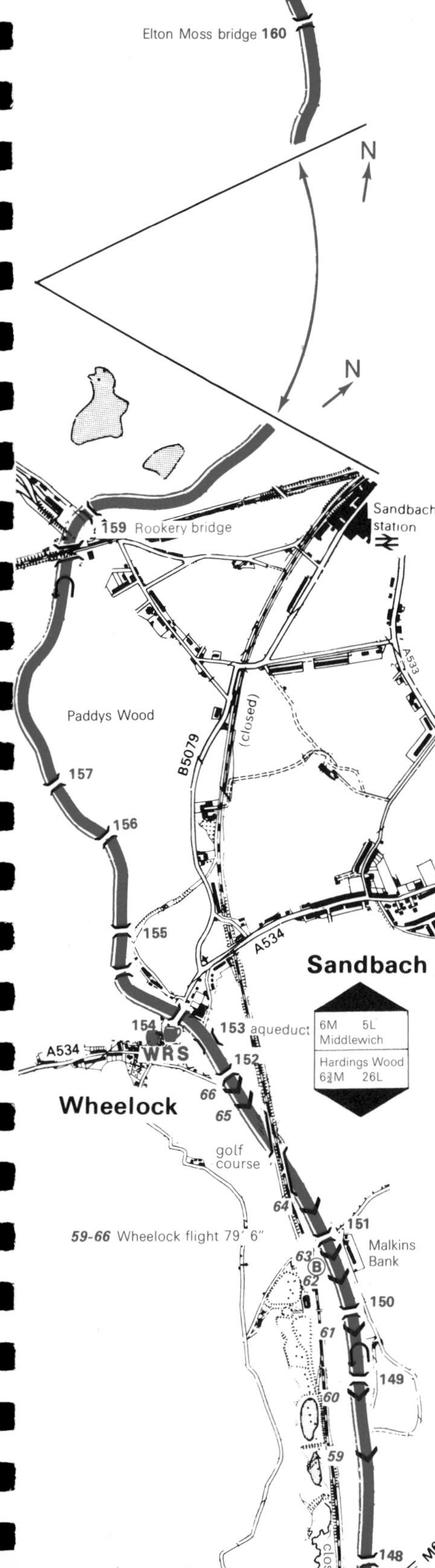

Wheelock

The canal now descends the Wheelock flight of eight locks, which are the last paired locks one sees when travelling northwards. The countryside continues to be quiet and unspoilt but unspectacular. The pair of locks halfway down the flight is situated in the little settlement of Malkin's Bank, overlooked by terraced houses. The boatman's co-op used to be here, in the small terrace of cottages. At the bottom of the flight is the village of Wheelock; west of here the navigation curls round the side of a hill before entering the very long-established salt-producing area that is based on Middlewich. The 'wild' brine pumping and rock-salt mining that has gone on hereabouts has resulted in severe local subsidence; the effect on the canal has been to necessitate the constant raising of the banks as lengths of the canal bed sink. This of course means that the affected lengths tend to be much deeper than ordinary canals. Non-swimmers beware of falling overboard.

Sandbach
Ches. EC Tue, MD Thur. PO, tel, stores, garage, bank, station. 1½ miles north of Wheelock. An old market town that has maintained its charm despite the steady growth of its salt and chemical industries.
Ancient Crosses In the cobbled market place on a massive base stand two superb Saxon crosses, believed to commemorate the conversion of the area to Christianity in the 7thC. They suffered severely in the 17thC when the Puritans broke them up and scattered the fragments for miles. After years of searching for the parts, George Ormerod succeeded in re-erecting the crosses in 1816, with new stone replacing the missing fragments.
St Mary's Church High Street. A large, 16thC church with a handsome battlemented tower. The most interesting features of the interior are the 17thC carved roof and the fine chancel screen.
The Old Hall Hotel An outstanding example of Elizabethan half-timbered architecture, which was formerly the home of the lord of the manor, but is now used as an hotel.
Wheelock
Ches. EC Tue. PO, tel, stores, garage, fish and chips. Busy little main road village on the canal.

BOATYARDS

Ⓑ **Malkins Bank Canal Services** (0270 764595). W Overnight mooring, long-term mooring, slipway, chandlery, boat building and restoration. Breakdown service.

PUBS

Cheshire Cheese Wheelock. Canalside pub serving Tetley's real ale and food. Garden with children's play area.
Commercial Near bridge 154, Wheelock. Once a home-brew pub, now you can enjoy Boddingtons and Marstons real ale.
Nags Head Near bridge 154, Wheelock. A small black-and-white pub serving Chesters and Whitbread real ale. Garden.
Market Tavern The Square, Sandbach. Opposite the crosses. Food, garden.

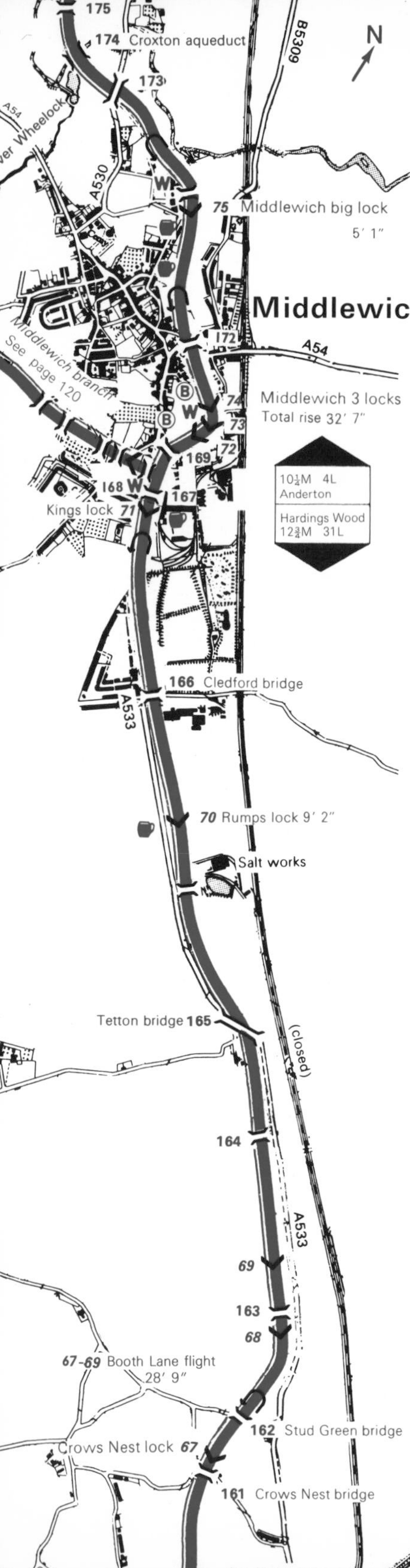

Middlewich

The navigation now begins to lose the rural character it has enjoyed since Kidsgrove. Falling through yet more locks, the canal is joined by a busy main road (useful for fish and chips and Chinese take-away) which accompanies it into increasingly flat and industrialised landscape, past several salt works and into Middlewich, where a branch of the Shropshire Union leads off westwards towards that canal at Barbridge. The Trent & Mersey skirts the centre of the town, passing lots of moored narrowboats and through three consecutive narrow locks, arriving at a wide (14ft) lock (which has suffered from subsidence) with a pub beside it. This used to represent the beginning of a wide, almost lock-free navigation right through to Preston Brook, Manchester and Wigan (very convenient for the salt industry when it shipped most of its goods by boat), but Croxton Aqueduct had to be replaced many years ago, and is now a steel structure only 8ft 2in wide. The aqueduct crosses the River Dane, which flows alongside the navigation as both water courses leave industrial Middlewich and move out into fine open country.

Middlewich
Ches. EC Wed. PO, tel, stores, bank, garage. A town that since Roman times has been dedicated to salt extraction. Most of the salt produced here goes to various chemical industries. Subsidence from salt extraction has prevented redevelopment for many years, but a big renewal scheme is now in progress. The canalside area is a haven of peace below the busy streets. The Tourist Information Centre is by bridge 172.
St Michael's Church A handsome medieval church which was a place of refuge for the Royalists during the Civil War. It has a fine interior with richly carved woodwork.

BOATYARDS

Ⓑ **Andersen Boats** Wych House, St Anne's Road, Middlewich. (060 684 3668). W Pump-out, gas, narrowboat hire, overnight mooring (*not weekends*), books and maps, toilets.
Ⓑ **Middlewich Narrowboats** Canal Terrace, Middlewich. (060 684 2460). R S W D Pump-out, gas, narrowboat hire, overnight mooring (*not Fri*), long-term mooring, dry dock, groceries, chandlery, books and maps, boat building, engine repairs, toilets, laundry service, breakdown service. Useful tool hire shop next door.

PUBS

Big Lock Middlewich. Canalside. Food.
✕ **Boars Head** Kinderton Street, Middlewich. (060 684 3191). Large rambling pub offering Robinson's real ale and *lunchtime* meals. Children's room and garden in hotel restaurant (*L & D*) next door.
Newton Brewery Inn By Big Lock, Middlewich. Marstons real ale in a small, popular local. Snacks, garden.
Cheshire Cheese Lewin Street, Middlewich. Food.
Kings Lock Middlewich. Canalside. Fish and chips opposite.
Kinderton Arms Close to canal 1 mile south of Middlewich, by lock 70. Ignore its dour appearance and walk in.

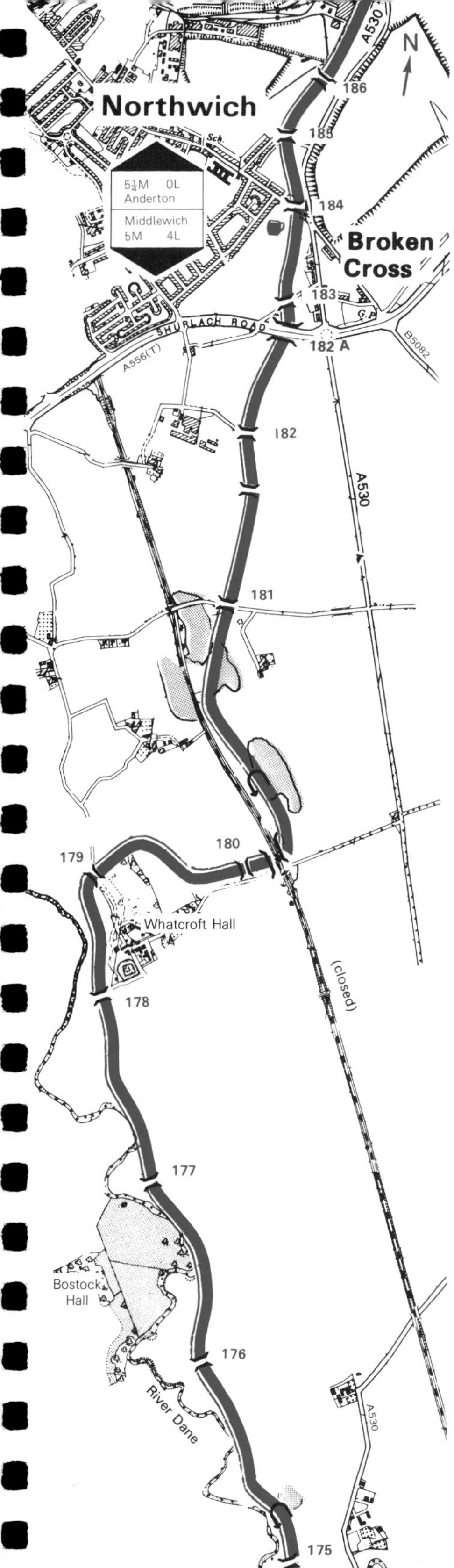

Dane Valley

Initially, this is a stretch of canal as beautiful as any in the country. Often overhung by trees, the navigation winds along the side of a hill as it follows the delightful valley of the River Dane. The parkland on the other side of the valley encompasses Bostock Hall, a school for children with learning difficulties. At Whatcroft Hall (privately owned), the canal circles around to the east, passing under a derelict railway before heading for the industrial outskirts of Northwich and shedding its beauty and solitude once again. The outlying canal settlement of Broken Cross acts as a buffer between these two very different lengths of canal.
Note: There are several privately owned wide 'lagoons' caused by subsidence along this section of the Trent & Mersey, in some of which repose the hulks of abandoned barges and narrowboats, lately being salvaged. Navigators should be wary of straying off the main line, since the offside canal bank is often submerged and invisible just below the water level.

Northwich
Ches. EC Wed, MD Fri, Sat. All services. Regular buses from Barnton. A rather attractive town at the junction of the Rivers Weaver and Dane. (The latter brings large quantities of sand down into the Weaver Navigation, necessitating a heavy expenditure on dredging.) As in every other town in this area, salt has for centuries been responsible for the continued prosperity of Northwich. (The Brine Baths in Victoria Road are still open throughout the year for the benefit of salt-water enthusiasts.) The Weaver Navigation has of course been another very prominent factor in the town's history, and the building and repairing of barges, narrowboats, and small sea-going ships has been carried on here for over 200 years. Nowadays this industry has been almost forced out of business by foreign competition, and the last private shipyard on the river closed down in 1971. (This yard – Isaac Pimblott's – used to be between Hunt's Locks and Hartford Bridge. Their last contract was a tug for Aden.) However the big BW yard in the town continues to thrive; some very large maintenance craft are built and repaired here. The wharves by Town Bridge are empty, and are an excellent temporary mooring site for anyone wishing to visit the place. The town centre is very close; much of it has been completely rebuilt very recently. There is now an extensive shopping precinct. Although the large number of pubs has been whittled down in the rebuilding process, there are still some pleasant old streets. The Weaver and the big swing bridges across it remain a dominant part of the background.
Salt Museum Weaver Hall, London Road, Northwich. (0606 41331). The history of the salt industry from Roman times to the present day, housed in the town's former workhouse. Look out for the remarkable model ship, made from salt of course. *Open daily, except Mon.* Charge.

PUBS

Old Broken Cross Canalside, at bridge 184. An attractive old canal pub. Shops and launderette a short way past the pub.

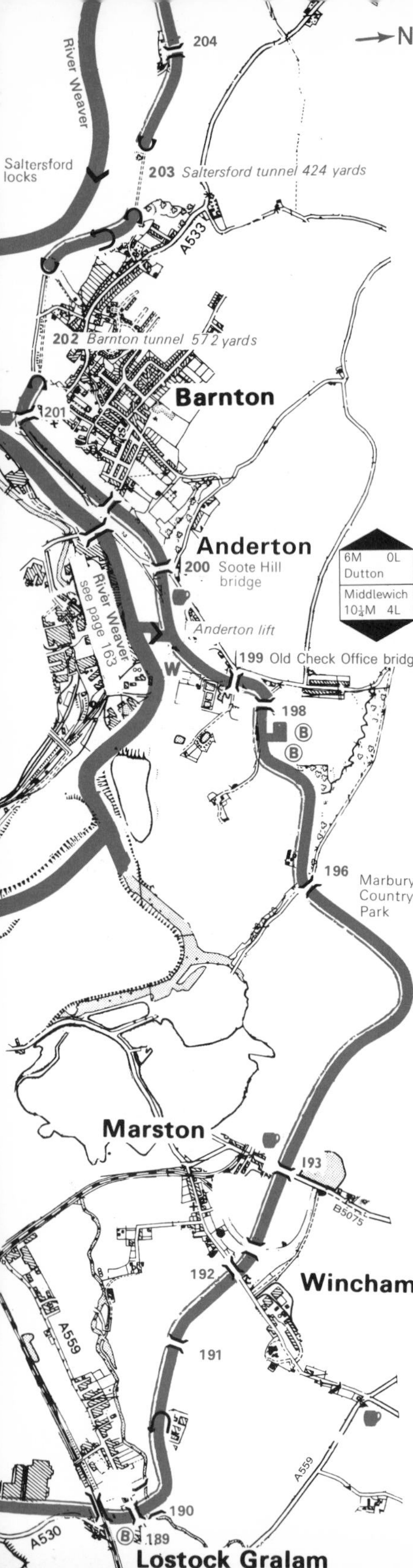

Anderton Lift

This is another length in which salt mining has determined the nature of the scenery. Part of it is heavily industrial, with enormous ICI works dominating the scene; much of it is devastated but rural (just), some of it is nondescript, and some of it is superb countryside. Donkey engines can still be seen in surrounding fields pumping brine. Leaving the vicinity of Lostock Gralam and the outskirts of Northwich, one passes Marston and Wincham (*PO, tel, stores*). Just west of the village, one travels along a ½-mile stretch of canal that was only cut in 1958, as the old route was about to collapse into – needless to say – underground salt workings. Beyond the woods of Marbury Country Park (attractive short stay moorings) is Anderton (*PO, tel, stores*) – the short entrance canal to the famous boat lift down into the Weaver Navigation is on the left. The main line continues westward, winding along what is now a steep hill and into Barnton Tunnel. At the west end one emerges onto a hillside overlooking the River Weaver, with a marvellous view straight down the huge Saltersford Locks. Now Saltersford Tunnel is entered: beyond it, one finds oneself in completely open country again. Henceforth, the salt extraction industry can be safely forgotten.

Navigational note
Both Barnton and Saltersford Tunnels are crooked, affording only a brief glimpse of the other end. Two boats cannot pass in the tunnels, so take care they are clear before proceeding.

Anderton Lift
An amazing and enormous piece of machinery built in 1875 by Leader Williams (later engineer of the Manchester Ship Canal) to connect the Trent & Mersey to the flourishing Weaver Navigation, 50ft below. As built, the lift consisted of two water-filled tanks counterbalancing each other in a vertical slide, resting on massive hydraulic rams. It worked on the very straightforward principle that making the ascending tank slightly lighter – by pumping a little water out – would assist the hydraulic rams (which were operated by a steam engine and pump) in moving both tanks, with boats in them, up or down their respective slide.
In 1908 the lift had to have major repairs, so it was modernised at the same time. The troublesome hydraulic rams were done away with; from then on each tank – which contained 250 tons of water – had its own counterweights and was independent of the other tank. Electricity replaced steam as the motive power. One of the most fascinating individual features of the canal system, it draws thousands of sightseers every year. Currently being extensively rebuilt and restored, ring (0606) 40566 if you plan to use it, to check if it is operational.

Marston
Ches. Tel. A salt-producing village, suffering badly from its own industry. The numerous gaps in this village are presumably caused by the demolition or collapse of houses affected by subsidence. Waste ground abounds.

BOATYARDS

Ⓑ **IML Waterways Cruising** Anderton Marina, Uplands Road, Anderton. (0606 79642). R S WD Pump-out, gas, narrowboat hire, overnight mooring, long-term mooring, slipway, books and maps, restaurant. *Closed Mon.*

Ⓑ **Clare Cruisers** Uplands Basin, Uplands Road, Northwich. (0606 77199). R S WD Pump-out, gas, narrowboat hire, overnight mooring, long-term mooring, winter storage, books and maps, engine repairs, toilets.

Ⓑ **Colliery Narrowboat Co** Wincham Wharf (bridge 189), Lostock Gralam, Northwich. (0606 44672). R WD Pump-out, day hire craft, overnight mooring, long-term mooring, crane, dry dock, chandlery, books and maps, boat building, boat sales, engine sales and repairs.

BOAT TRIPS

Golborne is a 48-seater restaurant boat with a bar, operating from Wincham Wharf. Ring (0606) 44672.

PUBS

Red Lion Barnton, just east of bridge 201. Food, garden, children's room.

Stanley Arms Canalside, right opposite the Anderton Lift. A friendly real ale pub with a lovely family room, where children are welcome. Food *lunchtime and evening*. Putting green.

New Inn Marston.

Black Greyhound ½ mile east of bridge 192. Good food, garden, children welcome *lunchtime*.

The Anderton Boat Lift. *Derek Pratt*.

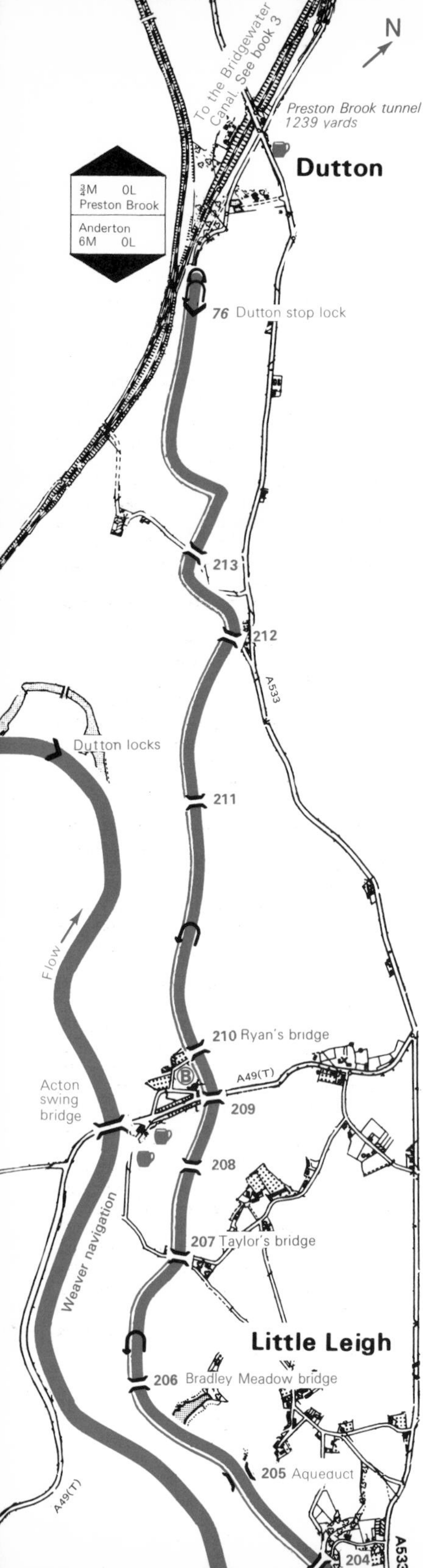

Dutton

This, the northernmost stretch of the Trent & Mersey, is a very pleasant one and delightfully rural. Most of the way the navigation follows the south side of the hills that overlook the River Weaver. From about 60ft up, one is often rewarded with excellent views of this splendid valley and the large vessels that ply up and down it. At one point one can see the elegant Dutton railway viaduct in the distance; then the two waterways diverge as the Trent & Mersey enters the woods preceding Preston Brook Tunnel. There is a stop lock just south of the tunnel; it has only one gate. At the north end of the tunnel a notice announces that from here onwards one is on the Bridgewater Canal, covered in detail in Nicholson/OS *Guide to the Waterways Book 3: North*.

Navigational note
North of Preston Brook Tunnel (see below) you are on the Bridgewater Canal, which is owned by the Manchester Ship Canal Company, and is described in detail in the Nicholson/OS *Guide to the Waterways Book 3: North*. Your BW licence is valid for three consecutive days on this canal.

Dutton
Ches. PO, tel, stores, garage. Small settlement on top of Preston Brook Tunnel, at the end of the lane uphill from the south end of the tunnel. There is a large hospital up the road, and a pub.

Preston Brook Tunnel
1239yds long and forbidden to unpowered craft. No towpath. *On summer weekends and B. Hols* entry is as posted on the notices at each end. It is crooked, like Barnton and Saltersford Tunnels, and two boats cannot pass, so at other times, make sure it is clear before entering.

BOATYARDS

Ⓑ **Black Prince Holidays** Bartington Wharf, Acton Bridge, Northwich. (0606 852945). R S WD Pump-out, gas, narrowboat hire, day hire craft, overnight mooring (*not weekends*), groceries, chandlery, books and maps, boat sales, engine sales and repairs, toilets, gifts.

PUBS

Talbot Arms Dutton. Food, garden.
Horns (0606 852192). 200yds south of bridge 209 on A49. Restaurant and bar meals *all day*, garden with children's play area, B&B.
Leigh Arms ¼ mile south of bridge 209, beside the Weaver. Sandwiches.

PLANNING A CRUISE

It is wise when planning a cruise to establish a means of calculating the time it takes to travel any given length of canal. This ensures that you can reliably work out whether you will reach a shop or pub before closing time. And of course for those who have hired their boat, it is vital to return to the starting point on time.

The time taken to navigate any canal depends, of course, on the average cruising speed of your boat and the amount of time it takes to negotiate the locks along the way. Remember that there is in any case an overall legal speed limit of 4mph on all canals. In practice, 3mph is a realistic canal cruising speed for most boats and 2mph is the maximum which can be achieved on shallow canals, such as the Peak Forest.

To the uninitiated, 3mph may sound an unbearably slow rate of progress through the countryside; but a few hours of gentle cruising on a fine day is usually enough to convert most people to this pace. For only by proceeding at walking pace can you appreciate the peace and beauty of the countryside, watch the bird life, and see the scurry of voles, rats and other creatures as they suddenly notice the slowly approaching boat.

The length of time taken to work through a lock depends on several things: whether the lock is full or empty, wide or narrow, deep or shallow. It depends on the number and size of the paddles that control the sluices, on the presence or otherwise of other boats near the lock, and of course on the number and competence of the boat crew. Most people take between 10–20 minutes on average to work through a typical lock – or, to put it another way, they may take as long to get through a lock as they would have taken to travel another mile at 3mph. Herein lies a basis for a simple method of estimating time required to travel along a given length of canal: take the number of miles to be travelled and add the number of locks to be negotiated on the way. This gives the number of 'lock-miles'. Divide this by 3, and the result is the approximate length of time it will take, in hours. Thus if you intend to travel 30 miles, and there are 12 locks along the way, the calculation is as follows: 30 + 12 divided by 3 (mph) = 14 hours. So this particular journey will take you around 14 hours, assuming your average cruising speed to be 3mph and assuming you take about 20 minutes to get through each lock (if they are all narrow locks in good condition then you may well better this time). The length of your journey and the number of locks can easily be calculated using the 'milestones' that appear on every map in this series of guides. To refine the system, simply tailor it more closely to the actual cruising speed of your boat and the efficiency of your lock-operating technique.

An excellent fortnight's trip, for example, would be the circuit formed by the River Soar and Trent & Mersey, Coventry, Oxford and Grand Union (Leicester Section) canals. This is 152 miles and 100 locks long (about 84 hours' cruising time), and takes you through some of the very best parts of Leicestershire. You will see the Foxton staircase locks, Braunston Tunnel, the delightful canal village of Shardlow and have time to explore the lock-free Ashby Canal (22 miles long – two days there and back) or the meandering course of the unspoilt Market Harborough arm, 5 miles long.

For just a one-week holiday, a good round trip with plenty of contrasts could encompass the Staffs & Worcs north of Aldersley Junction, the Trent & Mersey from Great Haywood to Fradley, the Coventry to Fazeley Junction, the Birmingham & Fazeley to Farmer's Bridge and returning along the Birmingham Canal Main Line. With 75 miles and 79 narrow locks, this should take no more than 50 hours' cruising time. You will enjoy the old locks and bridges of the Staffs & Worcs as it follows the pretty valleys of the rivers Penk and Sow, culminating at Tixall Wide. After a visit to Shugborough Hall you continue past the eccentric footbridge at Drayton Manor before starting the long climb to Farmer's Bridge. There's a choice of routes on the Birmingham Canal Main Line to complete the circuit.

These are just two examples of the many circular cruising routes available – a glance at the planning map on pages 4 and 5 will reveal many more. Of course, there is also much to be said for a straight out and back cruise – it will all look different when you are coming the other way, and you can arrange to re-visit that favourite pub again. The whole secret is to *allow plenty of time*, for shopping, for exploring and for gentle cruising. Many a holiday has been spoilt by becoming a race against time. The most comprehensive source of information for planning a waterways cruise is Nicholson's *The Ordnance Survey Inland Waterways Map of Great Britain*.

See also 'Stoppages' in the **General Cruising Information** *section.*

A BRIEF HISTORY OF BRITISH CANALS

River navigations, that is rivers widened and deepened to take large boats, had existed in England since the Middle Ages: some can even be traced back to Roman times. In 1600 there were 700 miles of navigable river in England, and by 1760, the dawn of the canal age, this number had been increased to 1300. This extensive network had prompted many developments later used by the canal engineers, for example, the lock system. But there were severe limitations: generally the routes were determined by the rivers and the features of the landscape and so were rarely direct. Also there were no east-west, or north-south connections.

Thus the demand for a direct inland waterway system increased steadily through the first half of the 18thC with the expansion of internal trade. Road improvements could not cope with this expansion, and so engineers and merchants turned to canals, used extensively on the continent.

One of the earliest pure canals, cut independently of existing rivers, was opened in 1745, at Newry in Northern Ireland, although some authorities consider the Fossdyke, cut by the Romans to link the rivers Trent and Witham, to be the first. However, the Newry is more important because it established the cardinal rule of all canals, the maintenance of an adequate water supply, a feature too often ignored by later engineers. The Newry Canal established the principle of a long summit level, fed by a reservoir to keep the locks at either end well supplied. Ten years later, in England, the Duke of Bridgewater decided to build a canal to provide an adequate transport outlet for his coal mines at Worsley. He employed the self-taught James Brindley as his engineer, and John Gilbert as surveyor, and launched the canal age in England. The Bridgewater Canal was opened in 1761. Its route, all on one level, was independent of all rivers; its scale of operations reflected the new power of engineering and the foresight of its creators. Although there were no locks, the engineering problems were huge; an aqueduct was built at Barton over the River Irwell, preceded by an embankment 900yds long; 15 miles of canal were built underground, so that boats could approach the coal face for loading – eventually there were 42 miles underground, including an inclined plane – the puddled clay method was used by Brindley to make the canal bed watertight. Perhaps most important of all, the canal was a success financially. Bridgewater invested the equivalent of £3 million of his own money in the project, and still made a profit.

Having shown that canals were both practical and financially sound, the Bridgewater aroused great interest throughout Britain. Plans were drawn up for a trunk canal, to link the four major rivers of England: the Thames, Severn, Mersey and Trent. This plan was eventually brought to fruition, but many years later than its sponsors imagined. Brindley was employed as engineer for the scheme, his reputation ensuring that he would always have more work than he could handle. The Trent and Mersey, and the Staffordshire and Worcestershire Canals received the Royal Assent in 1766, and the canal age began in earnest.

Canals, like the railways later, were built entirely by hand. Gangs of itinerant workmen were gathered together, drawn by the comparatively high pay. Once formed these armies of 'navigators' – hence 'navvies' – moved through the countryside as the canal was built, in many cases living off the land. All engineering problems had to be solved by manpower alone, aided by the horse and the occasional steam pump. Embankments, tunnels, aqueducts, all were built by these labouring armies kept under control only by the power of the section engineers and contractors.

The Staffordshire and Worcestershire Canal opened in 1770. In its design Brindley determined the size of the standard Midlands canal, which of course had direct influence on the rest of the English system as it was built. He chose a narrow canal, with locks 72ft 7in by 7ft 6in, partly for reasons of economy, and partly because he realised that the problems of an adequate water supply were far greater than most canal sponsors realised. This standard, which was also adopted for the Trent and Mersey, prompted the development of a special vessel, the narrowboat with its 30-ton payload. Ironically this decision by Brindley in 1766 ensured the failure of the canals as a commercial venture 200 years later, for by the middle of this century a 30-ton payload could no longer be worked economically.

The Trent and Mersey was opened in 1777; 93 miles long, the canal included five tunnels, the original one at Harecastle taking 11 years to build. In 1790 Oxford was finally reached and the junction with the Thames brought the four great rivers together. From the very start English canal companies were characterised by their intense rivalries; water supplies were jealously guarded, and constant wars were waged over toll prices. Many canals receiving the Royal Assent were never built, while others staggered towards conclusion, hampered by doubtful engineering, inaccurate estimates, and loans that they could never hope to pay off. Yet for a period canal mania gripped British speculators, as railway mania was to grip them 50 years later. The peak of British canal development came between 1791 and 1794, a period that gave rise to the opening of the major routes, the rise of the great canal engineers, Telford, Rennie and Jessop, and the greatest prosperity of those companies already operating. At this time the canal system had an effective monopoly over inland transport: the old trunk roads could not compete, coastal traffic was uncertain and hazardous, and the railways were still a future dream. This period also saw some of the greatest feats of engineering.

A contemporary view of canal promoters. *Eric de Maré*.

The turn of the century saw the opening of the last major cross-country routes; the Pennines were crossed by the Leeds and Liverpool Canal between 1770 and 1816, while the Kennet and Avon (opened in 1810) linked London and Bristol via the Thames. These two canals were built as broad navigations: already the realisation was dawning on canal operators that the limits imposed by the Brindley standard were too restrictive, a suspicion that was to be brutally confirmed by the coming of the railways. The Kennet and Avon, along with its rival the Thames and Severn, also marks the introduction of fine architecture to canals. Up till now canal architecture had been functional, often impressive, but clearly conceived by engineers. As a result, the Kennet and Avon has an architectural unity lacking in earlier canals. The appearance of architectural quality was matched by another significant change: canals became straighter, their engineers choosing as direct a route as possible, arguing that greater construction costs would be outweighed by smoother, quicker operation, whereas the early canals had followed the landscape. The Oxford is the prime example of a contour canal, meandering across the Midlands as though there were all the time in the world. It looks beautiful, its close marriage with the landscape makes it ideal as a pleasure waterway, but it was commercial folly.

The shortcomings of the early canals were exploited all too easily by the new railways. At first there was sharp competition by canals. Tolls were lowered, money was poured into route improvements; 14 miles of the Oxford's windings were cut out between 1829 and 1834; schemes were prepared to widen the narrow canals; the Harecastle Tunnel was doubled in 1827, the new tunnel taking three years to build (as opposed to 11 years for the old). But the race was lost from the start. The 19thC marks the rise of the railways and the decline of the canals. With the exception of the Manchester Ship Canal, the last major canal was the Birmingham and Liverpool Junction, opened in 1835. The system survived until this century, but the 1914–18 war brought the first closures, and through the 1930s the canal map adopted the shape it has today. Effective commercial carrying on narrow canals ceased in the early 1960s, although a few companies managed to survive until recently. However, with the end of commercial operation, a new role was seen for the waterways as a pleasure amenity, a 'linear national park 2000 miles long'.

Water supply has always been the cardinal element in both the running and the survival of

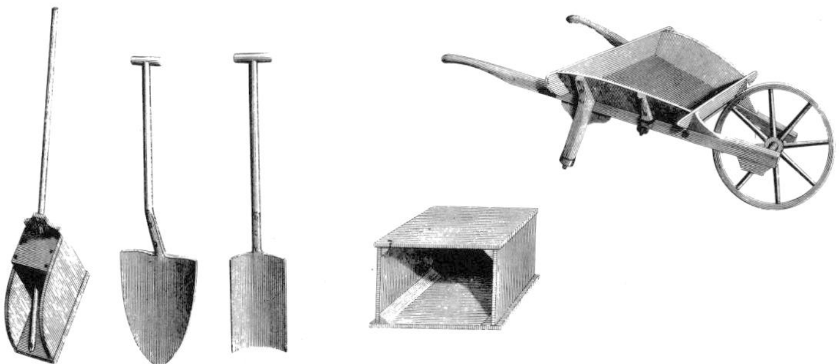

The rudimentary tools of the early 'navvies'. *Hugh McKnight*.

Worcester and Birmingham Canal.
LOWESMERE WHARF, WORCESTER.

Canal Company's Machine. 181
Cheque, No.
Carriage, No.
Tons. Cwt. Qrs.
Gross Weight . .
Tare . . .
Neat Coals, Cwt.
Weighing
Clerk.

Mr.
Bought of
£ s. d.
At per Ton
Carriage
Clerk.

Printed by R. Jabet and Co. Herald Office, High-street, Birmingham.

Worcester and Birmingham Canal Company toll ticket dated 1816. *Hugh McKnight.*

any canal system. Locks need a constant supply of water – every boat passing through a wide lock on the Grand Union uses 96,000 gallons of water. Generally two methods of supply were used: direct feed by rivers and streams, and feed by reservoirs sited along the summit level. The first suffered greatly from silting, and meant that the canal was dependent on the level of water in the river; the regular floods from the River Soar that overtake the Grand Union's Leicester line show the dangers of this. The second was more reliable, but many engineers were short-sighted in their provision of an adequate summit level. The otherwise well-planned Kennet & Avon always suffered from water shortage. Where shortages occurred, steam pumping engines were used to pump water taken down locks back up to the summit level. The Kennet & Avon was dependent upon pumped supplies, while the Birmingham Canal Navigations were fed by six reservoirs and 17 pumping engines. Some companies adopted side ponds alongside locks to save water, but this put the onus on the boatman and so had limited success. Likewise the stop locks still to be seen at junctions are a good example of 18thC company rivalry; an established canal would ensure that any proposed canal wishing to join it would have to lock *down* into the older canal, which thus gained a lock of water each time a boat passed through.

Where long flights or staircase locks existed there was always great wastage of water, and so throughout canal history alternative mechanical means of raising boats have been tried out. The inclined plane or the vertical lift were the favoured forms. Both worked on the counterbalance principle, the weight of the descending boat helping to raise the ascending. The first inclined plane was built at Ketley in 1788, and they were a feature of the west country Bude and Chard canals. The most famous plane was built at Foxton, and operated from 1900–10. Mechanical failure and excessive running costs ended the application of the inclined plane in England, although modern examples work very efficiently on the continent, notably in Belgium. The vertical lift was more unusual, although there were eight on the Grand Western Canal. The most famous, built at Anderton in 1875 (and currently being rebuilt) stands as a monument to the ingenuity shown in the attempts to overcome the problems of water shortage.

Engineering features are the greatest legacy of the canal age, and of these, tunnels are the most impressive. The longest tunnel is at Standedge, on the Huddersfield Narrow Canal (not navigable throughout, but restored in part). This tunnel runs for 5716yds through the Pennines, at times 638ft below the surface. It is also on the highest summit level, 644ft above sea level. The longest navigable tunnel is now Blisworth, at 3056yds long. Others of interest include the Dudley Tunnel, 3154yds long, which can be seen from the electric trip boat which operates from the Black Country Museum; the twin Harecastle Tunnels on the Trent and Mersey Canal – the first 2897yds long and now disused, the second 2919yds and still in use; Sapperton, which carried the Thames and Severn Canal through the Cotswolds and Netherton on the Birmingham Canal Navigations. This last, built 1855–58, was the last in England, and was lit throughout by gas lights, and at a later date by electricity.

The Netherton Tunnel was built wide enough to allow for a towing path on both sides. Most tunnels have no towing path at all, and so boats had to be 'legged', or walked through.

The slowness and relative danger of legging in tunnels led to various attempts at mechanical propulsion. An endless rope pulled by a stationary steam engine at the tunnel mouth was tried out at Blisworth and Braunston between 1869 and 1871. Steam tugs were employed, an early application of mechanical power to canal boats, but their performance was greatly limited by lack of ventilation, not to mention the danger of suffocating the crew.

An electric tug was used at Harecastle from 1914 to 1954. The diesel engine made tunnel tug

Islington Tunnel during construction. *Hugh McKnight.*

services much more practical, but diesel-powered narrowboats soon put the tugs out of business: by the 1930s most tunnels had to be navigated by whatever means the boatman chose to use. Legging continued at Crick, Husbands Bosworth and Saddington until 1939.

Until the coming of the diesel boats, the horse reigned supreme as a source of canal power. The first canals had used gangs of men to bow-haul the boats, a left over from the river navigations where 50–80 men, or 12 horses, would pull a 200-ton barge. By 1800 the horse had taken over, and was used throughout the heyday of the canal system. In fact horse towage survived as long as large-scale commercial operation. Generally one horse or mule was used per boat, a system unmatched for cheapness and simplicity. The towing path was carried from one side of the canal to the other by turnover bridges, a common feature that reveals the total dominance of the horse. Attempts to introduce self-propelled canal boats date from 1793, although most early experiments concerned tugs towing dumb barges. Development was limited by the damage caused by wash, a problem that still applies today, and the first fleets of self-propelled steam narrowboats were not in service until the last quarter of the 19thC. Fellows, Morton and Clayton, and the Leeds and Liverpool Carrying Co ran large fleets of steam boats between 1880 and 1931, by which time most had been converted to diesel operation. With the coming of mechanical power the butty boat principle was developed: a powered narrowboat would tow a dumb 'butty' boat, thereby doubling the load without doubling the running costs. This system became standard until the virtual ending by the late 1960s of carrying on the narrow canals. Before the coming of railways, passenger services were run on the canals; packet boats, specially built narrowboats with passenger accommodation, ran express services, commanding the best horses and the unquestioned right of way over all other traffic. Although the railways killed this traffic, the last scheduled passenger service survived on the Gloucester & Berkeley Canal until 1935.

The traditional narrowboat with its colourful decoration and meticulous interior has become a symbol of English canals. However this was in fact a late development. The shape of the narrowboat was determined by Brindley's original narrow canal specification, but until the late 19thC boats were unpainted, and carried all male crews. Wages were sufficient for the crews to maintain their families at home. The increase in railway competition brought a reduction in wages, and so bit by bit the crews were forced to take their families with them, becoming a kind of water gipsy. The confines of a narrowboat cabin presented the same problems as a gipsy caravan, and so the families found a similar answer. Their eternally wandering home achieved individuality by extravagant and colourful decoration, and the traditional narrowboat painting was born. The extensive symbolic vocabulary available to the painters produced a sign language that only these families could understand, and the canal world became far more enclosed, although outwardly it was more decorative. As the canals have turned from commerce to pleasure, so the traditions of the families have died out, and the families themselves have faded away. But their language survives, although its meaning has mostly vanished with them. This survival gives the canals their characteristic decorative qualities, which make them so attractive to the pleasure boater and to the casual visitor.

FISHING

Many anglers start their fishing careers on the canals and navigable rivers, mainly because our system of waterways has always offered excellent opportunities for the thousands of angling enthusiasts throughout Great Britain.

Most of these cross-country waterways have natural reed-fringed and grassy banks, and in addition to the delightful surroundings the fishing is generally good. In most areas there has been a steady improvement in canal fishing in recent years and in many places new stocks of fish have been introduced. The popular quarry are roach, perch and bream, but the canals also hold dace, tench, chub and carp in places, in addition to pike and other species in particular areas.

Canals afford good hunting grounds for those seeking specimen fish (that is, fish above average size) and these are liable to be encountered on almost any water. The canals also make good venues for competition fishing, and in most places nowadays matches are held regularly at weekends throughout the season.

The Statutory Close Season for coarse fish is March 15 to June 15 inclusive, but in some areas, notably the Yorkshire River Authority, the Close Season is from February 28 to May 31. The Close Season for pike in some areas is March 15 to September 30.

Permits and fishing rights

Most parts of the waterways system are available to anglers. The big angling associations – e.g. the London AA, Birmingham AA, Reading & District AA, Coventry & District AA, Nottingham AA plus many smaller clubs – rent fishing rights over extensive areas on the system. In most cases, day tickets are available.

On arrival at the water-side it is always advisable to make enquiries as to who holds the fishing rights, and to obtain a permit if one is required *before* starting to fish. Remember, also, that a River Authority rod licence is usually required in addition to a fishing permit. It is essential to obtain this licence from the relevant River Authority *before* starting to fish. Some fishing permits and licences are issued by bailiffs along the bank, but local enquiry will help to determine this.

A canalside pub or a local fishing tackle shop are good places to enquire if permission or day tickets are required for the local stretch of water. Canal lock keepers are usually knowledgeable about the fishing rights in the immediate locality, and often a lock keeper may be found who issues day tickets on behalf of an angling association, or owner. It is likely that he will also know some of the better fishing areas, as well as local methods and baits which may be considered most successful.

The fishing rights on most canals are owned by the British Waterways Board and many miles of good fishing are leased to clubs and angling associations. They also issue day tickets on certain lengths, so it is worth enquiring at the local British Waterways office when planning a trip. Special arrangements are made for fishing from boats; again, enquire with the BW locally.

'Private fishing' notices should *not* be ignored. If the owner's name and address is on the board then application can be made for permission for a future occasion. Once permission has been obtained it would be advisable to find out if there are any restrictions imposed, since some clubs and associations ban certain baits, or have restrictions on live-baiting for pike: and on some fisheries pike fishing is not allowed before a specified date.

Other restrictions may concern size-limits of fish, and this certainly applies to the London AA canal fisheries. Some River Authority by-laws prohibit the retention of under-sized fish in keep nets. A local club holding the fishing rights may have imposed their own size-limits in order to protect certain species. Such restrictions are generally printed on permits and licences.

Tackle

In the slow moving, sluggish waters of canals the float tackle needs to be light and lines fine in order to catch fish. When fishing for roach and dace lines of 1½lb to 2lb breaking strain are the maximum strength normally needed in order to get the fish to take a bait – particularly when the water is clear, or on the popular reaches that are 'hard-fished'.

Fine tackle also means small hooks, sizes 16 and 18 – or even as small as 22 at times. Such light gear is also effective when fishing for the smaller species, such as gudgeon and bleak. This tackle will require a well-balanced float to show the slightest indication of a bite.

Bait

Baits should be small, and maggots, casters (maggot chrysalis), hempseed, wheat, tiny cubes of bread crust, or a small pinch of flake (the white crumb of a new loaf) may take fish. It always pays to experiment with baits; bait that is effective on one occasion will not necessarily prove to be as effective the next. With slight variations, similar fishing methods can be used effectively on the majority of waterways.

Northern anglers who regularly compete in contests on canals use bloodworms as bait. They have become extremely skilful in using this tiny bait and often take fish on bloodworms when all other baits fail. Bloodworms are the larvae of a midge, and are a perfectly natural bait. The anglers gather the bloodworms from the mud and, apart from a wash in clean water, the baits are ready for use.

A popular groundbait that has had great success is known as 'black magic'! This is a mixture of garden peat and bread crumbs mixed dry and carried to the water. When dampened and mixed it can be thrown in in the usual way. The basis of most groundbaits is bread, and many other materials may be added, although stodgy mixtures should be avoided when canal fishing. Canals are not waters which respond to heavy groundbaiting tactics. It is far better to use a cloud-bait, and this can be purchased ready for use. Some successful Midland anglers wet their cloudbait with milk instead of water to increase the cloud effect.

Methods

Once the swim – that is the area of water to be fished – has been decided upon, and the tackle set up, use a plummet to find the depth and adjust the float, but be cautious when doing so in clear waters. At times it may be best to find the depth by trial and error. Often most fish will be caught from around mid-water level, but always be prepared to move the float further up the line in order to present the bait closer to the bottom, where the bigger fish are usually to be found. At frequent intervals toss a few samples of the hook-bait into the top of the swim to keep the fish interested.

Fish in different waters may vary in the way they take a bait and this creates a different bite registration. It may be found that fish take the hook-bait quickly, causing the float to dip sharply or dive under the surface. The strike should be made instantly, on the downward movement. On some canals the fish are even quicker – and perhaps gentler – not taking the float under at all, and in this case the strike should be made at the slightest unusual movement of the float.

Roach and dace abound in many lengths and although working the float tackle down with a flow of water takes most fish, better quality fish – including bream – are usually to be taken by fishing a laying-on style, with the bait lying on the bottom. This method can often be best when fishing areas where there is no flow at all. This is done with float tackle, adjusted to make the distance from float to hook greater than the depth of water, so that when the float is at the surface the bait and lower length of line are lying on the bottom.

The alternative method of fishing the bottom is by legering, the main difference in the methods being in the bite indication. Without a float a bite is registered at the rod-tip where, if need be, a quiver-tip or swing-tip may be fitted. These bite detectors are used extensively on Midland and Northern waters. Legering is a method often used in the south, where in some southern canals barbel and chub are quite prolific. These species grow to good sizes in canal waters – chub up to 7lb and barbel up to 14lb have been taken – but these are exceptional and the average run of fish would be well below those weights. Nevertheless, both species are big fish and big baits and hooks may be used when fishing for them.

Many bigger than average fish – of all species – have been taken by fishing the bait on the bottom. Whatever the style of leger fishing, always choose the lightest possible weight, and position it some 12 to 18in up from the hook. There are no hard and fast rules governing the distance between weight and hook, so it pays to experiment to find the best to suit the conditions.

Anglers who regularly fish the Northern and Midland canals invariably use tiny size 20 and 22 hooks, tied to a mere ¾lb breaking strain line, and when float-fishing use a tiny quill float – porcupine or crow quill. A piece of peacock quill is useful because it can be cut with scissors to make it suit prevailing conditions. Such small floats only need minimal weight to balance them correctly, and usually the Midland anglers position this on the line just under the float so that the bait is presented naturally. Once the tackle has been cast out, the bait falls slowly through the water along with hook-bait samples, which are thrown in at the same time. This is called 'fishing on the drop'. A fine cloud-bait is also used with this style.

Canals which have luxuriant weed growth harbour many small fish, which are preyed upon by perch. These move in shoals and invariably the perch in a shoal are much the same size. Usually the really big perch are solitary, so it pays to rove the canal and search for them. They are to be caught from almost any canal and although they may be caught by most angling methods, the most effective is usually float-fishing. The fishing depth can vary according to conditions, time of year, and actual depth of the canal, so it pays to try the bait at varying depths. The usual baits for perch are worms, small live-baits (minnows etc) and maggots. Close by wooden lock gates is often the haunt of large perch.

In certain places canals and rivers come together and take on the characteristics of the river (i.e. with an increased flow) and different methods are needed. These places are often noted for splendid chub (and sometimes barbel) in addition to roach and other species. Trotting the stream is a popular and effective fishing style.

Weather

Weather conditions have to be taken into consideration. Canals usually run through open country and catch the slightest breeze. Even a moderate wind will pull and bob the float, which in turn will agitate the baited hook. If bites are not forthcoming under such conditions then it may be best to remove the float and try a straightforward leger arrangement.

When legering, the effects of the wind can be avoided by keeping the rod top down to within an inch or two of the water level – or even by sinking the rod-tip below the surface. Anglers in the North and Midlands have devised a wind-shield for legering that protects the rod-tip from the wind and improves bite detection. Nevertheless, in some circumstances a slight wind can be helpful because if a moderate breeze is blowing it will put a ripple on the water, and this can be of assistance in fishing in clear waters.

Where to fish

Most canals are narrow and this makes it possible to cast the tackle towards the far bank, where fish may have moved because they had been disturbed from the near bank. Disturbance will send the fish up or downstream and often well away from the fishing area. So always approach the water quietly, and remember to move cautiously at all times. When making up the tackle to start fishing it is advisable to do so as far back from the water as possible to avoid scaring the fish. It pays to move slowly, to keep as far from the bank as possible, and to avoid clumping around in heavy rubber boots. If there is cover along the bank – shrubs, bushes, tall reeds and clumps of yellow flag iris – the wise angler will make full use of it.

There are some canals that are no longer navigable, and these are generally weedy. At certain times in the season the surface of the water disappears under a green mantle of floating duckweed, which affords cover and security for the fish. It is possible to have the best sport by fishing in the pockets of clear water that are to be found.

Some canals have prolific growths of water lilies in places, and are particularly attractive for angling. They always look ideal haunts for tench, but they can also be rather difficult places from which to land good fish. Tench are more or less evenly distributed throughout the canals and the best are found where weed growth is profuse. It may be best to fish small areas of clear water between the weeds. Groundbait can encourage tench to move out from the weed beds, and to feed once they are out. Sometimes it is an advantage to clear a swim by dragging out weeds or raking the bottom. This form of natural groundbaiting stirs the silt, which clouds the water and disturbs aquatic creatures on which the fish feed.

Bream seem to do well in canals and some fairly good fish up to 5lb may be taken. Any deep pools or winding holes (shown as ⌒ on map) are good places to try, particularly when fishing a canal for the first time.

Other places worth fishing are 'cattle drinks' regularly used by farm animals. These make useful places to fish for bream, roach and dace. The frequent use of these drinking holes colours the water, as the animals stir up the mud, and disturb various water creatures. The coloured water draws fish into the area – on the downstream side of the cattle drink when there is the slightest flow.

Pike are to be found in every canal in the country – they are predators, feeding on small fish (which gives a sure indication of the most effective baits). Any small live fish presented on float tackle will take pike. The best places to fish are near weed beds and boats that have been moored in one place a long time.

Many of our canals are cut through pleasant and peaceful countryside, and this enables anglers to spend many delightful hours along the banks – and always with the chance of making a good catch. As a general rule, never fish in locks on navigable canals, or anywhere that could obstruct the free passage of boats. Remember that you will inconvenience yourself as well as the boatman if you have to move in a hurry, or risk a broken line. Never leave discarded line or lead weights on the bank, and never throw these items into the water. Waterfowl become entangled in the line, and are poisoned by the lead shot, which they swallow when grubbing for food. All responsible anglers take their spoilt tackle and litter home with them, where it can be disposed of safely.

British Waterways produce a 'Waterways Code for Anglers', which can be obtained from local BW offices or from Customer Services, Greycaine Road, Watford, Herts WD2 4JR. (0923 226422). All who intend to fish on BW's waterways are strongly advised to obtain a copy, as it contains information regarding safety, health and pollution.

BRITISH WATERWAYS OFFICES

CUSTOMER SERVICES
British Waterways, Greycaine Road, Watford, Herts WD2 4JR. (0923 226422). General enquiries.

REGIONAL OFFICES
Will deal with enquiries regarding stoppages, long-term moorings and specific problems on a particular canal in their area. Also try the Canal Managers, whose telephone numbers are given at the start of each section.

Midlands Region 6th Floor, Auchinleck House, Broad Street, Five Ways, Birmingham B15 1DL. (021-633 3666).
Ashby Canal
Birmingham & Fazeley Canal
Birmingham Canal Navigations
Coventry Canal
Grand Union Canal (Leicester Section)
Staffordshire & Worcestershire Canal
Stourbridge Canal
Trent & Mersey (east of Fradley)

North-East Region 1 Dock Street, Leeds LS1 1HH. (0532 436741).
River Soar

South-East Region Wynyard House, 99 Langley Road, Watford WD1 3PE. (0923 31363).
Oxford Canal (North)

North-West Region Navigation Road, Northwich, Cheshire CW8 1BH. (0606 74321).
Caldon Canal
Llangollen Canal
Shropshire Union Canal
Trent & Mersey Canal (west of Fradley)

For assistance from operational staff outside of normal office hours, and at weekends, dial 100 and ask for FREEPHONE CANALS.

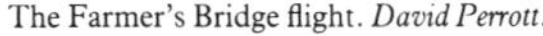

The Farmer's Bridge flight. *David Perrott.*

INDEX